TRICKSTER THEATRE

AFRICAN EXPRESSIVE CULTURES

Patrick McNaughton, editor

Associate editors
Catherine M. Cole
Barbara G. Hoffman
Eileen Julien
Kassim Koné
D. A. Masolo
Elisha Renne
Zoë Strother

TRICKSTER THEATRE

The Poetics of Freedom in Urban Africa

Jesse Weaver Shipley

Indiana University Press

Bloomington and Indianapolis

This book is a publication of

Indiana University Press
Office of Scholarly Publishing
Herman B Wells Library 350
1320 East 10th Street
Bloomington, Indiana 47405 USA

iupress.indiana.edu

© 2015 by Jesse Weaver Shipley

All rights reserved

No part of this book may be reproduced or utilized in any form or by any means, electronic or mechanical, including photocopying and recording, or by any information storage and retrieval system, without permission in writing from the publisher. The Association of American University Presses' Resolution on Permissions constitutes the only exception to this prohibition.

∞ The paper used in this publication meets the minimum requirements of the American National Standard for Information Sciences—Permanence of Paper for Printed Library Materials, ANSI Z39.48-1992.

Manufactured in the United States of America

Shipley, Jesse Weaver, author.
   Trickster theatre : the poetics of freedom in urban Africa / Jesse Weaver Shipley.
      pages cm. — (African expressive cultures)
   ISBN 978-0-253-01645-4 (cl : alk. paper) — ISBN 978-0-253-01653-9 (pb : alk. paper) — ISBN 978-0-253-01659-1 (eb)
   1. Theater—Ghana—History—20th century. 2. Theater and society—Ghana. 3. Tricksters in literature. I. Title. II. Series: African expressive cultures.
   PN2990.4.S55 2015
   792.09667—dc23

                                            2015009098

1 2 3 4 5 20 19 18 17 16 15

For Martin Weaver
　an artist always in the making

Wɔ kum Ananse a, Ɔman no be bo.
[If you kill Ananse, the nation will break.]

Akan proverb as told by playwright Yaw Asare

Contents

Acknowledgments	xi
Introduction: Poetics of Uncertainty	1
Part I. History and Mediations in Making Theatre	**23**
1 Making Culture: Race, History, and a Theory of Performance in the Gold Coast Colony	25
2 The National Theatre Movement: Urban Art Infrastructures and a Contested National Culture in Independence-Era Accra	53
3 Revolutionary Storytelling: Pan-African Theatre and Remaking Lost Futures in 1980s Ghana	83
4 A Man of the People: Mohammed Ben Abdallah as Artist-Politician	103
Part II. Stagings in Millennial Ghana	**113**
5 Total African Theatre: Language, Reflexivity, and Ambiguity in *The Witch of Mopti*	115
6 "The Best Tradition Goes On": Audience, Consumption, and the Structural Transformation of Concert Party Popular Theatre	147
7 Fake Pastors and Real Comedians: Doubling and Parody in Miraculous, Charismatic Performance	175
8 Copying Independence: Backstage at the Fiftieth-Anniversary Reenactment of Nkrumah's Independence Speech	204
Epilogue: Unfreedom as Critical Theory	226
Notes	237
Bibliography	253
Index	273

Acknowledgments

This book is the result of the work of many people. I thank my families. I thank my intellectual companions. I thank my artistic collaborators. I thank those who taught me things about art and life, forms of sociality, and techniques of being alone. I thank my editor, Dee Mortensen; my manuscript readers; Henry Howard; Paula Durbin-Westby; and everyone at Indiana University Press for their incredible support and patience. I thank Wenner Gren Foundation, Fulbright, Bard College, Achebe Center, Haverford College, Institute of African Studies at Columbia University, and Carter G. Woodson Institute for supporting this research.

For their guidance for this research from its early stages I thank William Addo, Korkor Amarteifio, Esi Ansah, Kofi Anyidoho, Nana Akua Anyidoho, Andy Apter, Sandy Arkhurst, Samuel Dawson Asaam, Awo Asiedu, Edinam Atatsi, Africanus Aveh, Y. B. Bampoe (Opiah), Bernard Bate, Bill Beeman, Ama Boabeng, Nana Bosompra, Catherine Cole, John Comaroff, Tom Cummins, David Donkor, David Dontoh, Sarah Dorgbadze, Ekua Ekumah, Laurie Frederick, Lina Fruzzetti, Susan Gal, Shane Greene, Jane Guyer, Mike Hanchard, Al-Mumuni Ishak, Diana Kofitiah, Loren Kruger, Margaret Kudjoe, Paul Liffman, Efo Kodjo Mawugbe, Nii Addokwei Moffatt, Nancy Munn, J. H. Kwabena Nketia, Judith Nketia, Cynthia Delali Noviewoo, Albert Mawere Opoku, S. K. Oppong, Agyeman Ossei, Martin Owusu, Birte Hege Owusu-Addo, Agnes Panfred, Beth Povinelli, Brew Riverson Jr., Solomon Sampah, Mawuli Semevo, Oh! Nii Kwei Sowah, Esi Sutherland-Addy, Ice Water, Gavin Webb, Kelvin Asare Williams, and Asiedu Yirenkyi.

For their aid in this work's extended development I thank Sareeta Amrute, Mensa Ansah, Koffi Anyinefa, Rab Bakari, Mario Bick, Kwadwo (DJ) Black, Leon Botstein, Diana Brown, Tina Campt, David Akramah Cofie, Rob Culp, Mamadou Diouf, Michele Dominy, Brent Hayes Edwards, Kim and Mike Fortune, Kobby Graham, Bayo Holsey, Habib Chester Iddrisu, John Jackson, Debra Klein, Laura Kunreuther, Jason Lee, Zilla Limann, Candice Lowe, Anne Maria Makhulu, Wende Marshall, Adeline Masquelier, George Mentore, Ato Quayson, Reggie Osei Rockstone, Jemima Pierre, Tyrone Simpson, Yuka Suzuki, Ben Talton, Deb Thomas, Michael Warner, Brad Weiss, and Hylton White.

For their support in bringing this book to its final phase I thank Ama Ata Aidoo, Nikhil Anand, Ben Angmor, Amy Appiah, Grace Ayensu, Linda Bell, Kim Benston, Dominic Boyer, Khadija von Zinnenburg Carroll, Jeff Cobbah,

Maris Gillette, Laurie Hart, Tom Keenan, Paul Kockelman, Saskia Koebschall, Brian Larkin, Kathy McGee, Joshua Moses, Stephanie Newell, Zolani Ngwane, Rodney Quarcoo, Chris Roebuck, Zainab Saleh, Chika Unigwe, and Binyavanga Wainaina.

For continuing inspiration I thank Akos Abdallah, Aminata Abdallah, Farouk Abdallah, Anne Balay, Kwesi Brown, Mildred Dennis, Alex Dent, Dzino, Bill Katz, Candice Lowe, Angela and Conall Macfarlane, Rhianne McCalip, Samuel Otoo (Ghana Boy), Burke Shipley, Neal and Nan Shipley, Ruti Talmor, Freddy Weaver, Giles and Roz Weaver, Jo Weaver, Danielle Verrett, Pya Verrett, Whitney Verrett, and Shawn Wilkerson.

The conceptualization of this book would not have been possible without ongoing encouragement from Virginia and Thorne Shipley, who believe profoundly in the timeless significance of intellectual pursuit. Jean Comaroff inspired the theoretical foundations of this work. John Collins with his analytic breadth lent me a conceptual map. Tabetha Ewing's brilliance helped build and sustain its architecture. James Gibbs provided generous readings of my work and shared his encyclopedic knowledge of Ghanaian theatre. Marina Peterson creatively challenged me to link scholarly and artistic modes. Christie and Chinua Achebe supported me with patience, radiance, humility, jokes, and questions that resonate in my head. Mohammed Ben Adballah provoked and taught me, laughed with and at me, and gave endlessly and generously of his time and work. I hope his passion about political aesthetics is in some small measure felt in these pages. This book has a ghostwriter, my brilliant friend and teacher the late Yaw Asare, playwright, journalist, dancer, director, who passed away in 2002 but whose thinking and work profoundly shaped this project. I hope the following words strung together in a linear fashion adequately reflect the energy and multiple views of living, art, scholarship, and ethics that all of these people given me.

TRICKSTER THEATRE

Introduction

Poetics of Uncertainty

> To take part in the African revolution it is not enough to write a revolutionary song; you must fashion the revolution with the people. And if you fashion it with the people, the songs will come by themselves, and of themselves.
>
> Sékou Touré (in Fanon, *The Wretched of the Earth*)

GHANA'S NATIONAL THEATRE MOVEMENT emerged as the nation achieved independence from British colonial rule in 1957. Playwrights and performers molded a modern theatrical style by adapting Akan-language Ananse the Spider trickster tales for the proscenium stage. State culture, education, and media infrastructures were built on a logic that performance was crucial to making the nation. The elaboration of a shared cultural tradition legitimated state sovereignty and tied a rising urban Ghanaian identity to a rural origin, on the one hand, and to transnational African and African diasporic liberation politics, on the other. Rising popular and formal theatre styles were built on established trickster storytelling techniques of genre blending, improvisation, and semiotic appropriation. However, there are consequences for a nation whose hero is Ananse, a trickster who is the owner and teller of stories as well as their protagonist; he seeks power using guile and cunning and is notorious for his cravings, intricate plotting, and duplicity. This book examines the contradictions that emerge from the ideal Ghanaian citizen being an urban figuration of a folkloric hustler, one who stands at the crossroads of tradition, everyday city life, and centuries of struggles against European trade domination and colonial rule. This trickster takes on changing significance in postcolonial contexts as the idealistic state drama of early independence is reinvented in the populist revolutionary 1980s and again in various electronic and digital genres around the millennium. The unintended consequences of presenting the trickster as a model of Ghanaian cultural belonging create a complex blend of sincerity and parody as social values. Trickster tales endure as emblems of social risk that both celebrate and warn of individual desire. As political futures, technologies, and labor conditions change, the tendency of actors to act and publics to interpret performances on two levels simultaneously defines formal Ghanaian drama and shapes its relevance as a broader form of public knowledge. In the process, this theatrical poetics of uncertainty shapes social action across a variety of popular, religious, commercial, and political realms. I begin with showing how the line between the real and the performed, on stage and off stage, is produced and contested in the shadow of Ananse the trickster.

Mohammed Ben Abdallah's play *The Trial of Mallam Ilya* is the story of a fictional African nation in the midst of a warrior's revolt. The title character is a religious elder and former revolutionary hero who is arrested and tried for treason. Not long after the actual second coup that brought Flight Lieutenant Jerry John Rawlings to power on December 31, 1981, in Ghana, Abdallah, one of the foremost playwrights of his generation, directed a production of his play at Accra's Arts Centre. This troupe consisted of radical young actors for whom theatre was a part of the new populist politics. The playwright/director delighted in tweaking the boundaries between spectators and actors and seated the rebel leaders in the audience as Mallam Ilya took center stage for his trial to argue for the beliefs that shaped his political choices.

Like Sophocles's Antigone, considered by the state to be a traitor for burying her brother against the wishes of her uncle who is the king, Ilya argues that he has followed his moral convictions even when they go in and out of political fashion and are against legal right. Mallam Ilya's trial becomes a play within a play raising questions of sovereignty for both the fictional rebel leaders and the audience. Abdallah's work is part of a broader tradition of African political theatre that posits drama as Brechtian provocation, in both form and content pushing people to speak and act out of moral conviction rather than through what is strictly legal.[1]

As his captors sit among the spectators, Mallam Ilya argues that while his actions appear seditious they have always been morally consistent. In the final scene, as the trial continues, a new group of rebels storms the stage to overthrow the previous coup's leaders. Explosions resound as a new insurgent shouts to the audience, "Block those entrances! See that no one escapes. If anybody resists, shoot him!" Ilya and his previous captor stand mute on stage as yet another coup swirls around them, their struggle rendered mute. A court crier announces, "Shortly after sunset today, while our latest group of warrior rulers were busy trying *their captors,* another warriors' revolt was afoot. . . . It has not been revealed who the leader of the revolt is. . . . The victors wish me to announce that they are here to stay! They will stand no opposition and take no nonsense." This satire of the frequent coup-making and regime changes that dominated African nations from the late 1960s through the 1980s was simultaneously an indictment of radical change and a call for it.

In 1999 Abdallah told me that at the end of one of the first performances of *Ilya* the audience was uncertain if the final revolt was real or staged. "In those days, people were so used to coups . . . everyone was really jumpy. So when an actor playing a soldier shouted 'block the entrances,' the audience panicked. . . . They thought it was another [real] coup. The atmosphere in the country was so explosive . . . everything became about politics." As one of the actors recalled to me, patrons jumped up and rushed for the exits. While Abdallah had not anticipated that audiences would confuse his staging with a real coup, he relished the mischievous potential of live theatre to unsettle people and question authority. Both the form and the content of Abdallah's play were intended to challenge viewers' assumptions about authoritative speaking and to stand by their moral beliefs even when faced with collective pressures. Its parody of endless political transitions and moral judgments resonated with recent state instability. For audiences in the early 1980s who had experienced so much recent political upheaval, anxiety collapsed the potential for theatrical narration and moral reflection. The staged action too closely mirrored spectators' expectations of public life.

Soon after this performance, Abdallah the radical playwright became an influential member of the new government, remaining as a cabinet minister for most of the 1980s and 1990s, shaping state policies in culture, education, religion, media, and urban planning in the midst of Ghana's uneven transition from a socialist revolutionary collective to a privatized corporate-oriented state. When in 1999 he recounted to me the story of audience panic, he had only recently returned to civilian life. When I asked him if he would call his plays political, he chuckled, deferring responsibility and denying artistic intent. "I can't control what people think. I just write the plays; if they see political messages in them, that's up to them." Pause. "But I don't know what audiences think these days. It is a different country . . . than it was in the revolutionary times. . . . There is not much chance of that confusion happening these days." As I researched theatre and its social implications, I kept thinking about the mix-up between staged theatre and political upheaval occurring in a key moment of national transformation, and about Abdallah's skepticism about it occurring in a later epoch. Maybe audience panic at the end of *Ilya* marked the performers' failure to direct audience interpretation, to properly mark their frames of reference; or perhaps it showed they were too successful by sincerely inhabiting roles meant to be satirical. Instead of offering a critique of conviction, the confusion of interpretation revealed a feeling of instability, not just in the state but at the root of public performance itself.

The misrecognition was a clue to how blurring the line between the staged and the real underpins much Ghanaian public performance across various genres. This episode—and the playwright's reflection on its historical contingency—raises questions about how various types of performances across Accra's urban landscape operate as types of cultural mediation that thrive on uncertainty. The confusion between the scripted and the contingent in the early 1980s and Abdallah's lament that this conflation was implausible twenty years later points to the changing significance of theatre as a way people remember, forget, and reconfigure the past for new eras. The on-stage mixing of politics and performance mirrors how Abdallah was able to be at once a leading social critic and powerful state minister, a dissident artist and a politician for over a decade. The blending of aesthetics and politics in turn reflects the complexities of colonial rule and liberation struggles in postcolonial states like Ghana. Abdallah, as an acolyte of Ghana's National Theatre Movement, was influenced both by the postindependence Akan folkloric revival and various strands of anticolonial Pan-Africanist thought. Throughout the twentieth century, Accra was a center for radical artists, politicians, and thinkers from West Africa as well as around the world: Jamaica, Trinidad, Haiti, and the United States. As a youth in the 1950s and 1960s, Abdallah recalls sneaking off to see various Pan-African leaders based in Accra, including Frantz Fanon, who briefly lived in Accra as ambassador of the provisional Algerian government.

In *The Trial of Mallam Ilya* the ambiguity of moral storytelling frames questions—whether intentional or unintentional—about the boundaries between the stage and the audience, politics and entertainment. The confusion between sincerity and artifice reveals how moments of social upheaval channel indeterminacy around political futures, as well as the productive instability of performance and its interpretive frames. In this sense, uncertainty drives interpretation and creativity and makes participants hyper-reflexive in discerning how performers claim voices and establish authority and when they fail to do so. Understanding a poetics of Ghanaian theatre involves not just looking at what happens on stage but at infrastructures, practices, and debates that frame how artists and audiences make and contest meaning, what semiotic registers guide the interpretation of words and actions, and how theatre becomes at times important and in other moments banal. As this book shows, reflexivity is highly developed in Ghanaian theatre, as it is rooted in a logic of appropriation central to proverb-rich Ananse trickster moral storytelling in which the boundaries between the stage and the audience are fluid and observers can easily become active participants. Self-consciousness about the rules of performance is also linked to how colonial spectacles objectified and ordered African political, cultural, and spiritual life displaying the power of the colonial protostate in racial terms. In the subsequent drive for independence, Gold Coast performers and intellectuals reconfigured colonial logics of race and culture in part through remaking the rules of performance and their political significance.

Since independence, in various ways, the Ghanaian state fought to consolidate a centralized national imaginary through institutions and policies of national culture, while over time the state ceded control by privatizing its institutions. Since the 1980s, in the face of global political-economic pressure to marketize its economy, Ghana has struggled with what Rinaldo Walcott (forthcoming) has termed the "incoherence of contemporary neoliberal unfreedom." I use "unfreedom" to describe how ideas and forms of liberation and resistance hold people in place, undermining ideas of collective and personal freedom in the process of imagining future possibilities. The logic of the market is built on a contradiction often described in the language of freedom: it requires the promotion of an individual's rights to sell his or her labor, buy things, and be mobile to some extent, but it also requires that the labor and market potential of marginalized peoples are always made available to capital. Struggles in theatre institutions and performance interpretation provide one way to understand the conundrum of how market potential and its structural constraints are inscribed in the name of freedom.

Because of its particular history, Ghanaian theatre values unresolved narratives, moral ambiguity, and obscuring the line between the staged and the unstaged, unlike theatre genres that, for example, value narrative resolution and the suspension of disbelief. I take theatre not as a set of static texts or representations, but rather critical theories and representational practices emergent in how artists and audiences embody the processes of acting and interpreting. This book takes an actor-centered, semiotic approach in following how performers, directors, culture workers, and playwrights develop theatre as a form of critical public knowledge that shapes Ghanaian national, racial, and cultural identities since independence. It traces how a critical genre of storytelling—and its associated signs, styles, and stances—migrates across social spaces, incorporating multiple influences repurposed for new contexts. As Stuart Hall points out, critical theory is built on highlighting reflexivity, especially in the context of the end of empire, where cultural meaning becomes intensely politicized. In this sense, Ghanaian performances and the discourse that revolves around them act as a critical theory that emerges in ongoing tensions around what constitutes Ghanaian culture and how to define Ghanaian theatre as well as how to calibrate their significance for public life in a nation struggling for political sovereignty in the face of ongoing foreign influences. As critical practice, theatre discourse configures the present and future, as past struggles, revolutions, and political stances get recalibrated through active processes of remembering and forgetting, lamenting and reviling. In marking the relationships between culture and politics, past and present, on stage and off stage, Ghanaian theatre points to the malleability of these temporal and spatial distinctions and to the contested nature of ideas of freedom. Critical theory retethers representations and actions to their historical and social contexts, and links stances, signs, and practices to the power that animates them. This book endeavors, then, to understand the emergent contexts in which Ghanaian performances as events and potentials are experienced and theorized as critical engagements with social power.

Theatre as Cultural Mediation—A Political-Racial History of Performance

The aesthetics of contemporary Ghanaian drama refract a set of tensions between the appropriation of Akan Ananse trickster storytelling by a state-centered cultural reclamation project, evolving ideas of modern stage drama, the use of the arts to forge a transnational Pan-African liberation movement, and the significance of theatre as medium for private media, religious belief, and corporate marketization.

British rule across its empire used ideas of culture to define non-European peoples as primitive, unmodern, and incapable of managing their own political and economic affairs (Cohn 1983, 1996). As British colonial states were being formed in the 1920s across Africa, educational, religious, and political institutions were built on the racial ideological opposition between European citizenship and African cultural being. The British saw Africans as susceptible to the power of performance. Cultural spectacles displayed traditional adornment, dance, and ritual as objectified forms for classifying and administering African peoples. Defining Africans as primitive and culture-bound disempowered educated elites and negated arguments for African political and economic sovereignty (Mamdani 1996). That is to say, racial inequality was naturalized in the language of cultural difference and its display. This colonial legacy of culture as objectified performance, in some measure, defined the terrain on which nascent postcolonial national publics were produced and contested. From the 1920s debates about the significance of culture and the arts for identity facilitated the emergence of new political imaginaries focused on the interrelationship between "tribal," linguistic, and racial affiliations.

Accra became the capital of the Gold Coast colony in 1877, and while Sekondi, Cape Coast, and Kumasi remained important Gold Coast cities, after World War I, Accra became a West African regional center of commerce, migration, politics, and popular culture, a place of excitement and possibility. Urban civil servant and laboring classes served rising mining industries and trade networks and the civic infrastructure they required. The rise of wage labor helped open local markets to foreign consumer goods. Taste, style, and entertainment both blurred and reinforced rising class divisions. American and English films were popular as were visiting performers from abroad; African American singers, musicians, and actors were highly anticipated. Educated elites and civil servants formed English-language literary and theatre groups and went to highlife big band shows at exclusive urban clubs. Wage laborers and aspirational youth patronized more impromptu venues with highlife guitar bands and concert party popular theatre shows—eclectic vaudevillian variety shows that intermingled music, dance, dramatic storytelling, and comedy.

After Ghana's independence from British rule in 1957, its first leader, Kwame Nkrumah, advocated for centralized state economic control and for African political and economic sovereignty. The Ghanaian state created spectacles out of traditional cultural practices to stage the new nation. These styles were also meant to forge linkages with other African and African diasporic peoples as Pan-African expression. Theatre was part of the national vision of political sovereignty and economic freedom. The National Theatre Movement, founded by intellectual urban artists, experimented with adapting rural storytelling and irreverent concert party theatre into a modern dramatic style that could be at once African and Ghanaian, the embodiment of traditional culture and a formal emblem of a rising urban-oriented nation. Artists and intellectuals from across the African diaspora flocked to Ghana to be part of its political and artistic transformation. Artists debated how to reconcile black and African culture with the development of a Ghanaian national imaginary. Nkrumah advocated for a modern "African personality," drawing on debates raging across Anglophone and Francophone Africa about how ideas of tradition should be reinvented for a new future. In this vein, Ghana's leading dramatist Efua Sutherland and her students created *Anansegro* or Ananse plays, positing that Akan-language Ananse the Spider trickster storytelling, or *Anansesem,* could be adapted to provide a moral-cultural grounding for new dramatic works. Artists and ethnographers researched rural folk storytelling, condensing and transforming their formal, stylistic elements for the temporal and spatial constraints of modern staging. Ghanaian scholars explored how the formal logic of Anansesem morality tales set in a mythic world inhabited by animals and humans allowed for the eclectic integration of multiple languages, music, dance, humor, and narration (Sutherland 1975).[2] They also explored the links between storytelling and vernacular concert party popular theatre (Sutherland 1970). While theatrical tastes had been defined by class before independence, with working-class folks enjoying popular concert party in Twi, Fante, Ga, and other African languages and elites preferring intellectual English drama and literature, the National Theatre Movement endeavored to link these styles. And while women had been excluded from performing in popular theatre, the new dramatic movement with its socialist ethos of worker inclusion encouraged numerous female playwrights, directors, and performers. Subsequent generations of intellectuals, writers, actors, educators, and culture workers were trained within this theatrical idiom of reflexive cultural appropriation.

Ghana's political history has been defined by the tension between those advocating for a socialist, Pan-African state and those arguing that liberation comes through free markets that connect entrepreneurs and corporations to consumers and resources with minimal state regulation. This ongoing opposition, as this book shows, has profound implications for ideas of theatre and public culture. Nkrumah's Pan-African socialist approach won out in the move toward independence, but his government was overthrown in 1966 in a Western-supported military coup. Popular sentiment had seemingly grown weary of his global focus and centralized state control. Subsequent military and civilian regimes were more sympathetic to Western liberal capitalist models. But after almost a decade of elite military rule characterized by spectacular pageantry and consumption, corruption, and instability, Flight Lieutenant Jerry John Rawlings came to power through a soldier's revolt on June 4, 1979, and a second coup on December 31, 1981. Rawlings's populist government critiqued widespread corruption and growing poverty, calling for grassroots "people's power." Between 1966 and 1981 there had been five successful coups d'etat and numerous other failed attempts. As Abdallah's *Mallam Ilya* points out, idealistic public calls for change began to seem empty to many Ghanaians. Rawlings attempted to instill moral and fiscal discipline and rebuild national pride. He recognized the power of street theatre and led by example, personally cleaning gutters and working with farmers in their fields as news cameras rolled. He established a Cultural Revolution that revived the idealistic cultural nationalism of the 1950s and 1960s. One actor recalls the excitement of radical political theatre in the early Rawlings years, explaining that there was "private and state-sponsored political drama ... celebrating Ghanaian identity through new African-oriented plays.... We were proud to be Ghanaian like we had been in Nkrumah's time."

In 1983, the state accepted the conditions of an International Monetary Fund (IMF) Structural Adjustment Program (SAP). In doing so, the new socialist state was mandated to enact free-market reforms and privatize state resources. The political-economic tension between the public displays of populist revolution and the infrastructural movements toward the free market was reflected in culture policy and theatre. The extended moment from the early 1980s through the 2000s marks Ghana's slow, inexorable transition from socialist uprising to a liberal political economy. By the turn of the millennium, marketization led to the growing centrality of private electronic and digital media and a public shaped by intertwined state, corporate, and religious institutions that distanced populism and theatre from politics, prying audiences and performers apart. Increasingly, the type of staged confusion—or confused staging—that happened at the early 1980s performance of Abdallah's *Mallam Ilya* seemed unlikely, though uncertainties about what constitutes culture, sincerity, and authoritative voicing continue to shape the power of performances.

Blended Performance Genres in Urban Performance Research

Popular and national theatre genres across mid-twentieth-century Africa were crucial to the emergence of centralized urban publics and of nascent aspirational classes with money and leisure time (Barber 2000; Cole 2001; Fabian 1998). Politicians like Nkrumah recognized that capturing the imagination of an emerging urban Africa—one seemingly caught between ideas of traditional, rural life and foreign ideas of modernity—was key to consolidating a popular base. The rich scholarly literature on popular culture, performance, and media in Anglophone Africa—especially Ghana and Nigeria—tends to be organized around particular irreverent popular genres, formal official styles, virtuoso artists, or material technological forms.[3] However, as Karin Barber (1987) notes in relation to Yoruba oral traditions, genre blending underpins much West African performance, giving it a malleability and mobility. Indeed, focusing a scholarly lens on the links among purportedly distinct genres gives new insight into how state orders, corporate and religious forms, irreverent sensibilities, and informal economies intermingle through signs and practices across a variety of contexts.

In the neoliberal moment, theatre is part of a broader dispersed set of contexts, genres, and technologies contributing to the development of a diffuse national public and a class of mobile and precarious youth. I show how formal staged drama, political spectacles, cultural performances, popular theatre, video, popular music, radio call-in shows, and Charismatic sermons appear as purportedly distinct genres, though they are linked through shared symbols, languages, and referential practices. Urban vernacular styles and fantasies are made in how people move among these putatively separate realms that, taken together, constitute a dynamic and multifaceted public life (Sasha Newell 2012; J. Shipley 2013a; Weiss 2009). Changing labor patterns, flows of capital, and new media technologies reconstitute lived experience through aesthetic practices that focus on mediation and circulation in themselves (Ferguson 2006; Hirschkind 2006; Larkin 2008).

This project is based on ethnographic research with theatre groups and archival research on the history of performance and cultural institutions conducted in Accra from 1997 to 2013. I began by working with and studying Abibigromma Theatre Company, the country's preeminent professional theatre group, but my research evolved into a study of a more abstract poetic configuration of performance. Abibigromma was founded in 1983 by Abdallah as a group to experiment with dramatic form and "to explore the transformative potentials of the storyteller . . . in mediating between the audience and the play." He coined the term *Abibigro* to expand Sutherland's concept of Anansegro into a broader, eclectic Pan-African aesthetic. The name Abibigro is an amalgamation of the Akan words *Abibi,* meaning "Black/African," and *agro,* meaning "play, trick, or joke," the slippage being appropriate to the company's style. For Abdallah, Abibigro is a "total African theatre" integrating various multimedia music, dance, and drama traditions from around Africa as a modern Pan-African theatre.

Beginning in 1998 I spent several years in official residencies with both branches of this professional, state-funded company: Abibigromma Theatre Company at the School of Performing Arts, University of Ghana, Legon; and

Abibigromma, the National Theatre Players at the National Theatre of Ghana. I observed and participated in rehearsals, traveled for performances around the country, conducted formal and informal interviews and recorded life histories with artists and workers, traced questions about political history and culture policy into the archives, and learned the groups' extensive theatrical repertoires. In these groups the ethos of participation and improvisation was prevalent, and people were quick to take advantage of my presence. I was a video documenter, production assistant, actor, speech coach, director, and stagehand. As Karin Barber and Catherine Cole both point out in relation to their own experiences acting while doing performance research, I was sought out as a stage and screen actor not only for my performance skills but for the symbolic value that a white male performer conveys in Ghana. Primarily, I acted in English, playing roles like a colonial officer, a missionary, and an Interpol detective. I also had a semirecurring role in *Cantata,* a popular weekly television soap opera musical comedy in which, because I spoke Twi on screen, I played various Ghanaian characters. Speaking Twi and being white provided an effective comedic juxtaposition for this irreverent show and revealed some Ghanaian notions of white bodies. On the one hand, they continue to represent authority, moral salvation, and access to resources. On the other, they stand for the history of exploitation from the slave trade to colonialism to contemporary forms of corporate expropriation and Western immigration restrictions (Pierre 2012; J. Shipley 2013b). Being part of staging race attuned me to the historical legacies of how power and inequality have been discussed and erased, visualized and performed.

As I branched out from working with Abibigromma, I got to know other networks of artists, writers, civil servants, corporate executives, video directors/producers, and media entrepreneurs associated with state-owned Ghana Television, private TV3/GAMA Films, Metro TV, TV Africa, state-owned Ghana Broadcasting (GBC) radio, numerous private radio stations, cultural troupes, the Accra Arts Centre, the National Commission on Culture, the Ministry of Information, and the Concert Party Union. I traced the continuities and divisions among dispersed genres, groups, media, and events and followed the public circulation of people, signs, and practices. Ghanaian theatre has been made as artists and culture workers objectify and restage "culture" as a form of public knowledge. State and private cultural institutions, in turn, legitimize theatre as a realm of authentic cultural expression. To trace a theatre poetics, I followed the ways in which live theatre events mediate relations among various participants across contexts. My "object of study," so to speak, became a theory of embodied and discursive knowledge implied in theatre.

I was amazed at the breadth of artists' skills and their ability to switch rapidly among various styles of staging, language use, and body movement. Abibigromma's repertoire is divided into four categories: staged versions of traditional music and dance from across Ghana and Africa; choreographed dance-dramas; scripted English-language plays, including works by British, American, South African, Nigerian, and Ghanaian playwrights; and Abibigro plays, multilingual scripted mixes of music, dance, and drama structured as storytelling narratives. During a single week the group might rehearse and perform a number of different shows at venues across Accra. In rapid succession they performed formal stage productions at the National Theatre and the University of Ghana's Drama Studio in English; choreographed traditional music and dance for tourists at hotels and executives at corporate launches; presented cultural spectacles for government events and visiting foreign dignitaries at the Conference Centre and the State House; and produced community-based theatre in nearby rural villages, using humorous plays to impart social messages about hygiene, safe sex, and voting, sponsored by private corporations, nongovernmental organizations (NGOs), and state organizations.

Despite the virtuosity of Abibigromma's artists, theatre in the late 1990s was beset with financial and structural problems. As in many locales around the world, theatre is not a respected profession. While popular entertainers are widely celebrated and writers, directors, and performers are seen as local cultural experts, they are also often understood to be morally suspect and, in an era of economic anxiety, their work unimportant. As state funding for cultural institutions was dwindling, corporate advertisers, private media companies, and religious institutions were using cultural performances for other purposes. As their state salaries dwindled in the face of rapid inflation, performers made money through side jobs performing in private productions, cultural displays for hotels, and television commercials for things like laundry detergent, bouillon cubes, and local alcohol. Some gave private dancing and drumming lessons mostly to foreigners; others began acting in private video-films; Brew Riverson Jr. did English voice-overs for popular television broadcasts of Latin American soap operas; David Dontoh hosted *Agro,* a weekly television quiz program; Maame Dokonoe became a popular radio call-in show host.

Conducting ethnography in a city like Accra with mobile, creative, irreverent artists made me constantly uncertain about how to define or focus on a field of research and how to understand the relationship between on-stage and off-stage activity in the midst of the myriad styles of theatre performed across a variety of venues (Hannerz 1987). Youth from across West Africa have come to Accra for work and pleasure since before independence, though they maintain ties to extended cultural, linguistic, and kin networks. While the city was built around several Ga towns, it became a multiethnic and multilingual space with Ga, Dangme, Akan (especially Fante, Asante Twi, and Akuapem Twi), Ewe, Dagbani, and Hausa, among other languages and cultures, intermingling. Akan language and social conventions—to the frustration of many Ga people—dominate much public culture in Accra with Twi as a lingua franca. Many Accra denizens continue to identify authentic African life and culture with rural villages and modern life with international travel and the West. Aspirational youth imagine life in urban Accra as temporary and unstable, always hoping for the future though also feeling the pull of social obligations (Piot 2010). Accra is a place of possibility as well as frustration and struggle. It juxtaposes the foreign and the local, extreme wealth and poverty in making a particularly Ghanaian cosmopolitanism (Quayson 2014).

Life as a performer entails moving across Accra's urban landscape among rehearsal spaces, live venues, video shoot locations, and radio and television studios as well as shifting between state and private realms and styles of performance. As James Ferguson (1999: 18) points out, the uncertainties and contingencies of urban life often conflict with expectations of urban field workers; he notes that researchers "have commonly lamented the lack of the sense of a knowable social whole."[4] Theatre artists in Accra constitute a small class of highly mobile performers and culture workers who shift among a diverse set of genres, groups, and media. They come from multiple linguistic groups. Some are highly educated from middle-class families, while others are working class, though their status in the culture and performance scenes remain determined by level of education and English fluency. Accra's theatre artists are drawn from across the social spectrum by the excitement of the stage. But their lives are shaped by uneven infrastructural support, economic anxiety, constant movement, long commutes, the uncertainty of regular work, and the threat and potential of video, digital, and mobile entertainment forms. Their routines entail long periods of boredom, waiting for work, missed rehearsals, and canceled events punctuated by the personal thrills and camaraderie of preparing and performing. Most hope that theatre leads to wealth and travel opportunities, though continual frustration at low wages and lack of patronage is often disillusioning. The malleability of theatre forced me to account for how artists react creatively to the contingencies of the city as an evolving built environment. I came to see constant movement as a way of being and to understand circulation as a central social principle rather than an impediment to understanding (Ferguson 1999: 84; Munn 1986).

As actors and culture workers moved among supposedly discrete traditional, popular, and modern dramatic genres, I traced how minute fragments of performances—bodily gestures, phrases, dance moves, drum rhythms, narrative structures, formal staging techniques—migrated among distinct forms and media. In tracing how a particular hand gesture from a dance or proverbial phrase from a song, for example, moved across various stagings and contexts, I began to understand the complex interdiscursivities and playful use of multivocal signs that defines much Ghanaian urban performance. A popular comedian might juxtapose in one tale *adowa,* an Akan funeral dance done at courtly events, a hand gesture referencing a political party, a hip-hop style of comportment, and a Charismatic preacher's speaking flow. As practices and signs move among distinct arenas, they provoke audiences and performers to debate aesthetic assumptions through incongruous juxtapositions: the appropriateness of using traditional cultural styles on a modern stage, defining respectful forms of address, or the distinctions between urban and rural, foreign and local. Actors play with generic boundaries, recombining signs to produce new interpretive registers. Debates about the respectful and legitimate use of symbols within specific events provoke reflexive recognition of styles of appropriation themselves.

By tracing principles of performance through disparate events and genres, I explore how Ghanaians negotiate the overlapping and sometimes contradictory relationships among class, gender, culture, religion, language, nation, race, and Pan-African identifications. Actors, directors, and playwrights shape eloquent speech and dynamic action by playing with the boundaries among multiple performance genres. By interweaving signs and references and forms in unexpected ways, they challenge audiences and publics to pay close attention. Performers of all sorts—politicians, pastors, comedians, actors, musicians—invoke authority by showing their mastery of multiple texts and contexts. In the production of viable performance stances—for speaking, acting, listening, and so on—within specific events, actors align incommensurate discursive registers, recontextualizing familiar signs to claim new types of speaking authority. The rise of the Ghanaian neoliberal state, then, is reflected in the uneven and contested transformations of the public sphere from focusing on Pan-African imagery and state-oriented performances of culture to dispersed corporate, religious, and popular practices and their electronically mediated enactments.

Ananse the Spider and Poetics of Mediation

Ananse the spider remains key to ideas of Ghanaian performance across eras and contexts as a transgressor and genre blender (Donkor 2008). Early-twentieth-century anthropologists, religion scholars, and folklorists identified trickster characters in various societies as mediators between spiritual and material realms (Radin [1956] 1972). In Native American societies trickster characters have been described as culture-heroes who make the world safe for human habitation (Radin [1956] 1972). In African diasporic cultures various tricksters demonstrate connections to Africa and are icons of guile and humor, figures who survive and achieve success against the odds (Gates 1988; Hyde 1998). R. S. Rattray's 1930 account *Akan-Ashanti Folk-Tales* examines Anansesem or spider tales as essential to Akan folkloric tradition. He criticizes earlier descriptions that focus on the tales' mythic and religious significance, instead arguing that rather than sacred, they are comments on daily life available to everyone. Tales are "told in public for amusement" (1930: xii) as villagers gather "in a circle after dark" (1930: vi) to listen to storytellers (Danquah 1928). In Anansesem, "subjects ordinarily regarded as sacred . . . appear to be treated as if profane, and sometimes even . . . become the subject of ridicule" (Rattray 1930: x). To Rattray, stories were functionalist, socially sanctioned outlets for "pent-up feelings," giving insight into the character of the Asante people (Rattray 1930: xii). For mid-twentieth-century concert party theatre artists and highlife musicians, Ananse tales inspired the use of irreverent humor as social commentary (Donkor 2013).

One story explains why all folktales are called Anansesem: Ananse wants all of the stories—in some versions for himself and in other versions to be set loose in the world. Nyame (God) owns the stories. When Ananse asks for the stories, Nyame says he will give them to him in exchange for various nonhuman creatures—python, hornet, leopard, and *mmoatia*, a malevolent magical fairy. Using elaborate traps and lies, Ananse deceives and captures the animals, bringing them to Nyame to claim the stories. Nyame is impressed with Ananse's cunning and true to his word turns over the stories. Ananse becomes the owner of the tales. This foundational narrative shows how Ananse is both the teller of stories and at their center. According to Kwesi Yankah (1983), tales focus on Ananse's "wily character." His cunning is linked to the spider's skills. "The adroitness of the spider in spinning an intricate web out of its own saliva is admired, as is the artistic value of the web . . . the spider's web is like a hangman's noose; the more you try to free yourself of it, the more you get entangled" (Kwesi Yankah 1983: 10). He schemes to achieve his desires by exploiting others' weaknesses. Ananse gets his prey "without any effort on his part" (ibid.). Ananse is both the antihero and the narrator of tales, simultaneously in the story and mediator of the lines between its characters and audiences. He is both human and animal, a normal village denizen and a supernatural creator, a charlatan and sympathetic character, an overly masculine fool and a wise elder, a loner and head of a family (Carroll 1984; Vecsey 1981). Ananse is a man who often takes advantage of his wife and children and neighbors. He avoids work but spends much time and energy telling lies to claim the wealth and value of the community and his family. His cunning comes in his ability to hide his intent. Stories often emphasize the moral tensions between his individual desire and collective moral obligation.

Ananse is understood in the popular imaginary as connected to a fundamental sensibility of rural traditional life, even as he moves into national and urban contexts. For Nkrumah's cultural nationalists, Ananse became an adaptable icon embodying the characteristics of the new nation meant to create unity in shared tradition and inspire future creativity. Drawing on the eclectic multiplicity of Anansesem, urban dramatists created multimedia, multilinguistic, ambiguous morality tales for national stages. Ghanaian modern theatre employs formal European staging conventions built on the illusion of the fourth wall separating audiences from staged action, though its fluid storytelling framework simultaneously opens a space for irreverent interplay between the performance and the audience (Donkor 2013). A scripted storyteller character is present on stage in many modern dramas. Drawing on the sense that Ananse is both owner of and protagonist in stories, this character is fundamentally dual, both complicit with the audience in watching the action and a character in the tale. This encourages theatre audiences to reflect on how the performed and the mundane, the narrated and the lived are made and unmade in the event. In recent decades, Ananse tales are appropriated in urban contexts by hip-hop, political discourse, television drama, film, radio, internet memes, and social media users. In these movements, Ananse's cunning and irreverent adaptability create a model of appropriation for navigating social transformations.

This book builds on performance and media studies by using an actor-centered, sociolinguistic approach to theatrical performances and performance discourse in Accra. Linguistic anthropology provides tools for understanding local notions of performance, critique, and agency by starting with social action and seeing contexts, actors, and texts as emergent in ongoing pragmatic interactions. As Kelly Askew (2002: 12) argues in examining popular music and Tanzanian politics, scholars are still reticent to explore the performative dimensions of African politics in historically and culturally specific ways (cf. Haugerud 1997). Many studies of performance focus on individual and collective notions of identity (Silvio 2010). Some theorists, building on the work of Émile Durkheim and Victor Turner, tend to examine rituals and performances as transformative events that produce subjects linked to collectivities by affective ties. Leading from Judith Butler and Erving Goffman, other analysts examine small-scale daily actions and language use as reiterative practices that make and critically engage identity. Both strands of performance theory tend to presuppose the universality of performance as public enactment and what it does. There is a tendency to underestimate the contextually specific nature of performativity itself and its relationship to subject formation. A theory of performance built out of the theatrical remediation of storytelling in Ghana implies that on one level performances produce stable national subjects. However, these subject positions simultaneously subvert the collective project they purport to celebrate. To show the contextual specificity of this contradiction, I focus on local understandings of performance and performativity. Ghanaian theatre relies on a critique of the link between performance and identity. The idea that an individual is oriented in performances is at the root of how nations tend to imagine the importance of ceremonies and spectacles of affirmation as making citizen-subjects. Ghanaian theatre condenses various histories, creating a shared cultural past linked to an aspirational present and a potential future. However, theatre and performances built out of trickster storytelling seem to unravel in their purported task even as it is presented, in favor of satirical self-awareness. If we take Ghanaian performance theory seriously, stances and subject positions emergent in a particular performance or genre may not spill over into other contexts. Ritual and performance theorists posit that theatrical performances, "in the act of addressing audiences, constitute those audiences as a particular form of collectivity" (Barber 1997: 354). However, in the socio-historical contexts of postindependence Ghana, this theoretical presupposition is itself scrutinized by participants and becomes part of an event.

In contrast to other traditions of postcolonial African theatre that engage in politics directly, Ghanaian drama is built on indirection. Whereas in South Africa and Nigeria, for example, theatre is interpreted as a form of praise or criticism of politics and society, Ghanaian theatre is more oblique (Kruger 1999; Olaniyan and Quayson 2007). Even plays like *Mallam Ilya* that are on one level explicitly political are framed and interpreted to focus on mediation itself rather than engaging power and authority directly. As I demonstrate, some practitioners lament the lack of a straightforward link between performance and political authority, but this shows an underlying poetics of reflexivity in which Ghanaian drama is often about performance and the process of appropriation itself. Actors and audiences make performances and simultaneously contemplate and interpret the process of making them.

Artistic genres emerge in a public's awareness of them as they deploy the indexical and referential aspects of performance to focus participants' attention on poetic functions of expression. For Roman Jakobson in verbal poetry, "the poetic function comprises the focus within the verbal message on the verbal message itself" (Waugh 1980: 58). The poetic aspects of any semiotic text, speech act, or performance orient participants toward the unique, specific configuration of the message in context. All texts-in-performance have a poetic function, but certain types like poetry, theatre, and visual art are socially recognized as emphasizing the poetic aspects of signification rather than the referential aspects. Texts that are explicitly poetic emphasize their own internal logics and how their various parts relate and make sense as a totality and in relation to what they are not. As Jakobson (1960: 358) elaborates, "The poetic function projects the principle of equivalence from the axis of selection into the axis of combination." Poetics focuses attention away from the syntagmatic co-occurrence or combination of terms—for example, the formal relations between a costume and a dance—and away from the referential aspects of signs—for example, the meaning of the costume and dance in isolation. Instead poetics focuses on substitutability or how elements are chosen from potential alternate selections and combined in new ways. An immanent paradigm underlies all performances that shapes the relationship between the signs used and other potential signs not used. All performances, then, reflect back on and reshape their underlying paradigms.

A critical aspect of making Ghanaian national theatre into a genre, as I will elaborate, was writing scripts with dialogue and directing plays with formalized choreography and established durations and blocking. Struggles over the codification of oral storytelling and dance into modern theatre are contestations over how to fix performance styles and how to objectify the idea of improvisation and the dialogic relationships among actors, dancers, musicians, and audiences. As a result, this theatre is characterized by a highly developed, reflexive discourse in which performances are explicitly about the process of performing. Participants focus on the formal aspects of acting, assessing aesthetic value through the performer's ability to control double meanings, multiple forms of address, and polyvalent, shifting registers. Critical debates about staging are a major part of any genre, and in Ghana they are particularly significant as performances often focus explicitly on how to be a convincing actor. Audiences and performers, on stage and off, spend a lot of time thinking, talking, and performing about the processes of performance. Participants tune in to assess trickery and sincerity of characters and storytellers. Ghanaian performance discourse emphasizes language about language use and how characters shift among various roles. In opposition to formal proscenium staging, Ghanaian modern theatre highlights the role of the storyteller, sometimes explicitly and sometimes by formalizing the storytelling function in how characters recognize the fact that they are acting. Storytellers mock and play with the line between narration and action shaping the space and temporality of performances in reflexive deliberation. Characters and actors point out and manipulate the constraints of institutions and argue with each other and with audiences about what they should be doing. Audiences assess performances often less on the content of the story than through its formal features. While reflexivity is part of all social action—on stage and off—here it is particularly pronounced.

Moving away from a universal theory of performance requires focusing on participation roles rather than general notions of subjectivity (Goffman 1981). Participants move among multiple social registers within events and as they move among different events. They adopt stances within specific contexts, aligning themselves with established, recognizable social roles in order to incorporate new values and signs. As new stances emerge, they realign past, present, and future discursive registers. An actor can shift positions and her or his identity in one event in ways that may be contradictory to another stance she or he takes in a different context. In Ghanaian performance, the trickster authorizes participants to claim contradictory moral positions across various contexts. Stance gives analytic and contextual specificity to local notions of agency, highlighting its cultural and historical conditions.

In Ghanaian theatre, poetics are defined to a great extent by struggles over the practice, interpretation, and staging of theatre and its relevance for broader aspects of social life—in a sense a reflexivity of reflexivity. Participants often focus on the aspects of performances that are about the making of performance and the ability to be a performer. All performances entail self-aware activities and language through which performers and audiences reflexively negotiate the rules of acting and interpreting. Trickster storytelling encourages heightened awareness of the making of performance and how on stage is separated from and collapses into off stage. Similar to the Hausa spider trickster Gizo, the Akan spider trickster Ananse "provides performers with a means to discuss language through the metalinguistic terminology of his own speech" (Hunter and Oumarou 1998: 157). In Ghanaian theatre, focusing on the message is highly recursive in that the message is often primarily about the process of performing itself. The art of storytelling in Ghana—turn-taking, the role of the storyteller, playing with audiences, referencing language shifts, inserting unexpected and subtle references seemingly apposite to the narrative—becomes, in and of itself, an object of contemplation.

Various performance practices congeal into a recognizable genre through reflexive awareness of them, in the process calling into being a community of interpretation. In this case, the genre values the ability to play multiple roles rather than inhabiting a singular subject position. Participants recognize themselves as members of a collectivity through actively and self-consciously adopting a set of potential stances (Kockelman 2006b). Poetic principles are relations of relations that organize the values and interpretive frames in an event; that is, they point to how referential and indexical connections are made and contested. A performance's moral and aesthetic values are assessed through participants' affective, bodily, and intellectual reactions to how these connections are made. Analyzing configurations of words, gestures, and stagings reveals how poetic frames link small-scale real events to historical and institutional contexts (Agha 2005a: 1).

For a performance to be legible, participants and audiences must share and understand the generic conventions at play. Proper adherence to established performance conventions and generic frames gives performances the authority of tradition. At the same time, artists play with and challenge these conventions with unexpected recombinations of references, humorous asides, and parodic copies of sincere actions, in order to reorient performances. As the juxtaposition of diverse styles and languages is central to life in Accra in general, actors irreverently intermingle various genres within single events and skillfully shift their performance styles to suit multiple genres across the social landscape. Focusing on how generic boundaries are produced and maintained in some contexts, even as these boundaries are transgressed in other contexts, shows theatre as a dynamic set of urban practices with an evolving poetics rather than a set of static conventions. A genre's distinctiveness is contingent on how its spatial, temporal, and stylistic borders are made and maintained. As Ghanaian theatre is explicitly a blended genre, it relies on actors' abilities to skillfully manage intertextual gaps and pull references from among various events in different contexts (Bakhtin 1982; Bauman and Briggs 1990: 75; Hill 2005).

The transformations of Ghanaian theatre over the twentieth century have fine-tuned the elegant use of indirection as a key principle of effective performance (Kwesi Yankah 1989). Generally across communities of interpretation of Akan peoples and in Gold Coast/Ghana, the arts of mediation and artful indirection are key to how authority and the right to speak are configured. Indeed in Ghana, "there is a built-in aesthetic within any mode of communication that consciously avoids directness and promotes suspense" (Kwesi Yankah 1995: 182). This logic of indirection also resonates with the broader sense that Akan ontology is built on a set of doublings between soul and inheritance, bodily presence and spatio-temporal abstraction. As philosophers Kwame Gyekye (1987) and Kwasi Wiredu (1996) argue, multiplicity defines Akan concepts of personhood. Debates about the nature of communication and African personhood and personality have been part of the ways that Ghanaian artists, scholars, politicians, and historians conceive of performance in relation to national/Pan-African identity and sovereignty. Some have argued that indirection and duality are autochthonous traditional aspects of West African cultures, while others see them as products of a centuries-long history of contact between European companies and empires and West African polities that required African peoples to develop complex forms of translation and diplomatic mediation. Public discourse on contested topics such as political elections or personal tragedy uses a variety of face-saving techniques to protect both speaker and listener from embarrassment and harm. For example, in Akan chiefly courts, the chief speaks indirectly through an Okyeame, a linguist who translates, embellishes, and disperses the force of royal words and mediates the potential dangers of outside forms of talk directed at the chief (K. Anyidoho 1983; A. Asare n.d.; Kwesi Yankah 1995). Indirection is highly valued in Ghanaian speech culture and "permeates all formal encounters involving face-to-face communication" (Kwesi Yankah 1995: 182). As Samuel Obeng (1997: 55) points out, in Ghana, "a 'good' speaker employs circumlocution to manage a wide range of face-threatening communicative situations." Because of the high value placed on mediated speaking, actors develop sophisticated ways to divide speaking roles—specifically separating the authorship or responsibility for words from the speaker or animator of them—predisposing participants to offer complex interpretations of intent and meaning (Kwesi Yankah 1995: 11). The particularly dense referentiality of proverbial speech creates flexible poetic paradigms through which new symbolic registers are incorporated into established forms of communication (Nketia 1962).

In contrast to the desire for certainty, theories of Ghanaian performance thrive on the productive potentials of uncertainty. Charles Peirce disagreed with the assumptions of analytic philosophers who argued that logic necessitates certainty of interpretation. For Peirce uncertainty is a part of language use and therefore logic must account for it. The political philosophy that underpins the nation-state model relies on a singular consistency between internal moral belief and external social persona. That is to say, the model national citizen is sincere, certain, and stands for enduring, consistent values. In contrast the trickster is cynical and polyvalent, drawing on multiple sometimes contradictory symbolic registers, driven by desire while obfuscating personal intent. As the figuration of the trickster endures in various aspects of Ghanaian public life, his poetic ambiguity seems to only increase in significance as the sincerity of national citizenship aligns with the skills required by neoliberal entrepreneurship. For those who live on the margins, trickery is a pragmatic and morally justified response to disempowerment (Hart 1973; J. Scott 1990). Ananse provides a ready model of self-fashioning for those who aspire to reinvent themselves and aim for personal fortunes and power in the midst of long-term collective struggles. Contemporary representations of the trickster valorize personal desire, complicating links between individuated business-mindedness and national projects. While traditional authority and modern politics are often seen as opposed, the trickster provides people with performance strategies for linking them and navigating aspirations in a contemporary landscape. Trickster sensibilities shape performances on and off stage, grounding a moral public in the desire for success and in the pleasures and dangers of persuasive speaking as actors struggle to negotiate the institutional pressures of state withdrawal and new corporate demand.

Chapter Outlines

This book's ethnographic, historical, and literary tales of urban theatre and its circulation trace the emergence of a poetics of theatre. This poetics is characterized by a particular concern with the malleability of the line between what counts as the staged and the real. In making and contesting this line, participants shape ideas of cultural, racial and national belonging and imagine the potentials of critical agency. If this book has a main character it is Mohammed Ben Abdallah, whose theatrical and political work provides a framework and perspective for telling this story of Ghanaian theatre.

Chapter 1 examines how British colonial ideas of African culture emerged in the 1920s and 1930s through theatre, education, anthropology, and media institutions. The British saw African performance as a way of depoliticizing modern African subjects by linking them to objectified tradition. A rising urban African elite subsequently reconfigured these colonial ideas of African culture to fight for economic and political rights. Theories of African culture and their theatrical enactment, then, were central to struggles over sovereignty.

Chapter 2 explores the historical development of culture policy and the National Theatre Movement in relation to Ghana's independence in 1957 and subsequent political transformations. Ghanaian intellectuals used ethnographic research to transform Ananse the trickster from a sign of passive rural life into a marker of Ghanaian cultural nationhood and urban guile. Moral storytelling became the basis for a modern national theatre.

Chapter 3 examines how, in the midst of a populist revolution in the 1980s, Nkrumahist notions of cultural nationalism were reinvented to reflect challenges faced by a state caught between critiques of neocolonialism and pressure to liberalize. The 1980s Cultural Revolution was a form of nostalgia for a lost future, a revitalization of the hopes of independence. New Pan-African theatre aimed to reinforce national moral integrity and racial connections in the face of the threat of foreign Western influences. Though as the state attempted to launch a theatre revival, artists and arts institutions were entangled in the struggles of marketization and rising Pentecostalism.

Chapter 4 examines the ethical, artistic, and intellectual struggles faced by Abdallah as he worked simultaneously as theatre artist and policy-maker through the 1980s and 1990s. His dilemmas were indicative of the conundrums many artists face when confronting the pragmatics of the state and the entanglements of moral right and sovereign rule.

Chapter 5 examines how Ananse storytelling provides a formal structure for mediating theatrical and social relations and the centrality of reflexivity to staging Ghanaian drama. I follow Abibigromma Theatre Company on and off stage through the production process of Abdallah's *Witch of Mopti,* a play about a moral and spiritual battle between a king and a witch in an ancient kingdom that is also a critique of modern political leaders caught between the desires of their people and ideas of moral right. The storytellers mediate between audience and actors, living simultaneously in both worlds.

Chapter 6 examines the contradictions that emerge in corporate appropriations of storytelling and theatrical traditions. It traces the sponsorship of concert party popular theatre by the multinational corporation Unilever at the National Theatre and on state-run Ghana Television to show how theatre institutions and performances refract political-economic transformation. What appears to the public as a performance of cultural nationalism at the National Theatre is, in fact, a complex intermingling of popular culture, corporate marketing, and state-centered ceremony mediated through newly private media outlets.[5]

Chapter 7 focuses on the excitement and anxiety of the fake. It shows that Charismatic pastors and popular theatre comedians rely on similar styles of performance rooted in adaptations of trickster storytelling while occupying inverted positions in the public moral imagination. With the growing authority of Charismatic pastors, public anxieties arise about fake preachers. Those who claim divine powers in highly theatrical ways though all too often turn out to be false prophets. Charismatic performances orient national publics toward both the potentials and dangers of personal aspiration. Popular comedians parody and adopt styles of performance akin to pastoral preaching. By mimicking theological authority they reveal the potential and dangers of fakery. In the ever-present fear of the fake, people seek the promise of the real that is discerned through performative authority.[6]

Chapter 8 examines copying as critical performance. It focuses on the 2007 fiftieth-anniversary reenactment, staged by popular actors, of Kwame Nkrumah's midnight speech on March 6, 1957, declaring Ghana's independence. Reenactment is a performance genre that allows audiences and performers to reflexively assess the closeness and distance between the current moment of performance and the moment being replicated. In nostalgically staging Ghana's past glory, this performance objectifies and inverts the nation's foundational ritual moment. The uncanny exactness of the reenactment acts as accidental parody, further distancing contemporary neoliberal uncertainties from the transformations and hopes of independence.

The epilogue describes Ananse as a sublime figure and points to how a Ghanaian performance theory provides a contextually specific model of productive uncertainty and multiplicity that emerges through a mix of historical patterns, semiotic appropriations, and creative reconfigurations.

PART I

HISTORY AND MEDIATIONS
IN MAKING THEATRE

1 Making Culture

Race, History, and a Theory of Performance in the Gold Coast Colony

THIS CHAPTER TRACES how culture becomes an object and technology, defined and circulated by a series of institutions and administrative projects oriented toward producing a modern, urban African populace through art and performance. Culture is consolidated in the 1920s and 1930s in the Gold Coast as a rural, ahistorical object of study within a British imperial logic. It is identified in practices, signs, and material aspects of art, religion and performance. In the late colonial period, as culture becomes a technology of rule, various British and Gold Coast factions vie to define and control modern Gold Coast identity. An evolving language of culture and nationhood is circulated by educational institutions, new media, arts programs, and administrative projects as well as informal, syncretic popular performance styles. In the Gold Coast colony—as throughout the British Empire—theories of culture were used to codify and administer local groups. Scholars and bureaucrats focused on the visual, public elements of social life, furthering stereotypes about non-Western people's predisposition for and susceptibility to the power of performance (A. Apter 2005; Barber 1997). From the 1920s, cultural performances were choreographed and institutionalized through colonial infrastructures as highly visible forms of identity. For the British, art and culture education were ways to help young Africans develop moral character based on their true identity and to prepare them to contribute to a civilized, modern society.

As scholars have shown in a variety of contexts, ideas of culture and tradition are invented: that is, various practices are bundled together and rendered as ahistorical markers of origins and identities (Hobsbawm and Ranger 1992). For the Gold Coast's aspiring urbanites, at times culture and debates about it were highly politicized, while in other instances expressive culture provided syncretic forms of leisure and entertainment through literary clubs, music, popular theatre, and film that shaped new urban cosmopolitan collectives. This chapter shows, then, how cultural forms of belonging become modes of control, organization, commodification, pleasure, and resistance within state, imperial, religious, and corporate orders. In the Gold Coast colony, processes and debates around art and performance develop a reflexivity through which intellectuals, artists, students, and audiences define what culture is and what it is good for (Cohn 1996; Comaroff and Comaroff 1992; Cooper and Stoler 1997).

Over the course of the twentieth century, debates about race and culture shape an emerging theory of performance which then becomes central to cultural-national and Pan-African identities and crucial to the making of Accra's urban public sphere. I am particularly interested in how an emergent theory of performance is defined by a specific reflexivity, one built on awareness of a duality of meaning and assessments of the relationship of culture to moral being and social power. Rural culture was appropriated as content for urban observation. Colonial performance relied on a logic of appropriation that despiritualized and depoliticized practices, making them into signs of ahistorical tradition. This logic reinforced polarizing oppositions between European as modern and African as traditional. Popular artists' syncretic approaches to musical and theatrical entertainment laid bare these simplistic oppositions of what was African and what was European, traditional and modern. The colonial, state-oriented project of culture was also contested by artists and intellectuals who reclaimed a logic of cultural belonging to support the political rights of Africans (cf. Povinelli 2002). Indeed, ideas of culture became a rallying point for African and African-descended radical thinkers and artists in the Caribbean, South America, Africa, Europe, and the United States, providing a language for imagining Pan-African connections and mobility. Conflicting ideas of African identity—caught between notions of rural cultural origins and modern progress—were debated by Gold Coast–educated elites, aspiring semieducated urbanites, uneducated workers, and rural poor. But a shared logic of eclectic appropriation defines Accra's various popular and artistic genres, shaping the city's self-image as it becomes a cosmopolitan capital. The rebundling of rural culture through institutions such as Achimota College is central to a rising urban public culture. Folkloric storytelling, "tribal" dance, and related forms of adornment and plastic arts are framed as key elements of Akan culture that are used to form a Gold Coast protonationalism. As subsequent chapters show, the development of culture as a form of knowledge that is displayed and circulated through theatre remains central to the institutional mediation of national belonging and the rise of modern urban life in Ghana.

Culture, Arts, and Urban Life under Indirect Rule

Culture was crucial to how British missionization, trade, and colonial rule in Africa were organized. Significantly, culture became a tool to limit the political and economic power of educated Africans. The importance of culture to control of trade and political authority fostered conflicts around its definition (Cohn 1996). The logic of colonial rule relied on regimenting highly visible cultural traits. Cultural logics were used to organize administration, public ceremonies, and school curriculums and to maintain chiefs rather than educated Africans as intermediaries between populations and British district commissioners. The British saw performances as ways to celebrate British power through events like Empire Day and durbars of chiefs, especially as racialist stereotypes portrayed Africans as particularly enamored of dance and music (A. Apter 2005; Cannadine 1983; Cohn 1983; Plageman 2012: 39). However, ideas of the inherent racial-cultural difference of Africans led to concern about how to maintain rule, control and regularize trade, and prepare Africans for inevitable social transformations. Stereotypes of what constituted African culture—traditional, ahistorical, rural, folkloric, customary—allowed the British to proclaim Africans as unready for modern life and identify African culture as the opposite of the modern. In this light, urban, cosmopolitan Africans were rendered inauthentic, caught between legible categories. Definitions of culture, particularly fostered through ideas of performance, were part of debates about political representation, economic responsibility, and the logic of African sovereignty. Twentieth-century expressive genres developed in the midst of struggles over what is African and what is European and the complex blurring of race and culture as categories of identification. In the process, white/European and black/African were produced as mutually exclusive, opposing types (Mudimbe 1988).

Nineteenth-century European missionaries in the Gold Coast were the first to learn African languages and local ways of life, creating written scripts and biblical translations, preaching, even if badly, in various African languages and teaching reading and writing to win converts (cf. Comaroff and Comaroff 1997). Missions encouraged some aspects of African languages and culture by delinking them from what they saw as demonic and primitive traditional religious practices. They tried to separate identity (culture) from belief (religion). Despiritualizing culture was a way of reaching Africans in familiar terms with Christian messages (Coe 2005).

In 1877 the capital of the Gold Coast colony was moved from Cape Coast to Accra. In 1901 Asante and in 1902 the Northern Territories were formally annexed and were administered by the Gold Coast colony. Accra became the regional center of trade and politics. Bourgeois Africans threatened the centralization of colonial power and British economic control. For late-nineteenth-century Gold Coast intellectuals, lawyers, journalists, and businessmen, moving toward self-rule meant claiming legal and political rights in the language of trade and international law. They claimed universal legal and political rights in preparing to manage their own affairs. The British Colonial Office saw the rising power of African Western-educated elites as a threat and sidestepped them in favor of customary chiefs. British policies of indirect rule across Africa recognized "native institutions" like chieftaincy and endeavored to rule through established political entities rather than impose a foreign system on local peoples (Lugard

[1922] 1965). Indirect rule sought to control traditional chieftaincies and use them as legitimate intermediaries between local populations and the colonial government in relation to taxation, land ownership, and representation (A. Apter 2005; Mamdani 1996). Colonial education under mandates of indirect rule celebrated and depoliticized cultural practices as ways to encourage the development of local moral character. Focusing on Africans as culture-bound subjects marked them off from the rights of citizenry and political sovereignty.

The Native Administration Ordinance of 1927 built on late-nineteenth-century colonial regulations that recognized the power of paramount and divisional chiefs to enforce colonial laws but left ambiguous the jurisdiction of customary law as "the government took on the bulk of administrative duties instead of sharing them with the chiefs" (Bourret 1952: 47). Sir Frederick Gordon Guggisberg, governor of the Gold Coast colony from 1919 to 1927, was unconventional and reform-minded, and concerned with both fostering and controlling African participation in the development of a liberal trade economy. Born in Canada to a merchant family, he attended military school in England and then joined the Royal Engineers. He served in Singapore before coming in 1902 to work for the Colonial Office as a surveyor in the Gold Coast and Asante and later in Nigeria. He was later accompanied by his second wife, Lady Decima Guggisberg (Decima Moore), a well-known actress who starred in numerous Gilbert and Sullivan productions and other West End shows. After serving in France in World War I, Guggisberg was appointed the Gold Coast's governor. In 1919 the populations of the colony, Asante, and the Northern Territories were together just over two million. The population was spread out, but increasing wealth and infrastructure drew people to urban centers: Accra at 25,000, Kumasi 30,000, Cape Coast 12,000, and Sekondi 12,000 (Agbodeka 1977: 1). By 1931 Accra had grown to an estimated 61,558 (Plageman 2012: 43). After the war, increasing revenue from gold and cocoa exports made the colony wealthy. Guggisberg's administration invested heavily in civil infrastructures, building roads, railways, ports, hospitals, schools, and telephone and radio communications networks to meet needs of import and export markets and growing urban populations.[1] Administratively, the colony followed the model of indirect rule, strengthening, organizing, and elevating the role of chiefs rather than bringing in English administrators or recognizing educated Africans (Bourret 1952: 49–50). In 1925 a new constitution granted elected representation to Africans, with paramount chiefs elected from provincial councils. Educated elites opposed the new constitution for its starkly limited form of enfranchisement. It gave most representation to rural chiefs, with only three representatives elected from the main urban areas of Accra, Cape Coast, and Sekondi.[2] Even as political organizations such as the Aborigines' Rights Protection Society and the National Congress of British West Africa criticized the investment of chiefs with power by the colonial state, the 1927 Native Administration Ordinance further recognized and controlled the power of the chiefs through the colony's provisional councils (Eluwa 1971: 205).

The political consolidation of power in chiefs and their regulation by the colonial state was accompanied by unprecedented urban growth (Parker 2000). Accra developed into an economic and cultural center in the 1920s as people of various cultural and linguistic groups came from all over the subregion. British, European, Lebanese, and Indian traders and administrators based in the capital worked in trading houses and government offices increasingly requiring the infrastructures of a modern city.[3]

The links between various literary and theatrical arts, urbanization, and class differentiation in the early-twentieth-century Gold Coast are well documented (Cole 2001; Stephanie Newell 2002; Plageman 2012). Coastal elites developed literary clubs and book culture in the 1870s and 1880s that flourished through the interwar period (Stephanie Newell 2002; Prais 2014). Highlife music and concert party theatre evolved out of eclectic musical and dramatic influences as English-language entertainment for coastal African elites in the early twentieth century (Cole 2001; Collins 1994a; Plageman 2012; Sutherland 1970).

Dramas, songs, variety shows, and dances were performed along the coast in forts at the center of slave and commodity trading and schools for mixed-race and white elites and for commemorative events since at least the eighteenth century (Cole 2001: 53; Lokko 1980). Missionary schools and churches performed nativity plays and Bible scenes in the nineteenth century (Lokko 1980: 315). Governor George Maclean and his short-lived wife, the famous writer Letitia Elizabeth Landon, reportedly put on plays like *The Merchant of Venice* in Cape Coast in the 1840s (Lokko 1980: 315). In 1901 *Antigone* was performed by Gold Coast former students in Sierra Leone (1980: 315). Cape Coast in the late nineteenth century saw the origin of syncretic Gold Coast theatre. It had an intelligentsia with a literary tradition and was a center of education. In 1876 the Methodist Wesleyan High School, now Mfantsipim School, was established as the first secondary school in the Gold Coast. In 1910 the Anglican S.P.G. (Society for the Propagation of the Gospel) Grammar School, now called Adisadel College, was established, becoming the second oldest secondary school. Theatre and interest in literature emerged from them. Elite social clubs for Africans and Europeans did play readings. The elite Cosmopolitan Club in Cape Coast premiered Kobina Sekyi's seminal play *The Blinkards* in 1916 (Gibbs 2009; Stephanie Newell 2002: 169). Unique as a formal scripted play in Fante and English, it satirizes the pretentions of coastal elites making fun of their desire to speak, act, and dress in European ways. This intellectual play presented themes and characterizations that have occupied popular and formal theatre, as well as public debates about what constitutes African and Ghanaian identity, for the past century (Cole 2001: 56–63; Stephanie Newell 2002: 157–77).

From the late nineteenth century, African teachers, students, pastors, and church members began to bring together disparate African, African American, and European performance traditions in performances put on for ceremonial occasions. Early concerts were influenced by vaudeville and minstrel shows, the silent films of Al Jolson and Charlie Chaplin, and church cantatas (Agovi 1990; Barber, Collins, and Ricard 1997: 7; Cole 2001; Collins 1994b). Initially, performances were in English for British and African coastal elite audiences. The term "concert" refers to a variety of eclectic musical dramatic shows. According to Catherine Cole, its first recorded uses were by a Wesleyan missionary in Cape Coast in 1895 describing a performance in which an actor satirizes a drunk Englishman in vernacular language for "natives" and a 1903 "Ball and Concert" held in Cape Coast Castle itself for black and white elites that featured music, magic, and comedic skits (Cole 2001: 63–65). Concert variety shows became regular events in the 1910s and 1920s held in schools and social clubs in Accra, Sekondi, and Cape Coast. By the 1920s, the loose configuration of styles became a recognizable genre in itself. Teacher Yalley popularized concert variety shows for "very big people, lawyers and other professional men of social standing" (Efua Sutherland, quoted in Agovi 1990: 1). With the influence of Bob Johnson, groups evolved into regular performing trios with more elaborate plays (Sutherland 1970). Performers "created a stock comic persona known as 'Bob,' a character with a bulging stomach who, like the trickster Ananse of Akan folklore, lived for his appetite and survived by his wit" (Cole 2001: 79). Concert party theatre revolved around the trickster/comedian character. These shows appealed "to a wider and a more proletarian audience" (Agovi 1990: 1). As groups began touring throughout the Gold Coast and performing for more working-class urban and rural publics, they increasingly used local languages, particularly various dialects of Akan. Increasingly concerts took on more Akan characteristics, including adopting a storytelling structure. Indeed, as Cole shows, artists explicitly recognized their methods of creative appropriation as being in line with Ananse's trickster sensibility. Professional performing trios featured three stock characters—the Bob or Joker/Houseboy, the Gentleman, and the Lady Impersonator—who parodied daily concerns and aspirations of their audiences (Collins 1994b). While the Joker is the most literal figuration of Ananse, it is more accurate to say that Ananse's various attributes are divided among this trio.

Because of its transformation from an elite style to increasing associations with rural farmers and uneducated workers, concert party came to be seen as rough, disreputable, and slightly dangerous, hence the ambivalence with which it came to be regarded by more elite Ghanaians and the reticence to include female performers. The rise of cocoa farming and mining developed a class of mobile wage laborers, with concert party catering to the interests and concerns of this rising audience (Cole 2001). The development of rail and road transportation aimed at exporting cocoa, gold, timber, and other products also facilitated the movements of local populations, including traveling performance troupes.

While the term "concert" referred to increasingly working-class-oriented popular concert party theatre troupes that dominated entertainment from the 1930s to the 1970s, its loose usage points to the ubiquity of blended genres that mixed music, dance, drama, comedy, and even magic across class divisions in the Gold Coast. Eclectic events catered to various European, African elites, and nonelites. Moving out of private social clubs, performers increasingly catered to aspiring classes with income from rising cash economies (Cole 2001). Highlife music and ballroom dance venues, literary clubs, newspapers, department stores, cinema houses, and theatre venues catered not only to elites but also aspiring urban classes (Stephanie Newell 2002; Plageman 2012). Some venues remained for whites only, others were for the African elite, and others were for lower-class patrons. Private clubs for elite Africans and Europeans, like the Rodger Club in Accra (which opened in 1904) and the Optimism Club in Sekondi, dominated entertainment and elite social life, holding dances and theatre and literary events for members and for paying publics. Entrepreneurial commercial ventures also proliferated to take advantage of those with money to spend seeking to enjoy leisure time.[4] The Merry Villas cinematograph palace was built in 1913 as the first dedicated entertainment venue in Accra (Cole 2001: 72). The Palladium, the Cinema Theatre, and others followed.

Mid-twentieth-century urbanization and entry into a wage-labor economy shaped the form and content of concert party theatre and highlife music (Cole 2001; Plageman 2012). From the 1950s, concert party troupes—reflecting migration to urban centers—evolved into larger groups with multiple characters, performing complex, musically based narratives (Cole 2001). Instead of brass band and ragtime, which the earlier groups had used, "proverb-laden" guitar-band highlife music became the focus of concert party groups (Cole 1997: 370; Plageman 2012)—though other types of music, including rumba, jazz, and funk, were used. Most concert party troupes were built around a popular highlife band, and their dramas revolved around the group's original songs. These dramas offered strong moral messages within the epistemic order of Akan proverbs and storytelling. Concert party became a primary social form through which working-class people engaged political change, social mobility, urbanization, and poverty not through direct comment or criticism, but rather through an indirect, humorous pastiche of styles, symbols, stories, and characters. These performances entailed an aesthetics of disjuncture, juxtaposition, and irony, embodying the contradictions of modern life as locally experienced (Cole 1997). In the mid-twentieth-century Gold Coast, youth aspired to financial success and mobility but were denied access to resources to fulfill their modern aspirations (Cole 2001: 100–103). Concert parties "performed Western culture—for a fee—to migrant populations in the new mining towns, cocoa trading centers, and international ports created by colonial development" (Cole 2001: 103). Plays often followed the melodramatic domestic, spiritual, sexual, and financial struggles of aspirational families dealing with modern social transformations. But these dramatic mimetic styles did more than copy European life. Evolving theatrical styles allowed actors and audiences to fantasize about how to imagine themselves as new types of agents capable of performing a fantastical world of possibility into existence.

The rise of modern colonial state infrastructure in the 1920s and 1930s facilitated the vernacularization of public culture for Gold Coast elites, aspiring civil servants, and workers. Elite English-language styles and venues transformed into eclectic popular genres that appealed to various publics in the 1930s.[5] A pan-ethnic, mobile, semiliterate urban aspirational class was being raised with a complex mix of influences and languages in Accra and other cities (Agovi 1990; Allman 1993; Stephanie Newell 2002). This rising class of unattached youth maintained ties to traditional kin, gender, and generational hierarchies and networks while aspiring to urban pleasures and entrepreneurial potentials (Plageman 2012). In the early 1930s, as global economic depression hurt the Gold Coast's export markets, reducing state and private revenue, an aspirational lower middle class was emerging, thinking in terms of personal desires and voicing, extra cash income, mobility, and leisure.

Highlife and concert party theatre, initially oriented toward Western-educated audiences in elite venues in coastal cities, gave way to vernacular language use and irreverent, eclectic styles. Music and theatre groups traveled across the country for urban masses and the rural poor (Cole 2001: 78; Plageman 2012: 98). By the 1930s, concert party troupes used bawdy vernacular language, traveling the country to play for farmers, the urban poor, and uneducated and semieducated crowds. While large ballroom and highlife orchestras persisted for fancy urban venues, smaller guitar-band highlife groups toured in conjunction with concert party shows (Collins 1994b, 2007).

English-language literary clubs for highly educated coastal intellectuals gave rise to more eclectic groups whose literary, theatrical, and musical tastes suited aspiring semiliterate audiences (Stephanie Newell 2002: 32). Nonelite literary and theatre publics emerged that blurred lines between literature, drama, and music as well as between observing and participating in these practices (Agovi 1990). According to Musing Light, music and drama critic for the weekly *Gold Coast Spectator* from 1929 to 1932, there were five clubs "whose aims and objectives ... are to give concerts" (Agovi 1990: 14) and numerous others that did drama alongside other entertainments. The five main ones Light identifies were the Accra Philharmonics, Half Moon Club, Astorias, Samaritans, and West African National Club.[6]

Concerts mixed amateur and professional dramatists and musicians. The influence of African American artistry and showmanship was notable as an embodied critique of British public sensibilities (Cole 2001: 37; J. Shipley 2013a: 47). Newspapers reviewed performances of black singers and actors in the United States for the interest of their readers, while some came to perform in West Africa. Gold Coast performers admired and copied African American and black Caribbean performers, seeing them as "free and natural" performers.[7] But concerts displayed a range of influences and were advertised and reviewed in the papers. The Musical Dragons performed *Ghost of Count Bolshevik* on March 28, 1932, alongside a "play-hit titled 'Sambo's Lucky Number' and another series of Negro Spirituals." Philharmonics did a "well organized Cabaret Show" at Merry Villas, preceded by a "musical playette titled 'Home Made Sunshine'" and including "a variety [of] Instrumental, Songs, and Ballet, accompanied by the Accra Orchestra, to be followed by Dance" on April 2, 1932. The West African National Club, nicknamed "the West End Comedians," was known for "excellent and wonderful Vaudeville Entertainment" such as was performed on April 30, 1932. Dapper Williams, a playwright, actor, and singer from Sierra Leone, staged two of his plays, *Music Hath Charms* and *Life*, at his Half Moon Club. Musing Light praises him for being a great singer and for "inducing girls to act on stage" for the first time.[8]

Elites and aspiring middle classes were drawn to eclectic syncretic performances, as were uneducated audiences of bawdy concert party shows, though the middle classes were more anxious about categorizing their tastes as eclectic and blurred, endeavoring to differentiate themselves from lower-class rural tastes by aspiring to and imitating European styles. The 1933 performance of *Antigone* by St. Nicholas' Grammar School "adds to the cultural advancement of the country,"[9] and an Empire Day performance of *Britannia and Her People* at Presbyterian School was "a truly patriotic play."[10] A 1931 Accra High School performance of Shakespeare's *Twelfth Night* at the Palladium was a success in creating an "Elizabethan air. . . . Each character of the play seemed to be the ghost of a sixteenth century person materialized in a Negro skin."[11] Musing Light argues that critics should take drama more seriously, recognizing it as a form of literature, and calls for separating dramatic clubs from dancing clubs. Light sees leisure and entertainment as different from theatrical and literary art, stating, "Serious dramatic effort is however incompatible with pleasurable pursuits. There should exist clubs which are mainly for drama."[12] The concern with categorizing and separating performances reflects how theatre was caught up in the making of class, race, and urban identities in prewar Accra. Aspiring middle classes imagined that modern life sought to imitate European literary and dramatic sensibilities, though it was only through an eclectic mixing of forms, locales, interests, and styles that these purported imitations took shape.

By the early 1930s, gramophone records and wireless radio were important to the transformation of public culture. Listening to them was seen as both for entertainment and education. In a speech at the Young People's Literary Club in

1933, reported in the *Gold Coast Spectator*, Ruby Quartey-Papafio, headmistress at the Government Girls' School in Accra, expressed that "listening-in" to either rare personal radios or gramophones was something that should "occupy the child's time at home."[13] Brunswick Gramophone and Record Service advertised that if "you cannot always spare your time to come to the pleasure-house every night. . . . You need not despair. We can convert your house into a miniature Palladium."[14] These technologies blurred lines between classes of listeners and between genres of entertainment, education, and propaganda. While radio and records allowed for private listening for elite homes, schools, and places of business, listening was often a public spectacle in and of itself. On Christmas Day 1932, Accra's postmaster general arranged to broadcast the British Broadcasting Company's (BBC's) transmission of His Majesty the King's "message to the Empire" at the Old Polo Grounds in Accra and central locations in Sekondi and Kumasi. This speech was re-created as an electronically mediated, spectacular ceremony with His Excellency the Governor presiding.[15] Whereas radio personalized listening practices in Britain, in the Gold Coast and other African colonies radio became a public participatory form (Larkin 2008).

The rising aspirant middle and working classes in Gold Coast's emerging cities were caught between persistent notions that opposed rural African culture to modern urban practices and values. However, while self-conscious debates about art, culture, and identity tended to polarize these oppositions, increasingly eclectic mixes and stylistic influences were remaking public tastes and forms of expression.

Making and Contesting Culture at Achimota College

Educational institutions were crucial to constituting and contesting ideas of culture. Achimota College was central to shaping debates around the significance of culture to political power and protonational identity. As part of his tour of the Gold Coast colony on Easter in 1925, His Royal Highness Edward, Prince of Wales—who would later become, briefly, Edward VIII—ceremonially dedicated the Prince of Wales College and School at Achimota, established to be a premier school in Africa. Establishing this school was one of Guggisberg's most celebrated achievements. It was meant to concretize policies of indirect rule in the short run and prepare Africans for self-governance in the long run. Situated on a hill several miles north of Accra, the school educated many children of chiefs and elites and exceptional students from across the Gold Coast and West Africa, training numerous future leading Gold Coast intellectuals, politicians, artists, and teachers (Coe 2005). Indeed, many aspects of independent Ghana were crafted by former Achimota students, including the first prime minister, most of Ghana's subsequent heads of state and many of its ministers, the founder of the Ghana Dance Ensemble, the writer of the national anthem, the founder of the

National Theatre Movement, and the sculptor who designed the symbols and images of the new state (Agawu 2003). Its influence came also in training numerous teachers and civil servants placed across the colony. The 1932 school assessment report noted the uniqueness of the school, stating, "Achimota hopes to produce a type of student who is 'Western' in his intellectual attitude toward life, with a respect for science and capacity for systematic thought, but who remains African in sympathy and desirous of preserving and developing what is deserving of respect in tribal life, custom, rule and law. This African outlook is noticeable in the cultivation of tribal dances as well as in the study of the vernacular language and the collection and investigation of folk-lore."[16]

Achimota was an educational experiment, one of a handful of elite, showcase schools across the African colonies designed to educate a rising class of civil servants who when "properly civilized" could be entrusted to take over the running of the colonies. But this was an ambivalent project as educated Africans continued to pose a threat to British legitimacy. Educating Africans to be leaders was a highly contested project in the early twentieth century, exacerbating white European anxieties about the threat of black colonized peoples. As the Colonial Office "Africanized" the civil service, students and teachers were caught between competing ideas of a future black sovereignty.

The mission of the school reflected the tensions of training a colonized elite, instilling in pupils the principle that service was a form of duty. As Achimota's founding principal, Reverend Alexander G. Fraser explained, the "aim of African education should be to develop the character, initiative, independence and ability of her youth, so that they may be reliable, courageous, and intelligent in the rapidly changing life and circumstances of their own people" (1933: 817). To do this, he continued, they must "create an atmosphere of freedom." The project of training children for the modern world was caught in competing ideas of culture and its relationship to universality. For some, teaching Africans through their "native" language and culture would help raise the level of primitive Africans, easing their progress into the universal and modern; for others, African culture was a sign of radical difference that marked the potential for alternative futures. Of Scottish origin, Fraser was the son of a lieutenant governor of Bengal. He came to Achimota after being principal of Trinity College in Ceylon, where he built its reputation as a leading international school. Achimota opened in 1926 with 6 boys around seven years old (Fraser 1933: 814). In 1927 Achimota took over the Government Training College, which was founded in 1909 to train teachers, and these older students joined the younger ones. By 1929 there were 400 students from kindergarten through postsecondary levels, 49 of them girls (C. Williams 1962: 40–41). By 1933 the student body totaled 500, with approximately 270 boys and 130 girls (Fraser 1933: 814). A central tenet of the school was that it was coeducational. Despite opposition from those who feared the moral problems of mixing the sexes, Fraser and James Aggrey, the founding principal and vice principal, both saw the education of girls as beneficial to the broader community. Pupils were divided by language groups—Ga, Ewe, Twi, Fante, the few northern Hausa and Dangbe speakers lumped together, and a few students from Nigeria and Togoland. One former student recalls how the few northern students were looked down on: "They arrived almost naked carrying their supplies on their head ... we [southern Ghanaians] saw them as natives ... they did not dress properly and seemed provincial."[17] Coming to Accra to study at Achimota provided students—many of them children of chiefs and elites from around the region—a space to imagine the Gold Coast as a collectivity composed of various cultures and languages.

In line with broader vernacularization policies, students were taught in one of the four recognized languages in their younger years. Principal Fraser argued that this allowed students to focus on their education in their native tongue without distraction of foreign influences. Older grades were taught in English. The 1925 Education Code mandated that Gold Coast children must be taught to read and write in their first language up to Standard IV (Stephanie Newell 2002: 65). For proponents, this was meant to emphasize character education for the sons of chiefs as future leaders rather than simply providing practical training of civil servants to fill administrative posts. From the perspective of African intellectuals, English-language fluency allowed for political organizing, and reducing its instruction in favor of local cultural and linguistic practices hurt efforts at international Pan-African organizing and opened local peoples to exploitation by capitalists (Stephanie Newell 2002: 66). Indirect rule was linked to celebration of African culture over Western education. The rise of indirect rule engendered increasing interests in studying African culture as well as debates about the relationships of language and culture to both identity and sovereignty.

Albert Mawere Opoku was sent to Achimota from Kumasi; he was a grandson of the Gyasehene, a subchief of the Asantehene, leader of the Asante. He remembered with great fondness being a student at Achimota from 1931 to 1934. He went on to be founding director of the Ghana Dance Ensemble. He recalls Achimota in the 1930s as "a place of excellence" that gave its students a feeling of superiority and authority and a sense of leadership through service. "We were ... taught ... the Achimota song. 'Born but to rule through service given. The ages all belong to thee. It was there that God ... God first made us his freedom of his grand employ.' You were not there just because you were a superior person. But you were to be trained for service to the country. This was what was drilled into us."[18]

This school encouraged its African charges to see service as a Christian moral duty for community leaders, in the process raising questions about the cultural, national, and racial makeup of the community being served. One reporter at the time points to a growing sense of Gold Coast identity but also to broader global racial links, stating, "Achimota is the hope of the Gold Coast, broadening to the larger hope of the race...."[19] Achimota encouraged public reflection on the links between education and identity. The school gave "Africans of the Gold Coast opportunities of an education and training that [would] fit them to take their place in the coming era of Western civilisation, the methods of which are inevitably sweeping over British Africa, while at the same time endeavoring to help them to retain their African nationality and characteristics."[20] Liberal English people argued that Africans had to adapt to colonial rule and the influence of Western civilization but that maintaining an innate cultural-national sensibility was crucial to maintaining stability and contributing to the development of society. The contradictions between universalizing ideas of progress and civilization and ideas of national particularity linked nationhood to language, territory, and culture, played out in the growing role of local culture at Achimota.

The organization, teaching, and daily life of the school were based on a British boarding-school model and its pragmatic approach to making well-disciplined, productive modern citizens. Every weekday, students awoke at 5:30 a.m., did chores and parade drill, and prayed. Games, sports, and social service were held every afternoon. Students played games and sports; cricket, football, hockey, boxing, and swimming were popular. Students were encouraged to cultivate and discipline their minds and bodies. The maintenance of daily routine was important. Visitors noted how impressed they were with the proper English phonetics of the students, which the school emphasized (C. Williams 1962: 42). The English school curriculum included math, science, literature, history, geography, and basic requirements to pass English school certificate examinations while also being oriented to the specific interests of Gold Coast students. Observers of the school were concerned that there were too many subjects, leading to student confusion because added to the "necessary" subjects were African subjects and "a wide range of cultural subjects."[21]

From the beginning there was concern about understanding the specific characteristics and traits of local cultures and their implications for education. For Governor Guggisberg, Achimota's mission was to shape a particularly African mode of development. In addressing the crowds at the opening of the school, he celebrated the school's potential for shaping a specifically African future. "I am sure Africans do not desire to become Europeans or to become like them. But... whatever difference may remain it must not be a difference of capacity.... The children of our countries are the country" (Guggisberg, quoted in C. Williams 1962: 23–24).

European teachers were brought to the Gold Coast before the school even opened to study one of four languages—Fante, Twi, Ga, or Ewe. The numerous other linguistic groups of the Gold Coast were divided into these main "vernacular" linguistic and cultural traditions. Research on cultures and traditions of the Gold Coast was encouraged among the staff. Lectures were given by invited "chiefs and other leading Africans. These may be on tribal history or custom, on African constitutions or customary law, on manners and etiquette, on local traditions or any other topic of national or local interest."[22] Students were taken on trips to do research in villages and collect ethnographic material[23] and encouraged to research "the four vernaculars, African music and local history."[24] Some even wrote monographs of their own languages;[25] local history writing was encouraged by awarding essay prizes (C. Williams 1962: 42).

Primarily European music was taught. For example, a concert in 1934 featured works by Wagner, Bach, Schubert, Handel, and Mozart (C. Williams 1962: 72). Orchestral training was important and took place in the evenings and on weekends.[26] Choral singing was popular as well. The 1932 school report notes that vocal and instrumental training is important at Achimota and seems to occupy "an honourable, and we believe in tropical countries an unusual, part." The assessors were impressed by the "very lively orchestra" as well as the "tribal drumming," noting that they were assured "that it is possible for Africans to enjoy Haydn and Mozart without being 'detribalised.'"[27] The country's leading art and religious music composer and musicologist, Ephraim Amu, had a strong influence on "Africanizing" music and its teaching, drawing on Ewe and Akan music for his compositions (Agawu 1995). He joined Achimota in 1934 as a music teacher after famously being disciplined for wearing African cloth rather than a Western suit while preaching in church in Akropong. Later Philip Gbeho—the composer of Ghana's national anthem—also was an influence on the inclusion of African music at the school.

Achimota's organization was a microcosm of how the Gold Coast colony imagined a modern African polity: structurally European modern with some local content (Coe 2005). It embodied the contradictions of colonial state-building. Achimota's focus on developing modern ways of living suitable to African sensibilities structured how ideas of African culture entered into students' lives. African culture was separated from regular study, religion, and ideas of proper comportment for modern living that the boarding school taught its charges.

Two regular events—Tribal Night, held once a month, and Tribal Drumming Night, usually held on Saturdays rotating with other entertainment—encouraged students to learn about their own "tribe's" characteristics through historical lessons and drumming and dancing. Opoku recalls their significance: "At Achimota there were two things which you could not miss: On Tribal Night, unless you were sick and in hospital, you had to be there. . . . The second compulsory thing was Tribal Drumming Night . . . on Saturday nights. . . . You had to go to it. So we learned to dance and tribal drumming at Achimota, whereas it was forbidden in churches."[28] The college purchased drums and brought in local masters to assist in the teaching.

Over sixty years later, Opoku recalled with passion the significance of dividing and teaching "tribal" identity. Despite the cultural diversity of the Gold Coast, all students were categorized accord to four principal written languages—Fante, Ewe, Ga, and Twi. "For Tribal Night, they brought in somebody, according to these four tribes, to come and talk to you about Ga, Ewe, Twi, or Fante culture and things like that. So, that you were having your education, not for tests, but it was to learn about ourselves. . . . It was done all in the local languages . . . you had to stay within the tradition . . . and within your tribal group. Tribal Night, they came and talked to you. . . . It was education—finding out more about tribal law: What is the social etiquette? When you are going to see a chief? What is the procedure, the protocol? You have to learn it. So, traditional experts came up and talked to you, just as they would in the village."[29] Tribal law and language were defined through public displays that were meant to strengthen moral character by highlighting specific traits that united people along cultural-racial-national lines.

The performance of tribal drumming and dancing made sense within broader British beliefs in the significance of public display for maintaining social order and revealing personal character. Students paraded each morning by house and marched and drilled for special events like the annual Empire Day according to English marching protocol. They displayed themselves for inspection by school officials and honored visitors. Tribal displays were held for distinguished visitors such as the committee sent to inspect Achimota in 1932. Opoku recalls that annual ceremonies like Empire Day and Founder's Day were times for displaying tribal identities. "The different groups were given funds to bring in drummers and so on to come and teach each tribe a new dance to present, for entertainment. On Founder's Day, we got together and exchanged these things between tribes. We came out to the forecourt in front of the Administration Block and people would go and dance and had these performances. There was high competition."[30] Traditional drumming and dance became spectacular public markers for organizing tribal identities. Language, custom, and law were codified and displayed identity within the order of Western knowledge. The presentation of traditional culture as an aspect of education reveals a tension between tribally bound identity and the ideal of a well-rounded, duty-bound, civic-minded Christian.

In encouraging drumming, Achimota was "consciously opposing traditional educational theory, which at the time was inclined to frown on things unfamiliar to the European" (C. Williams 1962: 72), although a number of British colonial schools like Achimota endeavored to help Africans, as stated in reference to students in Sierra Leone in 1906, "acquire a good education, without loss of their natural attachment to their respective tribes. Tribal patriotism is to be strengthened" (Clarence-Smith 1994: 67). European educators debated whether Africans were fully capable of being modern or whether they were limited by their race and culture.

Guy Warren, later known as Kofi Ghanaba, the internationally known jazz drummer and innovator of African jazz, had been a student at Achimota in the early 1940s. He was born in Accra in 1923. His father was a school headmaster. In his recollection, many students laughed at and looked down on Tribal Night. "Tribal celebrations" were the only times that the students wore African-style dress and played traditional music; many participated with reluctance. "We were taught to prefer being white to black. Subtle racism. Aspire to live like the English. Get civil service jobs and be good administrators." Students in Warren's recollection "mocked Africanness. We did not like [Tribal Night] . . . it did not mean anything to anyone. We felt we were British living on the Gold Coast. I thought Africa was a masquerade ball. On Tribal Night we felt we were whites playing Africans for a night."[31] Another contemporary agreed, recalling that concert party groups never came to Achimota, as students saw popular entertainments as "coarse and beneath us." European classical and scripted English-language drama constituted proper music and theatre, in their estimation.[32] For Warren, Achimota was more connected to England than to the Gold Coast. "Everyone mocked Africanness and African languages . . . the African teachers were more British than the English ones. We did not speak pidgin or local languages but English with a Cambridge accent. . . . Debates were held to show how to speak English properly. We thought we were at Eton." Ephraim Amu, the music teacher, was the only one who was different, in sandals and African top and shorts. Many laughed at him. A key aspect of culture pedagogy at Achimota was that each student was supposed to stay within his or her tribe, learning only its music and culture. "This encouraged tribalism and divisions to make you feel superior and think against other tribes. The British fanned tribalism and encouraged divisions among us." If a student's cultural/linguistic group was not represented, he or she had to pick one. But Warren was restless. He did not like music classes, as learning music theory bored him. Gbeho and Amu taught Beethoven in music class. Even though they played Ewe music for Tribal Nights, that was not in music class. Even though he was not supposed to, Warren moved between the school's different tribal groups "to learn different music because I got bored." Student were shaped through a double mirroring of expressive practices (Bhabha 1994). The experience of racial objectification meant that Europeanized African elites imagined "playing African." This reflects the contradictory legacy of cultural performance as a celebration of African identity but only in isolation of its elements and ossification and dehistoricization of their legacies.

Warren's personal and musical journey was driven by his profound, ambivalent reaction to how African culture was understood in his youth. He moved to Chicago and then New York, immersing himself in jazz and Afro-Caribbean music, though he felt African American music misrepresented its African roots.

He recalls that it was only after going to the United States and returning to Ghana that he became strongly Afro-centric. Back in Ghana, he Africanized his name to Kofi Ghanaba (literally "child of Ghana" in Twi), became known as "The Divine Drummer," and began blending a "truly African jazz." Musically he was known for his innovative use of complex West African polyrhythmic traditions and various hand drums within a jazz idiom (Feld 2012). On stage and around Accra he shocked audiences with his irreverence, dressing in traditional cloth and aiming to respiritualize traditional music and culture. His later performances brought Ga traditional drumming idioms to the modern stage.

The older Ghanaba recognized the significance of African performance traditions in a way the younger Warren had not. In school, "I was so English that is why I went so far the other way . . . I was brainwashed. After the United States disillusioned me I wanted to resurrect the African component of jazz. African interpretations of jazz were different than African American versions I heard in the U.S. I discovered Africanness in the U.S. Jazz is really European music. Chicago was a colonial environment too. I wanted to do African music." The separation of tribal groups shows the significance of cultural performance to the divide-and-rule tactics of British colonial rule—African pupils were encouraged to have cultural-tribal pride rather than learning music and dance from other cultural groups or African political history. Ghanaba's later musical work focused on showing commonalities of African performance traditions as embodied assertions of Pan-African cultural unity.[33] For Ghanaba it was Nkrumah's notions of pride and unity that changed things. "Nkrumah encouraged Africanness. He ignited people. . . . Ghanaians were a happy bunch of niggers until Nkrumah interrupted."

In this sense, colonial education posited culture, drumming, dance, and storytelling as depoliticized practices that could foster positive self-image, forging Africans into docile subjects. Crucially, difference was amplified through these objectifications of culture. The performance of cultural tradition set the terms within which colonial rule was both justified and contested. As Mahmood Mamdani argues, indirect rule "at once reinforced ethnically bound institutions of control and led to their explosion from within. Ethnicity (tribalism) thus came to be simultaneously the form of colonial control over natives and the form of revolt against it" (1996: 24). "The native question" became not just an issue of state administration or ceremony but shaped the very forms of knowledge and their contestation. The introduction of elements of "tribal culture" was supposed to help adapt British education to suit African pupils. For some students such as Ghanaba, the recontextualization of local practices initially emphasized their distance from Africanness as they embraced British education. This distance produced dissonances that led to much reflexive consideration of the relationship of culture to self.

From Anthropology to Art to Criticism

Anthropology was important to imperial rule in defining social and political structures to aid British administration of local polities. Ethnographic research also facilitated the identification and codification of various expressive practices as art. A Department of Anthropology, with Captain R. S. Rattray as its first director, was established by the Gold Coast government in 1921. Meyer Fortes also soon came to do ethnographic research in the Northern Territories.[34] Rattray and Fortes, whose ethnographic work became foundational in British anthropology, were both involved with Achimota. Rattray reported to the *Times* of London on the central role of culture at the college and the significance of the school in relation to developing education specifically related to local folklore and tradition. "The Gold Coast [government] has launched into a truly great experiment . . . the founding of a great school. . . . Here the African will be encouraged to study the folklore, the traditions and the past history of, and the institutions of his own race, instead of to despise and neglect them, and so perhaps will not lose what must be a priceless heritage to any people, their own national soul" (Rattray, quoted in C. Williams 1962). As H. S. Harrison of the Royal Anthropological Institute's Committee on Applied Anthropology wrote to the secretary of state for the colonies, anthropologists sought to aid in the "preservation and development of native institutions as a cardinal element in British policy in Africa" and to show the "value of anthropological research as a guide to policy."[35]

The inclusion of African culture in elite education opened up new anxieties and new terrain regarding the rising generation. The call to establish an Institute of West African Research in Arts and Industries and Social Studies (later referred to as the Institute of West African Culture) at Achimota shows rising concern among some teachers about how to shape the character of African students without alienating them from their true needs and sensibilities. H. V. Meyerowitz, of Russian Jewish origins, a main advocate of the institute, became head of arts and crafts in 1936–1937, arriving at Achimota from South Africa with his wife, Eva, an anthropologist. Some teachers felt that Achimota had been too oriented toward European ideas of art education, arguing that "during the eleven years of its life, Achimota has been able to build up a very efficient system of education on lines almost entirely European, while professing so far as possible not to disturb the old loyalties."[36] Initial documents on the institute appear to have been written in a collaboration between art teacher H. V. Meyerowitz, anthropologist Meyer Fortes, a South African Jew with leftist inclinations, and leading musician and composer Ephraim Amu (Agawu 1996).[37] One note to the Colonial Office arguing for the establishment of the institute posits that local cultural particularity was crucial to educational success. "Unless Higher Education in West Africa is to be a purely European importation, planted upon alien soil, it must be based upon a thorough understanding of the mentality, customs, religion, homelife, and economic and spiritual needs of the Africans who are to be educated."[38] As the note points out, Achimotans emphasized the links between plastic and performing arts and that customs must be understood in context of "native life" explained through professional expertise. "Accordingly it is strongly and rightly felt . . . that there ought to be at Achimota those who have studied and are studying the real native life of the African tribes from which the students come; and these must include anthropologists very highly trained in such research, and of proved ability to enter into and understand native life, ideas and customs; as well as persons intimate with African arts—not only carving, weaving, etc. but drumming, music and dances—as they enter into the religious and social life of the tribes."[39]

In the 1930s school life revolved around the central administration block with a small museum and library and hall that was used as a chapel. It had a farm, a model village for laborers, a printing press, and playing fields. The printing press at Achimota printed local-language materials for use in schools around the country.[40] As agriculture and practical education were placed alongside science, training in the plastic and performing arts linked the practical to the literary and abstract forms of thinking as well as providing productive and moral training for students to use "leisure for the profitable enjoyment of their neighbours and themselves."[41] Traditional arts and crafts were linked to the development of technique and critical faculties. Woodcarvers and kente cloth weavers were brought in to teach and demonstrate their crafts. Under Meyerowitz, arts and crafts also included ceramics, painting, drawing, metalwork, and bookbinding (Agbodeka 1977: 107). Kofi Antubam, who would later make the ceremonial scepter, sword, throne, and state seal for the first Republic of Ghana, was Meyerowitz's star student and returned to teach at Achimota after independence. Plastic arts were seen as being of great "cultural importance" and crucial to "African economic and social life" and the development of potential new economies. While some observers saw teaching African arts as a form of preservation of a "dying culture," Meyerowitz emphasized "free expression" to his students in younger years and at the secondary level, and to those training to be teachers. Illustrations, metalwork, tiles, cloth, and wood carvings made by students were used around the college. Students designed costumes for plays, equipment for the kitchen, book covers, and posters (Agbodeka 1977: 108).

While to some, non-Western culture could all be lumped together as not modern and uncivilized, advocates for the institute argued for understanding cultural particularity. "West African culture has its own characteristic features, and the problems cannot be solved by analogies drawn from America and the West Indies, or even from South or East Africa. . . ."[42] Other British residents, administrators, and educators recognized the specificity of West African culture but saw nothing worth saving in local art with perhaps the exception of kente cloth weaving in comparison to Western art as well as to more "advanced" societies found in India and the East. But others argued the need to inspire African youth by connecting their heritage to modern education. As one report suggests, an Institute of Arts and Culture would address the fact that in "the entire life of Achimota there is involved a tension between the African culture and ideas of the tribes and homes from which the students come and the strongly European and Christian character of most of the life and work of the College."[43] There was widespread belief in the fragility of Africans in the face of coming modern changes. The report continues, "There is, on the one hand, the immense energy and vitality of the peoples of West Africa—their pride of race, commercial enterprise and acumen, and their avidity for education. On the other hand there is a noticeable feeling of malaise, a sense of impending change, in the whole social system.... The future of African civilisation depends on a solution of these problems. A satisfying cultural adjustment must be worked out; from both cultures must be selected those elements best adapted to the needs of the new society now coming into being in Africa."[44] The malaise of modern life could be assuaged by identifying and sustaining foundational cultural elements. Rapid changes on the horizon and uncertain futures would leave Achimota's young charges vulnerable to the unknown. The school was meant to look out for its students' interests not only in its idealized environment but into possible futures. "By the students it is probably felt only half occasionally, if at all, until after they leave and re-enter a life which in different degrees is African. The College professes to aim at combining what is best in European civilization with what is best in African tribal and social life, and carries out this aim by the encouragement of tribal dances and plays, African art, etc. But most of the staff can know little about native African life and mentality, and they are hardly in a position to judge . . . what is good or bad in it, or what is consistent with the European and Christian education which Achimota gives; still less whether dances, drumming and native art, torn from their roots in native religion and social life, must not lose their reality and meaning. . . ."[45] Here education should combine the best of African culture with European Christian training to follow Guggisberg's focus on building character. This required expertise in local culture to identify and refine the best elements of local art and social life.[46]

The drive to develop discerning critical faculties emerged in the development of theatre. In early years student residential houses performed vernacular-language Ananse stories and other folktales that were primarily "buffoonery" (Agbodeka 1977: 117). This tradition came from the old Government Training College, where every year each boardinghouse put on "an African play in one or other vernacular."[47] Houses competed with each other to mount powerful shows. While local plays were forbidden in most schools, Achimota encouraged them. These plays often used improvised, unscripted dialogue in local languages rather than English (C. Williams 1962: 62–63). Plays were done on Saturday nights with "little rehearsing . . . with simple plots, some of them Ananse stories, no parts written out in full, rich in local colour: village scenes, scenes on farm, chief's courts, 'fetish' ceremonies, humorously presented. There was pathos and tragedy, but the popular line was buffoonery" (C. Williams 1962: 62).

In the 1930s, drama at the school was formalized. As teacher and critic George Hood explained, Achimota's drama committee, consisting of students and staff, planned to produce three major English-language productions a year: a straight drama, a musical comedy, and a religious play (C. Williams 1962: 63). Observers noted the students' abilities but also their lack of performance technique and technical skill. They endeavored to raise the level of stagecraft and formalize theatre norms. The staff put on a particularly well-received production of Gilbert and Sullivan's *Mikado* in 1933—among a number of Gilbert and Sullivan productions (Lokko 1980)—which apparently led students to decide "almost unanimously never to put on a vernacular play again," turning instead toward English formal theatre (C. Williams 1962: 63).[48] Staff and students experimented with various usages of language, narration, and staging. *Caesaris Incursio in Oram Auream* (Caesar's incursion into the Gold Coast) portrays Caesar's founding of Achimota and was performed in a mix of Twi, Fante, Ga, Latin, and French (C. Williams 1962: 62). Shakespeare and Gilbert and Sullivan were popular. Performances included versions of biblical stories and local adaptations of well-known European plays; *The Pirates of Prampram*, which relocated Gilbert and Sullivan's *Pirates of Penzance* to West Africa, and *Chu Chin Chow*—a popular adaptation of *The Arabian Nights* staged in London in 1916, with film versions coming out in 1925 and 1934—were also successes. Another production was *Bardell v. Pickwick* taken from sections of Charles Dickens's *Pickwick Papers*.

After several years, in 1942 the Colonial Welfare and Development Act funded the Institute of West African Arts. It combined practical concerns of wartime economics, making water coolers formerly imported from Germany and roofing tiles, with more abstract concerns about developing vibrant expertise based on traditional local arts, building critical faculties, and including culture in education.[49]

The development of arts programs is significant because they show a belief in the significance of criticism to art and society that fosters the emergence of a reflexive public discourse regarding culture. Debates about the importance of culture to educating Africans focused on developing critical skills and cultural self-consciousness, especially in the arts. Advocates for the Institute of West African Arts argued that the development of critical skills is the cornerstone of civilization. Art can reveal the best aspects of a society but also the threat of being tricked by the appearance of value. "It is curious that a people who produced such great artists did not produce also a culture in our sense of the word. This shows that two features are necessary to produce the cultures which distinguish civilised peoples. There must be, of course, the creative artist, but there must also be the power of conscious critical appreciation and comparison."[50] The problem with African society, by this logic, is the lack of self-conscious reflection and the development of criticism and taste. "If we imagined such an apparatus of critical appreciation as the Chinese have possessed from the earliest times applied to this Negro art, we should have no difficulties in recognizing its singular beauty. We should never have been tempted to regard it as savage or unrefined. It is for want of a conscious critical sense and the intellectual powers of comparison and classification that the Negro has failed to create one of the great cultures of the world, and not from any lack of the most exquisite sensibility and finest taste. No doubt, also, the lack of such a critical standard to support him leaves the artist much more at the mercy of any outside influences. It is likely enough that the Negro artist, although capable of such profound imaginative understanding of form, would accept our cheapest illusionist art with humble enthusiasm."[51]

Central to this was a belief in objectifying, condensing, and modernizing key elements of African culture. Crucially, according to the argument, great civilizations emerged not solely from skilled practitioners and aesthetic beauty but self-consciousness, scholarship, and criticism that recognized and encouraged positive moral and aesthetic values and avoided the dangers of "illusionist" art. Art and culture are reflections and producers of personal and social character and identity. Through heightened critical faculties, observers can both discern and encourage the moral and aesthetic best aspects of culture. But without critical reflection, the development of moral character, and proper study, excellent art goes unappreciated, and indeed observers might be deceived by appearances. The teacher George Hood expressed concern that the dual development of formal English-language theatre and informal vernacular drama could prevent the development of theatrical expertise and a new tradition of formal theatre (C. Williams 1962: 63). The interest in developing formal drama that reflected both local experience and European expertise and dramatic traditions represents broader debates about using vernacular and local culture in education.

Contesting History and Racialized Education

The role of African culture at Achimota remained controversial, as students and teachers were caught in the anticolonial struggle and international Pan-Africanism expressed in debates about race, culture, and language. For some, Achimota was a liberal project too independent of British political interests, while for others it was the embodiment of colonialism (Jenkins 1994). In disputes about the role of education and development in the colony, culture and its public manifestations was often a central point of contention for differing political positions. Moderate African nationalists and more conservative chiefs worked for development through social and political cooperation *within* the colonial system (Agbodeka 1977: 45–46).

In the early 1920s the Phelps-Stokes Commission toured the Gold Coast and much of British Africa to assess education and see what lessons Negro and Native American education in the United States could bring to education in Africa (King 1971). James Aggrey was born in Anomabo, an old coastal center of the slave trade west of Cape Coast. He attended Methodist school and excelled. He was invited to travel and study as a missionary at Livingstone College in North Carolina and later taught there. He also studied at Columbia University. He returned to the Gold Coast as part of the commission. The Phelps-Stokes Commission saw a great need to improve education in Africa and advocated recognizing local conditions and educating students in familiar terms. These studies followed American racial theory of educational adaptation, which advocated teaching the Negro race industrial and craft-oriented skills, practical techniques that were needed for upliftment without threatening the white establishment and facing the perceived dangers of modern thought and abstract pursuits that might destabilize their fragile minds. Teaching through culture and language could preserve Africa's moral character and traditions as they rapidly disappeared in the face of modernization. The American model of Negro education coincided in some ways with the needs of British colonial education. Guggisberg was impressed with Aggrey and they became friends. Aggrey returned to become the first vice principal of Achimota. His extensive travels and educational experience made him a strong believer in the significance of education for young Africans. It could "awaken his people's aspirations and to show the way by which they should climb; not the way of Westernizing but through the development of their own racial individuality" (Wallbank 1934: 110). Aggrey used the metaphor of a piano keyboard in designing the college's seal to visually signify that both black and white keys were needed to make proper music, an image of racial difference and synchronicity still evoked with pride (Agbodeka 1977). As Aggrey argued, institutions such as Achimota would allow Africa and its people to develop in their own specific ways by achieving a "synthesis of African and European cultures" (E. Smith 1929: 226). Though many of his more radical ideas foreshadow later advocates of self-rule, to critics, the Phelps-Stokes Commission and Achimota were reminiscent of racist arguments for segregation and separate but equal development.

For the Gold Coast intelligentsia, including those associated with the Aborigines' Rights Protection Society, the National Congress of British West Africa, and newspapers such as the *Gold Coast Leader,* this seemed an excuse to give Africans second-class education oriented toward industry, the arts, and culture—an education, as Booker T. Washington seemed to advocate, that did not aim too high or provoke white anxieties or violence—rather than serious subjects that would further their economic and political conditions (King 1971).

Some Gold Coast journalists were highly critical of Achimota. As one editorial read, "there cannot be one sort of education for the European and another sort for the African" (*Gold Coast Leader,* February 16, 1924, reproduced in Agbodeka 1977: 134). Some parents of children at Achimota were upset because they saw the focus on African culture as a sign that their children were being treated as inferior to Europeans (Agbodeka 1977; C. Williams 1962). The preservation of culture and its public performance, to some, became an excuse for denying people in the Gold Coast, as in other parts of Africa and the empire, access to modern rights and the political sphere.[52] Many elites did not see traditional music and dance and popular concert party as proper music and theatre.

Radical Gold Coasters were outraged at the assumptions about racial inequality embedded within these theories of education. "If a method is right in England, why is it wrong in Accra? . . . Do you think our children are less intelligent than yours? Is this another version of the 'hewers of wood drawers of water' theory?" (C. Williams 1962: 58–59). Indeed, Gold Coast intellectuals, many of whom were involved in the 1919 Pan-Africanist Congress, saw education as a key to moving the colony toward independence. But in their eyes education was a way to engage modern forms of knowledge and ways of being in the world rather than focus on African traditions. Critics wondered, "Why send [English]men out, on huge salaries, to idle about doing nothing? Study local conditions! They are not here to teach local conditions, but universal subjects like science! Learn the vernacular so as to be able to teach it? We do not need Englishmen to teach us the vernacular; we know it . . . we want English" (E. Smith 1929: 237). Irreconcilable images of African society as both idealized and backward were fostered by the dichotomy between modern society and traditional culture leading to oscillations in colonial policy and public opinion (Baku 1990: 39).

One particularly intense conflict demonstrates the significance of the teaching of history to identity. In 1935 J. B. Danquah, William Ofori Atta, and Nnambi Azikwe publicly accused W. E. F. Ward, head of history at Achimota, of being "an anti-Negro propagandist" as seen in the textbooks he authored: *Africa before the White Man Came,* for nine- to thirteen-year-olds, and *A Short History of the Gold Coast,* for secondary school and teacher training (Jenkins 1994: 172–73). In the press, his ability as a historian and his "personal and professional integrity" were questioned (1994: 172–73). Ofori Atta, a former student of Ward's at Achimota, argued, "From first to last the book aims to prove two amazing facts: first, that the only place Africans, especially those living in West Africa, have occupied in history is that of slaves; secondly, that Africans have never made any original contribution to world civilization."[53] Ward was accused of not showing his sources and not considering evidence in not showing Negro historical relationships to Sudan, Egypt, and ancient Ghana. Danquah's interest in the links between Akan and ancient Ghana would later lay the foundations for naming the new nation.

This incident occurred one year after the Sedition Ordinance of 1934, which was sparked by anxiety about radical writing from America, Russia, and the Caribbean among other sources (Stephanie Newell 2002: 67). The colonial government was anxious about the spreading of radical ideas and recognized that English was crucial to the "development of anti-colonial . . . and pan-African pan-Atlantic community of interest" (2002: 67). Gold Coast newspapers and intellectuals reacted to this, seeing Ward's type of history as part of a broader attempt to limit black internationalism by writing it out of the past.

Ward was one of the original teachers at Achimota and a founding member of Accra's Young People's Literary Club, and he spoke Twi (Stephanie Newell 2002: 53–56). His focus on African history was in fact in opposition to the colonial state's civics course (Jenkins 1994: 178). In many ways he represented a liberal anticolonial stance. The accusations against him from more radical intellectuals show the stakes in teaching culture and history. Azikwe, a journalist and radical intellectual living in Accra who was to become the first president of Nigeria, warned "'Renascent Africans' to be wary of those 'Europeans who have been with Africans for decades' and who 'pose as friends.'" He attacked Ward in the context of seeking "'mental and physical emancipation' from the 'grip of imperialism'" (Azikwe, quoted in Jenkins 1994: 179). These attacks are in line with broader critiques of European accounts from the mid-nineteenth century that present "a history of the Gold Coast and Asante, in which the heroic acts of Asante in resisting colonialism, for example, were seen as obstructing progressive development and the march to civilisation" (Baku 1990: 38). Ward countered that he wanted to "teach young Africa to understand and appreciate its past" and "if I did not believe that the Negro has the power to make a great and distinctive contribution to the future civilisation of the world, I should not waste my time on him in Achimota" (Ward, quoted in Jenkins 1994: 177). Ward's critics were less concerned with his intent than with the effects of teaching a history based on the idea that African life was primitive and focused on performance and ritual, ignoring Africans' relationship to broader historical, political, and social issues. To some, the emphasis on local language, tribe, and culture misrepresented Africa in racist, romanticized ways—reproducing the worst form of colonial mentality—no matter the "good intentions" of liberals like Ward who saw themselves as critical of colonialism (Du Bois 1947; Esedebe 1994; King 1971).[54]

For some radical intellectuals, "African traditional culture" was an impediment to African modernity. However, postindependence politicians and artists would appropriate these recontextualized cultural practices in the name of African and national unity and liberation. Events like Tribal Drumming Night show how culture provided content for public discourse from which race had been eradicated. British ideas of cultural display transformed potentially contentious political issues of citizenship into concern for cultural tolerance and preservation. Advocacy for cultural nationalism and Pan-African unity emerge from the inversion of these forms. In the colonial imagination, African peoples could aspire to modernity but never achieve it. Ofori Atta and Danquah became two of Ghana's Big Six who led the country to independence, though they were criticized for their English mannerisms and appeasement of British rule in the face of Kwame Nkrumah's call for immediate self-rule. Azikwe, a mentor of Nkrumah's, became the first president of Nigeria. Debates about historiography raised questions about potential futures open to Africans from a variety of perspectives and about the African people's claims to universal citizenship. The contradictions inherent in colonial liberal views of Africa emerge in Achimota's ideas of culture and history, where African self-recognition seems to necessitate an exclusion from the potentials of the modern universal subject.

While in later years Danquah, as leader of the main opposition to Nkrumah, was often criticized for being too Anglicized, his work foreshadowed the turn to local language and culture in formulating national identity. In 1941 he wrote *Nyankonsem* (Fables of the celestial), a Twi-language play based on a folk story (Agovi 1990: 15; Cole 2001: 57; Stephanie Newell 2002: 76), and in 1943 he wrote another play, *The Third Woman*. In 1943 F. K. Fiawoo wrote *The Fifth Landing Stage*, an Ewe drama. These scripted dramas—following Kobina Sekyi's 1916 *The Blinkards*—represent the movement to indigenize formal literary drama in the Gold Coast.

Another instance in which public technologies of drama, entertainment, and education ignited differences concerning language and culture was the introduction of local radio service to the Gold Coast. Until the beginning of World War II, Gold Coast broadcasts were from the BBC in Britain, focusing on news and European entertainment. But Accra's own transmitter was inaugurated and began broadcasting on October 24, 1940. Broadcasts could be heard across the Gold Coast and in Nigeria, Sierra Leone, and the French colonies. The governor saw the "many advantages of being able to broadcast addresses, local programmes, commentaries, ceremonies, direct from Accra to remote centres of the Gold Coast."[55] The governor emphasized local radio transmission's significance for "general organization of the Colony" and its "educational value ... maintaining [an] intellectual standard" for school leavers [graduates] and those with "limited library facilities." Radio service most immediately was meant to consolidate support for the war, spread news of immediate issues in the colony, and counter Dakar broadcasts of Vichy France propaganda. Gold Coast transmitters began broadcasting news in English, French, and six Gold Coast languages. These broadcasts also played a mix of local and foreign recorded music. District commissioners and chiefs were put in charge of radios around the country to manage and take care of the radio receivers. Listening was not a simple affair (Larkin 2008). The government was concerned that educated authoritative leaders properly mediate and interpret the broadcasts for the populace. They organized audiences to listen to news, music, and other programs in village meeting places and chiefs' palaces.

Radio provided a number of conflicts over how to balance representations of multiple languages and cultures. For example, there was concern that broadcasting news in Asante Twi would upset listeners in the Akuapem-Twi-speaking Eastern Region. Also English and elite listeners immediately began to complain that the BBC empire news from London and their *Hi Gang!* and *Garrison Theatre* programs, "essential form[s] of recreation," were being interrupted by Accra transmissions of news in Hausa and other languages.[56] The British were concerned with establishing a sensibility to define the new radio transmitter. Accra's broadcasts first used the sound of Bow Bells from St. Mary-le-Bow church in London as its "call," which seemed inappropriate. But the governor wanted a "distinctive and uncommon call" suggesting "the beating of a small African drum . . . I am sure it would be popular with all Africans as the drum is so much used in their national life."[57] In response, government officials wrote of their concern with inciting conflict. "Each tribe has its distinctive drum music and I fear that a Ga or a Fante piece, for example, would irritate Ashanti or other tribal areas. It seems desirable that a piece of drumming without a marked tribal character should be used."[58] To this end, Ephraim Amu was enlisted to write an original composition, which was used as the new station's call.[59]

Defining identity through cultural particularity helped separate and control Gold Coasters. But it also had unintended consequences, igniting tensions in a variety of arenas, including historical writing and radio broadcasting. It also laid the foundation for subsequent projects that used cultural performance to produce a pan-cultural anti-imperial nationalism particularly among mobile urban classes.

Structuring Theatrical Reflexivity by Arguing about Culture

My main point so far has been to show an emerging critical discourse on arts was grounded in perduring debates about culture and its significance. Crucial to the making of Ghanaian theatre was the emphasis on reflexivity in aesthetics that emerged through the politically charged focus on how to write history and understand cultural signs. Furthermore, a logic of staged eclecticism emerged in concert party theatre variety shows, the logic of trickster storytelling, and the colonial project of racial-cultural objectification. The making of culture and the arts as genres of intellectual study and leisure entertainment in the Gold Coast was a highly contested project tied to uncertainties about the relationship between past and present and between personal experience and collective legacy. In many contexts, "invented traditions" have become crucial aspects of national identities. In the Gold Coast/Ghana, the processes of objectifying and organizing cultural performances became themselves a culture, providing a semiotic logic of appropriation that shapes rising expressive genres through active debates about the boundaries and definitions of culture. For the British, it was widely believed that while Africans were "highly susceptible" to the powers of spectacle and performance, they had no recognizable tradition of drama in the European sense and did not know how to interpret "proper" theatre.[60] Drama was not mere entertainment but a way of disciplining the colonial subject, of inculcating Western notions of personhood and civilization by reshaping African viewing practices, aesthetic sensibilities, and critical facilities. Gold Coast intellectuals countered this project by imagining culture through more syncretic historical dynamics. Theatre and performance became central to public life not as vehicles of "traditional culture" but by highlighting debates and contradictions inherent in the culture concept itself.

Achimota institutionalized the public performance of African culture as signs of traditional life for the contemplation of urban educated publics. Education at Achimota relied on the belief that rural culture could be objectified and projected back to young Africans for their own self-recognition within the hierarchy of colonial rule. While authentic Africa was represented through rural traditions, urbanized elite African students were meant to draw on these forms to reinvent themselves as modern. Culture was linked to an idea of national-racial character that codified and naturalized colonial narratives of difference while providing a grounding for ongoing tensions around the relationship between culture and contemporary African life. In defining culture as a set of visible displaced performance forms, Achimota set the terms through which the following generations of artists would understand theatre and dance.

Colonial educational institutions produced a separation between African and European essences through definitions of arts and culture. Colonial and state political systems appropriated from local communities "a figuration of their very locality as a mechanism for stimulating in their subjects the 'imagination' necessary for hegemony (or at least the presumption of such) over them" (Silverstein 1998: 404). But the performance of cultural identities also provided practices through which Africans reappropriated ideas of culture as critical agency (A. Apter 2007), setting the very terms through which cultural nationalism and new political imaginaries were formed. Through the recontextualization and formal institutionalization of tribal performance, nascent fields of cultural production emerged for urban cosmopolitan youths. The rise of Accra as a metropolis populated by workers and civil servants searching for new, collective identities was tied to the development of the language of culture in which contemporary African identity was built on a tension between ideas of timeless rural cultural origin and future modern aspiration. Reconfigured performance genres presented African identity as dual, at once culture-bound and striving for universal, modern recognition. In the process, duality itself became a trope of public performance in the postcolonial state (Fanon 1963).

2 The National Theatre Movement

Urban Art Infrastructures and a Contested National Culture in Independence-Era Accra

In 1961, at the height of first president Kwame Nkrumah's power, the Ghana Drama Studio opened in downtown Accra, and the Institute of African Studies opened as part of the new University of Ghana, Legon. The Drama Studio was founded by theatre pioneer Efua Sutherland with the mission "to create, stimulate, and discipline the new Ghana Theatre Movement."[1] It became a hub of theatrical experimentation, a space for artists, writers, intellectuals, and students from Ghana and around the world. Accra was becoming a cosmopolitan black city, and the Drama Studio was at its center. After Ghana's independence from Britain on March 6, 1957, and its transformation into a Republic on July 1, 1960, the Institute of African Studies was meant to provide the intellectual foundations to underpin the new nation-state. For Nkrumah, culture and the arts were key to Ghana's political future. As he stated at the institute's official launch, "Our African theatre must help our people to appreciate the reality of the changing society, for it is only when there is a complete fusion between African culture and African politics that the African Personality will find its highest expression."[2]

These two institutions were at the heart of how Ghanaian theatre and its underlying theories of performance helped shape new national sentiments. This chapter traces how colonial-era debates around culture were reoriented to link rural traditions to national and Pan-African collectivities and produce a modern theatre for an urban populace after Ghana's independence. Within a British colonial logic, expressive practices were removed from religious, historical, and political contexts to make them acceptable as signs of traditional life within a civilizing framework. Colonial rule fixed Africans in a mythic past. Early-twentieth-century colonial notions of culture were used to deny Africans political authority, while Pan-Africanists and independence fighters sought various ways to link African identity to political sovereignty and culture to history (Fanon 1963; Pierre and Shipley 2003). These dynamics were refracted in theatre projects of the 1950s and 1960s. In reanimating dance and storytelling as National Theatre, postindependence artists aimed to reactivate the spiritual force of these forms for new purposes. Drawing on established styles of cultural appropriation emerging in both colonial education and popular concert party theatre, the National Theatre Movement used Ananse trickster storytelling, with its eclectic style of staging and multivocality as the basis for a state-supported, modern artistic movement, which in turn shaped Ghanaian performance across a variety of urban media and genres.

Ananse, a figuration of Akan culture grounded in the mythic past, reemerges in the context of the new nation's Pan-African political project that configures the arts as anti-imperial critical practices. One goal of postindependence theatre was to authenticate a history of performance as a legacy for modern arts that would ground future creativity and political freedom in African and Ghanaian cultural-historical forms. Theories of performance were formulated and debated as artists tried to ground the validity of their work in relation to various purportedly European and African genres and identities. Indeed, disagreements about the relationship between European and African modes of performance shaped differing ideas about what should constitute Ghanaian theatre. In the process, theatrical variations emerge with long-term consequences for public culture in Accra and across the nation.

Debates about dramatic form in Ghana had an urgency that reflected a broader postindependence-era sensibility across the continent of the importance of literature and arts to the political projects of decolonization and sovereignty. Most notably, disagreements between Nigerian writer Chinua Achebe and Kenyan writer Ngugi wa Thiong'o about language and nationalism show ongoing concerns about conversations across Africa about form, language, and art. Beginning at the first continental English-language-oriented African writers' conference at Makerere University in Kampala, Uganda, in 1962, Ngugi critiqued Achebe and others for writing in English, a colonial language, arguing that language shaped the poetic potentials of expression and by extension the arts' potential for social and political agency. Later, Ngugi would decide to write in his mother tongue, Kikuyu, for a time. Achebe, on the other hand, claimed what he saw as a pragmatic approach, arguing that postcolonial writers should use English and French even though they had been brought to Africa as colonial languages, because they could unite disparate colonized peoples who were divided by linguistic differences. For Achebe, while English and French had been foreign languages, Africans had remade them in local poetic idioms for their own purposes. Achebe crafted English writing in ways that invoked proverb use, pidgin, and code-switching of contemporary African life. For artists of the independence era, language use and artistic form in theatre and literature were seen as crucial to formulating new African identities and political forms. Debates about language use took place not only publicly among scholars and writers but also within the discrete institutional frameworks of Ghana's national theatre movement.

Examining the making of national theatre in Ghana is critical to understanding nation-formation and rising public cultural formations in the independence era that resonate with art movements across the African continent. It also shows how performance theory and linguistic analyses are embedded in the making of these artistic genres. Ghanaian theatre is a loose set of theatrical styles, projects, and institutions defined by a storytelling structure incorporating music, dance, and a concern with translation and language.[3] It is built on performance theory defined by complex intertextual references, stylistic layering, cultural appropriation, and the rebundling of various multivocal signs. In telling stories, performers both narrate and demonstrate the performance process itself. National theatre is made in part as participants define a local theory of performance. In making and arguing about drama, participants are oriented toward a specifically Ghanaian poetics that, in the process of reframing and restaging storytelling, emphasizes reflexivity and duality. Metalanguage and metapragmatic elements of storytelling genres actively point to the line between performers and audiences, directing participants to reimagine the role of performance in public life. The staging of trickster storytelling as national theatre creates a double reflexivity, an awareness of awareness, because metapragmatic elements reveal themselves and remain open; rather than directing participants to claim authority, they open up questions of voicing, emplacement, and stance-taking. The self-conscious remainder of reflexivity in performance gives participants flexibility in the ways they inhabit social roles.

The ways that this type of theatre fosters national identity are not simple; instead of pointing to or contesting a type of moral subject, the reflexive elements of theatre focus attention on the very process of being a public figure and good citizen. Ghanaian theatre's reflexivity reveals the debates at the heart of the local project of identity-making. The language of performance becomes metonymic for political authority. National subjects inhabit culturally legitimized participant roles that point to good citizenship as good performance, and good performance as defined through the skills of trickster storytelling. On the surface, Ananse is a stock character, the teller of folktales that appear as the embodiment of traditional culture. But Ananse is irreverent, greedy, and duplicitous, crossing gender and species lines as well as subverting and subsuming supernatural and worldly authority. R. S. Rattray notes that many Ananse tales, when told live, are pointed, indirect parodies of particular people and topical issues, though when they are collected as written folktales their immediate relevance is channeled into more general forms of parodic irreverence. Ananse can be a hypermasculine hustler out for personal gain at others' expense, but his invocation brings both reflection on national belonging and critical engagements with gender, wealth, and authority.

Independence: Infrastructure and Ideologies of Nationalist Expression

In the drive to independence, competing ideas of African nationhood were played out in the refashioning of cultural theories, institutions, and tastes. While wealthy elites argued for a decentralized political order that maintained chieftaincy and its established economic hierarchies, Kwame Nkrumah advocated for a radical overturning of chieftaincy as part of the colonial project. Nkrumah's Pan-Africanists developed centralized socialist state infrastructures with the aim of consolidating resources and eliminating conflicts based on linguistic and cultural differences. Culture and the arts were seen as crucial to making the identity of this new nation by melding various rural, traditional, and popular performance styles into a shared aesthetic. Formal theatre was part of a broader project of making a new political kingdom that would reflect past African glory without being trapped by the limits of particularistic cultures and languages.

As a youth Kwame Nkrumah came to Accra from Nkroful in the Western Region to study at Achimota College, where he notably admired James Aggrey. He later went to study at Lincoln University in the United States, then relocated to the United Kingdom, where in 1945 he worked with Trinidadian George Padmore to organize the fifth Pan-African Congress in Manchester. This global meeting brought together activists, scholars, and future leaders from across Africa and the Caribbean. In 1947 Ebenezer Ako-Adjei, who knew Nkrumah from Lincoln University, J. B. Danquah, George Alfred Grant, and others in the newly formed political organization the United Gold Coast Convention (UGCC), invited Kwame Nkrumah to return to the Gold Coast to be the party's general secretary. Soon after returning and taking up this post, he broke with the intellectual activists who had invited him, whom he perceived as interested in protecting commercial interests through reform and compromise rather than advocating for independence and immediate change. Nkrumah formed the Convention People's Party (CCP), advocating for self-governance now for the Gold Coast. In Europe and America, Nkrumah had forged links to Négritude and Pan-African radicals from America, the Caribbean, and around the African continent as well as Asian and Eastern European intellectuals and politicians concerned with fighting Western imperialism in ways that shaped his political and cultural projects. His concern throughout his career as a politician remained torn between focus on Ghana as a nation and broader anti-imperial and Pan-African alliances. Nkrumah was elected to the legislative assembly in 1951 and then prime minister in 1952 as preparations were under way for British withdrawal from the Gold Coast.

Nkrumah invested in political party and state projects to develop cultural forms in line with his vision of a nation with Pan-Africanist sensibilities. Infrastructures were built to manage culture and the arts. In 1954 a provisional Arts

Council was set up with Philip Gbeho as its first interim director. The Ghana Arts Council was formally established in 1958. Gbeho, a musician, had been a student at Achimota and later a teacher there. A key figure in establishing the aesthetics of the new state, he composed Ghana's new national anthem and was a founder and director of the National Symphony Orchestra. The old elite Rodger Club was transformed into the Arts Centre on Accra's High Street. The Institute of Arts and Culture was also established (Agovi 1990). Ghana Broadcasting Corporation (GBC) was established using radio and later television to showcase Ghanaian musicians, writers, and drama groups. Soviet and Communist Chinese projects of centralized, state culture influenced Nkrumah's ideas of how to forge a unified nation, though within an African idiom (Nkrumah 1961). Building on Soviet and Eastern European state-building models, Ghana established organizations like the Young Pioneers and the Workers' Brigade to foster unity through state patronage and propaganda.

Independence ceremonies in 1957 were accompanied by the first National Festival of the Arts. Philip Gbeho was a key organizer who traveled around the country to find musicians and dancers for the performances.[4] Held over ten days at various venues around Accra, festivities included a dramatization of the installation of an Akan chief; Shakespeare's *Taming of the Shrew;* traditional drumming and dancing from around the country; highlife music; an English play, *Zuchariah Fee,* and a Fante play, *Papa Ye;* and arts, crafts, and photography exhibits. Its eclecticism reflected the principles that tied cultural performance to national identity, juxtaposing diverse styles, groups, and genres to represent the unity and legitimacy of the modern state. After independence, durbars, cultural performances, and other ceremonies drawing on traditional cultural practices were used to celebrate the new nation. While the idioms of cultural performance were established in the context of colonial rule, politicians and artists sought to reintegrate the dichotomy between tradition and modernity on which colonial authority had been built, trying to give shared historical grounding to African creativity and sovereignty. Because Ghana was the first sub-Saharan nation to gain independence, its leaders were anxious to present the African nation-state as modern and united for the eyes of the world community as well as of its own citizens. The official program for the 1957 National Festival of the Arts described cultural display as crucial to producing a national imaginary for both Ghanaians and foreigners:

> Those of our guests who are strangers to Africa may take away something from our display of drumming and singing and dancing, of handicrafts and musical instruments and photographs, of drama and folklore, that is different from the other impressions that may have derived from the great political and social ceremonies . . . Ghanaians may . . . [also] realize how goodly a heritage we have to build on for the future. Both may recall the wisdom of an English

poet, who said that the makers of a people's song are no less important than the makers of a people's laws.[5]

Various genres and styles of artistic expression are brought together to represent the uniqueness of Ghana; a national identity emerges through the totality of public cultural forms—drama, music, dance, handicraft, political and social ceremony, photography, and so on. Song is seen to be as important, and as specific to a people, as law. The programs for independence in 1957 and Republic Day in 1960 represented Ghana within internationally legible frameworks of nationhood, in which public displays of national selfhood through artistic expression had preeminence, grounding sovereignty in the country's moral, cultural character.

Accra around independence continued to grow as an economic, political, and cultural capital, with its population expanding to an estimated 338,369 by 1960.[6] The city continued to draw migrants from around the country and subregion looking for work and excitement (Akyeampong 1996; Allman and Parker 2005; Allman and Tashjian 2000; J. Shipley 2013a). Popular highlife guitar bands and dance orchestras and traveling concert party theatre troupes dominated entertainment along with American and European film screenings (Cole 2001; Collins 1994b; Plageman 2012). In the lead-up to independence in the late 1940s and early 1950s, concert party groups became increasingly nationalistic, orienting their performances toward a rising national public. Nkrumah drew on the popularity of musical and theatrical stars, sponsoring numerous highlife and concert party groups by buying instruments and paying them in exchange for their praise in music and dramatic performances and support for CPP rallies (Cole 2001).[7] He also took artists with him when he traveled to nearby countries to represent Ghana through its music.[8] Perhaps the most popular highlife artist of the 1950s, E. T. Mensah, traveled to Nigeria, Guinea, Sierra Leone, and other countries playing in support of Nkrumah.[9] State and para-state organizations also had highlife and theatre groups associated with them, most notably the Workers' Brigade Drama Group. The Information Services Department hired groups to put on plays with "messages for the civic good."[10] To Nkrumah's critics, using culture as unifying principle was part of a centralizing socialist agenda that diverted resources and attention to the state and its leadership. While the opposition saw Nkrumah's support of popular music and theatre as part of a larger propagandistic manipulation of the masses rather than artistic patronage, for his supporters the celebration of local culture was meant to provide a basis for state-centered nationalist political belonging.

Art and culture were also crucial to education reform. In 1948 the postsecondary section of Achimota College became the University College of the Gold Coast (UCGC) under the supervision of the University of London. Kofi Busia became the first lecturer in African studies in 1949, though he argued for African studies to be subsumed into more traditional disciplinary structures; he became professor and chair in the Department of Sociology (Allman 2013: 184). Busia had taught at Achimota and received a D.Phil. in social anthropology from Oxford under Meyer Fortes's supervision. He would become leader of Nkrumah's opposition and later prime minister of Ghana's Second Republic. St. Clair Drake, the influential African American anthropologist, was head of the Department of Sociology at the University of Ghana from 1958 to 1961 and helped shape ideas for African studies. Ethnomusicologist J. H. K. Nketia was appointed a research fellow in music in sociology and was also central to discussions on the Institute of African Studies. Peter Shinnie, John Fage, Jack Goody, and others also were part of these conversations.

The Institute of African Studies (IAS) was established as part of the newly autonomous University of Ghana, Legon, in 1961 to foster the study of African culture established at Achimota, even though many students and faculty continued to think higher education should be Western-centric.[11] Thomas Hodgkin came from Oxford to be the institute's first head. Following Achimota's Institute of West African Culture in the early 1940s, the new IAS emphasized ethnographic, linguistic, artistic, and historical research and scholarly production on various African societies. The institute was crucial to Nkrumah's vision of linking scholarship to political projects of making a specifically African modern society. As Jean Allman describes, Hodgkin argued for "Africa-based and Africa-centered" scholarship to "expose racist colonial myths" (Allman 2013: 190). He aimed to build a "comprehensive body of source material" (Hodgkin, quoted in Allman 2013: 190), what Allman terms the "archiving of an 'African Revolution'" (Allman 2013: 190). In 1963 Nkrumah officially inaugurated the Institute of African Studies at the University of Ghana with these words: "One essential function of this institution must surely be to study the history, culture, and institutions, languages and arts of Ghana and of Africa in the new African-centered ways.... We must reassess and assert the glories and achievements of our African past and inspire ... a vision of a better future" (quoted in Arhin 1993: 68). For Nkrumah, rethinking Ghana as an independent society "devoted to the achievement of pan-African unity" (Allman 2013: 190) required building knowledge of African cultures, and the institute was the cornerstone of this. Pedagogy and scholarship at IAS focused on African-centric learning to reframe past ignorant and racist assumptions about Africa in relation to new pride and hope for the political future. The vision of IAS placed the arts at the center of the study of Africa. At the IAS inauguration, Nkrumah continued:

> An Institute of African Studies that is situated in Africa must pay particular attention to the arts of Africa, for the study of these can enhance our understanding of African institutions and values, and the cultural bands that unite us ... develop new forms of dance and drama, of music and creative writing,

that are at the same time closely linked to our Ghanaian traditions and express the aspirations of our people at this crucial stage in our history.[12]

Colonial and missionary projects objectified African culture as tools of civilization and divide and rule. At IAS the arts were part of a Pan-African/national aesthetic of unity, crucial for understanding a shared Ghanaian past as a grounding for new creative projects (Nkrumah 1961). The Music and Related Arts sector of IAS developed into the School of Music and Drama in 1962.[13] It first offered a certificate and then a diploma.[14] Splitting off from the Institute of African Studies, it was later called the School of Music, Dance, and Drama and then the School of Performing Arts (SPA).

The National Theatre Movement

The provisional Arts Council initiated the National Theatre Movement in 1955 (Altbach and Hassan 1996), and it remained a central focus of the Arts Council after independence. While the British preservation of African culture provided a technology of moral control and a way to separate African identity from political power, the Nkrumah state redeployed art and culture as vehicles for forging a centralized identity to undergird the project of self-rule while labeling their political opposition as colonial apologists.

The National Theatre Movement emerged as a state-based project to inspire and develop creative theatre through studying and developing various performance traditions rooted in the experience of African peoples. Its creative push and infrastructural underpinnings intertwined various competing views on the significance of theatre in contemporary urban Africa into an emerging performance logic that linked storytelling to European theatrical traditions. National theatre aimed to unite disparate linguistic and "cultural traditions" separated under colonialism, within the modern frame of a Pan-African state (Arhin 1993). One critic described theatre as freedom fighting: "The imperialists, acting as impertinent cultural arbiters, have employed among other powerful means the theatre as a means for recolonizing Ghana. The theatre in Ghana must therefore utilize the same means to combat neocolonialist culture by resuscitating the rich cultural heritage of the African and crush it once and for all" (Akpala 1964). Theatre practitioners reframed styles of narration, forms of reference and indirection, and modes of address typical of rural performance genres into an overarching style suitable for urban institutional contexts. Juxtaposing music, dance, and costume from Akan, Ewe, Ga, and other Ghanaian peoples was meant to show national and Pan-African unity. In training artists, writing plays, and designing performance spaces, intellectuals, dramatists, choreographers, and actors condensed and combined various genres into a shared aesthetic to be performed for rural and urban workers and citizens. The moral and cultural legitimacy of the new nation was made by recontextualizing and redirecting cultural practices as aestheticized signs of Ghanaian identity.

Efua Sutherland, playwright, teacher, impresario, and institution-builder, was the driving force behind the National Theatre Movement (Adams and Sutherland-Addy 2007). She was born in Cape Coast in 1924 and won a scholarship to St. Monica's Training College in Asante-Mampong, where she later started teaching (Gibbs 2009: 92–97). She studied at Cambridge and the University of London for several years before returning to the Gold Coast, where she worked at several schools, including Achimota College. She married African American Bill Sutherland, a Pan-African peace activist. Joe de Graft was also crucial in the development of National Theatre as actor, playwright, director, and teacher. De Graft was also born in 1924 in Cape Coast. He attended Mfantsipim School and the Gold Coast's University College. He returned to Cape Coast to teach English and drama at Mfantsipim (Gibbs 2009: 157). He was teaching at the University of Science and Technology in Kumasi when he was invited to Accra to be the Drama Studio's first director.[15] Sutherland and de Graft were both charismatic larger-than-life figures at the center of a small group of politically influential writers and artists revolving around the Drama Studio. At times "they argued intensely about the direction of National Theatre. Efua said that Joe was a new colonialist,"[16] while de Graft was critical of cultural revivalism as, at times, uncreative. The clashes between de Graft and Sutherland on what should constitute national theatre demonstrate a profound, ongoing conflict over Ghanaian identity, though at the same time, they worked together in building drama institutions, training students at the School of Music and Drama, and building an active theatre scene in 1960s Accra. Sutherland's position was more in line with Nkrumahist cultural nationalism (K. Anyidoho 1996). She wanted to formally reinvent drama, to revive and creatively reinvent traditional African genres to counter colonial mentalities and build a postindependence Ghana. In contrast, de Graft focused on developing modern theatre as it pragmatically addressed contemporary urban Africa. As a teacher, playwright, and director he emphasized precise English-language use, technical excellence in proscenium staging, and script interpretation and analysis. Nketia recalls thinking de Graft "was not interested in African culture."[17] Indeed, de Graft argued for separating the School of Music and Drama from the Institute of African Studies. To his mind theatre and the arts should not be limited by being seen as African projects per se.[18] The productive tension between these perspectives defines the ongoing ways that polarized definitions of culture—as Western or African—heighten reflexivity in Ghanaian theories of performance.

Sutherland in particular recognized the importance of building infrastructure and institutions to foster artistic creativity. In 1957 she helped found the Ghana Society of Writers. She set up the Experimental Theatre Players in 1958 under the auspices of the Ghana Arts Council, which toured Accra and Ghana with Ananse-inspired productions (Gibbs 2009: 107). In 1961 she worked to establish the literary magazine *Okyeame,* which became an important forum for poetry, research, excerpts of plays and stories, and debates on new developments in African theatre and arts. One former theatre student recalls how in the 1960s "everyone waited impatiently" for the latest issue to come out because "there were such heated debates about the importance of theatre we were engaged in."[19]

After independence, several ambitious, detailed architectural blueprints, models, and proposals were commissioned for building a monumental National Theatre, though none were immediately implemented. The Ghana Drama Studio, opening in 1961 in downtown Accra, became the center of the theatre world. Sutherland helped to acquire financial backing for its construction. Joe de Graft was its first director. With funding from Ghana's Arts Council, the Institute of Arts and Culture, and foreign sources, including the Rockefeller Foundation, the Ford Foundation, the Farfield Foundation, and Funds for Tomorrow Incorporated, Sutherland helped envision its construction in downtown Accra (Banham, Gibbs, and Osofisan 2001: 125).[20] Monies from various American sources were later revealed to be tied to CIA cold-war operations to fund arts and cultural projects around the world. The funding of a Pan-African socialist grassroots theatre project in such a manner reveals what Gibbs (2009: 108) has called "the complexity of the situation in which Sutherland operated."

Sutherland worked closely with Nkrumah to develop the arts but was also wary of too much state and foreign control and wanted to create space for the arts to evolve independently. "She was reluctant to be seen as too political and be seen as the mouthpiece of the African Revolution and get sucked into government. But Nkrumah was smart about the role of culture in politics and they remained close."[21] Nkrumah attended the opening performance of Sutherland's *Odasani,* a Ghanaian Twi-language version of the early modern morality play *Everyman* performed by her new group Kusum Agromma. She wanted to develop a play "in which you had very Ghanaian characters and every man's problems, about living carelessly and then finding to what complications there would be in the end" (Sutherland, quoted in July 2007: 163). The Drama Studio was central to Accra's intellectual life, as international and local artists and students congregated in making, thinking about, and watching theatre. It was founded to be the center of an idealistic artistic vision: "National Theatre [must be] sustained by a Movement of persons dedicated to the art of Drama and equipped to work at the various activities that make the life of a theatre."[22] The Experimental Theatre Players became the Studio Players, which were the Drama Studio's resident company as well as numerous other groups, including the International Drama Group, the Ghana Playhouse, the Young Artistes, the Freelance Players, and student groups and classes from the University of Ghana, Legon, the University of Science and Technology in Kumasi, and other children's groups.

In 1963, after de Graft and Sutherland became research fellows at the University of Ghana's Institute of African Studies (IAS), Sutherland handed over the private control of the Drama Studio to IAS.[23] It became the "University Theatre in town,"[24] with drama students shuttling back and forth to the Legon campus eight miles north. Overall, the studio was "intended to stimulate experiments in new forms of Ghanaian theatre, to provide a centre for the training of actors and an outlet for Ghanaian playwrights." It was to link the "University of Ghana and the Institute of African Studies in particular with the National Theatre Movement by providing a centre where the results of research in the Arts of Ghana undertaken in the University can be fed into creative experimental programmes that can be seen by the general public."[25]

Sutherland wanted the Drama Studio to be designed like an African compound house, to invoke the informal, intimate spaces of African rural performance.[26] It was an open-air theatre allowing artists to experiment with both proscenium staging and theatre-in-the-round (Gibbs 2009; Kerr 1995). Sutherland wanted to create a modern performance space that would reflect "the fluid stylized mode of theatre with close contact between audience and performers" crucial to concert party and rural storytelling traditions (Kerr 1995: 119). For Sutherland, theatre-in-the-round fostered interactions between audiences and actors, as in indigenous styles, and was important for imbuing modern African drama with the spirit of improvisation and the power to provoke audiences. Artists at the Drama Studio debated how the use of space in performance reflected the legacies of African theatre versus European theatre. De Graft was less concerned with the liberational potential of drama and focused on perfecting established European dramatic techniques of proscenium staging and English-language scripting. His attention to detail presented a theatre concerned with the struggles of contemporary life rather than a grand epic romanticism.

Competing Theories of African Theatre

For Sutherland a modern Ghanaian drama should draw on Anansesem and its eclectic, irreverent offspring, concert party popular theatre (K. Anyidoho 1996). She wanted "to root a modern theatre programme in the dramatic traditions of this country" (Sutherland, quoted in July 2007: 163). In experimenting with traditional forms through various groups and projects, she aimed to identify the crucial structural elements of storytelling to "condense and heighten [storytelling's] potency and add stagecraft and modern theatrical effects."[27] For Sutherland, Anansesem was "the body of stories *and* the storytelling *performance* itself" (Sutherland, quoted in Donkor 2008). Ananse tales are built on a proverb-like structure that provides indirect messages usually through morality tales (Cole 2001: 109; Kwesi Yankah 1989). According to Nana Ampadu, a highlife musician famed for making hit songs out of folktales, Ananse stories are fundamental to

Ghanaian public culture. They provide the basic "language for highlife music and all popular culture in Ghana" by telling tales in which "events in the animal kingdom [are] metaphors for . . . social life."[28]

In the early twentieth century, ethnographers, folklorists, and religion scholars around the world became fascinated with trickster tales. They were seen as mythic tales easily collected and comprehensible as primitive literature, representative texts that portrayed the essence of a culture. Comparative religion projects and folklore collectors brought together stories from disparate primitive peoples for comparison. Folktales about tricksters were seen as harmless morality lessons or mythic tales of cultural origins, semireligious texts that could be abstracted from the local issues and contemporary concerns. Significantly, Rattray's seminal 1930 account, *Akan-Ashanti Folk-Tales,* does not describe Ananse as a trickster. Fitting these tales into a universal motif came as part of interest in a trickster archetype that followed Paul Radin's (1956) work on Native American trickster cycles, C. G. Jung's ([1956] 1972) comparative essay arguing that the appearance of tricksters around the world gives insight into the human psyche, Claude Levi-Strauss's (1955) use of the trickster in his foundational structuralist analysis of myth, and later Robert Pelton's (1980) compilation and reanalysis of studies of tricksters from around the world.

Ananse tales were seen by ethnographers and folklorists as removed from history and politics. Rattray's collections of Hausa and Asante folktales were published as separate volumes, simple collections of stories in comparison to his complex ethnographic treatments of religion, art, and politics in Asante. For Rattray his text *Akan-Ashanti Folk-Tales* completed his comprehensive multivolume "survey" of Akan people showing them "at their worst no less than at their best" (Rattray [1923] 1969, 1927, 1929). For his final major work, Rattray collected "stories at their source; that is, in the remoter villages, as told at night by the old folk, under the stars. . . . After an evening's story-telling, the best tale would be noted, and the story-teller asked to come to back later on, when the tale would be repeated, written down, and finally read over for correction" (Rattray 1930: vi). The stories give to "Western peoples a vision" of "the soul of an African people" (Rattray 1930: xii–xiv). In the colonial logic of culture, trickster tales were aspiritual and apolitical and unlikely to stir up political upheaval or nationalist conflict. Rattray divides this body of stories into humorous stories, morality tales, and etiological or origin stories (Rattray 1930: xiii).

Rattray argued that Anansesem were complex allegories meant to be interpreted on multiple levels simultaneously. In contrast, many of his contemporaries subscribed to the idea that characters in folktales are hybrids of animals and humans because the "savage" mind of a "primitive" human cannot "grasp the difference in kind 'between animals and himself'" (Rattray 1930: xii–xiii). Ananse stories relied on *akutia*, or innuendo, to talk metaphorically about someone or use other forms of indirection to address the sacred and the powerful (McCaskie 2002: 81; Kwesi Yankah 1995). In this way, storytelling provides "a period of licence [sic]" such that they could humorously depict Nyame (God), fetishes, ancestors, sickness, and sex, and even ridicule chiefs (Rattray 1930: x). "The names of animals, and even that of the Sky-god himself, were substituted for the names of real individuals whom it would have been very impolitic to mention" (Rattray 1930: xii).

Colonial educators saw the potential of Ananse stories as a basis for the development of local drama that expressed a national character. They tried to "make a selection of native themes, so that a large amount of African folk-tales shall be ready for dramatic use."[29] Rattray noted Anansesem's multimedia theatrical elements: "During some story-telling evenings, between the various tales, and often indeed, in the very middle of a story, actors will sometimes enter the circle and give impersonations of various characters in the stories" (Rattray 1930: x). African teachers were "encouraged to make plays with their pupils and the adults of the village, and the highly educated African should wherever possible see these plays and note the methods and growth."[30] Interest in Anansesem as a potential national icon continued as a British observer in 1954 argued that a National Theatre should be based on Anansesem storytelling, drumming, and local festival traditions (Lawrenson 1954). Haitian poet Félix Morisseau-Leroy, who became a key figure after independence in establishing Ghana's theatre movement, also thought "traditional" performances of Anansesem stories could provide the basis for a National Theatre (Morisseau-Leroy 1965).

Sutherland termed her type of theatre *Anansegro*, meaning "Anansesem theatre," referring to how the formal style and technique of Anansesem storytelling could reshape more formal theatre. The Twi word *agro* as in, "I am playing," has a double meaning, referring to "joke" and "play." The doubleness of playfulness and playing reflects the sensibility of this theatre. Sutherland argued that in Akan storytelling traditions, Anansesem the spider as the main character of the action is dual: a trickster who is always scheming, and a storyteller who continually breaks the spatio-temporal frame to make metanarrative comments to the audience on his own action and that of others.[31] Storytelling sessions in rural settings are social events involving drumming, dancing, and acting, all of which are woven into the framework of the main story.[32] The action of the tale is regularly interrupted and taken on playful detours by *mboguo* songs and musical interludes and comic interjections from storytellers and audience members (Rubin 1997: 140). Anansesem embodies a multimedia sensibility. For Sutherland, storytelling predisposes people to pay attention on two levels at once as "people come to storytelling sessions prepared to be hoaxed" (Sutherland 1975: 5). Storytelling events often begin with the storyteller claiming the role of speaker/animator by invoking trickery: "Anansesem ye sisi!" (Anansesem storytelling, we are here to trick you!). Others respond, "Sisi me! Sisi me!" (Trick me! Trick me!).[33] Rattray records a variation of this exchange framing many of the tales he collected with "Ye' nse se, 'nse se o," which he translates as "We do not really mean, we do not really mean [that what we are going to say is true]." This performance frame demarcates participation roles and a space of performance at the beginning of a storytelling performance as one of complex double voicing, exaggeration, and hidden intents. By engaging audiences through trickery, Asansesem directs audiences to pay attention and to think reflexively (Kwesi Yankah 1998: 27).

For Sutherland, a modern Ghanaian theatre combines music, dance, drama, and storytelling, bringing "traditional" idioms to the formal stage to inspire new creative works. Anansegro often are set in traditional contexts or involve mythic elements. They interweave narrative and scripted dialogue with music and movement. The trickster/storyteller form provides the crucial structure around which the emergent genre of Ghanaian National Theatre revolved. It has set the poetic sensibilities through which subsequent forms of popular music, film, and theatre have been presented. Sutherland abstracted what she saw as the significant elements of these rural performance forms and trained a generation of theatre and media artists in this idiom. The trickster/storyteller provided Sutherland and her students with a form of critical agency. Sometimes the trickster is consciously invoked in formal and informal speech contexts; at other times he is unspoken, embedded in the ways that stage and social actors produce authority and public performance is made meaningful. Stories rely on an oblique style to communicate moral messages, akin to the indirectness of proverbial speech and the broader values placed on metaphor, circuitousness, and indirect references in public rhetoric (Kwesi Yankah 1992, 1998; Obeng 1997).

Sutherland's three major plays show her experimental approach to melding multiple influences. All three feature strong women leads faced with complex choices that dictate not only their future but that of their families and communities. *Foriwa* is about a woman who chooses to marry a foreigner, which presents risks and surprises but also leads to new successes for her and the community. It shows her linking a folktale about moral choice to grand-scale "festival drama" and "theatre for community development" (Gibbs 2009: xix). *Edufa* is a reworking of Euripides's *Alcestis*, revealing her interests in Greek tragedy. *The Marriage of Anansewa* most fully demonstrates the logic of how Ananse storytelling was formally adapted for stage drama and linked to indirect public discourse on state politics. The play also reflects the strong influence of Brecht as well as, according to James Gibbs, spectacular nonrealist Chinese theatre, in particular through S. I. Hsiung's play *Lady Precious Stream* (Gibbs 2009: 129–39). As Sandy Arkhurst, one of Sutherland's former students and main stage managers, explained to me, *The Marriage of Anansewa* "is not based on one specific folktale but brings several together . . . and is written in the style of Ananse."[34] The story was developed in rehearsals, with actors and playwright working to flesh out the dialogue and action. The play was first performed in Twi, though the written script and subsequent revivals have been in English. It was performed around Ghana and abroad, including as Ghana's drama entry at Nigeria's cultural festival FESTAC 77.

The play revolves around George Kweku Ananse, who has a beautiful daughter with several different suitors. They each try to win her hand in marriage, promising Ananse great wealth for the bride. Ananse uses the situation to get as much as he can from all the different suitors without ever making a commitment. In the play's climax the trickster/protagonist "either faces utter ruination or survives by the skin of his wiles" (Jeyifo 2007: 26). This play was seen by some as a metaphor for how Kwame Nkrumah negotiated the predicaments of cold-war political allegiances. He courted American as well as Soviet and Chinese connections, seeking aid from both sides until he was no longer able to maintain this balance. His attempt to juggle multiple interests at home and abroad was seen by many as what led to his eventual overthrow in 1966. *The Marriage of Anansewa* took the improvisational process of rural storytelling as Sutherland saw it and codified it in a formal English-language script. For her advocates, Sutherland's work translates and adapts signs of rural life for the national spaces of modern urban Accra. While to her critics her work was uncreative and derivative, she was accused of building an elitist theatre out of outdated obsolete indigenous-language populist styles.

Sutherland embedded the improvisational and unscripted styles of audience/performer interaction into the formal aspects of the storyteller as mediator. Ananse, in the way that Sutherland and subsequent artists deploy him, is characterized by humor and the ability to play all sides of a social situation for personal gain without letting anyone realize they have been tricked. At the same time, as Nigerian critic Biodun Jeyifo describes, "*anansegro* is, as Efua Sutherland herself so insistently urged, a communal art" (Jeyifo 2007: 26). In resolving Ananse's troubles in *The Marriage of Anansewa*, "every performer on stage contributes mightily to . . . a happy unraveling of the tangled web of Ananse's overachieving schemes" (Jeyifo 2007: 26). Jeyifo's interpretation reflects the importance of Sutherland's stylistic innovation in using the figure of the trickster/storyteller to embody processes of cultural mediation and moral deliberation. Ananse is able to balance multiple, often contradictory sources of power and meaning, made possible and revealed through the dialectic of personal interest and collective support.

The Marriage of Anansewa is emblematic of Anansegro, integrating various performance genres and media within a storytelling framework. The figure of the storyteller is taken as the mediator between audiences and actors and as the main protagonist on stage. Audiences and performers are predisposed to interpret political, theatrical, and spiritual activities in the language of the trickster with the protagonist as both problem-solver and mischief-maker, and the audience is both clued in to the duplicity of the trickster and following the tale from the perspective of the other characters.

Ananse tries to achieve his personal aspirations by hiding them and managing the line between the story and its telling and manipulating the social forces around him. He is often unable to maintain this public balancing act and is thwarted by the multiplicities he tries to contain. Ananse fails or succeeds through his ability to direct various social interests at play. However, he is ever resilient and finds new tricks and plans for success. Anansegro presents audiences with a figure of ambiguity, reversal, collective morality, individual gain, and humor. Tropes of hope and possibility emerge for Ghanaians faced with potentials of a new nation-state and the dangers of a hostile world. The threat of political instabilities and economic frustrations also provides new creative opportunities. In this theatrical idiom, value is judged by an aesthetics of indirection and doubleness. Transforming Ananse storytelling for the modern stage codifies the playfulness and improvisational aspects of storytelling, opening debates about acceptable modes of performance. Ananse as the embodiment of tradition also becomes a model for modern life, a figure both caught in moral dilemmas and a moderator of them, an antihero and an observer, linking rural and urban, past and future, on stage and off stage. Ananse's character traits highlight contradiction and duality as states of being rather than representing problems with simple solutions.

In contrast to Sutherland's concern with reinventing theatrical form, Joe de Graft's early plays focus on English dialogue and are set in urban contexts and bourgeois modern moral dilemmas. His work was criticized by some for not being "African" enough and for being detrimental to the development of cultural nationalism and the National Theatre Movement itself (Agovi 1992; Botwe-Asamoah 2005; Gibbs 2001: 73). To his detractors de Graft represented all that was wrong with the Europeanization of African society. In training students he showed a passion for Shakespeare and proper use of the Queen's English. The School of Music and Drama under his leadership focused on European intellectual theatre: Shakespeare, Ibsen, Chekhov. His plays were criticized in ways that show the highly contested nature of defining Africanity through theatre. For critic Obi Maduakor, de Graft's "preference for contemporary settings and his initial unwillingness to structure his plays on myth and legend makes his authenticity as an African writer questionable" (Maduakor 2001: 67). Despite criticism of de Graft as too European, he was interested in how theatre could forge connections among African countries bringing plays by Nigerians James Ene Henshaw and Wole Soyinka to Accra (Gibbs 2009: 159). He was noted for his "theatrical precision and passion for" stagecraft.[35] As Gibbs (2009: 158) shows, de Graft was indeed interested in popular theatre and supported students' use of "concert-party conventions" in their work, indeed encouraging Allen Tamakloe to do concert party versions of Chekhov's *Proposal* and *Bear*. Whereas Sutherland's cultural revivalism was concerned with creating a mythic time-space out of storytelling conventions that would make traditional forms legible to urban audiences, de Graft was interested in the pragmatics of urban life in contemporary Africa; syncretic mixes of African and European influences were ways to look toward a new future. Indeed, de Graft worried that Nkrumah's notion of the African Personality and the very idea of reviving "traditional culture" simply replicated colonial ways of seeing and reproduced "the African as a fossil," objectified for contemplation (de Graft, quoted in Gibbs 2009: 159).

Two of his plays, *Hamile* and *Mambo*, are reworkings of the Shakespeare plays *Hamlet* and *Macbeth* set in African contexts. His 1964 play *Sons and Daughters* portrays the conflict between a bourgeois father who values money and his children who want to be artists. Like much of his work, the play presents conflicts between those who value money and power and those who value beauty. *Through a Film Darkly* presents the intractable tangles faced by contemporary Africans: the ways that society gets distracted by wealth and materialism. It also shows his propensity for "involved English-language dialogue and setting his plays in bourgeois drawing rooms."[36] Central characters in his work are often sensitive, creative men caught in the pragmatics of contemporary urban Africa who are misunderstood by their intimates and the world around them. Joe de Graft became disillusioned with Ghanaian politics and in 1969 left for Nairobi, Kenya, where he spent several years teaching and working in theatre and film.[37]

His late play, *Muntu*, shows a radical departure from his earlier work in presenting mythic contexts, religious and cultural signs, and epic staging more in line with Sutherland's prevailing ideas of African theatre (Kemoli and Mwanzi 1981). De Graft directed the play and played the title role in its 1975 opening at Nairobi's Kenyatta Conference Centre (Gibbs 2006: 113–14). It is an epic retelling of African political history set in a mythical kingdom. It begins with an idealized portrayal of peace and harmony among Muntu's people before foreigners come to claim power. Muntu's children fight back, leading to a devolving series of violent conflicts. The play is a moral allegory critically engaging with the violence of colonial rule, the slave trade, independence movements, and subsequent military regimes. Unlike his earlier work, which focuses on the interior life of individual characters, this play is concerned with the broader movement of time and how past political struggles implicate the future of Africa (Kemoli and Mwanzi 1981: 48). When he returned to Accra in 1977, he seemed to have become, according to one of his students, "more African."[38] The contrast between Sutherland and de Graft as dramatists sparked heated and personal conflicts among politicians, artists, and students over the nature of African theatre and its significance for imagining the nation's future.

The next generation of intellectuals, poets, actors, writers, and artists, including Ama Ata Aidoo, Sandy Arkhurst, Mohammed Ben Abdallah, Martin Owusu, Kofi Awoonor Williams, and Asiedu Yirenkyi, grew up as artists in the midst of the creativity and debates at Drama Studio. Novelist Ayi Kwei Armah was critical of the artistic-intellectual movement, arguing in his novel *Fragments* ([1971] 1995) and elsewhere that Sutherland and her followers were elitist and self-deluding, though for many artists of the rising generation the atmosphere at the Drama Studio was inspirational. The space also linked a small but influential group of African American, Afro-Caribbean, and other African artists, intellectuals, and professionals living in Ghana after independence. They helped shape public discourse on artistic expression, emphasizing cultural links between Ghana, Africa, and diaspora. African American poet Maya Angelou became Sutherland's friend and confidante, helping with theatre productions, acting, and teaching at the School of Music and Drama (Angelou 1991; Gaines 2006). Philosopher and sociologist W. E. B. Du Bois moved from the United States to Accra at Nkrumah's invitation to work on the Encyclopedia Africana project. His wife, Shirley, became the first director of Ghana Television. George Padmore became Nkrumah's political advisor. Félix Morisseau-Leroy came from Haiti to develop socialist theatre and dance; Rex Nettleford came from Jamaica to work on national dance. Richard Wright, Fela Anikulapo Kuti, Chinua Achebe, Wole Soyinka, Malcolm X, Frantz Fanon, and Muhammad Ali, among other international black thinkers and public figures, spent time in Accra in the 1960s.[39]

Actor/director Sandy Arkhurst, a student of Sutherland and later a drama lecturer, recalls the idealism surrounding Drama Studio: "We trained in traditional techniques as well as modern stage drama. The Drama Studio was like our second home where we could experiment with new ideas."[40] Playwright and drama lecturer Asiedu Yirenkyi, who with his brother Kofi spent time at the Drama Studio, recalls its early days as times of artistic excitement. As aspiring young artists, they felt they were a part of a new arts movement. "As students a number of us would congregate at the Drama Studio where Sutherland presided.... She was a charismatic force ... we felt we were a part of something big."

Sutherland's experimentations with storytelling as modern theatre were shaped by a long-term collaborative research project in Atwia, a village in the Fante-speaking Central Region west of Accra. Some of the Ford and Rockefeller Foundation funds she garnered were used to construct the *Kodzidan* or "House of Stories" in the center of the village, built "to provide the right model for a national indigenous theatre" (Arkhurst 2007: 168). The building is a circular space designed to create intimacy between performers and audience members. Sutherland enlisted her students, including Sandy Arkhurst, to assist in the research and development of storytelling in Atwia. He recalls that he had a university graduate's ideas of "Western theatre technique, biased opinions of what dramatization ought to do, and a superiority complex" (Arkhurst 2007: 166). His self-confessed urban, "elitist assumptions" (2007: 166) were transformed as he began to question the assumptions of Western formal drama in favor of focusing on improvisation, audience participation, and the "dichotomy between performers and audience."[41]

Atwia's Kodzidan became a community center for visiting Accra-based artists and researchers and facilitated village artists going to Accra. Theatre became a research technique and form of dialogue to facilitate community development. Arkhurst recalls, "Atwia was a farming community with no electricity or running water and poor roads. We took our time working with the community to help them identify their needs and use theatre to help find communal solutions."[42] Sutherland and her students saw storytelling and theatre as a form of community mediation. "No . . . performance was 'manufactured' in someone's private study and dished out to a passive audience. . . . All activities were aimed at creating a platform for communal participation through theatre" (Arkhurst 2007: 172).

In Accra, Sutherland formed her experimental theatre group Kusum Agromma (meaning culture/tradition players) with artists from Atwia and rural parts of the Central Region. She encouraged women to perform and join the group. According to Asiedu Yirenkyi, "she was training [the group] to bring their local skills to the national stage."[43] Arkhurst became Sutherland's main assistant in running Kusum Agromma, directing and stage managing many of its rehearsals and performances. He recounts that the group had similarities to concert party, but "Sutherland worked on developing their rural craft for the modern stage. They performed in Akan language, Fante, though they did not use cheap techniques like only speaking into microphones like concert groups did. They learned to use their voices to project properly, develop proper stage blocking, and other more professional theatre techniques." Unlike concert party, this group included female performers trying to modernize "traditional attitudes to gender."[44] Kusum Agromma concentrated on how to translate and "modernize" storytelling techniques from rural village settings with no electricity to the spatio-temporal principles of a proscenium stage and an urban, multiethnic audience. They performed in stage plays, films, and television programs, eventually concentrating on educational theatre programming for rural development. Arkhurst would also later take these lessons to train theatre artists as community facilitators in "theatre for extension communication" and "theatre for development" programs at the School of Performing Arts. Kusum Agromma and other groups did musical and dramatic performances on air for GBC radio. When Ghana Television went on the air in 1965, they were among the first to do television drama.

Asiedu Yirenkyi recalls that Sutherland inspired his cohort to explore the roots of local artistic traditions in experimenting with theatre and being open to different kinds of drama. The Drama Studio Players were an amateur group consisting of educated elites and diasporic expatriates and included poet Kofi Awoonor Williams and Robert Lee, the leader of the African American community in Ghana. Yirenkyi at times led the group. Yirenkyi's own writing, he explained, had been heavily influenced by Chekhov, though he saw his work as a part of the National Theatre Movement. Yirenkyi went to Yale University for his M.F.A. in theatre arts, returning to Ghana in the early 1970s. Displaying a close affinity for de Graft's model, his dramas were elegantly scripted English-language tales set in contemporary urban contexts focusing on intimate emotional, psychological conflicts. They created new work by exploring how "popular arts of rural people, concert party and highlife music were based in the storytelling tradition." Though his plays eschewed the use of African languages and music-dance in favor of a modern bourgeois urban setting, "cultural-national" took on many different forms and his interest in African culture emerged in pragmatic concerns rather than in formal use of music, dance, and storytelling.[45]

In line with Danquah and de Graft, Yirenkyi saw the reliance on traditional form as a depoliticization. For example, Asiedu Yirenkyi's plays parody the conundrums of contemporary Ghanaian life but formally rely on Western-style scripting and narrative structure. Yirenkyi argued that Nkrumahist cultural nationalism that was focused on the formal aspects of performance had a Pan-Africanist political orientation but in fact depoliticized the arts by emphasizing traditional forms. He explained to me, "artists [of the older generation] were so focused on form they did not notice politics. Sutherland was worried about storytelling so did not pay attention to the political detentions going on. That is why to this day there are no politics in the arts directly; it is all innuendo and misdirection."[46] For Yirenkyi the metaphoric and dialogic aspects of storytelling at the center of so much Ghanaian theatre focuses attention away from direct institutional action and creative freedoms of modern expression. "Storytelling provides many possibilities, but it also constrains modern artists trying to uncover something new."[47]

The Story Ananse Told, a play by de Graft's student Martin Owusu, shows another way the intertwined legacies of Sutherland and de Graft led artists to experiment with form, language, and narrative. It is a staged adaptation of a folktale in which the trickster is both main character and narrator, mediating the on-stage action for the audience. Owusu's play is a literal English-language adaptation of an Ananse story for the modern stage. As an actor in one production of the play noted, "he took a story we all know and wrote it as dialogue and added blocking [stage movement] for the characters." In the play, Ananse exploits people's greed to forward his own plans to get wealthy. The story follows a lonely hunter who is transformed into a king by an enchanted antelope head, which then turns into a beautiful woman. The hunter is told he will maintain power if he holds to a few simple promises. Ananse tries to get the king to break his word, tempting him with the promise of even greater power. The king's eventual downfall is a result of his greed, exacerbated by the trickster's lies and crafty double-speak. The play is an example of how Ananse storytelling was restaged by making the storyteller simultaneously protagonist and teller of his own tale.

Various artists and groups struggled to balance what were seen as African and European—traditional and modern—elements of performance. The Workers' Brigade Drama Group (sometimes called the Workers' Brigade Concert Party) was a collection of concert party artists gathered under the Workers' Brigade, a state work-training collective with a nationalist and socialist ideology, as one of the few professional groups paid to devote all of their time to drama, but they were seen as too "local." Félix Morisseau-Leroy led the group. His work helped shape the National Theatre Movement, though he remained behind the scenes. He founded the private Ghana Theatre Club and was central to formulating a national theatre by intermingling local and international forms of drama, with a specific Ghanaian sensibility, professional theatre technique, and Pan-African connections.[48] Morisseau-Leroy was a Haitian writer whose work legitimized the Haitian Creole language in the Creole Renaissance movement. In 1960 the Arts Council of Ghana, later renamed the Ghana Institute of Arts and Culture, officially appointed him "to the post of Organizer of Drama and Literature with the Arts Council on a limited engagement for the period of three tours of duty," though he had already begun this work earlier that year.[49] In 1962, under Morisseau-Leroy's leadership, the Institute of Arts and Culture undertook an experimental training program built on "a socialist theory of the theatre" to both professionalize and politicize popular theatre styles. Its goals were "bringing the tradition up-to-date . . . playing on the emotions of the people . . . selecting plays with a community message well developed with the plot and dialogue, play[ing] on simple stage [sic] for the fellow worker and the villager."[50] It wanted to find and train the best performers from around the country. He also actively recruited and encouraged applications from female artists, initially seeking "a dozen girls" to complete the company, as most in theatre were men (cf. Sutherland-Addy 2002).[51] In March 1962, for example, artists, including ten girls, were brought from New Tafe and Takoradi to train for two months in Accra to learn "stage management, acting exercises, singing, drumming and dancing, and technical aspect [sic] of the Theatre."[52]

Morisseau-Leroy wanted to link Ghana's artistic development as part of an Anglophone Pan-Africanism to the Francophone Négritude movement and to socialist projects around the world. Indeed, after leaving Ghana in 1968, he moved to Senegal, helping to develop national theatre and culture there. Morisseau-Leroy and George Andoh Wilson saw Les Ballets Africains of Guinea and the Venezuelan Retablo de Maravillas as two performance companies using workers that "developed into a famous group" that they could emulate in developing Ghanaian performance.[53]

Morisseau-Leroy also worked with Sutherland on adapting concert party styles. He wrote a full-length musical comedy script while Bob Johnson and Bob Thompson undertook "a complete Ghanaianization of the story." The play, titled *Awo Ye* (Giving birth is good), is about nation-building. Speaking roles were given to Fante speakers while Ewe, Ga, Hausa, and Twi artists were given drumming, dancing, and singing parts. In acting exercises held at the Drama Studio, "it was discovered that instead of breaking the style of the cantata (concert party), it was possible to combine the acquired acting technique with modern technique."[54] Modernizing training consisted of stage management; technical aspects of production and design; acting exercises "to reduce ad lib relics"; singing, drumming, and dancing; body training; and voice projection.[55] In 1963, the group consisted of thirty-seven members and did an extensive tour of Ghana with *Awo Ye* and a second play *Afahye* (Festival), playing to thousands of fans in small and large towns in every region.[56] In Accra, theatre was a part of the state's celebration of Pan-Africanism for urban elites and visiting dignitaries. On November 1, 1963, for the inaugural meeting of the Defense Commission of the Organization of African Unity, the institute put on a lavish production of Fiawoo's *Fifth Landing Stage* at the Commonwealth Open Air Theatre. In official Institute of Arts and Culture documents, performances were in general reported to be highly professional and successful in reaching audiences around the country, though government officials expressed "concern with the heavy costs involved in supporting the troupe" in its extensive travels and over the long term.[57] The group was set up to train artists, not create a self-supporting professional group. Indeed, concern was raised that the "Institute subsidized by the Socialist Government should show any profit at all"; while making money was against the group's mission, its expenses were growing with its professionalization.[58] While the group was encouraged to perform across the country and as often as possible, detailed accounts of government expenditures to "equip a troupe," including salaries, props, costumes, technical equipment, lights, posters, handbills, hall hire, fees, accommodation, overnight allowances, fuel, and vehicles, show concern about the ability to continue full state support.[59] Between July and September 1963, ten different drama groups, including the Good Samaritans Society and the Accra Drama Group, of varying degrees of independence, were rehearsing at the Arts Centre and later the Drama Studio and, varying from "4 to 100 members," they performed seventy-four shows with the institute's support.[60] The Workers' Brigade performed twenty-two of these, though it used more than its share of the resources. An institute official was concerned about Morisseau-Leroy's centralization of the arts, complaining that "our theatre movement has been run at the expense of the individual groups."[61] It was further suggested that since the Workers' Brigade was fully supported as a "state subsidized venture," it should not be focused on developing the arts but be "available at all times to entertain: The

Armed Forces, The Police, The Workers of the Brigade itself, the Workers of the State Farms, The Schools and Colleges, State Visitors, Our Sister States and countries in Europe, Performances in the form of Debuts at the Arts Centre, Accra or National Theatre when it is built."[62] As Morisseau-Leroy continued to advocate for state funding for experimental artistic creative development from more reticent high government officials like the director of the Ghana Institute of Arts and Culture and the minister, the state was concerned with controlling resources, seeing concrete returns of investments in entertainment, and performing the nation for its citizens and in the eyes of the world. Morisseau-Leroy used his position as national Organizer of Drama and Literature to start the first National Drama Company.[63] He regimented their rehearsal and training routine strictly, aiming to professionalize this small selected group of artists. Archival records detail the fines he levied against artists for lack of discipline. He even drafted letters of resignation for artists who were continually late or absent, making them plead their cases for reinstatement.[64] The group rehearsed and performed his play *Antigone* in Haiti. Even after the overthrow of Nkrumah in 1966, Morisseau-Leroy produced an English-language version of Rev. F. K. Fiawoo's Ewe-language play *Tuniese;* with the National Drama Company and National Cultural Troupe, *A Dagger of Liberation* by Sebastian Y. Kwamuar "with traditional dances, songs, and dialogue" about the "migration of the Ewe from Notjie to Anlo"; and a version of de Graft's *Sons and Daughters*.[65]

Theatre groups sought at times to modernize and professionalize Ghanaian performance styles and at other moments to "Ghanaianize" international theatre sensibilities, though attempts to blend audiences and performers were not always successful. For part of the Workers' Brigade tour of *Awo Ye*, the Theatre Club, an elite English-language group in Accra, joined them, performing sections of *A Raisin in the Sun*. Beattie Casely-Hayford, the institute's chief promotions officer, pointed out the difficulty of mixing different classes of people and their styles of performance. He reported that "clearly there were two classes of persons engaged in this drama exercise . . . the mixture of these categories on a common event . . . entailed very real psychological difficulties."[66]

Tour organizers noted that the unstable political climate marked by a "state of emergency and bombings" affected their programs.[67] A bomb blast nearly killed Nkrumah at a rally in the northern village of Kulungugu on August 1, 1962. Several bombs went off in September and November, and another assassination attempt on Nkrumah occurred in December 1962, as well as another at a political rally at Accra Sports Stadium on January 8, 1963. The state increasingly imposed curfews and states of emergency, with new Preventive Detention Acts issued in 1960 and 1962 and numerous suspected state opponents jailed.[68]

In this political context, theatre artists struggled to balance creative artistry and state allegiance. Nkrumah's Osagyefo Players, founded in 1965 under the leadership of George Andoh Wilson, was the epitome of what Nkrumah felt Ghanaian National Theatre should be. Actor Solomon Sampah recalls that they were seen as the nation's most elite, talented performers "hand picked by Nkrumah" and were given all the resources they needed, making "other groups jealous," though they were more "Western oriented" than other experimental groups at the time, performing plays like the American classic *Our Town*.[69] Several performers had been sent to train in the Soviet Union and Eastern Europe. At the group's inauguration, Nkrumah stated, "I look upon this drama group to be the intellectual centre, artistic stimulus and driving force behind the theatre movement in Ghana and the cultural renaissance of Africa."[70]

Saka Acquaye's development of folk opera is another example of how artists blended local popular styles with modern staging. Acquaye was a musician, sculptor, and dramatist best known for the Ga-language opera *The Lost Fishermen*, performed by the Damas Choir.[71] He was not interested in straight staged drama or concert party. "He came up with folk opera in Ga more like Duro Ladipo's Yoruba theatre."[72] Arts journalist Nii Addokwei Moffatt describes the operatic tale: "It is about fishermen who went fishing on a day they were not supposed to and ended up on an island inhabited by only women. And as you know when men and women meet, there is bound to be jealousies, intrigues and all. It has a very elaborate set and the Ga songs are really wonderful."[73] Abdallah recalls that the work succeeded in being popular among mass audiences, though it was criticized by theatre elites. "They were jealous. Some people said they would put a huge pile of fish in front of the Arts Centre to show how they felt about the play. But Ga people loved it."[74] Various artists and groups saw themselves as doing radically different types of projects, though they all worked within a similar idiom of eclectic blended genres and complex intertextual reference. They were all struggling to come to terms with multiple theatrical traditions defined by a belief that the African and the European were radically different, and that one way or another culture played a role in creating and maintaining this dichotomy.

The Ghana Dance Ensemble: Dance as Cultural Unity

The Ghana Dance Ensemble represents another aspect of the National Theatre Movement built on a similar logic of appropriation and multiplicity. The National Theatre Movement and the Ghana Dance Ensemble used Akan storytelling, music, and dance as formal structures to organize various genres of narration, movement, and music from around the country. The Ghana Dance Ensemble was founded in 1962 at the Institute of African Studies with Albert Mawere Opoku as its first artistic director and under the guidance of J. H. K. Nketia.[75] For Nketia, as a musicologist, studying African music and performance was important to counteracting colonial misrepresentations of African culture as undeveloped and uncreative (Nketia 1962). Nketia was responsible for arranging

Asante courtly music and praise singing for ceremonies of the new Ghanaian state.[76] Jamaican choreographer Rex Nettleford, later founder of the National Dance Theatre Company of Jamaica, came to Ghana to advise Nkrumah on developing national dance.[77] Opoku learned "ritual, music, and dance as a youth in Kumasi," though, as I describe in the previous chapter, he was influenced during his years as a student at Achimota College by the forms of cultural staging of Tribal Night and Tribal Drumming Night. As a member of the Asante royal family, he approached "all African cultural traditions with pride," as opposed to a number of his classmates, children of urban and aspiring classes who were at times "ashamed of culture" and saw dance as backward, "outdated aspects of Africa."[78] From Guy Warren's (Kofi Ghanaba's) perspective, Opoku had been "brainwashed" by British ideas of Africa, but Nkrumah "[lit] a fire," inspiring Opoku to remake dance as a Pan-African project; "his dances were like fine compositions."[79] The Dance Ensemble had two main goals. First, it promoted "inter- and intra-ethnic harmony" as "people from all ethnic backgrounds were brought together to perform the country's many dances, which come from all sections of Ghana" (Iddrisu 2011: 114). Second, it sought to represent Ghanaian culture to the highest international standard to the rest of the world (Schramm 2000: 343).

Opoku's choreography juxtaposed dances from cultural groups from around the country to represent national unity in the harmonic juxtaposition of different dances.[80] The mandate of the Ghana Dance was "to act as a research laboratory of the arts and to preserve indigenous music and dance forms" (Iddrisu 2011: 113). According to Nketia they aimed "to create a national dance idiom for formal theater audiences and state ceremonial occasions," developing modern stagings of various music and dance traditions.[81] Opoku believed that in African societies, "drama, music, and dance are connected and essential" and could be used to make rural culture and traditional values relevant for contemporary life by "preserving and displaying the best aspects of diverse cultures."[82] Nketia and Opoku selected Dance Ensemble members from top musicians and dancers from around the country.[83] These performers became resident experts in their cultural performance styles, though it was important to the Dance Ensemble's mission that all performers could do all of the dances from different ethnic/cultural groups.[84] Opoku and Nketia led research trips around the country to find "dance forms that were both dynamic and visually appealing. Having spotted a genre that seemed suitable for . . . staged performance, the piece was first documented, and then later incorporated into the Ensemble's repertoire" (Iddrisu 2011: 113).

Opoku would identify "the most significant elements of a dance" and condense and abstract these movements in his choreography.[85] Choreographing dances to suit modern staging required distilling them so dancers unfamiliar with the cultural traditions, music, and language of a people could learn and repeat performances and audiences from other cultural groups could appreciate their "essence." According to Opoku, "Dances in ritual context don't have time limits and move across big spaces. We have confined areas and limited time so must condense the essence of the dance. They may also be hidden from public eyes. I have taken the essential gestures, rhythms, [and] costumes from the dances and oriented them so that an audience can see and appreciate each aspect."[86] Opoku decontextualized dances, scripting the improvisational, contingent, and communicative elements of a genre as beautiful gestures for artistic contemplation. He was crucially concerned with arranging dancers on a proscenium stage such that audiences in fixed seating could observe their movements properly.

Each cultural group within the nation was demarcated by a genre and a set of movements and rhythms. According to Habib Iddrisu, a Dagbamba musician, dancer, and musicologist, the Ghana Dance Ensemble's basic repertoire consisted of the "Agbekor/Atsiagbekor of the Ewe, the Bawa of the Dagara/Dagati, the Damba/Takai of the Dagbamba, the Nagla of the Kasina/Kasem, the Kpanlogo of the Ga, and the Kete and Adowa of the Akan" (Iddrisu 2011: 91–92). These various dances from different groups around the country were performed together to embody and display national unity through shared aesthetic values. Opoku posited that "members of a [cultural] group will recognize a dance as defining them; it is a familiar dance from their area, seeing the dance brings them joy; then they see this dance which they know next to another dance . . . they don't know . . . that stands in for their neighbor who is from another tribe. They gain joy from watching this performance and make the connection by the two dances being next to each other that they are the same people."[87] For some observers this eased the anxieties of cultural communication; "it was an honor to see an Ewe person drum and dance Dagbamba forms and an Akan person performing Ga music and dance forms" (Iddrisu 2011: 113–14). The Dance Ensemble redesigned and combined dances as recognizable and equivalent signs of different "cultural" groups into a poetics of national unity. Thus difference is both defined and overcome in performance. Each dance is a sign of a cultural-linguistic group that, placed in sequence with others, represents a modern national totality.

The first major piece Opoku choreographed was *Akan Ceremonial*. It stages "the celebration of a chief . . . in all his regalia . . . and his people at a durbar and the dances, ceremonies, and dress of the Asante court."[88] One dancer says it uses the progression of a chief as "a framework for us to do [various] Akan dances." Its choreography condenses numerous dances, styles of dress, and music that would normally be done in disparate contexts into a performance in which dancers progress across the stage; the chief sits on his royal stool surrounded by his court retinue facing the audience as dancers perform downstage. Adowa and *kete* dancers display the subtle hand gestures and powerful footwork of these dances for audiences to appreciate. *Fontomfrom* drummers invoke the sounds of thunder, tapping out proverb-laden rhythms on the giant drums. Performers take on the roles of members of an imagined Akan royal court with their regal body language and forms of dress. *Akan Ceremonial* remains an important piece performed by the Dance Ensemble for state ceremonies, theatre events, and tourist displays; like all of the ensemble's work, it has been replicated by many amateur groups (Iddrisu 2011).[89] *Akan Ceremonial* spatializes an idealized version of Akan life for easy observation and enjoyment by a naïve audience. But durbars have been used by British rulers in India, Nigeria, and elsewhere as public ceremonies in which imperial rulers displayed the political orders of colonized peoples for public inspection (A. Apter 2005; Cohn 1996). For some observers this piece replicated these colonial forms of display. But for others it reinvents chiefly and colonial political spectacles as part of a Pan-African logic.

In the context of national display, Asante dances represent pride in political grandeur through a celebration of royal and courtly display. For mostly southern performance researchers, northern groups' dances and cultural displays symbolize war-like, uncivilized traditions. Ewe performance forms represent potentially dangerous religious and spiritual potency. Fante and Ga performances point to a history of colonial compromise and urban living. So while these dances became points of identification for different groups within the national ecumene, to some they reinscribe hierarchies of social respectability and notions of genre based on Akan cultural grammars.

At times, condensing and abbreviating performances for modern staging is a form of disrespect and misrecognition to those with more personal knowledge of the dances. For example, Opoku choreographed the Ewe war dance *atsiagbekor* by identifying three key movements to create a "smooth and logical flow of atsiagbekor to stage presentation. Unlike the traditional atsiagbekor, where the lead drummer occasionally randomly picks a variation to play that the dancers must then embody, Opoku and his assistants intentionally arranged certain movements to follow one another" (Iddrisu 2011: 143). Improvisation and communication between musicians and dancers and audiences are key to dances in traditional contexts. Staging is meant to transform ritual contingencies into signs of identity to be assessed in terms of staged beauty.

But recontextualizing dances can have unintentional consequences for unleashing spiritual power in modern, urban spaces. Dancers at times refuse to do "spiritual" and "possession" dances from shrines out of fear of spirit possession. As one Dance Ensemble member recalls, "several women have danced spiritual dances and gotten possessed by accident on stage. We had to take them backstage and calm them down. We [are just] doing the movements but they are not just for watching, they have meaning; it can be dangerous. If you are a Christian you do not want to risk getting involved with these spiritual things."[90] The fact that dancers at times get possessed on stage raises questions about the relationship between form and force, action and affect, and leads audiences and performers to question the possibility of actually abstracting core values from the original contexts and intents of movements, rhythms, and signs.

Another question arises when performers do dances from cultural groups with which they are unfamiliar and do not understand the language or movements. Various types of talking drums used throughout West Africa can communicate complex proverbial phrases and direct dancers and in turn respond to them in a call-and-response manner. But they require deep linguistic and cultural knowledge to use and understand. In multicultural contexts of southern Ghana, cultural meaning is lost. For example, as Iddrisu notes, "Folklore groups performing Dagbamba music and dances have gradually stripped the lung'a drum of its original speech/voice, or talking role, and prominence. . . . Most notable, the lung'a drum has lost its voice in favor of sporadic, improvised, nonsensical rhythmic patterns that replace speech" (Iddrisu 2011: 39–40). The use of musical instruments and dance moves associated with remote locales lends national performances cultural legitimacy. For Iddrisu, however, decontextualizing music and dance forms to make them legible to linguistic outsiders makes them incomprehensible and even ugly to people who know them from original contexts.

Developing a Ghanaian Theory of Performance

In the move toward independence, culture becomes a technology of debate, ceremony, and circulation for integrating difference into a national imaginary. The aesthetic values of performance evolve in debates about the structural and emotional role of cultural belonging for developing a modern national citizenry. The history of modern theatre in Ghana is rooted in the reinvention of Ananse storytelling and numerous other performance traditions combined and reconfigured within a Pan-African aesthetic. Ghanaian theatre is a blended genre marked by competing ideas of what constitutes performance and what is authentically African. As practitioners try to define Ghanaian theatre, they delimit participation through reflexive boundary-making. Through the evolving formal structures of theatre, participants make intertextual links between signs of past, present, and future political and cultural affiliation, anchoring these signs in specific kinds of participation. The self-conscious negotiation of metacodes that structure performances underlie how words and actions are made meaningful (Duranti 2001). Participants point to and contest formal structures, implicitly debating participation, timing, spatial organization, content, and so on of an event through its metapragmatic elements. Reflexive moments of intersubjective communication and shared semiotic action are constitutive of contexts and concomitant subject positions in ways that show the culturally specific ways that reflexivity works.

Directors, playwrights, and actors struggle to imbue words and actions with authority. They attempt to balance the appearance of the natural animation of tradition with new creative authorship by actively managing the intertextual gaps while audiences strive to discern gaps between actors and their characters, signs, and various registers (Bauman and Briggs 1990; Kockelman 2005). Malleable codes of performance evolve as actors and audiences debate meaning and reflect on the relations between the form and content of events. Theatre participants debate the roles of creativity and intent in making meaningful performances. In the process, artists and audiences reimagine the past as a way to conceive of new possible futures. In the independence era, the precolonial past was at times romanticized and at other times seen as backward. For some, the colonial political order needed to be erased, while for others a pragmatic focus on daily life would provide a way forward (D. Scott 2004). Reimagining performance was a way to rethink the future in cultural terms. Signs and practices that point to and connect various images of the past and the rural potential futures are especially productive in cultural revival projects (Handler 1988). In the process, an urban present is reconfigured (Kruger 1999: 72).

The self-referential qualities of evolving semiotic orders call new forms of participation into being. The indexical and stance-taking aspects of social action link various registers into an emergent, shared genre (Parmentier 1994: 70–71). That is to say, as actors make references and inhabit social roles in performance, they are invoking new potential futures. As multiple established registers and contexts are realigned in performances, participants piece together a new language for discussing culture, nationhood, and Pan-Africanism through performance (cf. Eisenlohr 2006). The development of formal Ghanaian national theatre is an urban elite art project aimed at claiming and reinventing the folkloric, as in the development of Russian, American, German, and French inventions of modern national expressive idioms (Bauman and Briggs 2003). Ideas of what constitutes Ghanaian and African culture and tradition are made, debated, and reconstituted in the development of national projects that naturalize the process of producing a coherent notion of the past and the rural and link them to the urban present (A. Apter 1999). Traditionalized practices make new viable stances for artists who validate their creative activity by connecting it to past styles. Indeed, "much of what is important in a story or myth is not the 'content' but its 'intertextuality'" (Goodwin and Duranti 1992: 11). Through multiple kinds of referencing, performances restructure potential relations among audiences and performers within changing political, economic, and social contexts.

While advocating for a singular national narrative, Sutherland's *Marriage of Anansewa* and performances of Opoku's dance dramas like *Akan Ceremonial* also reveal the multiplicity and artifice that go into the production of a singular image of national belonging through performance. A director's or storyteller's abilities to reanimate established registers and author new utterances are central to legitimizing new dramatic forms (Goffman 1981). The relationships among audience members and performers are built on a type of performativity that must appear to be referencing past authority while making new utterances. Performativity classically delineates the nonreferential aspects of semiotic processes through which speakers and performers call into being viable subjectivities and collectivities (J. Austin 1975). Performative actions produce new images, positions, and ideas, often in the guise of referencing preexisting ones. As signs are delivered with new emotional inflections, recombined, and linked to new references or contexts, they take on different effects and meanings for participants. Performers call into being new nationally oriented subjects by aligning previously incommensurable signs, registers, and genres within events, redirecting their performative force (Keane 1997).[91] A theatrical community of interpretation emerges through debate and contestation of theatrical form that leads to shared styles of language use, reference, aspirations to urban cosmopolitanism, and attitudes toward the future. Intertextual references across genres and social spaces shape a shared set of values and principles in an enduring poetics.

3 Revolutionary Storytelling

Pan-African Theatre and Remaking Lost Futures in 1980s Ghana

With the overthrow of Kwame Nkrumah in 1966 and subsequent political uncertainty, Ghanaian postindependence dreams of unity and social-economic progress waned. For the urban intelligentsia and artists like playwright Mohammed Ben Abdallah, political disillusionment was cast in aesthetic terms: "National Theatre was a grand idea, a concept. Different people were doing different facets of what was supposed to come together. We had lost an opportunity. Some say through lack of self-awareness. Everyone was too focused on what they were doing. We [did] not recognize that all these various projects were all components of a National Theatre."[1] In this sense, the National Theatre Movement's potentials and failures reflected the nation's broader struggle for self-recognition.

After Nkrumah, state and public support for the arts and interest in the significance of culture declined. Many of the grand projects begun in the early 1960s limped along, though with little vigor. The Second Republic of Ghana, under the leadership of Dr. Kofi Busia, undid many of Nkrumah's economic and cultural programs. The state encouraged foreign investment, aligning Ghana more closely with global free markets, though Colonel I. K. Acheampong deposed Busia in 1972, soon after he radically devalued the currency. The new military government was noted for its spectacular displays of both grandeur and corruption, though it also recuperated Nkrumah's legacy, at least in name. In the absence of centralized cultural projects to display a nationalist sincerity, highlife groups and concert party popular theatre troupes flourished, playing for rural workers across the country, while more elite bands played for middle-class urban audiences. These entrepreneurial performance groups set the tone for Accra to increasingly become a vibrant center of nightlife and entertainment (Collins 1994b; Plageman 2012).

But with disillusioning political instability around the continent, the violence of the Biafran civil war in Nigeria, and the war in Algeria, Nkrumah's dream of a shared Pan-Africanism was fractured. Actor Solomon Sampah recalls that subsequent governments de-emphasized the importance of culture; they "did not spend money on developing our arts. They associated that with state socialism and Nkrumahist centralization. In the 1960s we [artists] were seen as important... part of a vibrant scene.... After Nkrumah, nothing."[2] Though state funding for arts decreased, some artists like Sampah and related civil servants were able to remain on the government payroll. Little work was accomplished, as governments changed numerous times and leadership in the higher state posts and the organization of the various institutions, ministries, and secretariats were regularly shuffled.

Sutherland and other leading artists who had not left Ghana continued to advocate for the significance of culture and the arts. In 1970, after receiving a request to assess "Ghana's cultural programme," Sutherland wrote diplomatically, if forcefully, to the Ministry of Education, Culture, and Sports, arguing that "a new approach to the promotion of artistic activities is seriously in demand."[3] She noted a lack of leadership and the need for surveys to identify "WHO the artists of Ghana are, WHAT they are doing, and WHERE they are."[4] She advocated for resources to develop venues and facilities and grants and loans be made available to *"fill a gap in Ghana's artistic output"*[5] (emphasis in original). She noted in particular that the number of "children's books of artistic quality" and "artistic plays" was "pitifully low."[6] Sutherland's assessment makes clear that state priorities shifted away from the arts and culture as experimental future-oriented projects. Indeed, a notion of culture as preservation—more in line with preindependence colonial ideas of African arts—had reemerged. Another searing internal document by Seth Cudjoe calling for reorganizing of the Arts Council in 1970 noted that while the council's goals were to "preserve and foster traditional arts,... encourage development of new art forms... [and] encourage appreciation of the arts,"[7] it failed to promote the arts at all. It notes that the "reasons for failure" to achieve these goals are that Arts Council members "have no living contact with the root sources of traditional arts and crafts... [and] are not deeply conversant with the nature of any of the arts... [or] with the artistic needs of the people... [or] the social role of art."[8] Both Sutherland and Cudjoe also point to a growing disconnection between urban and rural life with resources and populations increasingly concentrated in Accra and other cities. This became manifest in artistic terms as people in Accra seemed increasingly out of touch with "cultural traditions" and threatened by the dangers of Western influence. In a letter to N. Z. Nayo, director of the National Academy of Music, Cudjoe warns of the dangers of losing touch with culture. "The argument is not that Africans should shut their doors against all foreign influences, but that they should order them to attune with, and subordinate them to the special progress... [of] their own proven history.... FOR TO FAIL TO CONTROL FOREIGN INFLUENCES IS TO BE ENSLAVED BY THEM."[9]

Jerry John Rawlings came to power in a populist coup on June 4, 1979; his Armed Forces Revolutionary Council (AFRC) relinquished power to Hilla

Limann's democratically elected government only to overthrow them in another coup on December 31, 1981. Rawlings stayed in power as revolutionary leader of the Provisional National Defence Council (PNDC) until 1992 and then until 2001 as democratically elected president of Ghana's Fourth Republic. The Rawlings Revolution inspired a revival of Nkrumahist cultural nationalism as part of renewed critiques of neocolonialism and European control of global political economy. This renewed interest in recalling a lost cultural past and its previous revival in a moment of high nationalism is a nostalgic project, a form of remembering meant to redirect the nation. The state's political stances were institutionalized in various culture-oriented state policies and infrastructures and in the founding of Abibigromma Theatre Company and the building of the National Theatre in 1992. Building a Pan-Africanist theatrical aesthetic required cultural and urban infrastructure. These projects, however, came into tension with pressure to marketize the economy. The political-economic conditions in the 1990s of intensive state privatization shaped how theatre artists and cultural institutions reconfigured the legacy of Nkrumahist National Theatre.

In the 1980s artists tried to turn political lament for a lost future into renewed potential. Theatre was part of the Rawlings Revolution's cultural revival. In nostalgia for early nationalist political hope, a new Cultural Revolution was instituted to revive the use of art to create cultural unity. Young artists and politicians reinvented a lost moment, aiming to overturn established racial, gendered, generational, and class hierarchies. However, they soon confronted a contradiction in which the state simultaneously claimed a populist socialist revolution while turning to economic marketization. Through building cultural and media infrastructure, the Rawlings state imagined a national grassroots populism. Conflicts between socialist state control and continuing pressure to liberalize would play out in struggles over theatre and its institutions. Drama provides a point of mediation between changing civic institutions and competing popular imaginaries.

Theatrical genres have often been used to understand political events and the passage of time more broadly. Independence movements and revolutions connote radical breaks and discrete, self-consciously narrated, staged actions. Revolutionaries attempt to reshape ideas of the past to open up new ways to contemplate the future. In *The Eighteenth Brumaire of Louis Napoleon*, Karl Marx reflects on the significance of repetition in political transformations and in historiography: "Hegel says somewhere that all great events and personalities in world history reappear in one fashion or another. He forgot to add: the first time as tragedy, the second as farce" (Marx 1994). For Marx self-recognition emerges in the loss of the past and how it is given new meaning in its repetitions. Events become history and gain narrating and moralizing orders, which give them new meaning as they are copied, repeated, and recognized. In Marx's much-cited formulation the tragedy of failure and loss is repeated as a nostalgic farce. In Louis Napoleon, Marx sees someone attempting to replicate and surpass France's past political actions, though these historical repetitions become a type of self-parody. In reanimating events and ideas through emotionally and morally charged dramatic styles, revolutionaries create narratives and ways of telling history that, in turn, shape forms of remembering and forgetting required for conceiving new political futures.

Revolutions and tragedy, as David Scott points out, share "an uncanny but nevertheless adhesive intimacy" (D. Scott 2014: 35). The threat of violence and the potential of liberation and freedom are connected in revolution. Tragedy stems from the unpredictability of radical action and the devolving violence, physical and epistemic, it may incite. Indeed, tragedy may always be the flip side of freedom's promise (D. Scott 2014: 23). For many, Nkrumah's fall—whether it is marked by his increasing authoritarianism or by his opposition's inability to recognize his vision—was a tragic end of the dreams of independence. Tragedy is a genre that implies romantic hope that frames a conditional failure. The Rawlings coups corresponded with a secondary wave of revolts across the cold-war postcolonial world—in Burkina Faso, Grenada, Iran, Nicaragua—that marked renewed attempts to reassert local rule and critiques of global capitalism and neocolonialism as well as the intensification of cold-war opposition politics played out in numerous proxy wars. Ghana's 1980s revolution explicitly tried to claim the sincere vision of Ghana as a strong independent country, in some measure reviving and copying Nkrumahist projects. It was an attempt to re-create the lost future that freedom had promised. Marx's critique of secondary political actions as farcical implies a naïve hopelessness and further tragedy in comic failure. In Ghana's case, tragedy and farce meld into a poetics of theatre that uses humor to temper dreams of the future. But the trickster character—one who hustles to achieve his heart's desire—is at the center of national theatre and the idea of a Ghanaian citizen. Reading this moment of political transformation through theatre arts that are shaped by tropes of the trickster shows how humor and deferral are modes of reimagining a future not as a story of success or failure, freedom or tragedy, but rather as an ongoing struggle contingent on the latest set of insurmountable obstacles to be conquered.

A Dream Deferred

Rawlings's seizure of power at the end of 1981 was a complex moment of rupture from the immediate past that created uncertainty about how to reorganize life with a mind toward future independence and prosperity. The early days of the Rawlings regimes were terrifying for some and refreshing for others. Soldiers roamed the streets to keep the peace, meting out swift justice to those who disobeyed.[10] Families living near military and police installations often ate and slept on the floor to avoid stray bullets. Accra's main markets were razed to discipline private traders accused of hoarding commodities. Market women were publicly flogged for valuing profit over the good of the nation. Six former heads of state were executed by firing squad. The execution was broadcast on national television, cast as collective catharsis. The government's attempts to rein in perceived rampant corruption and moral indiscipline led to sporadic violence and extended curfews. Fuel shortages led to transportation crises and prevented farmers from delivering cocoa crops to the coast on time. State and corporate institutions faced numerous strikes and stoppages. Rampant inflation led to food shortages and market crises. With the forced return of one million Ghanaians from Nigeria, resources were stretched to the limit, with rich and poor alike facing austerity measures. The city of Accra was at the center of the struggle. By 1984 census reports gave the capital's population as 969,195.[11] It continued to grow and attract migrants, though the lean times of the early 1980s affected the life in the city. Transportation was unreliable, forcing people to walk long distances. Nighttime curfews and fuel shortages destroyed Accra's nightlife as well as the ability of touring groups to travel. But myriad crises also created social solidarity. Scarcity inspired new artistic promise, with new amateur theatre groups gaining popularity and venues holding "afternoon jump" dances, concerts, and shows to beat the curfews. One actor recalls the excitement at feeling that "artists could once again contribute to social change . . . we were hopeful concerning the role of art. Everyone was struggling but we were struggling together."[12]

Young intellectuals and artists saw the Rawlings Revolution as a critique of corruption and of the older generation's neocolonial complacency (Nugent 1995).[13] The new government's idealism attracted artists who revived Marxist and Nkrumahist political critiques. Writer Ama Ata Aidoo served as secretary of education, poet Attuquaye Okai was mayor of Accra, and playwrights Asiedu Yirenkyi and Mohammed Ben Abdallah and other intellectuals took high-level government posts, linking the tentative revolution's messages of unity and transformation to culture.

The day of the second coup, Rawlings addressed the nation on radio from Ghana Broadcasting House. His speech invoked Ghana's legacy at the forefront of Pan-Africanist politics: "Ghana may not be that rich but she is the political light of Africa. . . . As soon as Ghana realises her social and economic democracy, the rest of Africa will follow and will be on the road to a continental unity."[14] In recognizing the links between Ghanaian autonomy and the continent, Rawlings argued that political sovereignty for African societies was not tied to economic wealth but to a more profound shared history. To this end, culture and the arts were meant to counter neocolonialism by reconnecting the citizenry with national and continental heritages.

Ama Ata Aidoo's Theatre of Memory

Of the myriad artists who joined the radical AFRC and PNDC governments, writer Ama Ata Aidoo is one of the most striking. Her theatre work is particularly relevant to the political project of recuperating a cultural nationalism in that it focuses on themes of embodied memory (Gibbs 2009: 153). She became secretary of education for eighteen months after Rawlings's first coup in 1979. She recalls, "It was important for me as an artist because I went through a phase during which I felt, for the changes I wanted to see, writing was not enough." Her artistic and political sense developed in the context of the Drama Studio. Aidoo's plays, novels, and poetry elude easy generic categorization. Always an independent spirit, she bridges the gaps between the Sutherland/de Graft independence generation and younger artists. Many of her works center on strong female leads who reject normative female roles and are creative, misunderstood, and displaced. They persevere as renegades, observers of social conditions around them to which others seem oblivious. The semiautobiographical novel/poem *Our Sister Killjoy* follows a young woman who leaves Ghana and returns, and in the process struggles with conservative expectations of women. Through stream-of-consciousness inner narrative the story tells of the exoticization of black women abroad and the ignoring of their value at home.

Dilemma of a Ghost was her first play, written when she was a student and first performed in 1964. It portrays Ato, a Fante man who returns from abroad with Eulalie, his African American wife, and the complex struggles as Ato's family looks down on his wife as the descendant of slaves and she thinks local customs are backward and primitive. The play is about the immanence of the history of the slave trade as it haunts daily concerns and disturbs surface cultural logics and simplistic ideas of racial affiliation. According to Aidoo, *Anowa* is based on a folktale that her mother told to her.[15] The play is about Anowa, a young woman who defies her parents to marry a man named Kofi Ako. As Gibbs describes, the play is "full of stories" and "'shadows' of other narratives" (Gibbs 2009: 143–44). Stylistically it builds on Sutherland's Anansegro, blending proscenium staging techniques with storytelling and musicality. The storytellers are an old man and an old woman; together they are The-Mouth-That-Eats-Salt-And-Pepper who interject into the narrative to debate the tale's significances. The play is set in the 1870s, when the Gold Coast colony came into being. Kofi Ako, with Anowa's help, becomes a wealthy merchant, though he becomes impotent, symbolically sacrificing family and social reproduction for prosperity and trade. Anowa rejects his use of slaves and his focus on riches, in the end regressing to a childlike state, and both she and her husband kill themselves. The play shows the parallels between colonialism, capitalism, slavery, and patriarchy. Aidoo is concerned with the idea that "Ghanaians do not want to talk about the slave trade, or the connections between colonialism and racism . . . and the effects of not dealing with the past."[16] Like much of her work, this play is a critique of the way Ghanaians deal with history.

Aidoo's tales point to the ways that women often are trapped between ideas of traditional Africa and modern life. Her lead characters are highly ethical women pushed by the flux of contemporary life, forced to reckon with ideas of tradition that reflect historical dilemmas in unrealized ways. She has critiqued Western feminism by pointing to the importance of linking race and class to feminist critique and not rejecting African traditions but rather showing their significance and historical production in the context of slavery, colonialism, and inequality. Aidoo rejects the idea that female empowerment is located outside Africa; instead she positions her characters in racial and gendered dilemmas of cosmopolitan making and local articulation. As a critic and public figure she tries to address the intractable dilemmas faced by postindependence Ghana.

Sutherland, de Graft, and other pioneers of the National Theatre Movement were concerned with education reform. Aidoo entered government to reform the education system, extending the idea that literature, theatre, and pedagogy are central to decolonization. Sutherland, Morisseau-Leroy, and de Graft had pushed to include women in theatre, as had the socialist sensibility of Nkrumahist organizations like the Workers' Brigade. Aidoo's outspoken critiques of gendered inequality further opened up room for a rising generation of female theatre artists, including Patience Addo, Dzifa Glikpoe, Edinam Atatsi, Amy Appiah, and Akos Abdallah. Aidoo was particularly concerned with literacy for girls. She recalls her motives for going in to government: "I was going through a period when I was clear that the pen was not mightier than the sword. . . . Writing was not enough to help effect the change I wanted to see as a part of that whole revolutionary phase. Otherwise I like writing too much to give it up like that. So when an opportunity presented itself for me to go into . . . revolutionary politics, I didn't think twice. I was interested in changing the Ghanaian education system, contentwise, to make it more Ghanaian."[17]

In her short time in government she was not able to accomplish her goals. "I could not do what I wanted to do from inside of government."[18] As the characters in her plays know, there were no easy solutions. But she raised awareness of gender equality and cultural education and brought Ghanaian and African literature and theatre to the populace.

The Cultural Revolution

The Cultural Revolution was launched on April 2–3, 1982, under playwright Asiedu Yirenkyi's leadership as the PNDC's first secretary of culture and tourism. It was celebrated with performances by musicians, dancers, cultural troupes, and a parade to Black Star Square in central Accra. Yirenkyi delivered a speech titled "Towards a Creative National Culture" linking culture to political unity and economic potential.

> P.N.D.C. Secretaries, chiefs, members of the diplomatic corps artists, invited guests, and all gathered here, you are welcome to the launching of the cultural programme for the revolution. . . . The revolutionary process [that] began on 31st December 1981 offers opportunities to those who have been struggling to contribute to the development of a true national culture, to those whose talent and efforts have been inhibited and discouraged by the preponderance and perpetuation of barrenness and imitation. . . . The aim of the Ministry of Culture and Tourism is to instill in our people the self-confidence that our material problems can be solved by us and not the benevolence of any foreign investor.[19]

Equating the suppression of creativity with colonial domination and blind copying of foreign ideas, the Cultural Revolution reinvigorated precepts of the National Theatre Movement. The state sponsored durbars and public performances, linking culture to national pride. Popular, intellectual, and state ceremonial events took on a revolutionary feel, with themes and dress oriented to promote equality and critique established power hierarchies. Yirenkyi encouraged people in rural areas to restart traditional festivals, many of which had not been celebrated for years because of urban migration and financial constraints.[20]

In 1983 Mohammed Ben Abdallah, who had been deputy secretary under Yirenkyi, replaced him as secretary of culture and tourism. Abdallah had returned to Ghana the previous year after completing his M.F.A. at the University of Georgia and his Ph.D. at the University of Texas, Austin. He soon joined the inner circle of Rawlings's government, holding various cabinet positions until 1994, while continuing to write and direct plays (Asiedu 2001). Abdallah, Yirenkyi, and other artist-politicians aimed to build on the work of the older independence generation. Among colleagues in government focused on economic stability and military organization, Abdallah fought to position culture as foundational to state policy and national development across all realms of life: religion, media, education, tourism, privatization and the market, foreign policy, infrastructure, and development.[21] The PNDC set up numerous cultural and artistic exchanges with radical governments around the world, including Iran, Czechoslovakia, the German Democratic Republic, and Cuba.[22] An agreement with Cuba, for example, builds on one agreed upon between the two nations in 1964 that "provides for co-operation in education, scientific, and cultural matters . . . interchange of artistic groups . . . scholarships . . . interchange in the fields of radio, films, and television."[23]

For Abdallah, understanding cultural heritage would foster creative experimentation, and both were crucial to political autonomy. He approached policy with the eye of a theatre director, creating infrastructure to foster potential creativity. He noted the lack of attention that culture received: "When I became Secretary for Tourism and Culture . . . the first thing that confronted me was a document that was called the PNDC guidelines for the ministries . . . and for culture and tourism. . . . It was a very short paper, mimeographed."[24]

Following Yirenkyi's initiative, Abdallah revived long-moribund local rural festivals to encourage "pride in our cultural heritage and [to encourage] tourism."[25] Culture policy and institutions were meant to empower Ghanaians to take charge of their political-economic future. This entailed a radical decentralization. In extensive tours of the country, he assessed capacity, identified local cultural and artistic leaders, and set up cultural centers. In his passion to visit every corner of Ghana and inspire a cultural revival, he at one point was so exhausted he had a heart attack and was advised to stop traveling. In a speech inaugurating the Central Regional Cultural Committee, he explained that the government sought to establish "a true and democratic working programme for the development of arts and culture in . . . an aggressive campaign to arouse the consciousness of Ghanaians at all levels of society with particular emphasis on the youth and at community level. It is in this direction that the Ministry has called for the establishment of District Cultural Committees comprising all organs of the Revolution, the Traditional Councils, the District Administration, members of groups of artistes, and cultural experts to work out a functional Cultural programme."[26] In another speech setting up a district cultural committee, Abdallah argued that government decentralization was having a powerful effect. "It is not by accident that there is a great upsurge on the Cultural front at this time of our revolutionary journey. All over the country there is a proliferation of cultural troupes in response to the Government's Community and District Cultural drive."[27]

In 1989 Abdallah established the National Commission on Culture (NCC), with himself as its first chairman, which focused on culture as a field of administration. It established a decentralized national structure allowing regional and district-level autonomy, while centralizing control of all media, arts, and culture-related institutions and programs under the NCC. Abdallah explained, "We wanted to provide the structures to foster creativity among local peoples across the country."[28] The NCC established a Centre for National Culture (CNC) in each of the ten regions. Established cultural hubs such as the Arts Centre in Accra and Kumasi's Cultural Centre were reincorporated under this rubric. "Cultural activities in each of the 110 districts, in turn, connected with the regional centers."[29]

> We criticized previous regimes for perpetuating new colonialism, by not creating the kind of institutions that would help Ghanaians to see themselves more culturally, as Ghanaians; thinking independently of our former colonial

administrators. This was manifest ... in education ... the dominance of foreign cultural influences on Ghanaians. In music, in dance, in drama, in the arts, in clothing that people wore and even the attempts by some women to lighten their skins with all kinds of creams. Our cultural institutions, radio and television, the *dominance* of the airwaves by, again, foreign influences. Foreign music was played more than local music—programs generated from outside dominated our airwaves as compared to programs generated from within our country and the continent. We thought there could be new inspiration from *our* culture. So you know, all these things were very, very clear and we talked about the ... democraticization of culture, culture institutions and the products of culture.[30]

The NCC highlighted the dangers of foreign culture and commodities, promising an infrastructure to support cultural diversity centered on an ethical African-centered politics. "Accra should be a center of national pride as well as Pan-Africanism." Abdallah aimed to use state support for the arts and a strong culture policy to protect Ghanaian society from the global free market.

Reviving Nkrumahist links to the African diaspora, Rawlings's state built memorials to Pan-Africanist political history as centers of commemoration, tourism, and research. The George Padmore Library, the W. E. B. Du Bois Memorial Centre for Pan-African Culture, and the Kwame Nkrumah Memorial Park and Mausoleum in Accra were dedicated, all revolving around the reinternment of the bodies of these leading Pan-Africanists and their roles in building Ghana.[31] In 1992 Abdallah and Sutherland helped establish the ongoing Pan-African Historical Theatre Festival (PANAFEST) to "foster global dialogues and artistic exchange between people of African descent."[32] The National Commission on Culture controlled the Museums and Monuments Board, the National Theatre, the W. E. B. Du Bois Centre, the Kwame Nkrumah Memorial, the Folklore Board, the Copyright Office, the Ghana Dance Ensemble, the National Theatre Players, the National Symphony Orchestra, and all ten regional Centres for National Culture. Encouraging a shared idea of cultural tradition would encourage new creative energy. In this model, state control of national culture could help mitigate outside influences on Ghanaians. In religion, "foreign" religious institutions were regulated as they were seen as a threat to local cultural integrity (Coe 2005).

Following on Aidoo's earlier education reform attempts, school curriculums were redesigned to include cultural studies to teach students "African ways of life," philosophy, and arts. Language policy was oriented teaching "local" languages to youth and using local languages for early-childhood instruction. In school the younger generation read works by Ghanaian authors like Efua Sutherland, Ama Ata Aidoo, Kofi Awoonor (formerly Awoonor Williams), Asare Konadu, and Albert Adu Boahen, as their texts became part of set curriculums.

Abibigromma: The Logic of Pan-African Storytelling

In February 1983, Abibigromma was founded as the Resident Professional Theatre Company of the School of Performing Arts, University of Ghana, Legon, by a board consisting of Mohammed Ben Abdallah, Asare Newman, and William Adinku. Abdallah recalls that his initial resistance to working with the state had to do with his commitment to furthering theatre in the country: "I was trying to resist going into government. I told Jerry [Rawlings] that I didn't want to be in an office. I wanted to work on campus, to help implement things on the ground . . . to help the revolutionary movement directly." For Abdallah there was a sometimes-productive tension between government and theatre work. "We wanted to develop a vision of national cultural policy. We realized there had never been a ministry dedicated to culture so I wanted to develop that. But we needed to develop this policy through supporting local art structures and artists to instill pride and creativity in Ghanaians."[33]

Abibigromma was established to provide a forum for creative experimentation. Its name was coined to represent its artistic vision. Abibigromma is "an Akan name derived from three words: *Abibiman* (Africa / Land of black people), *agro* (players), and *mma* (children). The new concept of Abibigro loosely translated means 'African Theatre.'"[34] Defining a new genre, it expands Sutherland's notion of Anansegro to further develop the formal storytelling idiom in connection with broader Pan-African performance styles. For Abdallah it "reflects my attempt to expand the tradition of Anansesem [Ananse storytelling] to include other African performance traditions . . . in creating a modern African theatre out of the roots of traditional African performance."[35] The original mandate called for an elite, artistic vanguard also well versed in music, dance, and drama. It called for all members to have university educations, be fluent in English, and know Western theatre traditions as well as various Ghanaian languages and performance genres. The first two plays the group performed were Adinku's dance drama *The Eternal Idol* and Abdallah's *Verdict of the Cobra*, both formal experiments with blended genre storytelling. The group's performances fall into four main categories: dialogue-driven English-language formal dramas; choreographed "traditional" dances; dance dramas; and Abibigro plays combining multiple languages, music, dance, comedy, and reflexive narration.

Abibigro reflects a belief in "complexity of performance in traditional societies" and both the unity and the diversity of "artistic legacies of African peoples across the continent and the Diaspora."[36] Abibigro is a multimedia, blended genre incorporating music, dance, drama, multiple languages, experimental use of space, storytelling, and comedy. It was built on ideas of appropriation, reference, and condensation that Sutherland, Opoku, and other members of the

National Theatre Movement's first generation developed in codifying and staging a new style of performance.

Oh! Nii Kwei Sowah, an early member of Abibigromma, recalls the passion of the new group and its use of performance to link rural and urban to antineocolonialism. "Everyone wanted to be in the group at the time.... It was made up of the best actors, dancers, and musicians.... There was excitement about the arts and government support. We were going into the rural areas to do research on traditional performance forms. We would travel to Wa [in the Upper West Region], to the Volta Region, learning the real indigenous dances and dancing with rural folks and then we would come back to Accra and work the material into our repertoire. It was an exciting time; Rawlings made it feel like political change was happening and Abdallah was the arts side of that. We wanted to finish the decolonization project the older generation did not."[37] Abdallah felt that "we needed a serious professional theatre group in Ghana. In the early revolutionary years, there was a lot of energy for theatre but no one since Nkrumah's time had done anything to support the arts. Abibigromma was a group that would bring together the best of our dancers, dramatists, musicians. It was meant to raise the level of our theatre to the professional level."[38]

Edinam Atatsi, another early member of Abibigromma, recalls how the group was part of a renewed optimism and a moment of theatrical revival. "In the early 1980s there was artistic excitement in the air. Accra was alive with possibility for change.... The mission of Abibigromma was to ... develop a culture for professional, modern drama. There were no professional companies at the time. There was no money, no private media.... [But] we wanted to take theatre seriously and reach an international standard. Abdallah was the one who wanted to provide the resources for Abibigromma to be insulated from daily concerns. It reflected the concert party [popular theatre] tradition as well as the spirit of the revolution at the time. Abdallah took that ethos and tried to turn it into a professional theatre tradition."[39] Agnes Panfred, another Abibigromma member, recalls rising theatre interest: "The Arts Centre was always packed for afternoon jumps ... early evening performances ... because of the curfew. People queued to watch theatre.... At first, actors, we were not paid. We did it for passion, excitement. You would have to walk to the performance; there was no transportation in Accra."[40] The nascent socialist state supported theatre, linking its political legitimacy to the ability to stir populist sentiment. Revolutionary theatre groups, building on Sutherland's work, saw a rise in female performers. Panfred recalls that "theatre was respectable for women so a lot of us joined. Some had done it in school; others were not educated but liked talking and spreading ideas and being on stage. If a woman did concert party they would call you a prostitute, but we got some respect."

Theatre continued the formal transformation of the National Theatre Movement as a hybrid of intellectual literary drama, music-dance, concert party, and storytelling. Groups like Audience Awareness, Theatre Mirrors, Ghana Theatre Club, and Arts Council Concert Party, the remnants of the Workers' Brigade Drama Group, combined socialist theatre traditions of provoking audiences with Ananse storytelling and concert party's use of proverbial moral tales. For Atatsi the political climate brought social issues to the fore, asking people to think about their moral responsibility. "After the corruption and excess of the [1970s] military [regime], people were interested again in being responsible to the community."[41] Talents Theatre Company, led by Kofi Portuphy, formed as part of a national mobilization to perform in support of the revolution at schools and work sites and around the country. "They combined music, dance, and drama using people from the School of Performing Arts and did a lot of political plays reviving Nkrumah's legacy and supporting Rawlings's revolutionary vision. The goal was to bring culture back to the people." They performed, among other things, *The Teacher of Africa: Black Star*, a satire about Nkrumah by Nigerian Uwa Hunwick intermingling music, dance, and narrative;[42] *Events* portrayed the market hoarding and corruption that led to the Rawlings revolution; *The Trial of Kwame Nkrumah* addressed his political legacy; *Mambo* by Joe de Graft, *Jogolo* by Allen Tamakloe, and *Shaka* by Asiedu Yirenkyi, *The Struggling Black Race*, and work on "Woman Power" all addressed social issues and African history while experimenting with theatrical form.[43]

The Ghana Dance Ensemble also became more explicitly political. In 1976 the founder Albert Mawere Opoku's star pupil Francis Nii-Yartey took over directorship of the company. Nii-Yartey emphasized new creative dance dramas to reinvent African modern dance. While incorporating traditional elements into his choreographies, Nii-Yartey was not concerned with replicating original dances in cultural tableaus representing various cultural groups. He aimed to abstract dance elements to tell new stories through dance. "Professor [Opoku] had to do the work he did to allow me to create modern works, but I do not want to just repeat what has been done."[44]

Rawlings's government recognized the potential of television, film, and video. GTV, the one state-run television station, increased its cultural programming, imbuing it with educational political and moral messages (J. Shipley 2013b). *Akan Drama* was a regular drama program that televised morality plays. *Osofo Dadze*, and later *Obra* and *Cantata*, were ongoing soap operas that did weekly, improvised stories around proverb-like messages such as "Everyone should vote," "Keep your community clean," and "Be a morally responsible member of society."[45] The film *Harvest at 17*, about teenage pregnancy, was shot with Abibigromma.

Get Involved Drama Group in 1982 had a regular televised show every Thursday performing new, educational plays, and later did the *Jagger Pee* television series. As Atatsi recalls, the shows taught "how we all can get involved to solve the nation's problems. As with all of the cultural programming at the time the goal was to bring culture to the people." For Atatsi and others, theatre promised to build a shared cultural expression as a way to bring out potential of political change. Joyce Addo wrote scripts on "health, sanitation, hoarding; how we can all get involved to solve social problems." "These early films and theatre groups were all addressing social issues: love, home life, morality, social change, community."[46]

Theatre artists in the early 1980s were driven to find innovative ways to inspire collective moral development. But tension around lack of financial support and struggles over artistic control grew. Abdallah insisted that Abibigromma members receive good government salaries and not do propaganda dramas on "social and development issues" but "experiment artistically." Entrepreneurial concert party troupes remained dominant among popular audiences but struggled to find the backing to mount tours. Experimental and literary groups were energetic but erratic, were untrained, and lacked resources. State television paid low wages to artists. Private funding for theatre and film was minimal.

Building the National Theatre

The theatrical renaissance of the cultural revolution was a flashing-up of artistic energy in a moment of political danger. State-supported arts came under threat as the Rawlings government changed its economic orientation. In 1983 the state accepted IMF and World Bank loans in exchange for a Structural Adjustment Program (SAP), which mandated privatization of state resources, open markets for foreign investors, and Western-style democratic reforms. State cultural institutions and rising private media were intermingled in an uneven process of marketization.

While the Rawlings government invoked Nkrumahist Pan-Africanism and links between culture and the fate of the nation, as the state struggled to implement privatization policies, debates about culture were sidelined. Frequent shifts in the administration of culture show continued uncertainty about its significance and state vacillation between socialist revolution and free-market capitalist reforms. To Nana Brefo Boateng at the National Commission on Culture, government shuffling of culture portfolios during the 1980s represented an uncertainty about its significance. "It started with the Institute of Arts and Culture during Nkrumah's time, then it became part of the Ministry of Education, Youth, and Sports. Then it became part of Ministry of Education and Culture, then Ministry of Culture and Tourism, back to Ministry of Education and Culture. . . . Abdallah's idea was to let it stand on its own so that culture can be given the right emphasis as during the First Republic . . . Nkrumah's time."[47]

The National Theatre building in downtown Accra was meant to be the home of the National Theatre Movement. However, the movement's struggles embodied the contradictions of state institutions caught in the uneven processes of privatization. Nigeria's National Theatre was built in Lagos in preparation for the Second World Black and African Festival of Arts and Culture (FESTAC 77) as a spectacular sign of national power and Pan-African unity, a celebration in the midst of the country's oil boom and its public displays of excess (A. Apter 2005). Ghana's National Theatre was meant to be spectacular, but in the midst of socialist upheaval, tightening economics, and the transition to a market economy, the project was caught between competing ideas of public culture. The People's Republic of China aimed to gain influence in opposition to Western powers by supporting development projects throughout Africa. They offered a soft loan to finance either a new sports stadium or a theatre, two quintessentially national projects. After debate within the Rawlings government over potential benefits, on September 18, 1985, China agreed to finance a national theatre in Accra. Construction began on June 19, 1990. Its design and construction was completed for $20 million largely by Chinese workers, causing local resentment as its lure had included job creation. The government wanted the National Theatre to be recorded as an accomplishment of the PNDC era, pushing for the project to finish before the new constitution of the Fourth Republic of Ghana with its democratically elected government took effect in January 1993. This concern shows how the theatre became important as a monumental sign of politically driven development rather than as a space for artistic experimentation.

The National Theatre opened on December 30, 1992, under the administration of the National Commission on Culture and its chairman, Mohammed Ben Abdallah. The opening ceremony had the National Dance Company, the National Theatre Company, the National Symphony Orchestra, the Pan-African Orchestra, and others staging the history of the National Theatre Movement in Ghana. It linked various political histories to performance traditions. It also linked Ghanaian society to the diaspora. The event's climax was when the National Dance Company performed a scene from an Akan chief's enstoolment, with African American poet Maya Angelou coming on stage and dancing with kente cloth before sitting on the stool, which was symbolic of a chief's power.[48]

As the long-awaited physical manifestation of the National Theatre Movement, the new theatre was intended to "foster the development of traditional idioms of contemporary art forms and to preserve the roots, growth, and variety of the artistic forms that represent modern Ghana. Primarily it is about creativity."[49] However, arguments ensued about how to do this while balancing artistic experimentation, state support, and profitability. For Korkor Amarteifio, its artistic director in the late 1990s, the goal was "to foster a theatre-going public"; to sustain an arts institution born into financial uncertainty required attracting audiences who would come on a regular basis.⁵⁰ The Theatre boasted a fifteen-hundred-seat main auditorium as well as several smaller performance spaces, art galleries, and rehearsal halls. An unusual concrete-and-tile building amid the conjuncture of new glass high-rises and colonial-era bungalows in downtown Accra, it was meant to make a statement.

> When looked at from a distance [the National Theatre of Ghana] looks like a gigantic ship returning in victory from the Atlantic Ocean; or like a seagull spreading its wings.... Taking a critical look however you find the traditional Ghanaian stool with its curved sides and straight stands. The building is also embellished with both Chinese and Ghanaian style gardens with a number of African art pieces.⁵¹

This poetic description from *National Theatre in Retrospect,* an internal publication, tells how the building's multiple missions were part of its design. It combined the figure of a slave ship "returning in victory" to the African coast with an Akan chief's royal stool and Ghanaian, Akan, and Chinese elements. Its pastiche references represent Pan-Africanism and Ghanaian, precolonial, anti-imperial solidarity. In reversing the slave ship's trajectory, these are reunited in a modern hope intended to undo past violence through linking various semiotic registers.

The National Theatre was built on the site of Sutherland's Drama Studio, though she was adamantly against it. To placate her, Abdallah had the Drama Studio rebuilt at the School of Performing Arts at the university. Abdallah recalls, "While we named it the Efua Sutherland Drama Studio, she never set foot in it at the new location. She was the original inspiration for the National Theatre finally being built, but felt betrayed that it went on top of her site."⁵² Sutherland was disappointed, calling the National Theatre a "development venture.... Somebody came and said I'll give you a loan to build a big theatre.... But I'm sure when the artists want to do something again, they'll develop their own theatre ... this one won't allow developmental thinking ... it's a monument" (Sutherland, quoted in Osofisan 2007: 206). Abdallah agreed that a building does not constitute a movement, but hoped it would be inspiring for future generations. "Artists need a space and resources to create ... the building is just a shell."⁵³

Two Contradictions of a Privatizing State Institution

Some saw the National Theatre as the fulfillment of Nkrumah's cultural nationalist vision to develop Ghanaian art for the unity and progress of the nation. Others felt that monetizing and institutionalizing the artistic vision of the National Theatre Movement compromised its spirit and potential. Two institutional conflicts demonstrate the tensions between financing and artistic control that seemed to represent broader issues about the effects of institutionalizing an artistic movement. The first issue was the splitting of Abibigromma into two competing groups. The second issue revolved around a contradiction in the laws establishing the National Theatre that placed its resident groups in bureaucratic limbo. In both cases, the competition for dwindling state resources became manifest in debates about artistic freedom and marketability. These structural frustrations furthered the potential for the strange alliance that developed between Unilever, rural popular theatre, and this state-owned venue.

In 1994 Abdallah left government to return to teaching at the School of Performing Arts. In 1995 private consultants identified the theatre as one of the state-owned enterprises (SOEs) that could become economically independent of government support as a money-making venture. As one state official explained to me, this was a mixed economic venture. "The national theatre . . . will not be given to private people to run it. The government will still control it but it will be encouraged to run more like a business."[54] A new mission statement was added to reflect this new semicorporate status:

> A profitable and multi-functional National Theatre, professionally equipped to meet world standards with unique and viable customer-oriented programming in the contemporary and traditional arts and other special events, taking into account the growth of the National Theatre Movement.[55]

The National Commission on Culture estimated that within five years the National Theatre would be financially self-sustaining except for personnel salaries. But as its budget was decreased each year, the theatre could not meet its expenses. Komla Amoako, executive director of the National Theatre, argued for a pragmatic market-oriented response: "We must accept changes and adapt to the modern world. We must package and market our culture and art or else someone else will. . . . Since tradition never stands still, we have to make the best of a changing world."[56]

In the midst of artistic and financial disagreements, the theatre had trouble filling the auditorium, partially because of high ticket prices and, significantly, because the practice of going to formal Western-style theatre was unfamiliar to most Ghanaians. While playwrights and directors argued for the freedom to foster noncommercial experimental productions, administrators argued that they had to attract a broader popular audience to avoid being shut down.

The National Theatre was designated to have three main resident companies: the National Dance Company, the National Theatre Players (Abibigromma), and the National Symphony Orchestra. Abdallah recalls, "The National Theatre itself was simply a building. It was part of the original plan that they would house these companies when it was ready. Its real work necessitated the best musicians, dancers, actors, and theatre artists in the country to be given the time and resources to experiment with artistic form."[57] The Ghana Dance Ensemble had been based at the university since its establishment in 1962 and Abibigromma since its founding in 1983. Some at the university protested this move and felt Abdallah was betraying the original experimental vision linking the arts to research and education in favor of a professionalizing, national political agenda.

In the midst of the conflict, the groups were moved in secret. One Abibigromma member recalls, "One night the costumes, lights, props, and drums for the groups were moved from the University [of Ghana, Legon] to the theatre. We felt that these were our tools of the trade and we were meant to move into the National Theatre all along. The university was trying to hold us back from progressing. When we were at Legon no one treated us very well. It was only when we left that the university got upset. Technically, Abdallah did use the power of the state to take the group away, but it was also an excuse to rail against government power."[58] Abdallah recalls, "When we moved the groups there was some opposition and the university claimed that government had no right to house the groups at the theatre. They argued that it was illegal for the groups to be moved. The groups staying at Legon had simply been out of convenience, but in the long run they needed the best resources available, which is why the theatre was built."[59]

The groups' official base became the National Theatre. However, the university argued that this move was illegal, that the performers were university employees and under its control. Even though it was a state-run institution, this was seen as a threat to the university's independence from state intervention. The School of Performing Arts reformulated the groups using variations on the names and with some of the older original performers, students, and new artists. The unusual, dual existence of the groups creates ongoing confusion. The Abibigromma Theatre Company and the Ghana Dance Ensemble are based at Legon, while Abibigromma: National Theatre Players and the National Dance Company are based at the National Theatre.

This schism reflected the tensions between state centralization and ideas of artistic and educational independence. Abdallah's goal was "establishing the institutional structures to develop modern Ghanaian theatre to its highest level." He argued that the state needed to financially and institutionally subsidize artistic creativity to allow time for its development, especially in light of the growing influence of foreign media and market demands. "Education and research into traditional forms is crucial, but the mission of professional theatre groups is beyond that and requires protection from the academic drudgery as well as forces of the market. It takes time, money, and support for theatre to evolve. We see that in every country which has great art. African countries have not given the arts the chance to develop."[60]

The second conflict stemmed from the fact that the legal structures establishing the relationship between the theatre and its resident groups presented a contradiction. The root of the problem was a conflict between two laws. One law that established the National Theatre defined these groups as its resident companies under its administrative control.⁶¹ Another gave the three companies equal status to the National Theatre, stating they should report directly to the National Commission on Culture, which was administering their salaries.⁶² This legal contradiction exacerbated tensions between state control and creative production.

The National Theatre and the National Commission on Culture both claimed the right to direct the activities of the National Theatre Players, the National Dance Company, and the National Symphony Orchestra. The groups for their part wanted to organize their own artistic affairs rather than be dictated to by administrators. All sides were deeply frustrated by the impasse. The theatre's administration faced the daily realities of bills and governmental pressure to meet guidelines for economic self-sufficiency. The conflict was played out daily as the theatre turned the electricity off in rehearsal halls, forcing groups to rehearse in the dark without air-conditioning. Nii-Yartey, director of the National Dance Ensemble, was more successful at getting private funding and attracting crossover audiences for his modern dance dramas than Abibigromma was in funding experimental theatre. But the resident companies had to pay fees to the building to perform in their own theatre; they were often unable to afford to put on their productions and refused to perform at National Theatre–organized events unless they were paid separately.

Yaw Asare, the director of the National Theatre Players from 1992 to 1998, explained one day as we sat sweating in his darkened office, "We need to be able to experiment and perform without worrying about making money or constantly doing shows for a paycheck. The theatre is not paying us and we should not have to follow their commercial program."⁶³ The resident companies were intended to be a central part of a state-centered National Theatre Movement, which, according to Abdallah, needed to be protected from the "fluctuations and dangers of economic market forces and commercial interests" in order to allow "modern African theatre the chance to evolve creatively within an African idiom."⁶⁴ Artists were receiving state salaries, though because both wages and morale were low, they often spent their time moonlighting for private video/filmmaking production companies and advertising firms to gain exposure through new media. Upper-level theatre officials were academics and arts administrators. Some midlevel workers were educated civil servants, while others were uneducated performers tempted by a regular salary into administration. Tension spread as administrators, resident companies, outside groups, private media, government officials, and theatre administrators clashed over artistic and financial control.

The National Commission on Culture and the National Theatre were constantly at odds, resulting in paralyzing frustration for the main performance companies caught in the middle. Numerous small arguments pointed to larger structural conflicts between state interests and privatization.

The theatre administration created other residential groups, including Dance Factory and the Vision 2020 Band, and established programs to sidestep the commission's authority and help pay the theatre's operating costs. They created commercial events and programs like the children-oriented Fun World and Kiddafest, Key Soap Concert Party, and the Art Institute for Teachers and rented out space for business conferences, trade shows, pop concerts, beauty pageants, and album launches. They felt that while most of these activities did contribute to developing an artistic vision of a national theatre, they could attract audiences from working classes with concert party and audiences from the elites with conferences and pageants, over time developing "a modern Theatre Culture" in Ghana.[65]

Prevalent themes in Ghanaian stage drama from the independence era and later generations include political coups, madness, profound ambivalence to tradition, family disapproval, marriage conflicts, tensions between cultural and racial solidarity, effects of rural-urban-international movement, disillusionment, the temptations of strangers, poverty, and greed. These tropes were built into the critical storytelling structure of this blended dramatic genre.

Artist-politicians like Ama Ata Aidoo, Asiedu Yirenkyi, and Mohammed Ben Abdallah built on a poetics of performance to structure state institutions of theatre. This configuration was subsequently challenged by a privatizing urban public. A new generation of artists imagined culture as a way to foster dynamic creativity and relink Ghana to African identity. As marketization came into conflict with the ideals of a populist state, notions of culture and the theatre infrastructures that had been built in the image of a Pan-African state were realigned. The privatization of state resources called into question the role of culture in developing an African- or Ghanaian-oriented political economy.

4 A Man of the People
Mohammed Ben Abdallah as Artist-Politician

Both his friends and enemies would agree that playwright Mohammed Ben Abdallah is a man of passion. Through the 1980s and early 1990s, he held ministerial positions covering portfolios in education, tourism, information, religion, and culture. As chief architect of national culture policy, he has aimed to inspire Ghanaian and Pan-African sentiment by building an African cultural aesthetics from myriad influences. For Abdallah art and culture are significant in shaping a people's core values and actions across economic, political, and social realms. The arts could open up critical awareness to counter the legacy of colonial rule, structures of global racial inequality, and the rising threat of free-market capital. His work reflects the intertwined political and artistic orders of postindependence Africa. If history is framed as a series of revolts, losses, triumphs, and projects of recuperation, artist-politicians struggle with policy decisions and directorial staging choices, addressing societal notions of remembering and forgetting that lie just below the surface.

One afternoon in 2000, Abdallah and I sat on the screened veranda of his house on the University of Ghana campus discussing how the new chairman of the National Commission on Culture and the minister of communication were vehemently advocating for the privatization of cultural and media institutions, policies Abdallah had fought against. I wondered aloud about the long-term effects of ending state support and regulation of media and the arts. Presidential elections were slated for December 2000 and for the first time in almost two decades, Rawlings would no longer be head of state. Across the country, people reflected on old and recent political choices. The two major political parties were busy portraying themselves as leaders of liberalization, trying to erase traces of radical thought from Ghana's recent past.

We talked, as we often had, about the effects of commercialization and foreign cultural influence on Ghanaian public life and theatre and the significance of Pan-Africanism in the history of the Ghanaian nation. Abdallah reflected on the legacy of the Rawlings years and his own role in it. I pointed out that the new generation seemed to thrive in the turn to privatization and embrace the entrepreneurial spirit in music, theatre, radio, and video production, and they did not seem particularly concerned with Pan-Africanist thought or nationalist history. Abdallah paused over my remark: "I have decided to show you something private I wrote." He said it might help me understand the dynamics of culture and privatization in Ghana.

The next day Abdallah called to say he had a letter for me to look at, though he was still unsure if he was prepared to make it public. Back at his house, he explained that the letter had been a response to his monthlong trip in 1989 to the Soviet Union where he reflected on the global political transitions taking place. He recalled feeling a growing unease about the implications of the end of the cold war for Ghana. Upon his return to Accra, he outlined his concerns in a private communication to Rawlings, imploring the head of state to recognize that the negative effects of liberalization would soon overwhelm the moral and cultural foundations of the nation. He handed me the two-page typed letter. It begins, "I am convinced that we are on a collision course with disaster some 15–20 years hence."

In the letter, Abdallah expresses frustration with the Ghanaian state's inability to control its economic fate in the face of foreign pressures and changing international alignments. He had been, in his own estimation, an ambivalent participant in the political transformation of Ghana from early 1980s revolutionary populism to the marketization of the next decade. As Ghana implemented its International Monetary Fund (IMF) and World Bank Structural Adjustment Program (SAP), Abdallah was increasingly marginalized within government. His colleagues embarrassed him with petty concerns. Former Marxists turned liberal economists looked down on the significance of culture, instead acting as if fostering foreign investment was a radical political strategy.

For Abdallah, developing Ghanaian culture was necessary to defining a national identity and making political links with progressive allies around the world. A strong understanding of history built on social, educational, religious, and cultural organizations could lay the groundwork for political and economic sovereignty.

Abdallah's commitment to progressive politics emerges from myriad influences.[1] His life is entwined in a longer story of Pan-African movement and resistance. He was born in 1944 and raised in the city of Kumasi, the center of the old Asante Empire and a cosmopolitan trading crossroads.[2] On his mother's side, his grandmother was from Nigeria and his grandfather was half Fulani and half Gonja from northern Ghana. "Pan-Africanism and activism were part of my family," he tells me. "The house I grew up in is one of the oldest in Kumasi, built in the late nineteenth century. The house of Sherif Ali; everyone can direct you there. My original ancestor who came from Morocco to settle, on my father's line, was a rebel fighting French occupation of Morocco and Algeria, running guns through Tangiers. To escape being captured he ended up in Guinea when

Samory Touré [ancestor of the first president of Guinea, Ahmed Sékou Touré] was struggling against colonialism. So Sherif supplied them guns. When Samory fell, Sherif went to the next point of resistance, which was Kumasi, and brought with him his wives and family and slaves. We grew up with elderly men and women, some who had been slaves.

"He came just before the Yaa Asantewaa War in 1900. Sherif Ali had strong connections to Manhyia Palace and Asante power. He had four wives and wanted to be sure the family was taught Arabic and proper Islamic culture. Mohammed Abdallah, a learned friend, was a Moor living in Fez. Sherif Ali convinced him to come to Kumasi to teach his children and others. He married the eldest daughter of Sherif, Fatima, my grandma. They had two children, my father and uncle. The marriage broke and Mohammed Abdallah went to Nigeria; my grandmother remarried and had more children. People in Kano were trying to convince [Mohammed] to come, that it was a stronger center of Islam. He died in northern Nigeria. I was named after him. I was taken to see him in Kano before he died. I must have been around ten or twelve.

"My father, Ali Mohammed Abdallah, never went to formal school, he went to Islamic schools. But he read and wrote many languages: Mosi, Twi, Hausa, Arabic, Portuguese, English, French. He was self-taught. My uncle Hussein went to Achimota College; he was Western educated. He was one of the first people to be sent to the BBC school of broadcasting ... the first Hausa announcer on radio on Gold Coast Broadcasting, ... the first director to set up the West African Service of Ghana Broadcasting Corporation. Under Nkrumah it was the external service to reach across the continent for Pan-African broadcasts. I would visit and meet all the announcers at GBC speaking different languages: Swahili, Portuguese, English, Hausa, Arabic, French."

Abdallah had both Western and Islamic education and was influenced by the complex intermixed media and styles in postwar Gold Coast that would later shape his own theatrical and political work. "Culture and language mixing in Kumasi and later Accra, when I was a child, were amazing, especially in the Zongo [area for Muslims]. Growing up I heard Ananse stories in Akan. In the Zongo it was in mostly in Hausa and other northern languages. Gizo is the Hausa name of the trickster. In a compound house, children would gather and often an elderly woman would start. One person begins to tell the story, then gives it to someone else to finish. People interject songs and characters. Everyone waits for an elder to come to tell ones that they have never heard. But there is a lot of repetition hearing different versions of the same story. Popular culture was also important to us. We would go to the cinema and watch American films and act out the characters."

When his father died suddenly, he went with his brothers to live with his uncle in Accra who was working at Ghana Broadcasting Corporation. He attended

St. John's Secondary School and Wesley Teacher Training College and then enrolled at the University of Ghana, Legon, to study theatre arts.

His political passion was awakened as a teenager in the intellectually charged atmosphere of postindependence Accra. "I was a high school student when Nkrumah was in power. Charles de Gaulle was president of France. The Algerian war of independence was raging. Nkrumah was vociferously against the French testing atomic bombs in the Sahara. I remember concerned Ghanaians even threatened to drive across the Sahara to confront the testers."

Progressive thinkers and Pan-African politicians from around the world were his heroes. "A few students had a political debating/current affairs club in school and were in Nkrumah's Young Pioneers. We would visit embassies, almost as groupies. They tolerated us. Embassies of progressive countries were gathering points; countries like Cuba, Czechoslovakia, China had just opened an embassy, and all the North African countries which were progressive, Ethiopia, Tunisia, Egypt under Nasser, Libya, even Morocco. They were pleased to see young students interested in current affairs. We would hang around when the ambassador was arriving; he would walk with you, put his hand on your shoulder. We would invite them to give talks and we took pamphlets and magazines and revolutionary propaganda."

He met Ferhat Abbas, the president of the Algerian revolutionary government, and Frantz Fanon, who was the ambassador to Ghana of the Algerian revolutionary government in exile. "People like Fanon were aware it was good to appreciate young people. We did not have in-depth chats and at the time I did not fully appreciate what was happening, but it made a big impression. I remember distinctly Fanon had a mark on his right cheekbone like you would see among Asante people. We thought he looked like he could be Ghanaian."

Jaja Wachuku, Nigeria's minister of foreign affairs after its independence in 1960, "was in and out of Accra like many who were consulting with Nkrumah." Tanzanian leader Rashidi Kawawa was another Pan-African politician who came through. Abdallah "only saw him from a distance but he was a sort of hero. He called Britain 'a toothless bulldog' and refused to retract it."

Malcolm X visited Accra in 1964. "He had just returned from a pilgrimage to Mecca. I attended a lecture he gave at Legon and shook his hand, but we never really met one on one. He was very sober and reflective. Malcolm became my greatest hero. Black people treated him as badly as Ghanaians treated Nkrumah. The white establishment feared him and his legacy. That is why they have never lowered their guard against him. That is why I created the Malcolm X shrine at the Du Bois Centre which we had established."

Abdallah also spent time at the Drama Studio. "It was a very busy place. It was not just for drama. There were workshops, poetry, writing, experimental work. Besides Efua Sutherland there was Joe de Graft; Kofi Awoonor, known as George

Awoonor-Williams at the time; the poet John Okai, who later became Attuquaye Okai. People changed names to Africanize them; that was the atmosphere at the Drama Studio. We watched what was going on with great excitement. Efua noticed what was [happening] with young students and encouraged us."

Abdallah's play *The Slaves* first gained him attention when it was performed in 1969. The play is set in a slave castle's dungeon as a group of West Africans captured from across the region face the prospects of being sent across the ocean. Despite their cultural differences, the characters struggle to unite and hatch a plot to overcome the mulatto overseer. They are betrayed by one of their number, a woman who is sleeping with the guard. The play portrays the struggles to unite in the face of common oppression and the cultural, gendered, and racial aspects of the violence and fragmentation that emerges as the legacy of the slave trade for African peoples. This play signaled the author's concern with how unresolved moral dilemmas activate historical traces.

While at the School of Music and Drama in the late 1960s, Abdallah became a member of the Legon 7, an unofficial drama company that performed on campus and toured other schools and nearby venues and towns. It was founded and led by James Gibbs, a visiting lecturer and theatre researcher from Bristol, England. Legon 7 led Abdallah to form an offshoot company, the Legon Road Theatre. Abdallah recalls the influence Gibbs and these groups had on his work. "The School of Music and Drama was not inspiring at the time . . . they were doing mostly Shakespeare . . . and European and American plays, but the Legon 7 and the Legon Road Theatre gave us avenues to explore new productions, to travel with theatre . . . and to imagine what an experimental company could be." While both playwrights were already known in Ghana, Gibbs brought serious attention to influential works by Wole Soyinka and particularly Bertolt Brecht (Gibbs 2009: 194). *Mother Courage* starring Maya Angelou had been performed several years before, and Soyinka was already known for his bold political theatre (Gibbs 2009: 194). Gibbs, inspired by Soyinka's recent detention in Nigeria, dramatized his political and artistic views in a production called *The Trial of Wole Soyinka*. Set in a prison, it imagined Soyinka doing theatre as a prisoner (Gibbs 2009: 179). Gibbs and the Legon 7 also put on *Of Brecht*, a compilation of a number of Brecht's works. Abdallah played the leading roles in a number of Legon 7 productions (Gibbs 2009: 197). Soyinka, who was also one of Abdallah's external university examiners, and Brecht had significant influence on his radical philosophy of art and political consciousness.

Upon completing his studies at the University of Ghana, Abdallah was offered a prestigious Schubert Fellowship for playwriting but refused because "I did not think I could learn anything about African theatre by going to the United States." Instead he went to Kumasi to teach at Wesley College while working as the drama coordinator for the Anokye Players at the Kumasi Cultural Centre and the drama organizer for Ghana Education Service. He eventually left Ghana to complete an M.F.A. at the University of Georgia and a Ph.D. in theatre at the University of Texas, Austin. He returned to the country just after the Rawlings Revolution began.

In his letter to Rawlings, Abdallah wrote of culture's significance to politics:

> Our economic recovery programme is designed to achieve a certain minimum of economic stability which in itself depends upon several factors some of which lie outside our borders and totally beyond our control. Most importantly, however, any economic system, in order to be meaningful, gratifying and devoid of dehumanizing aberration, must be grounded firmly upon a sound philosophical bedrock of value systems, social and cultural structures compatible with the collective psyche of the society it is designed to serve.

Abdallah decries what he sees as the moral contradictions and dehumanizations of the state and economics. He worries about the threat of foreign influence. In his years in government he had advocated for developing "value systems" and "cultural structures" crucial to Ghanaian national consciousness and long-term economic stability. The letter continues, "the language factor is at the heart of the entire issue." Recalling independence-era debates, he argues for the "establishment of an official Ghanaian National language" and the "encouragement of a multi-lingual Ghanaian, beginning . . . with a knowledge of at least two Ghanaian languages." He also argues that the state must control electronic media, as they are threats to African creativity. "The areas of film and television are of major concern for educating our people, for halting the serious damage of cultural imperialism and for freeing the creative genius of our artists." Abdallah's most passionate plea argues that the rising generation lacks modes of self-recognition:

> The status quo, if allowed to continue for long, will lead to disaster. There is a sense of "unbelongingness" especially among urban youth that is dangerous. It is not alienation—like in Western society—how can you be alienated from what you've never been a part of? It is worse than alienation!

In the state's initial turn toward liberalization, more progressive Ghanaians recognized the conflict between state-centered anti-neocolonialism and the liberalizing policies of international aid in terms of moral choices between being true to the ideals of African independence and capitulation to the demands of the West. Rawlings's government maintained its populist legitimacy in its "return to some of Nkrumah's policies of African-centered, cultural nationalism which had [lain] dormant under the intervening governments."[3] By the late 1980s critics such as Abdallah recognized the dire need for financial aid but felt that the moral and cultural compromises that marketization entailed were too high a cost. The state was morally compromised in neglecting Nkrumah's legacy of Pan-Africanism and moving toward neoimperial, free-market economics. Central to the letter are anxieties about losing control. Abdallah appeals to Rawlings not to use state coercion to push through deleterious economic policies. In the face of growing hardships, the government should not give in to the illusory temptations of liberal reform:

> Your own image of a train that has lost its steam and is plunging rapidly backwards down a steep slope into an abyss is a very apt example indeed. Arresting the backward slide is difficult enough! Holding it in place once arrested is even more difficult! But the train does not just need repair. It needs thorough overhauling.
> It is perhaps now the right time to hold our fire and tell the World Bank that: yes we want a sound economy; yes we want growth and credit worthiness etc. But we also need to be allowed a free hand, now, to plan, shape, and direct our development according to the values of our own society.

Rawlings never acknowledged receiving the letter. For Abdallah this silence was final confirmation of the anticlimactic demise of Ghana's populist revolution. In writing the letter, Abdallah was testing himself to find out whether he should stay in government and continue to fight, even as things looked bleak, or leave because of the increasing impossibility of his task. His personal dilemma reminded me of his plays in which central characters struggle with inconceivable choices, questioning what it means to be true to oneself, to the law, and to the collective moral good.

As we sat on his veranda discussing the letter, Abdallah mulled over how personal choices and political conflicts had intersected for Ghana's leadership:

> Jerry [Rawlings] at some point stopped listening to us. He changed. He had decided that he would go with the IMF but try to maintain the original ideals. Maybe he had no choice. But I don't think he fully understood the implications of the compromises we were making. I knew that we were headed in the wrong direction; that the forces of global imperialism would not allow us to maintain our own path, but at the same time it seemed that state control was no longer possible.

Abdallah's disillusionment with the government reveals a growing polarization between the dream of a cultural nationalist state that forged anti-imperial, Pan-African solidarity and a society driven by its connections to global capital. Public and private debates raged about which model would better serve local interests and the role of culture for politics: How does cultural context relate to a universal moral, political subject and ideas of individual rights? Do peoples from historically exploited societies need particular, culturally based forms of solidarity to be equal members of a global world? What are the obligations of a society without the resources to support its people caught in a history of foreign economic extraction?

As Abdallah worked in government, he was actively writing plays and directing performances that were often critical of the political process. When I point out to him this contradiction, as I have a number of times, Abdallah replies by asking me questions: Why do I think there was not more controversy about the subversive aspects of his plays over the years? What could that reveal about theatre in Ghana? For years he expected conservative leaders of the Muslim community in Ghana to condemn his work. His plays display a secularist tendency, celebrate traditional African religious worship, are critical of organized religion, moral norms, and sexual conservatism, and call on people to question their leaders. But to his surprise Muslim elders have seen him as a good example for the community. "They are always pleased to see me and I don't know why." His work has also been consistently critical of government, but observers seem to ignore his plays' sharp edges. For example, in August 1991, his play *Land of a Million Magicians* was to be performed for Non-Aligned Movement leaders meeting in Accra. Olu Otunla, the Nigerian ambassador to Ghana, was good friends with Abdallah and came to watch a rehearsal for the production. Afterwards, Otunla warned the playwright that the production would land him in trouble with its thinly veiled criticism of the state. "'Your colleagues will jump on you and lock you up,' he told me. He thought I was treading on dangerous ground. There were all kinds of comments criticizing government by characters all over the play."[4] Its action is set in fictional Nimman though it explicitly satirizes the IMF, prevalent poverty, the role of the first lady in setting up the 31st December Women's Movement, and the construction of a highway that cut through the real Nima neighborhood of Accra, described in the play as bypassing people without helping them.

The drama is a loose adaptation of Bertolt Brecht's *Good Woman of Setzuan*, telling the story of a poor water-seller and a lowly prostitute who are asked by the gods to bring change to their society (Banham, Gibbs, and Osofisan 2001: 89–93). The production realized the things Abdallah was trying to do with Abibigro in combining styles and genres of local and elite artists. The company included a local Nima-based cultural dance troupe, Amore Cultural Troupe, and the Abibiman Concert Party based at the Arts Centre and led by superstar actor/musician Bob Cole, who was featured in the production. "It was a very popular production. It drew huge audiences. I was so disappointed when the run was over; that was it. There was not even critical commentary about some of the things that were being said. I was so disappointed.

"I said to Olu, 'It looks like the people you were worried about didn't even notice that something has happened or somebody has insulted their democracy.' He laughed and said, 'I am glad for you that this is not Nigeria. Our military leaders are so nervous. They would have jumped on you. Maybe it is a good sign that your military government is not as jittery as ours. Maybe that is why people like you can serve in government in Ghana even when it is a military one.'" But perhaps the success of Abibigro was its problem: the humor, the familiar context of urban daily life combined with mythic elements, the metaphoric critiques that could pass as an unrelated story if audiences chose to see it that way. A propensity for indirection in public speech culture allowed criticisms to pass and allowed those being insulted to save face and avoid confrontation by acting like nothing had happened. Ignoring rather than highlighting opposition was an effective way of sidelining rather than addressing political critique.

But the Nigerian comparison is instructive. Chinua Achebe recounts a story to me one evening after I ask his advice about how to interpret Abdallah's attempts to balance theatre and politics. In Lagos one evening in 1966, when Achebe was head of the Nigerian Broadcasting Corporation, he received a phone call at home from a colleague, warning him to go into hiding. Achebe recalls, "I asked him what was wrong and he said that a coup had just occurred and the soldiers were drunk and looking for me." Achebe's novel *A Man of the People*, which describes the unwitting entry of a young idealistic teacher into the corrupt and disillusioning world of state politics, had recently been published. The novel portrays a military coup. Achebe explained to me that when the book came out, a fellow writer, John Pepper Clark, had teased him that so much of his work was an accurate portrait of Nigerian life that he wondered if the coup was coming. When the coup actually did come, soldiers, journalists, and politicians wanted to know whether Achebe's writing was prescriptive or descriptive. "Apparently the soldiers were looking for me to find out which was actually more powerful, the pen or the gun." Achebe chuckles. "I am glad they did not track me down to find out."[5] Achebe's novel recounts political turmoil in such a prescient manner that some wondered if he was not an instigator.

Whereas Nigerian artists are often posited or posit themselves as provocateurs, this model of critical art, at times, sits uncomfortably with Ghanaian publics. As part of centenary celebrations of Kwame Nkrumah's birth, Nigerian playwright Femi Osofisan was invited to Accra to direct his play *Nkrumah-Ni . . . Africa-Ni* with Abibigromma at the National Theatre. The play celebrates Nkrumah as a Pan-African visionary, focusing on his life in exile in Guinea after the 1966 coup that overthrew his regime. While there, Sékou Touré made Nkrumah ceremonial co-president of Guinea. In the play the fictional Nkrumah reflects on his vision of African political change, revealing his heartbreak at Ghanaians' complicity in his ousting. The play is critical of Ghanaians for betraying him and not defending Nkrumah against his enemies. After the National Theatre performance, the lights went up and Osofisan, Nkrumah's daughter who was a member of Parliament, and one of Nkrumah's bodyguards who was with him in Guinea, mounted the stage to discuss the play and the real events. The Ghanaian audience was taken aback by the performance's stark criticism of Ghanaians for not defending Nkrumah and "being cowardly," though they remained quiet through the discussion. Osofisan was disappointed at the audience's apathy even when confronted with a direct insult in discussing Ghanaian lack of political grit.

Whereas in Nigeria artists have been vocal critics of the powerful, in Ghana the state invited artists into its midst in ways that confused opposition politics. The Rawlings government at first welcomed artists and intellectuals to participate in populist reformation, though it became increasingly unreceptive to their critical interventions. Abdallah was the last of the early idealists to leave government, perhaps the last to hold on to the dream of reviving Nkrumah's promise to place Ghana at the center of African political and cultural solidarity. By the mid-1990s, liberal transformations against which Abdallah had fought had taken hold. Believers in state cultural and economic centralization no longer had a public platform. The main political parties instead argued over how fast to implement liberalization policies.

After writing his letter to Rawlings and receiving no answer, Abdallah's belief in the revolutionary potentials of the state seemed to turn into nostalgia for what might have been. Fanon (1963) argues that the revolutionary ethics of national and Pan-African liberation emerge from the promises and obligations of shared racial-cultural belonging. Postrevolutionaries in Ghana adopt different kinds of remembering, desiring, and hoping. Solidarity and betrayal are central motifs of narratives of postcolonial African politics, though forgotten promises return in unforeseen and unspoken ways. The letter's presence recalled the now-faded transformative potential of the state and its centralized national culture project.

The letter is a token of an old ethical exchange and the impossible obligations and choices of leadership, for Rawlings and for Abdallah. It bears the traces of the commitment to tell the story of hope and loss, desire and frustration. But for whom and to what effect? To me, the letter marks an interconnected series of spectacular and mundane moments constituting a history of the conflict between ideologies of Pan-African liberation and market-based freedom. Liberation has many guises, and liberalization promises a community of individuals freed through their abilities to create and accumulate wealth. This has necessitated the erasure of other forms of collective memory, power, and obligation. Literary and dramatic artists often bring an idealism to their political engagements, perhaps wrought through the processes of writing and staging, where they have the power to shape imagined worlds and narrative endings. Abdallah increasingly struggled with Rawlings's inflexible military leadership style. As Abdallah joked to me, "Perhaps the train is not losing steam but has gone off the tracks." Receiving the letter made me think about how individuals imagine the telling of history and their roles in it. There is an enduring sense in modern African literature—from Achebe and Soyinka to Chimamanda Adichie's writing on the Biafran War and Binyavanga Wainaina's incisive critiques of global power and expressive arts in the digital age—that even with the loss of idealism, even in political and personal circumstances with no obvious solution, telling the story matters.

Cape Coast elites portrayed in an Abibigromma production of Kobina Sekyi's *The Blinkards* with leading role played by David Dontoh. Arts Centre, Accra, 1991. Used with permission of Abibigromma: National Theatre Players.

Kusum Agromma in one of the first Akan dramas on television, a production of *Yaa Konadu*, a love story. Ghana Television studios, 1970. Used with permission of Abibigromma: National Theatre Players.

The Storyteller (*left*) discusses Ananse's (*right*) dilemma. Abibigromma production of Efua Sutherland's *Marriage of Anansewa*, directed by Dzifa Glikpoe. National Theatre, 2012. Photograph by Jesse Weaver Shipley.

Ananse and his wife plot the fake death of Anansewa, his daughter. Abibigromma production of Efua Sutherland's *Marriage of Anansewa*, directed by Dzifa Glikpoe. National Theatre, 2012. Photograph by Jesse Weaver Shipley.

Anansewa, Ananse's daughter, receives gifts. Abibigromma production of Efua Sutherland's *Marriage of Anansewa,* directed by Dzifa Glikpoe. National Theatre, 2012. Photograph by Jesse Weaver Shipley.

Writer Ama Ata Aidoo as PNDC secretary for education greets chief, early 1980s. Used with permission of Abibigromma: National Theatre Players.

Hasana/Fuseni portrayed by David Dontoh kneeling before gods in disguise as an imam, a cardinal, and an Okomfo traditional priest. Mohammed Ben Abdallah's *Land of a Million Magicians*. Arts Centre, 1991. Used with permission of Abibigromma: National Theatre Players.

Mohammed Ben Abdallah while PNDC secretary for information in the 1980s. Used with permission of Abibigromma: National Theatre Players.

Oh! Nii Kwei Sowah as the priest in Abibigromma's production of Mohammed Ben Abdallah's *Verdict of the Cobra*. Drama Studio, University of Ghana, Legon, 1999. Photograph by Jesse Weaver Shipley.

Efritete Concert Party group performing a play using typical concert party three-microphone setup and selling soap. Performance near Koforidua as part of a National Theatre and Key Soap tour of the countryside in 1999. Photograph by Jesse Weaver Shipley.

Conflict between Christian and traditional priests in Joris Wartenberg's *Corpse's Comedy*. Ghana Television production, 1971. Photograph by A. D. Ocansey. Used with permission of Abibigromma: National Theatre Players.

Bishop Bob Okalla performing in the "Who Is Who" finals of a *Key Soap Concert Party* comedy competition at the National Theatre in 1999. Photograph by Jesse Weaver Shipley.

Speech by David Dontoh playing Kwame Nkrumah in the fiftieth-anniversary reenactment of independence. Kwame Nkrumah Mausoleum, 2007. Photograph by Jesse Weaver Shipley.

Ghana Boy (*right*) dressed in period Fante costume with Kofi (*left*) dressed in period Asante costume for the fiftieth-anniversary reenactment of independence. Kwame Nkrumah Mausoleum, 2007. Photograph by Jesse Weaver Shipley.

Akhenaten, Nefertiti, and the Egyptian court with the three storytellers downstage in Mohammed Ben Abdallah's *Song of the Pharaoh*. National Theatre, 2013. Photograph by Rodney Quarcoo. Used with permission of Abibigromma: National Theatre Players.

The three storytellers discuss the action and address the audience in Mohammed Ben Abdallah's *Song of the Pharaoh*. National Theatre, 2013. Photograph by Rodney Quarcoo. Used with permission of Abibigromma: National Theatre Players.

PART II

STAGINGS IN MILLENNIAL GHANA

5 Total African Theatre

Language, Reflexivity, and Ambiguity in The Witch of Mopti

> What would have happened if the King had not drunk from the Well of Madness?
>
> In the struggle for Mopti... Who was the winner... and who the loser?
>
> Storyteller in Mohammed Ben Abdallah's *Witch of Mopti*

Mohammed ben Abdallah's play *The Witch of Mopti* tells the story of a young king of the city of Mopti, who marries a poor fisherman's daughter and rebuffs his aunt, a powerful witch, who wants him to marry her daughter. The king and the witch battle for control of Mopti in both spiritual and material realms. When the king employs powerful sorcerers from across Africa to defend himself, the witch "makes a pact with the devil," casting a spell on the city's well water to drive anyone who drinks from it insane. Everyone goes crazy except the king, who has not drunk from the well. His mad people see their leader's apparently strange behavior and determine that *he* must be insane. In the play's climax, the king faces a moral dilemma that pits his beliefs against his people's needs. The conflict over sovereignty between the king and the witch is interspersed with music, dance, and storytellers' reflections on the conventions of staged theatre. The play is framed by humorous banter between two storytellers who move among the time-place of characters, actors, and audiences.

This play shows how the structure of trickster storytelling is reinvented and enregistered in making a Ghanaian cosmopolitan theatre. Various performance traditions are objectified, staged, and intertwined. The author/director reframes them to legitimize an urban theatre that aims to draw together local and transnational audiences. Examining the production and staging of this play reveals the tensions and contradictions that emerge in transforming a scripted play into a live event. Performers navigate the use of different languages, gender roles, spirituality, and humor in navigating audience expectations, performance frames, the staged character, and the sociality of the actor. In these shifts ambiguity and reflexivity develop as key principles of a theory of modern Ghanaian theatre.

The storytelling formula provides a method of theatrical, and by extension social, critique. Principles of storytelling shape the production of *The Witch of Mopti* both on and off the stage by emphasizing the reflexive elements of acting, embodiment, and authority. The play's action is driven by not one but two main storytellers, which, as Abdallah explains, reflects the idea "that the entire group is the storyteller. This play was a way for me to think about the process of telling a story and the multiple meanings that emerge in the telling and interpretation." On stage, characters argue about language use, turn-taking, code-switching, and appropriate forms of address. They discuss what to say and what not to say. These multiple storytellers debate among themselves how to tell a story. Arguments about storytelling parody and critique everyday forms of talk. The conflict between the king and the witch is highly gendered and places male and female forms of power at the center of political conflict in ways reminiscent of older debates about performance legitimacy. Off stage, in rehearsals and informal interactions, the play's self-consciousness provokes parallel arguments about language use, public speaking and class and gender hierarchies among performers. Examining language-related practices tells us about how subject positions are posited and enacted on and off stage. As Susan Gal explains, "language ideologies are never only about language. They posit close relations between linguistic practices and other social activities" (Gal 2005: 24). *The Witch of Mopti*'s main focus is formalist: it directs participants to contemplate its staging and structural features. In the process, it reveals social hierarchies and performance norms, challenging actors and audiences to critically reassess them. Its production and staging emphasize the relationships between the audience and the characters as mediated by the storytellers. The storytellers' ability to stand both inside and outside of social action provides a way for participants to reflect on the moral tensions between individual desire and collective obligation.

Splitting the storytelling figure in two provides a literal example of double voicing, in which debates about things such as what language to use and how to navigate the relationship between the audience and the characters in the play are staged between two narrators. However, the two characters represent opposite sides of a singular stock character. The split storytellers frame the action by constantly challenging the lines between theatre and the everyday, the staged and the natural. In this sense, the play reveals the gap between a character and an actor. If we take the play as emblematic of a Ghanaian performance theory, this ambiguity with which actors and characters relate to each other—and the split subjectivity it implies—challenges two basic assumptions of Western performance theory: that performance is about making identity, and that identities made in performance are singular, sincere, and sustainable across social life (Silvio 2010).

Leading from Émile Durkheim and Victor Turner, ritual theory posits that culturally sanctioned performances reproduce social organization as subjects are aligned with key symbols and totems in emotional, embodied moments of efflorescent action. While signs and rituals vary across societies, ritual theory tends to postulate that the process in which highly charged performances produce enduring subjectivities is similar. For Turner, while rituals are structurally ambiguous in their liminal phase, participants reproduce social norms by actively aligning themselves with definitive dominant symbols and functioning social roles. J. L. Austin's notion of performativity, as interpreted by Judith Butler (1990) and others, shows how semiotic practices produce social positions through the power of reiteration. For Austin and Butler, performative statements and acts require—and in turn produce—clarity and singularity that is repeatable in both reinforcing and challenging positions of power. Theories of theatre, media, and popular culture tend to rely on the notion that performances make subjects into members of broader collectivities through reiterated practices and events. But studies of media and performance need to take into account socio-historically specific ways that all social performances are linked to subject-making (Manning and Gershon 2013; Silvio 2010).

In examining the production process of this play I want to show that performance theories are specific to particular place-times and contexts in how they enregister the use of signs and references, and how they order the relationship among specific events, affects, ideas, and bodies. The uncertainty that surrounds *The Witch of Mopti*'s staging demonstrates a fundamental ambiguity at the center of Ghanaian performance values. Having multiple storytellers splits the subject at the center of this dramatic genre. In this context, performances do not focus on the singular presence of performers, the performance of identities, or the assertion of individuals through defining action and moral choices. Instead, even basic principles about the relationship between an actor and character are open to reinterpretation. Rather than point to moral certainties or provide a vehicle for announcing selfhood, Ghanaian theatre suggests the impossibility of definite perduring interpretation and the contingencies of inhabiting a social position. Theatre artists shape how publics conceive of the relationship between a character and an actor and its implications for personal morality and the sustainability of subject positions across social realms.

Ghanaian performances shaped by trickster aesthetics are successful when they are unclear, when it is uncertain who is animating speech and who is authoring it (Goffman 1981), when the pleasure of trickery and ambiguous meanings inspires further debate and responses (J. Shipley 2013a). In formalizing the ability to question the performed, both the real and the fictional are made uncertain, but in a playful way that encourages creative responses. Concerns with reflexivity and multiplicity in this production provide a template of how they are central to Ghanaian drama, and publics more generally. Theatre artists imagine the moral and spiritual parameters of social life in challenging the conventions of performance authority. In the interplay between on- and off-stage activities, drama reinforces established gendered, linguistic, and class-based hierarchies embedded in bodily action even as it lays bare their contradictions.

Theatre Work

On a Monday morning in October 1998 at the Drama Studio at the University of Ghana, Legon, theatre group members trickle in, walking from *trotro* (minibus) and taxi stands just outside the campus's gates. *The Witch of Mopti* was originally produced in 1986 by Abibigromma Theatre Players; I assist the writer as he directs its reprise twelve years later. Actors joke and talk as they change from street clothes into tights for rehearsal. Actors gather their scripts and head from the dressing rooms' privacy to the open-air stage to meet with playwright/director Mohammed Ben Abdallah. As the sun filters through the trees into the Drama Studio, everyone gathers in a circle at the back of the covered stage to find shade. It is an open-air theatre with a proscenium stage at one end. Degree and diploma students in music, dance, and drama as well as lecturers in the various departments of the School of Performing Arts pass through the studio on their way to lectures, glancing to see what the group is working on and curious about the presence of the sought-after playwright. The director of the School of Performing Arts, playwright Martin Owusu, passes through the theatre on his way to his office and nods a greeting to Abdallah. Another lecturer, Sandy Arkhurst, stops in the studio to joke with some of the actors. They have all known each other since they were students working with Efua Sutherland at the downtown Drama Studio and Joe de Graft at Legon. Now they are training the next generation of theatre and media artists.

The script for *The Witch of Mopti* was written in the production process as actors improvised around initial scenarios and directions given in 1986. Abdallah recalls, "We rehearsed a scene based on my early [written] versions of scenes.... We would try things out during rehearsal and I would go home and rewrite scenes and come back the next day with new pages for the actors."[1] In the process of creating the first production, a finished written script emerged. It was published by Woeli Publishing Services in Accra in 1989 with two of his other plays, *The Slaves* and *The Fall of Kumbi*. Worn books and photocopies of typed scripts are circulated to the cast.

Abdallah wrote the play while he was PNDC secretary of education and culture. In typical, enigmatic fashion for him, writing plays while being in government provided a critical outlet for things he "could not articulate directly" in political circles. It was first performed for the continent-wide Organization of African Unity (OAU) Conference held in Accra. He recalls, "It was a busy time for me. I was rushing back and forth between my [government] work and rehearsals. But it was also artistically exciting.... I felt that this play had a message for the government and people of Ghana at the time that related to the choices being faced by states across Africa. But some messages are better conveyed indirectly." It was again performed in 1989 with most of the original cast as a part of the Abibigro festival. In reviving it, Abdallah wanted to see how the play would be received more than a decade later, in a different political climate.

In contrast to his reputation as a tough politician, Abdallah is soft-spoken as a director. He lowers his voice to be heard, as actors concentrate to listen. He focuses on the big picture. He sees theatre as a creative collaboration and values input from actors and production crew. As he explains to the troupe one day, "I will tell you how I think something should be done, but if you have a better idea, then let's try it." He struggles to maintain the professional standards of the production with minimal financial resources. He lets group leaders work out technical problems rather than control every detail. I get the impression that, perhaps, he has let go a bit of his idealized vision for the transformative potential of the arts.

Abibigromma members are University of Ghana workers—officially government employees. Salaries are regular but low, and limited funds for productions make it difficult for them to maintain group morale and high production standards. Most are passionate about theatre and, as one member said, are "not doing it to become wealthy, but because it is my talent, my calling. We need art in this country."[2] But while they take pride in their status as a professional theatre company, members are continually frustrated by personal and group financial trouble. They also look out for the opportunities that theatre can provide to earn extra money and particularly to travel abroad and find a better life. As the economics of the group have gotten worse in recent years, members increasingly search for opportunities to study overseas or use their artistic talents to find creative ways, as one member explained, to go to Europe or America and escape the frustrations of life in Accra.

This group at Legon was re-formed after the original Abibigromma company was moved to the National Theatre in 1993.[3] Their original costumes, props, drums, and equipment were also taken downtown; they had to borrow and make new props and costumes for shows. Oh! Nii Kwei Sowah was a founding member of Abibigromma. After the split he was instrumental in re-forming the group at Legon and served as its artistic director from 1997 to 1998. He played to rave reviews in the original productions of Abdallah's *Verdict of the Cobra* as the priest and *The Witch of Mopti* as the witch. Playwright and dancer Yaw Asare recalls, "He was a great dancer. He made the roles come alive."[4] His nickname, Oh! Nii, reflects the exclamation "Oh!" people would gasp as seeing him dance. As he recalls, originally Abibigromma members were required to have both university education and be well versed in traditional forms of performance. "In the 1980s the group represented the best of Ghana's artistic tradition. There was an idealism as to the role of the arts in addressing social problems and bringing us together. The state supported the arts then . . . we had our own bus, lights, costumes. Everyone in the arts saw Abibigromma as being the elite."[5] By the late 1990s, he explains, it was hard to find well-trained university graduates willing to work for such low wages. "Instead of doing research in rural areas we hired musicians with traditional knowledge." Many of the best drummers and dancers had no education. They would train performers to learn skills they needed. "University and state resources for the arts are small. It is hard for the groups to afford quality props, musical instruments, and costumes. Salaries are also very hard to survive on for members, so we seek other sources of income generation and ways to perform for local audiences."[6]

When Abdallah left government in 1994, he returned to the Department of Drama at the School of Performing Arts as a lecturer, creating tension among the faculty. Some at the university were not pleased at his presence; they blamed him for taking the original Abibigromma and the Ghana Dance Ensemble to the National Theatre, seeing this as a betrayal of the university for the sake of state power. His supporters saw this criticism as a form of jealousy.

Through this period Abibigromma shares the Drama Studio with student projects and faculty lectures. Control of performance and rehearsal space is a constant struggle among students, school administration, and Abibigromma members, reflecting broader resource scarcity and conflicts over artistic experimentation, professionalization, and pedagogical work. One senior group member says that sometimes when students and lecturers complained about wanting to use the space or did not respect the group's need for time, Abibigromma would lock the Drama Studio "to stop people walking through disturbing rehearsals. At times this was a problem for the actors. This should be a private space for us to work." Group members, on the one hand, are seen as respected professionals, but students from wealthier families often look down on those without formal education and good English skills—ironically, because of the negative stereotypes associated with being in the arts.

The group has exclusive use of male and female dressing rooms backstage to change, work on makeup and costuming, rehearse lines, and so on. The backstage areas provide semiprivate spaces for these professional performers to gain some seclusion, eat, talk on cell phones, braid hair, and so on in the midst of hectic campus life and the inundation of the growing masses of tourists, visitors, and dance, drama, and music students demanding classroom and rehearsal space.

Members' salaries range from three hundred thousand to one million cedis a month,[7] often not enough to easily support themselves. But some poorer members must support individuals in / people from their extended families, and feel lucky to earn a regular steady salary and are often sought out by relatives in need. Most performers also make money in other informal ways. They try to use the theatre resources and their skills to find multiple income streams.

In the mid-1990s, the School of Performing Arts and the Institute of African Studies began to attract an increasing number of foreign students, researchers, and travelers from the United States and Europe. The 1992 democratic elections and privatizing reforms opened the country to tourism. And as Nigeria was increasingly seen as a dangerous place to visit, Ghana gained a reputation as safe and welcoming and a model example of neoliberal reform. Globally, Ghana is often seen as a center of drumming and traditional music, attracting white hippie spiritual seekers and African diasporic roots travelers alike.

Several male artists make and sell drums. Dancers and drummers give private and group lessons for formal school groups and informal visitors passing through. Visitors are rarely interested in formal theatre or dramatic acting, however. Ghanaians also come for lessons. David Cofie taught a contestant preparing for the national Miss Ghana beauty pageant to dance for the cultural performance aspect of competition. Unrelated to the arts, some of the female artists sell cloth, bread, and jewelry. These informal businesses sometimes cause frustration as members use time and space of the group for private lessons or selling things that more senior members do not see as professional. Many performers act in private video-film productions, in commercials, and on television, though they have to be careful not to get caught missing rehearsals to participate in other programs.

Some artists make money through cultural troupes, which perform at restaurants, hotels, and beaches for primarily tourist audiences. For example, dancer Habib Iddrisu leads a cultural performance group called Novisi, which included a number of other artists. When this group collapsed, Emmanuel Mantey, Albert Dzolu, Diana Kofitiah, and Maxwell Eshun formed Bomukasa, bringing in local performers who also work regular full-time jobs. Repertoires include versions of traditional dances from around Ghana choreographed to suit staging for both tourists and more formal audiences. Rehearsals are held after work and on weekends in a nearby half-built concrete-block house or an empty church hall, if they can find one.

Abibigromma's repertoire includes stagings of traditional dances and ceremonies from around Ghana; choreographed, opera-like dance dramas; scripted English-language dramas; and Abibigro plays that mingle music, dance, drama, mixed media and different languages. The group also performs under private contracts for commercial and government events, for which they are paid directly. These have included corporate openings, a calendar shoot for a private insurance company, a staging of Akan courtly dances (*Akan Ceremonial*) for tourists at La Palm Hotel, television and print ad campaigns, and NGO community outreach programs. In 1999 the group performed ceremonial traditional dances for the state dinner in honor of the queen of England's visit to Ghana. In 2008 the group was commissioned to write and perform a community outreach play for a private bank. They traveled throughout rural parts of the country, according to one member, "educating people to save their money in banks and making wise investment."[8] In each region the basic story was adapted to local languages and styles. For example, in the Volta Region the Ewe-speaking group members played leading roles, whereas in Akan areas the play was performed by Akan speakers. Revenue from contract work is often controversial and conflicts arise over whether it should go to the university, the School of Performing Arts, the group, the director, or the performers.

Rehearsals

Total African Theatre: Scripting Improvisation and Double Voicing

Abibigro's philosophy of "total African theatre" shapes *The Witch of Mopti*'s staging, requiring performers to master various dramatic, musical, and dance styles. Rehearsals begin with a script that was developed during the course of the play's first production. The scripted lines and minimal stage directions are memorized and transformed into blocking and stage movements. Lighting, costumes, music, and dance are added. While it is a modern, staged drama that relies on a formal script, a proscenium stage, and the timing of theatre events, the play is built on an ethos of improvisation, ambiguity, and dialogicality. The play tries to do something contradictory: to script and formalize the improvisational aspects of rural storytelling. Reflexivity dominates the play's staging as performers reveal to the audience the building of the production. Actors put on costumes and get into character on stage. Rather than emphasize the fantasy world of a staged play, the relationship between on and off stage is continually invoked.

As I have described, Abdallah's notion of Abibigro literally means "African play" but is more loosely understood as "total African theatre." He explains that Ghanaian performance is rooted in storytelling traditions but has been continually reinvented by eclectic influences and reinventions. "Efua Sutherland developed *Anansegro*, transforming *Anansesem* for the modern stage. I wanted to take her work and develop a Pan-African aesthetic." While Sutherland focused on using Akan storytelling to create a national aesthetic, Abdallah's theatre draws on eclectic influences from across Africa. He continues, "All of my plays have been formal experiments [in defining what] should constitute an African theatre . . . I wanted to draw on the structural principles that have driven African performance: its humor, improvisation, complex storytelling forms, and create a flexible framework adaptable to modern staging techniques, requirements of cosmopolitan audiences, and different venues . . . to convey the things that connect African peoples across the continent and in the diaspora." Abdallah has been concerned with understanding and revealing how performance works, expanding its potential by creating a cosmopolitan lexicon that references multiple diverse registers.

Abdallah sits in a plastic chair in the front of the audience with the company arrayed on the edge of the stage, listening. He explains the opening scene of the play to the cast, telling them that they will come in from all sides of the theatre and position themselves evenly across the stage to do an opening song introducing the group. The first person on stage will be Kwesi Brown, who will raise the song for others to join in.

Kwesi Brown also plays the role of the king of Mopti. He received his diploma in music education from what is now the University of Education, Winneba. He lived in Nigeria in the early 1980s, returning home when Nigeria expelled all the Ghanaians. He has experience with performance in a variety of religious and secular contexts. "Growing up, my grandmother was an Akom fetish priest and my father was a Methodist minister. When I went to perform at the shrine, my father would punish me by making me go to Bible study. I have always been tied to both traditions."[9] As with many professional musicians in Accra, he regularly performs in church services. But, perhaps more unusually, he remains equally interested in traditional forms of music from shrines and festivals. And he is critical of how African performance is characterized as static. "When I see foreigners come and write about our indigenous music and don't know what they're talking about . . . my goal is to record and preserve these traditional forms . . . and show how music is really a part of the lives we live."[10] After the group moved to the National Theatre, Oh! Nii and others struggled to rebuild the Legon group. Kwesi was running a concert party group and joined Abibigromma as a musician in 1995. He began to distinguish himself as a lead actor who mastered both improvisational traditions of concert party as well as the staging of Western-style plays.

Kwesi composes and arranges music for the group's dance and dramatic pieces. For the opening of their recent production *Fortunes of the Moor*—a retelling of *The Merchant of Venice* from the perspective of the Moor, written and directed by visiting African American director Carlton Mollette—Kwesi wrote a song to bring the group onto the stage. They reuse it for *The Witch of Mopti*. With the house lights down, Kwesi enters an empty stage and calls the group: "Abibibrommafueeee!" Slowly they hear the call and enter from the audience and backstage. They harmonize the song, welcoming the crowd with a slow set of synchronized steps and gestures. "I redid Yaanom Abibima [Black people], a tune by Ephraim Amu which is well known as the state radio signature tune. Amu is known as the founder of contemporary Ghanaian music."[11] Amu's tune indicates a traditionalist sensibility and a historical connection to nationalist arts. Kwesi wrote a second piece that followed. "I created a short melody with a South African sound, but the lyrics are nonsense. They use Fante intonation but it is not in a real language. People kept asking me what it meant and I said 'nothing!'"[12] Kwesi is known in the group for his wicked sense of humor. The inside joke that the tune has, on one level, no meaning while also being a sincere representation of the group's unity and evocation of an eclectic Pan-African aesthetic points to the pleasure of double-voiced performances.

The pleasure of ambiguity for the artists comes from knowing something that the audience does not and their inability to figure out a reference (or lack thereof) or double meaning. But an audience may not even be aware that they are missing something. Performers appear to reinforce the play's intent but also make a playful detour, giving them a sense of excitement and mastery over the event and the audience. In trickster storytelling and Ghanaian performance more generally, actors and audiences assume doubleness and are challenged to create, hide, and reveal layered meanings and references. "Because of Anansesem, audiences are looking to laugh and be fooled. It is part of the genre," Kwesi Brown explains. Modern theatre audiences assume this framework, relying on the duplicity of performance as incitement, a challenge to act with precision and watch for complex references meant to trick others.

Abdallah encourages his actors to think about "levels" in how they modulate the emotional rhythm of their lines, how they move through the spatial tableau of the stage, and how they regulate the timing of the play. The idea of levels creates a spatial-temporal point and counterpoint. In teaching the importance of emotional levels for conveying a narrative's significance, he points to a commonly seen dichotomy between acting in Ghanaian and Nigerian video-films: while Ghanaian actors tend to appear flat, unemotional, and overly formal, Nigerians appear too intense and overly emotional. "By varying levels, actors can direct the attention of the audience where they like. It is a basic form of control that good actors need to have: to be aware of their character through the course of the performance and to always know where you are on stage in relation to everyone else." In staging, Abdallah is especially concerned with making sure the simultaneity of the witch's home and the town is not taken too literally by the actors.

Abdallah tells the cast, "There are two main areas, the city of Mopti downstage and the witches' lair that will be raised upstage right. Action will shift between them . . . actors must use their bodies to direct the audience's focus. The concept of levels is important. . . . The two areas represent emotional . . . and physical levels." He further directs actors to fully inhabit their characters. "Even when the witches don't have lines it is important that they are always busy, plotting and moving around in their space . . . watching over people's actions."[13] These two spaces represent the ongoing tension in the gendered and moral struggle for power that drives the narrative. The main spaces are complemented by the space of the Great Baobab Tree and the town well, where the final confrontation occurs, and an undifferentiated empty space downstage left occupied by the two storytellers. These four spaces are simultaneously present throughout the play and continually occupied; audience focus is directed through lighting cues and dialogue. Sets for other scenes held in the middle of the stage are minimal, with actors pantomiming to indicate city streets, celebrations of the king's installation, the king's bedchamber, and so on.

Rehearsals progress unevenly as some artists struggle to remember lines and stage blocking. After two weeks, frustration boils over as a number of actors have not memorized their parts and are still reading from their scripts. Margaret ("Maggie") Cudjoe, who is playing the witch and is one of the group leaders, questions the professionalism of some members: "You should have memorized your lines by now! We will not be using our scripts in rehearsals any more . . . we are supposed to be the best of the best." While some struggle with this, the group begins to work on blocking their characters' movements for each scene and how to navigate the multiple levels of the set.

As actors learn their lines, blocking, and movements for the story, they are separately working on the music and dance sequences. Transforming the written script into a live, repeatable performance entails animating a text that has minimal stage directions and expanding it spatially and temporally through music and dance sequences. Music, dance, and drama are developed separately and then integrated over many weeks. The story itself is relatively short, and the musical numbers change the duration and structure of the tale. Performers see the explicit connections between the production and storytelling traditions. Kwesi Brown explains to me how the process of integrating music and dance into an Abibigro is akin to the role of *mboguw* (*mboguo*) songs in old storytelling sessions. "*Mboguw* is part of Anansesem. It breaks boredom. It makes storytelling fun. It wakes people. When you get a good storyteller all the songs, et cetera, have links to the story; it's not just random. Drumming, music, dance, and the story itself, and everyone takes turns telling the story. This is why Abibigro speaks to people both educated and uneducated. Different viewers will have different interpretations but they all understand what is going on."[14] As I describe earlier, mboguw literally means "a kicking aside," describing how audience members' spontaneous musical contributions lead to the "displacement of the storyteller's narration" and the creative fragmenting of the performance through musical and dance interludes (Donkor 2008: 43). In scripting these interludes, Abdallah attempts to capture the ethos of storytelling with the appearance of unscripted interludes. The first production of the play primarily used dances from across Ghana, but for its 1998 incarnation, the play reflects "a broader Pan-Africanist aesthetic. Our theatre should not just reflect Ghanaian traditions but those from across the diversity of African performance traditions."

Language Ideology: On-Stage and Off-Stage Code-Switching

The play foregrounds the politics of language use by mixing Twi and English and having the storytellers discuss the significance of code-switching and language choice. Language ideologies indicate how language practices are always embedded in orders of social power and both produce and contest authoritative forms of communication. In the process, language use shapes the lines between acceptable public and private action (Dent 2009; Gal 2005). On stage, characters argue about what contexts are appropriate for speaking Akan and English. They humorously point out the formal elements of their own performances, critiquing the value placed on English usage and the colloquial connotations of using "local" languages in urban contexts. Behind the scenes, however, actors re-create the social hierarchies embodied in language use. Although the play is meant to unsettle the values that link English with education, authority, and urban life, troupe dynamics during rehearsals show how this dynamic is replicated in assigning roles to actors and working through the script. Actors grapple with multiple linguistic registers in a complex intermingling of English, pidgin, and Twi meant to reflect the cosmopolitan, multicultural realities of urban Ghana. These dynamics emphasize the reflexive negotiation of language use behind the scenes.

In early rehearsals, group members pull chairs into a tight circle on stage and slowly read lines, stopping in various places as the director answers questions and elaborates on his intent and the script's meaning. During the first readings, some of the cast members who have not had much formal schooling struggle with complex English lines. Diana Kofitiah is a dancer and costume designer who has been in Abibigromma since 1996. She grew up in Accra, though her parents are Ewe from the Volta Region. She speaks Ewe, Ga, Twi, and English fluently, though she is not comfortable reading English scripts. She joked to Abdallah, "Please sir, the script is full of this *Abrofo kɛse* [big English]. Can we [perform it]?" He smiles, continuing with the read-through. This points to the difference between ideologies of standard and Ghanaian English. Whereas Ghanaian English is accepted for informal speech, it is not seen as appropriate for public speaking, and those who cannot speak with formal inflections are looked down upon. Later Abdallah explains, "Still, people do not respect the local English." Public language use in Ghanaian performance is a complex landscape. Most educated Ghanaian playwrights have scripted narrative dramatic works in English. In contrast, concert party theatre uses "local languages" reflecting traditional life, though they are understood by elite audiences as unsophisticated. In traditional formal contexts like Akan chiefly courts, speaking eloquent Akan is crucial to public respect and authority (Kwesi Yankah 1995). *The Witch of Mopti* blurs formal and informal genres of performance by mixing languages.

In the late 1990s, Abibigromma consists of twenty-eight members, though some are out of the country or on extended leave. They come from all parts of the country, representing the larger cultural/linguistic groups: Ga, Ewe, Fante, Asante, Hausa, Dagomba, and so on. A linguistic and class hierarchy existed within the group based on English fluency and literacy. While the group was originally intended to have only members with university educations, only some members have diplomas or degrees. Educated members play leadership roles, speak fluent English, and play most of the major acting roles in the scripted Nigerian, Ghanaian, and American English-language plays. Other group members had completed secondary school while some had little formal schooling. While everyone understood basic English, many members are not fluent enough to perform in English. Dancers and lead drummers concentrate on traditional dances from across the country and less on English-language-focused dramas. Supporting musicians are seen as less versatile and not expected to be major presences on stage or play leadership roles.

Code-switching remains contentious across social realms in Ghana. While English is valorized, as Maggie Cudjoe explains to the group one afternoon, one of Abibigromma's missions has been to support the "respectful use of African languages" on and off the stage. Emmanuel Mantey is cast as Togbi, the main English-speaking storyteller. This is part of the group's explicit attempt to encourage its junior members. Emmanuel is known as a drummer. The group is trying to develop and diversify the talents of the younger members of the group, and Emmanuel will have the opportunity to play his first big acting role. He is Akan and grew up in Accra. He completed junior secondary school, though he is not confident in English and has no formal training in theatre. He lives with his wife and young son in a rented room in a compound house with relatively reliable electricity but no running water in Madina, a rapidly developing peri-urban area just north of the University of Ghana. He is nervous about memorizing extended English lines for the first time but sees it as an opportunity: "This is my chance to show the group that I can play big roles and am not just a drummer."[15]

Ishak al-Mumminin is a senior member, and though he was a music major at SPA, he is one of the most experienced English-language actors and usually plays major roles. In this play, however, he performs as the storyteller who speaks only in Akan. Ishak is known for his deep, resonant voice that lends his characters gravitas on stage. "My character is a local guy who does not speak English but likes to talk."[16] This storyteller is a character of a familiar social type. His speech reflects the simplified Twi and linguistic code-switching typically spoken across urban, multiethnic Accra, delineating an informal, familiar speech community that has uneducated and naïve connotations while defining a familiar ease and humor.

Some members laugh at his stilted English pronunciation and stiffness as he reads his lines. During breaks his dedication to the task shows as he sits backstage near the men's dressing room quietly practicing his lines. Emmanuel practices his English lines with authority, though he feels self-conscious about his intonation. A crucial line addressed to the audience involves shifting the focus of the story away from the actors and toward the action. "Our story today is about a king and a witch." Another member of the group teases him about his accent:

"You sound like some bush boy. You haven't been to school and you want to speak English on stage. You will make the group look bad in public." Walking toward his house one evening he is contemplative; finally he says to me, "This play is a great opportunity for me. I can show people that I am fluent in English. It can help me get away from here, to travel. It will give me new chances. My English is good; people don't realize, so they hold me back."[17] Public authority and social respect are conferred through the fluent use of English, with its connotations as the language of business, cosmopolitanism, politics, and education. Demonstrating English fluency on stage promises new possibilities for performers in other realms. Abibigromma senior staff members encouraged junior members to play bigger roles and improve their English, often spending time with them after work helping them with their lines. As one explained to me, "We know they can do better, so we try to get them to improve their situation."

Rehearsals are conducted in English for the most part, though asides and informal talk backstage and in the dressing rooms are in a mix of Akan dialects, Ga, Ewe, English, and pidgin. On and off stage the dynamics between English, pidgin, and Twi language use point to broader forms of social difference. Language ideologies that delineate appropriate language use and related class hierarchies shape the relationship between narrating and acting for the storytellers. A few performers and many workers around the Drama Studio are Ga speakers from Accra or were raised in Accra and are fluent in Ga even though they self-identify as being from another linguistic group. Most members have a rudimentary knowledge of Ga, as they have resided in Accra for a period of time. A number of members from the Volta Region were native Ewe speakers, though it was rarely used except in private asides, as everyone assumed that no one else would understand and that using it could be construed as offensive.

Whereas fluency in formal English marks public authority, speaking heavily "accented" Ghanaian English or pidgin in formal institutional contexts is usually inappropriate. In most instances, speaking pidgin in public is seen as a sign of coarseness and impropriety, though it depends on the context (Huber 1999). At times, elites use pidgin as a way of "coming down" and showing solidarity with "local" peoples. For example, at university labor meetings and union discussions, lecturers and senior staff sometimes speak pidgin when addressing university workers as a way to demonstrate that they are all part of the same group. Secondary and tertiary students—especially men—also speak pidgin to demonstrate that they are "hip and with the people."[18]

Speaking "local languages" like Twi, Ga, or Ewe indexes traditional, rural life, and lower-class status (J. Shipley 2013b). Communication between the director and the group, as in most hierarchical relations, is mostly in English. Even group members not comfortable in English reply in it or remain silent when formally addressed; those less fluent at times feel uncomfortable or intimidated as a result. In rehearsals, when an actor does not understand an English word or reference in the script, others will explain it to him or her, though less educated actors often will not admit to not understanding something out of fear of public embarrassment or ridicule.

Diana Kofitiah is primarily dancing and designing costumes for the show but is also playing the queen's maidservant and has several English lines. She is nervous, as it is the first time she will perform in English. She completed primary school and is not comfortable in formal English. She describes the polyglot life of Accra that requires shifting between languages in various contexts. "If you are talking to people you don't always understand everything. But you have to learn different languages. If you are trading in Accra you have to learn Ga. A lot of traders are Akan or Hausa but if you don't speak Ga in Accra it is disrespectful as this land belongs to the Ga." She points out that not understanding everything in an interaction is a common experience. "Sometimes there will be so many languages in one conversation. And people might start speaking what you don't understand so you just try to listen and figure out what is going on. Sometimes if people want to say something so that you won't understand they will switch into their local language or say something proverbial so that others can't follow. So you try to understand all languages you can. But you don't always want to let people know you speak different languages so they don't know you are listening to them. I speak Ga fluently because I grew up in Accra so sometimes I won't tell people I am Ewe to avoid problems." Speakers and listeners use purposeful misunderstanding and misdirection to defer conflict and save face (Obeng 2000; Kwesi Yankah 1995).

Language difference can mark both connection and antagonism. Cecilia Yelpoe, from the Upper East Region, understands Akan but refuses to speak it for moral reasons and uses exclusively English. "It is not my language and won't be forced to communicate in it," she explains to a colleague. She is a respected senior member of the company specializing in dance and dance choreography, and she attended the University of Ghana. She is concerned with the power of language use and is remembered as one of the first Ghanaian artists to try to rap in an indigenous language. "I got on stage at a performance in Accra and someone asked why can't we try to rap in African languages. You know all these kids were trying to pretend to be American and gangster and rap in English. I improvised something in my mother tongue just to show what real African creativity is about." Her brother is a top police official under the Rawlings government. She communicates in English or her mother tongue, Dagaare. "I am not Asante and it is not my language. I won't be forced to speak someone else's tongue." Her principled stance reflects ongoing public debates about official and unofficial public language use and the "hegemony" of Akan-language use.

Storytellers: Scripted Ambiguity and Fractured Characters

In experimenting with dramatic form, *The Witch of Mopti* tries to script the potential for unscriptedness. The play formalizes an aesthetics of uncertainty and codified ambiguity. The idea that actors improvise and audiences can interject into performances are seen as key aspects of "traditional" storytelling. These informal elements are scripted into the formal structure of the play and enacted on a proscenium stage to display for an audience separated as spectators. The storytellers continually remind audience members and characters that they are in a play and of the idea of improvisation as an objectified representation of traditional life. This reflexive narration is located in on-stage debates about how actors inhabit participant roles and deploy linguistic registers. Its reflexivity is reminiscent of Beckett's *Waiting for Godot,* which focuses the audience's attention on the passage of time and notions of narrative structure through self-referential discourse on waiting. The play's two storytellers are its central mediators and narrators. They are scripted embodiments of the potential for improvisation and audience/performer interaction. Their interactions mirror various familiar real-world relationships. As they directly address the audience from the stage, they both reveal and naturalize storytelling as a type of narrative and spatio-temporal logic. They help develop the story's plot through reflexive reference to the process of storytelling and its moral implications. The performance is a play within a storytelling session, forcing actors and audiences to reflect on the process of narrating.

The names of the characters demonstrate how actors shift between off-stage self, storytelling, and character persona. Senior group member David Cofie recounts, "The names of the storytellers in the published script reflect the names of the actors who played the storytellers in the original production. They played themselves using their own names. That is why in our production we used the storyteller's real names. They were really playing themselves narrating the story."[19]

The tale begins with the storytellers discussing language use and speaking authority as an argument among actors/townspeople of Mopti breaks out about who will narrate the story. Everyone wears tight full-body brown spandex bodysuits, as they mime the activities of waking up in the city of Mopti. Actors debate in Twi and English how audiences respond to language use.

ABOTSI: My brother, stand aside and let me talk to these people, OK? . . . As I was saying before I was rudely interrupted; this is Abibigromma.

KOFI ONNY: Ose, wo fre yen Abibigromma. Asee kyere se yedi Abibigro. [He says we are called Abibigromma, Black Players, and we teach and perform Abibigro, Black theatre.]

Their uncertainty about the norms of speaking and staging is aimed at getting audiences to think about their expectations. The actors then debate and explain the meaning of Abibigro.

ABOTSI: Some people think we do concert.

NII SAI: Some think we are just jokers.

KOFI ONNY: Ebinom koraa se yen dee asa nko ara na ye sa. Ye bo donno nay ere sa.

TOGBI: Dondology? Some say we are dondologists.[20]

OSABUTEY: Some even say we do drama and play all sorts of musical instruments.

KOFI ONNY: Ebinom koraa se ye to anansesem.

NII KWEII: But the truth of the matter is . . .

ALL: We do all of those things and more!

They celebrate the eclectic inclusiveness of the genre and then move toward telling the tale at hand and argue over who has a right to be the storyteller.

NII SAI: You are probably wondering what we have in store for you this time. Well, I will tell you . . .

OSABUTEY: My friend, who made you the story-teller?

NII SAI: I did!

KOFI ONNY: Hwe, enne me na me to anansesem no oo!

NII KWEII: No! No! No!

TOGBI: OK, OK! I have an idea. I have a solution to the problem. We shall all tell the story.

Each claims the right to tell the story, creating humorous disagreements. Meta-language highlights how the storytellers claim speaking authority by simply enunciating it. As some characters speak Twi, others translate or interpret their words. The actors talk directly to the audience, arguing over who will tell the story and what kinds of activities constitute drama. Senior group member David Cofie explains that for this play, "the entire company are the storytellers."[21] In staging the debate about who gets to tell the story, this play highlights the issue of framing itself and discussions about language use, what is legitimate modern speaking, and who can claim it. Once the storytellers have been decided, a conversation about the uses of English and Twi reveals societal norms in which public respect and authority are conferred by speaking proper English and disrespect and lower class status through Twi usage in many modern urban public contexts.

ABOTSI: Good evening... My brothers and sisters! My name is Abotsi and this is Abibigromma. I am sure you are wondering what Abibigromma means and what it is we do.

KOFI ONNY: *(Whispers in Abotsi's ear.)*

ABOTSI: What?... What did you say?... Did you hear what Kofi said?... He says you are probably all staring at me so sheepishly because you don't understand a word of what I am saying... Kofi Onny says you don't understand a word of the white man's English...

KOFI ONNY: Oboa manka saa. Abotsi me mpe saa oo! Oboa, manka se monte Brofo. Me se, enye obiara a owo ha na ote Broni kasa ase. [He's lying. I didn't say that. Abotsi, I don't like that! I didn't say that they don't understand English. I said that not everyone here will understand the white man's language.]

ABOTSI: But Kofi, how do you know that all the people here understand Akan?

KOFI ONNY: Manka se obiara a ote ha biara te Twi... [I didn't say that everyone understands Twi...]

ABOTSI: But I am sure everybody here can understand English even if they cannot speak it.

KOFI ONNY: Ah! Abotsi paa. Wo dee woasei! Hwe! M'adamfo Kwashivi sei. Oye Ghana ni nso onte Akan kasa biara. Na, wo gye di se woantumi ansua Twi a eye Ghana ha kasa no anka ono ara ne kasa a yede woo no ho a, eye den na otumi sua Brofo kasa a eye Obruroni kasa ka? [Abotsi, what's wrong with you? Look! My friend Kwashivi is a Ghanaian and doesn't understand Akan. But if you can't learn Twi, a Ghanaian language, it will be hard to learn the foreign white man's language, don't you think?]

NII SAI: Ohh! You people are wasting our time. Do you think these people came here to watch you carry on your stupid argument?

The actors, who are not yet characters, directly address the audience, implicitly acknowledging the formal frames that are supposed to demarcate performance and audience. This humorous argument parodies and exaggerates common metalinguistic debates about turn-taking that happen in a variety of social contexts. During performances, the preceding exchange provoked laughter at the unexpected reflexivity around code-switching and appropriate language use among the mostly bilingual audience.[22] As a university student in attendance one evening said, "The play points to the issue of public language... why do we disrespect the public use of our own language and praise the use of foreign tongues... the exchange is humorous and familiar to all Ghanaians."[23] The play's opening points out the controversial hierarchical role of language in public speaking. When Abotsi addresses the audience directly in English, he is immediately stopped by a private comment from Kofi Onny, who does not speak English and is afraid that the audience will be alienated by this inhospitable use of "the white man's English."

Juxtaposing English and informal Twi in a debate about the etiquette of appropriate language use points to the contextual conditions that would allow their usage to overlap. Kofi's bashful question to Abotsi about whether a Ghanaian or African audience will speak Twi highlights the inappropriate nature of this sort of question and the embarrassment that a conversation about language can provoke. More than 40 percent of Ghanaians are native speakers of one of the Akan dialects, and most people understand it and speak it on a functional level. However, to some its ubiquity represents the historical domination of Asante culture and politics, and they resist its de facto transformation into a national lingua franca. As Ishak points out to me, it also demonstrates the high value placed on politeness and respect in public speaking: "Ghanaians are polite, too much. Even when there is an important issue or some problem we don't want to embarrass anyone even if they are hurting us."[24]

As a narrator, Kofi Onny translates for the audience into Akan, providing indirect, humorous metacommentary on the process of narrating. Throughout the play, Kofi Onny maintains his role as Akan storyteller, making comments on, joking about, and embellishing the English comments of his colleague, effectively highlighting the contradictions of public language authority. Social negotiation of language mediation and turn-taking are central to respectful public language use in many Ghanaian contexts. In particular, these forms of mediation and indirect speaking invoke the Okyeame, the court linguist of Akan chiefs who indirectly speaks for the chief, translating and mediating his words in official political, juridical, and ceremonial contexts (cf. Obeng 1997, 2000; Kwesi Yankah 1995).

The storytellers frame the narrative of the play through authoritative turn-taking, moral commentary, and language shifting. Actors joke behind the scenes about their English-language abilities, showing how the play reflects the local significance of public language choice and proper forms of address in the making of social standing and authority. In daily life and in ceremonial and theatrical events, Ghanaians reflect on the changing nature of public authority through the language of the storyteller. Fluent English-language use reflects an authoritative public stance, while Akan-language use acts as contextualizing commentary on this authority and frames it with questions of class hierarchy, ethnic difference, and historical power relations. The two storytellers link the realms of the story and of the audience, while maintaining distance by pointing to these as distinct realms. In the process, they mark the narrative as a fiction, repeatedly reminding characters that they are in a story and audience members that they are watching an unreal place-time. The moral and emotional force of the narrative depends on how well the two storytellers mediate between the audience and the rest of the play's characters, who are unaware that they are in a story: at times bringing them close together, at times keeping them apart. The centrality of the storytellers foregrounds the importance of the telling itself. They embody the possibilities of audience-performer dialogue and performer improvisation. The reflexive aspects of Abibigro beckon the audience to focus on the concept of theatre itself and the contexts through which Ghanaian public speaking authority is made.

The Pan-African Dance Aesthetic

Over the course of rehearsals, the minimalist stage directions in the script are transformed into complex staging. Actors begin to memorize their lines, define their characters, and learn blocking for each scene—the exact movements on stage in relation to other actors. As the narrative takes shape, the music and dance scenes are intermingled. There are a number of stage directions in the written script, such as "everyone dances to celebrate the king's enstoolment," that leave a lot of room for interpretation. Abdallah explains, "The script does not give much information on how the music and dance should fit into the story because I want my plays to be flexible. Anyone can take this script as a form and make it their own."

The main choreographed dance scene is the celebration of the installation of the king of Mopti and his marriage. For this production Abdallah wanted to use new dances and music rather than solely those from Ghanaian traditions to create a Pan-African aesthetic: mixing images, movements, and sounds from a variety of African locales as a way to denote the connectedness of African peoples. He enlists Amadou Bole Ndiaye, a Senegalese master dancer and teacher married to an American embassy worker, who is a visiting dance teacher at SPA.[25] The dancers and musicians are excited and nervous about learning new dances from Senegal and figure out how to stage these "traditional" forms within the spatiotemporal framework of the play. A number of dance students from the school are enlisted to join the dances to fill the stage. Abdallah explains how the scenes are to be structured but leaves the staging largely to Amadou and Habib Iddrisu, one of the lead dancers and drummers in the company. Habib is from a family of musicians near Tamale in the Northern Region. He completed his O-levels in Tamale and his advanced secondary education in Accra, and is finishing his undergraduate degree in dance. He would later complete his Ph.D. in performance. He is officially on leave from the group but still performs. He explains that dances from other parts of Africa bring a different aesthetic and sense of the body: "Group members all know [Ghanaian dances]; it's exciting to learn dances from another part of Africa, to learn about other cultures. . . . The way they use their bodies . . . in Francophone countries . . . for dance is very different. The movements are much bigger and sweeping, less controlled with smaller hand movements like a lot of the Ghanaian dances, especially from the south. But it will also be hard for some learning something that is African but foreign, that is totally new to us and not part of our tradition."[26]

In the afternoons, Amadou works with the dancers and musicians. He shows the drummers the rhythms to play. He demonstrates dance movements, first slowly without music and then in rhythm to the music. The dancers copy him over several days, repeating each movement and then learning to string them together into a fluid sequence. Once the performers learn the basic dances, they begin to integrate them into the script. They have great respect for the elegance and mastery of Amadou's dance skills; the basic dance movements are very different from those from southern Ghana. Whereas many Ghanaian dances involve small, intricate, exacting movements, the Senegalese dances that Amadou teaches use large gestures, sweeping arms, extending legs, going to the ground and up to the sky. Some dancers struggle to learn particular moves. One dancer discusses with another after a rehearsal how hard the moves are for him. "Hye! The way he shakes his rasta (dreadlocks) and drops his arms and waist, like a bird!" Amadou's dreadlocks stand out in Accra of the late 1990s, where this seems rebellious. When he dances, Abibigromma members agree he is one of those special dancers whose lanky elegance, as Abdallah says, "transcends the movements," and as Habib says, "demands respect . . . He flows like water." Amadou's dances are exciting, new, and unfamiliar. One experienced dancer explains that they are learning the new dances by copying movements and do not know their meaning or the dances' original contexts, which would help them understand them. They focus on emulating the flowing and sweeping gestures.

In earlier performances of *The Witch of Mopti,* Asante music, dance, and symbolism were used for the installation of the king. Choreography followed the model of the Ghana Dance Ensemble. In this performance a more eclectic Pan-African assemblage of dances and symbols was used. In the script, "enstooled" is changed to "enskinned," transforming a sign of Akan kingship into that of a northern chief. Many of Abdallah's plays draw on images and symbols from the Muslim Sahel, and Amadou's dances help realize that aesthetic. The king is represented through an eclectic combination of the bodily adornment of Dagomba and other peoples of northern Ghana, such as leather boots and woven smocks combined with the dances from Senegal taught to the dancers by Amadou. The chief is put into power by being enskinned, ritually placed on an animal skin rather than a stool. There is much discussion of how to translate and integrate various traditions. "Look, in the north they don't use stools; chiefs wear skins, so we will change the language of the script from enstooling to enskinment of the chief," Ishak says. This shift points to the move away from a familiar idea of national symbolism that relies heavily on Asante cultural signs toward an unfamiliar recombination of ethnic signs and practices that is explicitly cosmopolitan in its incorporative principle. Maggie's comments during rehearsals are indicative of these differences. For her, the new dances enliven Abibigromma's repertoire but also point to how little they have learned. "It's exciting to learn . . . culture from another part of Africa. I am tired of doing the same dances over and over, though I would love to understand more of what we are doing. I don't even know how to do these dances properly or really where they are from. Amadou is such a great teacher, but it is different learning on stage than really living a culture and understanding the meaning of what you are doing."[27]

The set and costume designs also promote an eclectic Pan-African sensibility. Mopti is a city in Mali famous as a historical center of Islamic learning and trans-Saharan trade. The play is set in a timeless Sahel, giving it a folkloric and malleable sensibility. Costumes include beads and cloth and adornments from across West Africa. Setting the action in this way marks the story as being in a generic, culturally diverse, African time-space. Abdallah intended the play to be adaptable. He recalls, "When it was performed in the U.S. with an African American cast, the Twi language was done in African American vernacular dialogue to contrast with standard English. This made the same point about how different kinds of speaking have different values." Ethnic, linguistic, national, and Pan-African sensibilities are framed by the genre of storytelling to invoke not a homogeneous sense of affiliation but rather a complex landscape of both familiarity and distance, understanding and miscommunication.

For local audiences these non-Ghanaian African dances do not evoke familiar symbolic grammars of Dagbamba, Asante, Ga, or Ewe performances, nor the hybrid poetics forged through the combination of their elements by the Ghana Dance Ensemble. On opening night, one young Ewe audience member was struck by the "beautiful" but unfamiliar Senegalese dances and compared them to dances from his region. "I love watching them and knowing they're African; that is true of dances from other parts of Ghana as well. But they don't affect me like the dances from [the] Volta region where I am from; those I can feel in my body. When they do the dance properly it just makes me so proud."[28] This reflects a broader principle of viewership that has informed the staging of performances from the colonial era through independence to the present: that cultural displays provoke emotional affiliation in audiences, which can be shaped toward an actor's or director's interests. Performance forms create emotional connections for local participants and observers by linking the familiar and the unfamiliar. New dances mark broader African affiliations while reinforcing Ghanaian specificity in opposition to their aesthetic sensibility. Ambivalence to difference marks the contested nature of national and Pan-African affiliation in Ghana.

Pan-African Spiritual Battles and Political Theology

The narrative crux of the play revolves around the witch's rage that her nephew, the king, refuses to marry her daughter and instead weds the daughter of a poor fisherman. The witch unleashes a spell that makes the king impotent. In response, the king brings priests, wizards, spiritual channels, and healers from across the African continent to help. His new wife gives birth to quintuplets and the town celebrates. The witch creates new plagues and spells, but the city and the king are protected by the priests. This spiritual battle is portrayed through musical and pantomime interpretations for casting spells. In the power struggle the witch hurls plagues onto the city: blindness, hate, itching, commodities—in which all of the townspeople desire to buy and sell everything, including each other. The visiting magicians are introduced and narrated to the audience in a conversation between the witch and her daughter as they watch celebrations of their defeat in the city below. Politics are cast as a spiritual battle and conflict is put in gendered terms. Mopti is portrayed in terms of political theology in which belief and spiritual power are intertwined with sovereignty, the rights and means of rule. These abstract notions of power are spatialized on stage. The king, standing for belief and respectability, is centered in the palace and public spaces of the city, which occupy center stage. The witch and her daughter, in contrast, inhabit the periphery and fight for power through devious means from their lair upstage.

The celebration after the witch is defeated by spiritual means is choreographed by Habib based on a dance from his Novisi dance group. Each priest also does a dance as the witches describe where in Africa they come from and what magical powers they possess. The performers each develop their dance through improvisation. For each dance the drummers followed the movements, inventing a rhythm to follow them. Kwesi explains that in rehearsal and performance, "the drummers followed moves of actors to mimic. We followed their rhythms. You have to improvise here, which is different than playing for traditional dances. But you have to think on your feet."[29] Members who play in the music ensemble shift in and out of their characters, as they are needed on stage. The musicians are assembled on the side of the stage visible to the audience.

The witch is so desperate to defeat the king and gain power herself that she calls forth the devil and sacrifices her beloved daughter to learn the secret of how to defeat the king. This sacrifice invokes a moral choice, the exchange of personal sentiment and family in blind pursuit of power. The devil teaches her to cast a spell poisoning the city well's water so that everyone in the town who drinks the water goes insane. Everyone drinks of the well except the king. He remains the only sane person, and the citizens roam through the streets. When the crazy mobs see their king, they assume *he* is a madman, as he is the only one acting differently.

Maggie, playing the witch, is a quiet leader giving advice to less experienced actors about how to impart proper emotion to their characterizations and how to master their stage movements. She is married and known within the group as a pious Christian. She had expressed slight misgivings about playing a role so contrary to her religious beliefs. She is upset when the actor who was playing the chief was teasing her about a scene in the play where her spiritual powers cause the chief to become impotent. After one rehearsal the actor jokes in Pidgin, "Be careful my prick no go come down for nobody. My spiritual powers are stronger than you, old witch! And I don't need the church to get them." The sexual innuendo of this joke make the men laugh and the women roll their eyes. This type of explicit gendered tension backstage is common. Another actress in the group who is also a member of a Charismatic church interjected, "Don't mind him. Witches can't stand the blood of Jesus. That is why many people join the church: to protect themselves from all these people who go in for using such things." The conversation turned to a recent radio program during which a young woman confessed to having been possessed by demons and doing ill to her family. Maggie later explains to me how spiritual power works: "It's always someone close to you who tries to hurt you, spiritually. You never know who you can trust. That is why you have to go to church and be a good Christian. These are uncertain times."[30] The on-stage spiritual war is about a struggle for sovereignty; this opposition refracts into off-stage concerns about the tension between theology and sexuality on the one hand and belief and political uncertainty on the other.

Drinking from the Well: The Impossibility of Moral Choice

Actors create bizarre characters to stage the scene in which the townspeople go insane after drinking the well water. The script says: "The general area of the stage is suddenly invaded by a parade of the citizens of Mopti, Lunatics of all kinds, shades, sizes, ages. The parade is a cacophony of different songs. . . ." This simple script direction is developed into a six-minute extended scene with mad townspeople trooping through the aisles toward the stage to confront the king. Maggie helps direct dancers, drummers, and actors as each is charged with improvising and developing a mad persona. "Remember any mad people you know. If you are in town or in the market, try to observe the way a mad person acts: their gestures, dress, everything." Actors are responsible for assembling their own costumes and creative pastiches of materials and styles. Another senior actor, Jesse Offei, says that she develops her mad character by observing people in daily life. "I just exaggerate normal gestures to the extreme. You know?" She is a senior member of the company who graduated from the University of Ghana and focuses mostly on drama. Her costume consists of a headband of palm seeds, raggedy skirts and clothes layered, and heavy makeup. She stamps her feet and rambles across the stage invoking both humor and danger. Maxwell, a musician, tromps through the audience to the stage, frenetically playing (out of rhythm) a *dondo* talking drum tucked under his arm. They improvise short frantic dances as they encounter the king.

First Lunatic: . . . Stop the music! Stop the dance! Stop everything!

Second Lunatic: Well! What is it?

FIRST LUNATIC: . . . Look at your King! Can't you see how different he behaves? . . .

THIRD LUNATIC: It's true. He is different. Hei, King? What's the matter with you? Are you crazy or something?

The king is not crazy. His frenetic citizenry in their madness interpret his difference—in fact his normal actions—as insanity. The lunatic townspeople give him an ultimatum. The king has until sunrise to act sane or they will depose him. The witch thinks she has won and will be made the new ruler of Mopti once the king is removed from power. But the king lies awake contemplating his predicament.

The climax of the play comes as the king suddenly is able to see the storytellers and contemplates what to do about the mad townspeople. The storytellers mediate between the worlds of the audience and the world of the story. By changing whom they address and the intended and unintended hearers of their words, the storytellers control how the interactions between these three distinct worlds shift throughout the play. Since early in the story, the characters in the play have not been able to see or hear the storytellers. At times they stand on the side of the stage, looking intently as if watching a play themselves. However, in the climactic moment when the king is faced with how to confront his imminent removal from power, they suddenly reenter the fray. They do not give the king solutions, but their appearance marks his ability to step outside the action and reflect on his moral dilemma and the possibilities for action. When the lunatic mob confronts the king, he tries to reason with them to recover their sanity. His sudden recognition of the presence of the storytellers blurs the separate spaces of narrating and acting. In the reflexive recognition of narration in which the storytellers indexically align participating and observing, thinking and feeling, the moral choice of the play is prepared for contemplation. The narrative hinges on a moral choice made not through rational discourse but rather embodied sentiment.

ALL: Regain your sanity by dawn! Or you shall be King of Mopti no more!

KING: Please! Please stop this madness! Please listen to me! Oh! God. Oh, people of Mopti come back. You are the ones who need help! . . . Somebody, please help me. *(Togbi and Onny step out of their corner and approach the king.)* Oh God! Who are you? Where do you come from? Have you come to help me?

TOGBI: We pity you and sympathize with you, oh, King! But we cannot help you.

Two storytellers reveal their presence, which creates a disjuncture that allows the king to step out of his own time and reflect on his ability to make choices and the possibilities available to him. At times the storytellers talk directly to the audience; at other times the audience members are relegated back to being observers, unintended recipients of an exchange between the space-time of the storyteller and that of the king and the witch.

TOGBI: We can only agree with you King; but we cannot help you. You see we are not even supposed to be here. We are not part of the story. We are only story-tellers from a different time and a different dimension. That well over there is the problem. The problem is between you and the Old Witch. And the solution may very well lie deep inside the well. We must go, King, for you have no time, and your people will be back! Good luck King of Mopti.

In the moment of his greatest need, the storytellers appear before him, again breaking the performance frame to mark the formal aspects of narrative conflict and resolution. The king decides, "I will never turn my back on Mopti. It needs me." As the sun rises he declares, "You know, those two clowns were right! The answer is in the well." He fills a calabash full of water from the well, and as the mad populace approaches, he drinks. The witch realizes she has been outwitted. "The King drops the calabash and immediately begins to dance around the well. Taking off his clothes, singing, muttering unintelligible words; he has gone stark raving mad, and does a solo Dance of Madness." When the citizens of Mopti see him, they celebrate his newfound sanity and all dance off the stage. Togbi and Onny directly address each other while facing the audience to conclude the play.

ONNY: Ei! Abibigro wei dee aba wo mu oo! [This African play has messages inside it!]

TOGBI: No! No! No! We cannot tell them the moral of the story. Can't you see they are all adults, many of them old enough to be our parents? But I only have one question.

ONNY: Edee Kwehen? [What's that?]

TOGBI: What would have happened if the King had not drunk from the Well of Madness? In the struggle for Mopti . . . Who was the winner . . . and who the loser?

The storytellers frame the king's action as the audience is directed to contemplate the process of narration itself in a final exchange between storytellers. Viewers witness the storytellers' disagreements about how to find narrative closure. Describing Abibigro as a form of moral proverb-like speech, Onny tells the audience the play has an explicit "message." But Togbi cuts him off, preventing him from revealing what it may be, and replaces it with a question. The storytellers are, as the king says, "clowns" and comic relief as well as controllers not of the action per se but of the performance frames, the participation roles that characters, actors, and audience members are allowed to inhabit.

Reflecting later, Kwesi describes his experience playing the king and how shifting in and out of character provided a lesson for him. "You know the play is supposed to impart a moral lesson. Even myself, in playing the part, I learned to be careful when you are dealing with people; you know they can harm you, especially those closest to you. The witch was the king's aunt, you remember? Anything can happen to you. . . . With my character, the most intriguing thing was when I went crazy I did things I would not normally do. It allowed me to play around in character with what is normally acceptable."[31]

Community of (Mis)Interpretation

The Witch of Mopti is performed at the Drama Studio on December 17, 18, and 19, 1998. It is also included in the group's Abibigro '99: A Festival of Total African Theatre Productions.[32] Maggie is proud of the production but disappointed that they don't have more chances to reach the public. "You know we rehearse for months and only perform for a few days. We have so many events and SPA programs that we can't do as much with marketing and sales as private groups." The play is well attended at these performances, mostly by students and others at the university, though some workers who live nearby attend. The Drama Studio is mostly full, with several hundred tickets sold each night. Despite relatively cheap ticket prices—admission is eight thousand cedis, about a dollar—the fee is still high for working people, reinforcing the sense that events at the Drama Studio are for elites. I ask a barber I know in nearby Madina if he attends performances at the Drama Studio; he reflects a common sentiment among working people when he says that he will not be welcome if he goes to the university. "The security guards don't treat you well. Anyway, what business do I have being there?"[33] As I have described, formal theatre venues like the National Theatre and the Drama Studio at Legon are seen as elite spaces, which discourages local audiences. Advertising is done by handwritten posters placed near the university and some radio announcements. The minimal attention paid to publicity is striking, particularly because electronic media and corporate sensibilities are inundating Accra in the late 1990s. State theatre has not aligned itself with commercial branding or media but continues to rely on the sense of a shared grassroots aesthetic.

Audience members' responses during and after the performances show that they are less concerned with political messages about choice, leadership, and integrity that were profoundly relevant ten years earlier. The characters' moral choices reflect Ghanaians' ambivalent reactions to privatization when it was still a publicly contested organizing principle. But for the rising generation, the logic of the free market seems unquestioned. One business student attending a performance felt that it brought up the question of "good leadership" and that a good leader should respond to his people's needs. Others saw a more nihilistic or pragmatic moral message, feeling that outside forces made leadership impossible and, according to a middle-aged viewer, "all we can do is go along with society and try our best with the situation we are given."[34] The storytellers' questions are meant to leave theatre audiences in a similar structural position to the one Ghanaians face as foreign interests and commodity culture take over local moral sensibilities. The king asks himself questions about leadership and how to regain moral speaking authority among his crazed people. Asking questions without easy answers presupposes an audience that can rise to the moral challenge of the storyteller.

Actors from the original mid-1980s production remember how the play attracted large audiences and was well received.[35] Abdallah recalls that audiences were provoked by performances. "It was seen as a critique of government's bowing to international pressure. In some ways it is a classic African morality tale, so people knew how to read it. It provoked discussion, though it is also a story that people could understand on many levels so others simply enjoyed it."

In contrast, audiences in 1998 and 1999 seem less interactive. Evolving audience expectations have been influenced by stylistic formality brought through increased television and film production work. Viewers seem bothered by slippages and inconsistencies in language and fluency. In interviews I conduct with audience members after performances, many comment on the discrepancy between the use of English and Akan dialogue. For example, one agriculture student, a native Akan speaker, who attended all three nights of the performance notes, "The actors seem so comfortable speaking Akan; they are really natural. A lot of them look stiff and not very good when they are delivering the English. Their intonation is wrong, like they don't know what they are saying."[36] While the play tries to show the fluidity of a multilingual society, the striking contrast between some actors' fluency in Akan and awkwardness in English reinforces linguistic hierarchies and the distance between the Ghanaian populace and a commercial English-speaking elite.

While senior staff works hard to help junior and less educated members of the group learn English, they also recognize their lack of fluency in English can be a problem. As Kwesi Brown explains, "Most of the junior staff learn lines without understanding meaning. They put the wrong stress in the English, throwing the meaning off. . . . The most difficult aspect of the play was working with performers who don't stick to the script. They never know their cues. One of the mad townspeople was supposed to cue me with his line; he only had one line! 'King of Mopti, change your life by sundown tomorrow.' But he could not get it right; he said, 'King of Mopti, change you life of the Sunday tomorrow.' Even the witches were laughing."[37] But this confusion and the laughter it provokes is not simply an issue of language fluency. It shows how slippages between scripted theatre and storytelling can become points for ridicule as well as critical thought. It also shows that at times there is as Kwesi Brown points out "a gap between locals and more elites in terms of what they mean by theatre." More local members confuse "doing concert," that is, slipping into more bawdy undirected styles of concert party, with "proper modern theatre," where they are staging improvisation. But humor—both intended and unintended—can provide a point for critical intervention; that is, laughter highlights not only the actors' wit but also points to where there is potential for double meaning and moral uncertainty in the making of a performance ideology (Barber 2000: 209).

This play, like Ghanaian performances more generally, operates on two levels simultaneously. Humor is often a way to temper the dangerous, divisive potential of political commentary or indeed any type of direct speech. On stage at the end of one of the final rehearsals for the play's climactic scene, one actor switches into pidgin to make a joking aside to one of the drummers about the absurdity of the king's choice. Such asides are common in rehearsals, often entailing linguistic and bodily code-switching. They are explicitly bracketed segments of informal language that are important for producing in-groupness among members as well as for marking moments of uncertainty of interpretation. While appearing to be peripheral, informal, improvised moments create a sense of intimacy for participants (Spitulnik 1996). Walking off stage, the actor quips in Pidgin, "This one ee no be hard, oh. They for chop. As for me, I no get choice. I go for sit my room, shut my mouth." (People in power will do what they have to do to stay rich. I don't have anything, so I have no choice but to go home and keep my mouth shut.) For him, choosing to go crazy to stay in power is not difficult. Indeed, the point of his joke is that having a choice at all is a privilege not afforded to most people.

Many people have commented on the fact that Ghanaian audiences often laugh at tragedy or when characters face serious moral dilemmas. Abdallah thinks it is a sign of anxiety. "We laugh at something to dispel the fear of tragedy or because of fear of embarrassment." Kwesi Brown is frustrated at audiences laughing at serious moments in the play. "There is a problem with our Ghanaian mentality; people treat serious issues by laughing. Even when the king went impotent, they laugh, or when the witch is overpowered. They see it as comedy; even some of the lines from Abdallah have profane and hidden things going on, it's the humor that dominates." Some performers encourage laughter. "Some play their roles to make the audience laugh, not knowing what the broader points were. Acting to them is concert, and anything concert is comedy. We were all rehearsing at the same time, but members have very different interpretations of the same play. Junior staff or dance students think it is concert party because that is what they know. They just try to go for laughs from the audience. Those who have been through college or have more experience see it on a different level."[38] Actors sticking to the script had trouble dealing with other performers' improvised asides and movements. Kwesi says that while "the mad people improvised their roles, they were supposed to stick [to] the script. Even when my character went crazy, . . . I stayed within the script because others took cues from my lines. . . . You can't stray too far. . . . The balance is difficult." Performers experience acting and creativity differently when they are improvising, picking up from each other through shared references, themes, and rhythms, compared to when they are following a script with precise blocking and timing.

Again, humor points to the ways this play operates on multiple levels. While for some it is just a comedy, for others it makes them think about social issues. Kwesi Brown says, "We try to make people laugh, but drama has multiple levels. It is there to send a message. This is one play, but it addresses several issues. Abibigro is what is going on in the community. People can relate to it. We have mixed feelings with Abdallah's plays. It's only one play, but it deals with everything in the community. Politically, socially, religiously, I mean everything. His plays have hidden messages. . . . Intellectuals who watch, really catch what is going on. If you are passing by you just see a comedy."[39]

As I describe in the book's introduction, during a performance of Abdallah's play *The Trial of Mallam Ilya* in the early 1980s just after two coups d'etat, the audience was scared and confused as to whether staged violence was theatrical or part of another "real" revolt. In that moment, the transformative potential of theatre was particularly self-conscious as audiences seemed predisposed to be active participants in staged deliberations. The prevalent spirit of populist solidarity and social transformation united dramatic and political stagings. However, the structural conditions fostered by an intermingling of privatization and ambiguous state control, and growing class divisions over the following decade, were refracted in increasing distance and mediation between actors and audiences, theatre and politics.

With the rise of electronic media, video-films, and commercial television, intellectual theatre in Accra reaches relatively small audiences, though it legitimizes popular theatre's dialogic and moral sensibility, spreading this formal logic through state, religious, and educational institutions and media. Modern drama establishes a network of personnel, institutions, and forms that shape public understandings of public performance. Intellectual theatre's translation and appropriation of traditional culture has shaped students, artists, business executives, and media workers who pass through schools and universities. These rising elites in turn shape private, religious, and national media forms that compete as Accra's public sphere is privatized and transformed.

Audience reaction to *The Witch of Mopti* demonstrates exuberance at the pleasures of dance and wordplay, but there seemed to be a lack of recognition of how its poetics linked to political critique only a few years after its writing. Comic exchanges and language shifts—often met by laughter from the audience—point to several of the poetic features of the trickster/storyteller as a figure of postcolonial power: indirectness/directness, ambiguity, humor, reversal, and the dichotomy between seamless performance and breaking the performance frame. The characters remain structurally relevant for young audiences and seemed to provoke discomfort in ways that Abdallah found comforting, even in light of his frustration at how increasing electronic media hindered formal theatre's ability to reach broader audiences.

The storytellers' presence encourages the audience to actively engage with the conundrum the play presents by marking the distinction between performers and viewers, thereby recontextualizing them within one interpretive frame. By explicitly refusing to reveal their opinions, they dare viewers to engage. In denying a straightforward ending, they highlight the fact that what is not enunciated is the main point of the performance. By not saying something, they draw attention to the implications of revealing and concealing, calling on participants to actively search for meaning rather than waiting for an answer. The implication is that the political message of the play must be powerful *because* it cannot be directly revealed. Talking *around* the main point is reminiscent of the logic of proverbial speech and Anansesem, in which meaning is driven by indirection, ambiguity, innuendo, and humor. Speaking authority comes from eloquence in not revealing meaning. Ultimately the king's unexpected trickery in reversing the witch's power play commands the day. The struggle between the king and the witch shows the contradictions of definitive individuated leadership in the face of collective delusion. As the storytellers explain, they cannot tell the audience the play's meaning, as it is inappropriate to speak in a direct manner to their elders; they are mocking the audience by invoking the convention that prevents direct forms of public address. They are also provoking the audience to respond even as they are left with the moral ambiguity of the king's choice and a sense that they have been purposefully misdirected.

Questioning as Self-Fashioning, Critical Discourse

Bertolt Brecht's radical theatre was meant to disrupt an audience's social complacency and provoke emotional responses. While radical Western dramatists have struggled to connect passive audiences to the stage, African theatre artists struggle to carve out space for theatrical contemplation. For Abdallah, experiments in theatrical form by twentieth-century dramatists in Europe and America recall basic tenets of African storytelling. "African storytellers use . . . theatre-in-the-round and other techniques which are seen as experimental and radical in Western drama."

An aesthetics of humorous exaggeration compels participants—actors, production people, and audience members—to exist in the moral ambiguity of performances that refuse singular references. The storytellers gently make fun of the characters, the audience, and each other and indirectly point out the slippages between on stage and off stage, reality and performance. Social interactions among artists during the production of the play replicate formal critiques made in the script, reinforcing how speaking practices index both social hierarchy and agency. The explicitly dialogic relationships between audiences and performers in storytelling, popular concert party, and other African traditions of dramaturgy are well established (Barber 2000: 228; Cole 2001; Gibbs 2009; Kerr 1995; Kruger 1999). What is significant in the Abibigro form is the ways in which improvisation and ambiguity are objectified, codified, and formally marked through scripting and performance. The characters in *The Witch of Mopti* spend a lot of time figuring out how to perform and how to talk. They formally encode the play's metapragmatic elements—the linguistic and bodily aspects of performance that comment on the process itself—as central to the process of telling stories and facing moral choices.

The king's moral dilemma is on the surface an absurd choice. It is also a reflection on the belief in abstract moral right—in the Kantian political tradition in which citizens should make moral choices through rational discourse based on abstract principles regardless of practical consequences. The king loses himself, going mad with his people, making his choice based on emotional affiliation, not abstract value. The absurdity of choice is exaggerated by equating collective will with madness and agreeing with mad people as consent. *The Witch of Mopti* both points out and critiques a sphere of moral deliberation. Actors and audience debate, embody, laugh at, and query a set of moral oppositions; these critical engagements are a crucial form of self-fashioning that begins with a staged performance and symbolically extends the performance off stage as actors and audiences circulate debates and jokes.

Abdallah often hints to me that when he wrote the play it was intended as an exaggerated parody of the impossible choices faced by Ghanaian politicians. "In the 1980s when we first did it, some people read this story as being about Jerry [Rawlings] . . . but I don't know." He laughs.

I joke, "Well, if you don't know, who does? You wrote the play!"

He teases back, "Ahh? Just because I wrote it, does that mean I am supposed to know what it is about? You tell me, you're the one who likes theory!"

6 "The Best Tradition Goes On"

Audience, Consumption, and the Structural Transformation of Concert Party Popular Theatre

> You are saying I have grown fat. Thank you.
> It is all because of Key Soap.
> If they sponsor you and you go to America, you also will grow fat.
>   Bishop Bob Okalla, National Theatre *Key Soap Concert Party*

On december 31, 2000, the National Theatre of Ghana witnessed an extraordinary upheaval. A standing-room-only audience filled the fifteen-hundred-seat auditorium to see a concert party popular theatre show. However, angered by a change in the format of the performance, the exuberant audience forcibly prevented the show from beginning, threw tables and chairs onto the stage, sang political protest songs, and even pushed and shoved the police when they arrived. The National Theatre was hosting its annual competition called "Who Is Who" to select the nation's best concert party performers. The organizers had decided to hold the finals competition over two days and, for the first time, separated the dramatic plays from the comedians. When the audience arrived and discovered that the highly popular comedians were not performing until the next day, they were livid.

Concert party troupes since the early twentieth century have been independent, traveling groups performing for mass rural and urban audiences.[1] With the rise of electronic media coinciding with economic and political struggles in the early 1980s, independent concert groups' success waned. In 1995 Unilever Ghana Ltd.[2] revived the genre by sponsoring drama groups to perform under the rubric *Key Soap Concert Party,* providing funding to the financially troubled National Theatre in exchange for linking Unilever's product, Key Soap, to theatre with the slogan "The Best Tradition Goes On." The weekly program held at the National Theatre in downtown Accra was also shown on Ghana Television (GTV) and led to renewed national interest in this eclectic theatre style. But because of Unilever's advertising needs and the demands of televising the shows, the National

Theatre began to transform the content and form of concert party in ways that unsettled fans and artists alike.

Theatrical transformations coincided with a heightened moment of political change, which on New Year's Eve 2000 turned a seemingly minor programming alteration into a flash of public frustration and anger. Jerry John Rawlings had been elected president of the Fourth Republic in 1992 and 1996, though the new constitution forbade his seeking a third term. For many Ghanaians, Rawlings—who had overseen the transformation of the nation from military state to populist revolution to liberal democracy—symbolized the contradictions of the past and uncertainty about the future. A majority seemed to feel that a change of government was long overdue. The day before the 2000 Key Soap Concert Party finals, it was announced that J. A. Kufuor, the New Patriotic Party (NPP) opposition candidate, had defeated Rawlings's current vice president, John Evans Atta Mills, from Rawlings's National Democratic Congress (NDC) in run-off elections for president.[3] The elections symbolized to many Ghanaians a culmination of the promises of liberalization and new possibilities of political freedom and economic prosperity. The nation, however, had never experienced a change of government through elections. Public anxiety grew as no one was sure how Rawlings, a man of notorious temper, would react to his party being voted out of power. Coincidentally, this show also coincided with the anniversary of the December 31, 1981 coup that had brought Rawlings to power. That morning, much to people's surprise and fear, soldiers marched through the streets of Accra commemorating the revolution and fanning rumors that Rawlings would not step down peacefully.

With these political dramas looming, thousands of men, women, and children, dressed in their Sunday best, bought tickets to attend the finals of the "Who Is Who" *Key Soap Concert Party* at the National Theatre. When the extremely popular comedians did not appear, the waiting audience rapidly became agitated. People shouted the rally slogan, "We no go sit down for nobody!" One young man excitedly told me, as he came to the side of the theatre where I stood: "We will not let them trick us! We have come for the comedians!" Perhaps drawing on the politically charged atmosphere in the country, the crowd seemed to revel in its unexpected power to shape the situation. The popularity of television viewing had also reinvented how audiences reacted to being at the theatre; the experience of liveness seemed counter to the normalized technological spectacle of electronic and digital circulation (R. Williams [1974] 1990). I was attending the performance in the company of several performers not on stage that afternoon and was watching this near-riot with one of the judges who had been at the university during the early days of the Rawlings revolution. Watching the students shouting in the aisles, he jokingly said to us that it reminded him of the 1980s calls for "people's power." The young protesters reveled in being heard in the midst of a central state institution like the National Theatre. So even when several of the most popular comedians were quickly called on their mobile phones and appeared at the theatre to perform, the crowd refused to cooperate. This minor programming controversy invoked ideas of rights, freedom, and collective power that the recent elections had awakened. The theatre management, for their part, were outraged at the crowd's "disrespect" for state power. Observing the protests, one National Theatre organizer angrily commented, "They will watch what we show them!" Riot police arrived with a show of force but were reluctant to respond to the crowd's antagonism and escalate the affair. Pushing and shouting at each other on the stage and through the aisles of the auditorium, the crowd and the police hung in an uneasy balance between voiced opinions, contained agitation, and real violence. The confluence of concert party's emphasis on indirection and double voicing, Unilever's disruption of audience expectations, and a national history of unstable political transitions meant that this National Theatre audience was predisposed to expect trickery on stage and off.

This tense moment was defused in a way that told of the increasing intermingling of corporate consumerism and state representation. Audience frustration at *Key Soap Concert Party* organizers appeared in their claims to be consumers who had a right to get what they had paid for. The impromptu leaders of the crowd decided that the only solution was to get their money back. Fearing permanent damage to the theatre, the officials agreed to return the entrance fee to anyone who wanted to leave. At first the crowd seemed pleased with the outcome. Slowly, most of the audience lined up through the halls of the theatre to be refunded their ten-thousand-cedi[4] ticket price and leave. For the National Theatre, however, this was only a minor irritation because several thousand people were waiting outside, ready to refill the auditorium. As the suddenly mute protesters filed out the backstage entrance and slowly dispersed, there was the anticlimactic realization by the spectators that, in achieving their goal of getting their money back, they had negated their cause and vacated their positions as audience members whose tastes and opinions matter. Their places as actors on the national stage were subsumed into their roles as paying consumers. People who had reveled in their brief sense of mass power at a site of state authority walked off anonymously. Individually, they had exchanged their collective participation in the event for cash. What appeared to be a citizen's right to enter the public sphere as part of a collective became a consumer's right to purchase a voice for a limited time. Indeed, value was abstracted, assessable in terms of practices of consumption mediated by a semiprivatized state institution. In the realization of their demands, the crowd vacillated between a national audience voicing demands and consuming individuals, easily discarded and replaced.

From State to Corporate Appropriation of Popular Theatre

This chapter examines how concert party—formerly a bawdy and disreputable theatre genre performed by small, financially independent traveling groups—is reframed as a commercially sponsored, centralized program at the National Theatre in Accra and on state television. Crucial to this move is the marketing of concert party as the embodiment of Ghanaian traditional culture. This process illuminates the significance of institutional and theatre contexts in the midst of an uneven process of privatization for evolving poetics of storytelling theatre. What is presented as an official state celebration of place-based national culture is, in fact, built on a complex intermingling of state and corporate interests in which a locally based affiliate of a major multinational corporation sells soap through the appropriation and reconstitution of what delineates the traditional and the national.

Ideas of traditional culture, codified in the 1960s National Theatre Movement, recirculate as saleable signs of authenticity at the new National Theatre.[5] Efua Sutherland's notion of Anansegro created a theatrical discourse for staging performances. She restructured and "professionalized" concert party theatre to remake it as a sign of traditional culture within the logic of modern staging. Abdallah's Abibigro expanded on this, emphasizing the indeterminate potentials of the storytelling form, particularly in relation to humor and moral dilemmas. Corporate-state entanglements both build on and clash with this evolving poetics of performance reliant upon symbolic appropriation and moral ambiguity. The audience upheaval at the National Theatre is a disagreement about theatrical form, not content. It illustrates one of this book's larger points, that Ghanaian drama foregrounds the formal process of storytelling itself as the subject of performance that leads to ambiguous, open-ended interpretations. The near-riot demonstrates the rising significance of the consumer as preeminent national citizen and the male comedian as individual performance star. At the same time, marketing soap as a domestic product aimed at women genders tradition as feminine. The transformation of concert party is not a straightforward tale of the domination of hypermasculine neoliberal individuation, but instead shows how theatre artists and audiences draw on an established poetics of performance to respond to theatrical changes wrought through a mix of state and corporate interests in their gender and class forms. While some theorists of liberalism argue that the withdrawal of the state represents the triumph of globalization and the inevitable individuation of local worlds, recent ethnographies of neoliberal transformation show the varied effects of how people respond to privatization and marketization (Chalfin 2010; Dent 2009; Greenhouse 2009; Peterson 2010; Piot 2010; Tsing 2004).

The remaking of concert party demonstrates how uneven state privatization produces complex corporate and government entanglements that recall colonial-era debates about the moral good of opening African markets to foreign commodities (cf. Burke 1996). Ironically, marketization draws formerly independent concert party artists known for their entrepreneurial savvy into corporate-state structures as wage laborers. Cole (2001) shows that concert party was driven by an entrepreneurship inspired by the improvisational aspects of Anansesem. Artists characterize their on- and off-stage improvisational talents as using intellect and wit in the face of need, the necessity for poor folks to be savvy in order to survive or as Cole translates it, the ability to "use your gumption" (Cole 2001: 78). Their changing labor conditions compel them to reshape their artistic work, not in relation to audience tastes but rather through the dictates of the state's image of itself and corporate branding needs. Television's electronic remediation also forces artists to restructure performances to emphasize the importance of short, easily broadcast, morally sanctioned individual comedy routines, called *gyimi*, over long, rambling musical dramas (cf. R. Williams [1974] 1990). Concert party has long had a contradictory public image: seen by nonelite audiences as modern and, in contrast, by elites as embarrassingly old-fashioned. In order to remake this genre, Unilever had to make traditional appear as morally positive and modern. As an authentic sign of cultural tradition, concert party is then resignified to ground a specifically Ghanaian modernity in which consuming goods and services underpins membership in an urban public that blurs national sentiment with monetized consumption.

In performances, established styles of indirection, exaggeration, and parodic, double-voiced humor guide performers and audience members as they adopt complex stances in relation to past performance events, political changes, evolving commodity forms, and new technologies of transmission and circulation (Kockelman 2004). As I describe in the introduction, I use poetics to refer to a shared set of evolving principles that dictate how participants create relationships among various registers and adopted stances. Building on an established poetics of staged moral storytelling, actors actively reimagine the valence of their performances in new contexts. The structural transformations of concert party objectify the form of performance itself as indexical of traditional belonging. Performers struggle to define how jokes are told and moral tales are conveyed. In the process, the reflexive aspects of these new performances are recodified, notably in the emergence of the stand-up comedian as the new theatrical star. A storytelling structure authorizes performers and audiences to reimagine their relationships to changing notions of urban public life. Concert party is objectified and reframed as a marker of tradition that, in turn, gives authority to a modern performance space and urban lifestyle. Reflexive debates among artists and audiences contest what constitutes the realm of the cultural itself. Purportedly distinct genres and institutional frames are separated and reentangled as participants use theatrical form to contest or go along with broader political changes.

Large-scale societal transformations are instantiated in the evolving conditions of theatre making and viewing. Actors make unexpected connections among disparate, culturally legitimized signs within performances, as they struggle to adopt and adapt roles prescribed for them.

Theatrical transformations encourage participants to critically reflect on their actions and on communication itself (Bauman and Briggs 1990: 60). The National Theatre, Unilever, and concert party actors struggle over the restructuring of performances. In the process, the performances themselves take on a particularly heightened sense of reflexivity for participants. All social action contains metapragmatic elements—practices and language that point to how social action is framed and made meaningful—through which actors negotiate the terms of intersubjective interaction (Kockelman 2006a). Reflexivity is crucial to performance especially when, under conditions of social change, the organization and interpretation of events themselves are actively contested (Silverstein 1976). In this sense, performances link microlevel events, such as the near-riot at the National Theatre wrought by changes in theatrical staging, to broader macrolevel transformations such as the privatization of the Ghanaian state and the ideological and structural transformations it entails (Agha 2005b: 38).

The Fall of Concert Party

At the end of the 1970s, concert party's popularity rapidly declined. Extended dusk-to-dawn curfews, fuel shortages, and ongoing economic crises curtailed the vibrant nightlife in urban areas and made it difficult for concert groups to reach the countryside. Increasing electrification brought television and recorded music to rural areas, making traveling theatre and its spectacle of lighting, costumes, and musical equipment seem old-fashioned. Demographic shifts that drew populations and economic resources to the urban centers of Accra and Kumasi also contributed to changing tastes, away from the rurally oriented concert shows that reflected on modern life from the perspective of the village looking toward the city.

The proliferation of video technology contributed to the decline of old live touring concert party troupes and live entertainment in general. The first video houses began opening in the late 1970s. As film director and producer Seth Ashong-Kitae recalls, at first they showed imported films, especially kung fu and Indian films, as well as Hollywood productions.[6] Impromptu video units were set up in urban areas and entrepreneurs traveled into the rural areas to show video copies of foreign films. In the mid-1980s, video production technology became widely available in Ghana. Soon local filmmakers began to produce new Ghanaian features cheaply and quickly on video and distribute them throughout the country. They became extremely popular, as Ghanaians were excited to see stories that expressed their own concerns and starred Ghanaian actors. These videos addressed many of the same topical issues as concert party. In Ashong-Kitae's estimation, "the rise of video led to the demise of concert party. Television and video told the same stories of daily life."[7] Early video-films mostly focused on issues of witchcraft and the supernatural, such as *Zinabu* in 1988 by William Akuffo and Richard Quartey and *Diabolo* in 1991 by William Akuffo (Garritano 2013; Meyer 2004b). Special effects to create supernatural creatures, lighting, fake blood, and fight scenes added to the excitement of the new technology of video. The creative new modes of video production and distribution developed by entrepreneurial directors and producers outside state and media institutional control allowed these videos to find large audiences. The rapidity of producing new videos allowed directors to respond rapidly to the specific desires of popular audiences (Garritano 2013). The spectacle of new video technology and the ease and portability of video screening further aided in the decline of concert party.

Rebirth of Concert Party: Advertising, Television, and Formal Change

Concert party at the National Theatre was transformed by the goals of Unilever, the structures of formal theatrical staging, and spatio-temporal constraints of television production and viewing. Unilever and the National Theatre foregrounded and objectified concert party's definitive formal elements such as nonnaturalistic acting, exaggerated makeup, the predominant use of Akan languages, and moral, proverbial storytelling. These features marked performances as authentic and familiar while allowing other corporatizing transformations. Unilever's advertising and branding goals for Key Soap at times coincided with and at times contradicted the National Theatre's desire to inspire Ghanaian theatre forms and foster a theatre-going audience. As one Unilever marketing manager explained to me, popular theatre was a culturally specific way to reach their target market: "The *Concert Party* idea is to look for and attract the consumer by using integrated stage approach[es] in order to achieve total communication with the targeted group.... Culture and tradition become the key operative words. We must look at how the potential user [of Key Soap] lives his or her life, with the major target group being the lower and middle class[es]."[8] The restaged concert party was reflexively framed as a sign of culture and tradition. It became a formal vehicle for specific corporate content aimed at nonelites.

In 1993 National Theatre officials approached Concert Party Union members to help organize a program. Many performers were initially suspicious of working under the auspices of a state institution. According to one artist, they had always operated independently and did not think a centralized state institution was the proper venue for attracting "their type" of audience. However, they needed money and publicity, and so they finally agreed to perform. The first concert party shows at the National Theatre were held at the small, open-air Folk's Place Theatre outside the main auditorium. Despite the presence of some of the more famous actors and highlife musicians, they were not initially popular and the organizers did not think the program would survive.⁹ "Local" working-class and rural people who enjoyed concert party were intimidated by the huge edifice of the National Theatre in downtown Accra. On the other hand, more educated middle-class and elite people often saw themselves as above the bawdiness of concert shows. In fact, many urban dwellers saw concert party as *colo* entertainment; *colo* is a term for something outdated and parochial that recalls the colonial era.

The National Theatre continued to struggle to meet its financial obligations, and, in February 1994, David Dontoh and the National Theatre administration approached Unilever Ghana Ltd.¹⁰ with a proposal to sponsor the concert party program. Unilever decided to sponsor concert party as a marketing vehicle for its all-purpose Key Soap,¹¹ to help revive the product's popularity. As the Unilever marketing executive explained, "Key Soap has become a part of the tradition and culture of Ghana. It is part of the family in this country. . . . So to have a traditional program [like concert party] fits well with the image that consumers [have] of Key Soap."¹²

The relationship between the National Theatre as a state institution and the local affiliates of Unilever as a multinational recalls liberal economic arrangements of early-twentieth-century British colonial economics in which corporations and trading companies focused on creating and exploiting new markets in Africa and Asia. Lever Brothers—later Unilever—first began importing soap to the Gold Coast in the 1920s. After independence in 1957, its local subsidiary initiated the production in Ghana of its popular hygiene products. During the politically turbulent 1980s, production stopped for several years because of economic embargo and foreign exchange problems.¹³ Lintas Ghana Ltd. is a private advertising agency founded through Unilever in 1974 that does the branding and advertising for Unilever and other companies in Ghana.¹⁴ It is a local, "wholly owned affiliate of Lowe Lintas and Partners, an agency with networks in over 100 countries." In Ghana they employ "university graduates and other creative professionals. . . . Half of the employees are Ghanaians from diverse ethnic backgrounds—some who have acquired their skills from outside the country—and half are British and American. Expats with special skills, copy writing, et cetera. . . . are managers, senior managers, directors."¹⁵ Some of their clients include Ghana Social Marketing Foundation (GSMF), Guinness Ghana Ltd., Ghana Textile Print, [and] Mechanical Lloyd.

As a crucial aspect of its marketing program, Unilever made a deal with Ghana Broadcasting Corporation (GBC) to televise the program. This national media exposure quickly popularized the show, and it was moved to the theatre's main auditorium. Many artists who were at first unsure about playing at the theatre became more enthusiastic when they realized the potential prestige and publicity of national television exposure. Audiences began coming to the program partly so that their friends and family would see them on television. Indeed, concert party gained a new air of respectability and crossover appeal, attracting both working-class and more elite audiences. An official publication of the National Theatre celebrated the revival of concert party. "The dying Concert Party Tradition . . . has been revived and transformed into a box office hit and a popular TV program."[16] For Unilever the main goal was to reach as wide an audience as possible. As an official explained, "even though we started with the stage, the real target was . . . the outside audience/consumer whose preference is to be solicited and dramatized using the relevant option of [the] television medium to reach a wider audience."[17]

Structural changes profoundly affected the ethos of the genre. The set designs made clear the new relationship between Unilever and concert party. The shows revolved around a giant bar of yellow Key Soap hanging above the stage with "Key Soap" written on its side, which always appeared prominently in the televised broadcast. The sets varied but they always included Key Soap boxes and logos. Often, performers brandished bars of Key Soap as props or mentioned the product in dialogue. Unilever sales booths were set up in the lobby of the theatre during some performances. In the past, when an older traveling concert party group went on tour through remote villages and urban areas, they would set up an improvised stage and begin performances late in the evening with several hours of music and dancing before the comedic and dramatic performances would begin. The shows were raucous, carnivalesque events involving much music and improvisation, often running into the early-morning hours. Interaction between actors and audiences was common. Audience members would respond directly to actors, repeating and commenting on the staged dialogue, transforming it into improvised asides with other audience members (Barber 2000: 228). Television formatting and formal theatre staging, however, demanded rigid timing, scriptedness and scheduling and formal separation of audiences and performers.

The National Theatre's raised proscenium stage and its fixed-row seating—as well as the constraints of performing for TV cameras—limited actors' improvisation and audience interaction as viewers remained at a distance from the action. In order to foster a respectable family atmosphere, *Key Soap Concert Party* at the National Theatre began promptly at 2:00 p.m. on alternate Sundays, attracting patrons after church. In the new format at the National Theatre, music, drama, and comedy were highly regimented and separated from each other. Formerly each group toured on its own. Group leaders were entrepreneurs and artistic directors, organizing all aspects of the show from marketing to ticket sales to staging to music. The National Theatre program marginalized these theatre impresarios. It was organized as a competition between groups, highly structured by corporate organizers.

Older artists complained that the dramas were not musical enough and were too oriented toward dialogue. A house band accompanied dramas; without rehearsing together it was difficult to integrate the music into the narrative. Programs opened with a quick song; then a comedian would perform for fifteen minutes; and finally, the dramatic sketch, strictly limited to forty-five minutes, was shown. These restrictions allowed for the shows to be easily edited into one-hour televisable segments. The National Theatre organized the live performance and GBC shot the program at the National Theatre. However, Unilever and Lintas Ghana Ltd. maintained direct control over every facet, editing the raw footage, adding the appropriate Key Soap advertisements, and delivering the tapes to GBC for transmission. In cutting the footage for television, a Lintas production assistant explained, Unilever "edits out nonrelevant portions of scenes that are not in the story itself. Bad language not good for TV viewership and children is also taken out. Everything that directly goes to enhance the image of the program and focuses on [Key Soap is included]."[18] Content was no longer controlled solely by group leaders and performers. In the past, group leaders had operated as theatrical entrepreneurs, orchestrating performances in direct response to the interests and desires of their audiences in order to elicit the biggest laughs and attract audiences. As old-time performer Bob Vanns explained to me, to that end they had "tried to exaggerate things as much as possible and push the boundaries of acceptability."[19] In contrast, at the National Theatre, artists were given a wage to produce and deliver a controlled product, packaged and circulated by corporate media workers.

A number of experienced concert party artists and those trained in the National Theatre Movement tradition were hired by the National Theatre to transform the concert party groups' content and staging techniques for the needs of the televised program. Willie Addo, trained at the School of Performing Arts, was in charge of organizing concert party groups. Ama Boabeng, an original member of Sutherland's Kusum Agromma group and Leroy-Morisseau's Workers' Brigade Concert Party and a highly respected actress, ran the costume shop and helped with acting technique, advising untrained performers on how to adapt their movements to the huge National Theatre stage (Sutherland-Addy 2002). Ice Water, a concert party group leader, was one of the few active performers on salary at the theatre and acted as master of ceremonies for the weekly programs. As a respected member of the Concert Party Union, he mediated between the institution of the theatre and the performers.

Concert party as a television show was an immediate success, particularly with female viewers. For television audiences across the country, GBC and the National Theatre were supporting a traditional art form in the name of national culture and African tradition. With some definite exceptions—especially soap operas from South Africa, the United States, and Latin America such as *Egoli*,

Sunset Beach, The Bold and the Beautiful, and *Esmerelda*—Ghanaian viewers tended to favor local television programs such as the weekly *Cantata* and videofilms by Ghanaian and Nigerian directors, which they felt were more directly relevant to their lives (J. Shipley 2013b). Many were surprised at concert party's renewed popularity considering the rising availability of more "modern" television and video. As a popular entertainment newspaper columnist reflected, "I thought it was one of those stage performances that could never be popularized and was meant for the rural folk."[20] *Key Soap Concert Party* was local programming that appealed to viewers across class and gender divisions, linking national cultural identifications to Key Soap's advertising agenda.

Corporate Takeover

As *Key Soap Concert Party* became more popular, Concert Party Union members grew increasingly resentful about the arrangement between the National Theatre and Unilever. The union met every other Tuesday at Accra's Arts Centre; while there were several hundred members, about fifty people usually attended meetings. David Dontoh was president, and most senior members were old stars whose popularity had peaked many years before. Some lived in run-down housing in back of the Arts Centre. Others, like retired star comedian and troupe leader Y. B. Bampoe, aka Opiah, came to meetings from as far away as Nsawam, several hours on public transportation. Artists who worked directly for the National Theatre, like Ice Water, remained union members. Over a period of months, union members were increasingly frustrated that the National Theatre and Unilever had negotiated financial contracts without artists' input. Unilever paid the theatre for all aspects of the program, including artists' fees, prizes, television and theatre support crews, and plant maintenance; the theatre administered the program and handled the performers. Performers were concerned about outside corporate control. As one older union member said, they were not told anything and then "all of a sudden the program had become *Key Soap Concert Party.*" He continued, "Gradually as the sponsorship package grew, the role of Key Soap also grew along with it, and wormed its way into all [our] activities. Gradually Key Soap became an inseparable element of the concert party."[21]

Unilever not only wanted their brand associated with the program, they wanted Key Soap to become integrated into every facet of it. While it was not mandatory for performers to discuss the benefits of Key Soap as part of their routines, doing so would get the artists "in the good books" of the sponsors, making it more likely that they would be hired for other Unilever programs. Some artists continued to perform but refused to mention Key Soap. Others stopped participating in the program rather than compromise their artistic integrity and financial independence. One prominent performer expressed to me his frustration at corporate control of their work: "We cannot see ourselves writing plays to perform and mention Key Soap in it just because [we] were told to do so. They [Unilever] should not tell me to incorporate something in my drama or they won't put me on stage.... Once [concert party] gets commercialized to the point where they [Unilever] dictate what must be put on stage then it ceases to be art. It becomes just an appendage of the corporate entity."[22]

In contrast to experienced performers, newer, unknown groups were eager to gain recognition by being on television and were willing to perform for less money and advertise for Key Soap. The National Theatre and Unilever made a point of promoting these artists in order to minimize the effect of the growing conflict between the more established performers and the program. For example, a local newspaper promoted *Key Soap Concert Party* by quoting an artist who "expressed gratitude to the management of the Theatre and Lever Brothers for making it possible for some of them to put their God-given talents to economic use."[23]

In early 1997, tensions came to a head when the Concert Party Union realized that they were getting less than 20 percent of Unilever's sponsorship money that was given to the National Theatre. Performers were paid per performance, had no financial guarantee, and were pitted against each other to compete for paying gigs. Many artists were not shy in confronting Theatre officials and telling the press that their talents were being exploited for corporate and state interests. From the perspective of the Concert Party Union, the program was meant to revive the concert party art form and financially support the artists, not sell soap. The National Theatre was caught between their reliance on Unilever funding and the interests of the artists. The theatre's long-term goal was in promoting local art forms in attracting and sustaining theatre audiences. Its representatives argued that the theatre was barely surviving, production expenses were high, they were working in the long-term interests of the artists, and they could not afford to pay the artists more.

The Concert Party Union felt they were being exploited and decided to boycott the program. This conflict jeopardized *Key Soap Concert Party*'s image since the show's success depended on the time-honored authenticity of its established artists. The Theatre decided to re-create the image of tradition and authenticity by persuading several well-known performers to create the Efiritete Concert Party group—*efiritete* roughly translates as "in keeping with tradition"—to advertise Key Soap.[24] Also, in the absence of most popular performers, the National Theatre began to promote younger artists and restructure the program. As new performers and groups gained national recognition through television, Unilever and the National Theatre began to use them for other advertising purposes, taking them on the road to perform "Theatre for Development" programs in rural communities.

Since the early part of the twentieth century, British colonial authorities and missionaries, as well as corporations, had used traveling theatre and film units as educative tools for reaching mass audiences (Gibbs 2009; Larkin 2008). Under Unilever's Direct Consumer Contact (DCC) program, drama groups, comedians, and musicians from the National Theatre now toured the country promoting products to potential consumers. Efiritete Concert Party in particular performed in Akan-speaking areas, while other groups were hired to perform in other local languages, including Ewe, Ga, and Hausa, throughout the country. These performances took into account linguistic and cultural differences in their marketing strategies. The National Theatre, in conjunction with the traveling groups, created plays revolving around Unilever hygiene and food products, which were advertised under the rubric of rural education programs. Unilever's approach to civic education through popular theatre drew on concert party's relationship to African proverbs and morality tales. Drama was used, according to one artist, "to educate the people on the use of select Lever products. . . . Through drama [we] educate people on how to use Pepsodent [toothpaste], Key Soap, and Blue Band [margarine] and what they can do for you." One play performed around the country in the late 1990s, for example, told the story of a child's aunt who was accused of witchcraft because the boy was rapidly losing weight. When the child ate Blue Band margarine and regained his health, they realized that the problem was not witchcraft but rather poor diet. Unilever organizers saw this play as doubly educational in that it explained both the nutritional benefits of Blue Band and the "unreality" and negative effects of believing in witchcraft.

During these performances, vans covered in colorful paintings of Unilever images and filled with Close-Up and Pepsodent toothpaste, Key Soap, Royco bouillon cubes, Blue Band margarine, and a host of other products accompanied performances to sell their products to village women. In order to encourage initial purchases, these vans sold items for cheaper than they would normally sell in the market. Even though the prices were still high for people living in rural areas, the spectacle of urban, cosmopolitan performers recognizable from television helped convince them of the desirability of buying these commodities for maintenance of proper "modern" domestic practices, and the vans were mobbed by people after shows.

While the National Theatre, out of financial necessity, was beholden to its corporate patronage, concert party artists became de facto corporate employees who could perform only through Unilever's institutional legitimation. With growing public recognition of new performers, the Concert Party Union was left without any bargaining power. Unilever and the National Theatre had gained institutional control over the genre, its particularities, and its social valences. In the past, "concert party" had referred to a loose musical and theatrical performance genre or specific performance groups within it. By the late 1990s, for most people it referred to the National Theatre program. Some performers recognized that *Key Soap Concert Party* had become synonymous with the genre and eventually returned to the National Theatre out of economic necessity.²⁵ The Concert Party Union and various groups tried to start new programs and tours without much success. Many artists were left with no financial or structural means of mounting performances. Others turned to making low-budget Twi-language video-films.

Producing and Contesting Authority

Key Soap Concert Party struggled to recontextualize concert performances as nostalgic markers of the local and the traditional within the modernized spaces of the National Theatre and electronic circulations of television broadcasts. Unilever's marketing campaign produced links between traditional domestic spaces, performance, and their product, Key Soap. In this logic, women were both consumers of soap and controllers of domestic economies. Whereas traveling concert party had often been about explicit sexuality and pleasure, the new concert party emphasized control and moral ordering of male and female bodies. By remaking tradition as being about domestic familial order and the control of hygiene and female sexuality, this program lent authenticity to both the soap and the new theatre, but also led to unanticipated conflicts over the meaning of tradition and control over performances. Structural transformations were intended to predispose actors to link performances to specific older forms of cultural legitimacy in which signs were validated through association with established contexts of origin and authorization. Performers reference the authority of rural concert party and storytelling to make new referential connections between soap and potential consumers in the guise of an urban nationalistic project. Through changes in concert party, Unilever attempted to regulate the moral boundaries of what constituted tradition, particularly in relation to issues of sexuality and hygiene, to sanitize culture for use in product branding.

For Unilever, sponsoring a local genre provided the company the image of a benevolent, responsible institution. In a newspaper interview, one executive stated that the "company was proud to be intimately associated with the Key Soap Concert Party programme which aimed to encourage the revival of the nation's indigenous art forms."²⁶ Initially Key Soap's tagline was "The Tradition Goes On." The rationale for this, as a Unilever marketing manager told me, was to differentiate "Key Soap . . . from the other competing products in the market. One distinguishing feature of Key Soap is . . . it has served the needs of their grandparents. It has been passed on to their mothers. And now they are currently using it."²⁷ However, after several widely publicized controversies in which Christian organizations criticized traditional African religious institutions, Unilever realized that "tradition" in local discourse could have both positive and negative connotations. Marketing executives were anxious not to be associated with what many elite Christian and Muslim Ghanaians saw as the detrimental and outdated aspects of "tradition" such as witchcraft and the supernatural. Along these lines, the tagline was changed to "The *Best* Tradition Goes On" to indicate that Key Soap is traditional but only in the positive, nostalgic sense of the term.

Indeed, Unilever also did not want Key Soap to appear old-fashioned and stodgy. Corporate officials realized that the authenticity gained from its association with concert party could also attract its colo image of rural poverty and backwardness. The program was therefore reshaped in terms of what National Theatre and Unilever officials saw as the changing demands of current audiences. An executive at Unilever explained, "Key Soap is perceived to be a traditional soap. . . . It is good to be traditional, but if we want to secure the groove of Key Soap [in the market] then we will have to contemporize it; make it such that the younger generation will not see it as something for the older generation, but something that they can associate themselves with."[28]

In line with this vision, Unilever and the National Theatre began regulating the topics presented in the performances. Old concert performances had often focused on ethnic and religious humor, supernatural themes involving witchcraft and "fetish" priests, and free sexuality and "loose" women. They had created extravagant routines with characters in outlandish costumes representing spiritual creatures like *sasabosom* (forest devil), snake demons, and ghosts. The organizers of *Key Soap Concert Party* tried to limit the groups' use of fantastical, profane, or sexual routines as well as of ethnic and religious stereotypes. The National Theatre and Unilever wanted to promote what would be seen as a more generic, Christian, family atmosphere. As one official at the National Theatre said, they discouraged the idea that the spiritual world was to blame for "real-world" concerns by not showing these phenomena. They also shied away from addressing issues relating to Islam because, while southern Ghana is mostly Christian, they were afraid of provoking conflicts between Christians and Muslims from the north of the country. An official at Unilever explained that they did not want the performances to "bring people against the concert party or the brand. As much as possible we want to maintain a neutral position."[29] Theatre and corporate officials were most concern with sustained popularity and were anxious to maintain a morally respectable image, which they saw as most likely to attract sustained audience interest.

Beginning with the 2000 season, the National Theatre and Unilever began prescribing specific topical themes for performances, such as teenage pregnancy, AIDS education, sanitation, and the importance of peaceful elections, which they considered relevant to contemporary life, educational, and uncontroversial. Unilever and their creative consultants picked program themes and theatre officials explained them to the groups, who created performances around these messages. Before a performance, groups rehearsed several times with National Theatre personnel to introduce "professional" production standards, theme, narrative structure, profanity, appropriateness, and time limit. Performances were formally regulated to provide "neutral," morally positive, socially relevant entertainment. For example, since 2000 was an election year, Unilever proclaimed that they wanted to "preach a message of peace" through the performances. Implied in this was that groups should present positive moral messages, promoting "good citizenship" and "proper behavior." The winning drama group in the "Who Is Who" competition for 2000 was the Adikanfo Concert Party troupe, which performed a play titled *Oman Ba Pa* (Good citizen or Child of the nation) that described a boy who was a responsible person in his hometown and in the end benefited from his good deeds. These plays continued concert party's tradition of storytelling in which characters are faced with moral choices. But as old comedian and Concert Party Union leader Y. B. Bampoe lamented during a union meeting, "we were cleaned up . . . and changed so that we don't even recognize what the new groups are doing as concert."[30]

Double Voicing

Obvious attempts to regulate performances and to create simplistic moral messages left audiences complaining that the old concert party had been more dynamic, exciting, and relevant to their lives, whereas the *Key Soap Concert Party* was obviously controlled and predictable. Audiences at rural concert party performances had responded to moral choices faced by characters with laughter, with direct responses to characters on stage and by repeating and circulating key phrases among themselves (cf. Barber 2000: 209–20). While this continued to some extent at the National Theatre, organizers tried their best to regulate shows and prevent unexpected interactions. As I overheard one audience member comment during a performance, "They want us to just sit back and consume! But we want to enjoy." When I asked him what he meant, he replied that to "enjoy" the show he needed to be "a part of it . . . joke, talk, and have fun with the characters." Watching necessitated an active form of participation for popular audiences, which the Key Soap organizers wanted to control in terms of content and spatio-temporal formatting.

While being televised and being associated with the National Theatre brought a sense of respectability and renewed popularity to concert party, for many viewers it did not engender the excitement of the older performances. In this light, the National Theatre began to focus on competition between different groups and comedians to garner interest. The competitive "Who Is Who" series was held annually to pick the best drama group and individual comedian. At each performance, several judges—academics, artists, or well-known public figures—compared the various drama groups and comedians, basing their assessments on a set of criteria, including how well the group followed the suggested themes and whether they stayed within prescribed time limits. For the 2000 *Key Soap Concert Party* finals the criteria were theme (five points), humor (five points), clarity of language (three points), relevance of songs (five points), costume (two points), and time (five points). For the comedians, exceeding fifteen minutes resulted in losing points, while the drama groups were penalized for exceeding forty-five minutes.[31]

Artists' flat fees were supplemented, with winners receiving monetary awards and opportunities to perform around the country and abroad. One older artist quipped that concert party was once again "a competitive business. . . . The popularity that comes from being a champion means that any time Lever needs a performance [launching new products] they call you."[32] In this sense, the commodification of concert party provided an institutionally mediated, performative spectacle of competition.

The assessment of performances was based on institutional prescription rather than audience input, which led to frequent conflict. Audiences at the National Theatre often vehemently expressed their disagreement with the judges' decisions. There were frequent accusations of unfair and biased judging in favor of groups supported by the National Theatre. For example, an older concert group based in the city of Kumasi came to perform in the 1999 "Who Is Who" competition. Their style was reminiscent of the older touring troupes, and the crowd shouted with delight as their performance began. They opened with three minstrel-like performers singing and dancing, recalling the style of the preindependence trios. The narrative of their play included many digressions and old highlife songs and did not focus on educational social issues as Unilever had suggested. Because of these digressions, the loose narrative structure of their play, and the fact that their performance went over the time limit, they received a low score and were eliminated from the competition. The crowd, however, had loudly proclaimed their support for them, and at the end of the night the audience shouted in protest at the judging as they filed out of the auditorium in disappointment.

The rise of evangelical churches in Ghana reinvigorated the moral aspects of storytelling tradition in *Key Soap Concert Party*'s transformations. Several popular Pentecostal churches—most prominently Kristo Asofo and Christ for All Mission—sponsored concert groups initially for the publicity offered through television. The increasing prominence of the comedic sketches—fostered, in particular, by the popularity of two comedians, Nkomode and Bishop Bob Okalla—was instrumental in shifting the focus of the genre from the older style of musically oriented, eclectic theatrical plays toward easily segmented, marketed, and televised individual comedic gyimi performances (Donkor 2013).

As evidenced by Okalla's use of "Bishop" in his stage name, the role of comedians as individual performers also refracted the rise of evangelical preachers as national public figures. Ghana Boy, a young comedic protégé of Okalla, explicitly described the affinity between comedians' routines and pastors' sermons, explaining to me that his comedy taught moral lessons to his audience, though often through risqué tales. In one routine, he described a young man who loved to smoke marijuana and have sex. One day, he locked himself in his room to smoke and, unfortunately, his house caught fire. He tried to call for help but, because he was high, he was misunderstood and burned to death. While the explicit moral lesson was that if you do drugs and are promiscuous you will "pay the price," the humorous manner in which this tragedy was described evoked huge cheers from the youthful audience and showed the contradictions between official moral prescription and lived daily life. In performance, the comedian adopts the stylistic bodily cues and linguistic rhythms of a pastor, telling a moral tale and then leading his audience to weigh various ways of interpreting it. This figure resonates with Ananse, playing all angles of an issue and leaving audiences wondering what the intended relationship is between a direct message and its critiques.

Indeed, despite the institutional regulations, stage performances were not always oriented in terms of the wishes of the corporate sponsors. Throughout its development, concert party has been characterized by subversive aesthetic sensibilities, often proclaiming particular ideas while simultaneously making fun of them, thus opening space for reframing social and political contradictions (Cole 2001). In one play performed in 2000 on the theme of the mistreatment of young girls, a girl forced into prostitution used the phrase "Wo ntumi ntake" (literally, "You are unable to tackle"; idiomatically, "You cannot beat me") in reference to her ability to elude having sex with a man. The phrase was a frequently used call slogan from Peace FM, a new radio station that went on-air in 1999, significantly as the first private station primarily using Twi and other local-language programming. Its use here is an example of the value placed on the ability to make quick and elegant double-voiced references in Ghanaian public oratory and performance more generally (Kwesi Yankah 1995). The saying became widely used in conversation as a humorous reference to myriad things. In the context of this play its invocation was met with audience recognition at the clever insertion of the phrase as an affirmation of the independence and strength of the young girl and her ability to control her sexuality as well as a sign of her skill as a social observer and of her ability to outwit the man chasing her.

Performers would sometimes advertise for Key Soap or address the social themes prescribed by Unilever, but the effect was often ironic and even contradictory to the purposes of Unilever. For example, Bishop Bob Okalla, a favorite comedian of Unilever who often included advertisements in his comedic routines, began his performance at the 1999 "Who Is Who" finals by praising Key Soap as he mounted the stage amid wild applause and addressed the audience, "Thank you! You have done well. You are saying I have grown fat." Okalla, an unusually tall and spindly man, spun around, revealing that his tattered costume trousers were stuffed with pillows, making his buttocks protrude in an exaggerated, comic fashion. The crowd burst into laughter as he proclaimed, "Thank you. It is all because of Key Soap. If they sponsor you and you go to America, you also will grow fat."[33] His vocal delivery, with rasping voice and curled lip, makes audiences reflexively question the sincerity of his endorsement. While promoting the product of the sponsors, this skit also highlighted the ironies of the consumption of commodities and the forms of personhood they entail. On the surface, these products appeared to be associated with wealth, foreignness, and modernity. However, the ironic juxtaposition of travel and success with the obvious illusion of fatness and the ragged clothing revealed the promises of Key Soap as contradictory at best, showing the illusion of corporate benevolence. Innovation appears in how actors configure their words and deeds in relation to previous instantiations of their social use (Silverstein 2005). Concert party performers improvised, juggling complex, often contradictory meanings of signs. Comedians like Bob Okalla and Ghana Boy imparted parodic value by pointing to the double-voiced aspects of their routines: on one level the words promote Key Soap, but the delivery and bodily presentation renders them self-critical.

In this sense, despite the structural transformations of concert party, performers and audiences did not always play their ascribed roles. Signs operate by compelling participants to make connections between disparate registers, stances, and emotions; a sign causes "something else, its interpretant, to stand in the same relation to the sign's object as the sign does" (Lee 1997: 117). Actors creatively manipulated new contexts, taking parodic, playful stances, while the National Theatre tried to regulate all possible digressions from the program. Comedic routines were double voiced, operating on several levels simultaneously to both reinforce the literal message of the program and simultaneously complicate and undermine it. Creative improvisation, then, provides a new poetic alignment, drawing together multiple registers in new alignments made into repeatable patterns of reference. Actors acknowledge and inhabit established regimes of power and registers of meaning in order to establish new referential strategies. Relying on established patterns of double voicing allowed artists and audiences to critically engage *Key Soap Concert Party* from within.

Audiences appreciate performers' creative references and improvisation, but rather than being assessed as pure invention, they tend to be understood in terms of how fluently artists realign semiotic registers in unexpected ways. As Richard Bauman and Charles Briggs point out, recontextualizing a sign or text is "an act of control, and in regard to the differential exercise of such control the issue of social power arises" (Bauman and Briggs 1990: 76). Performers indexically position themselves as authoritative by intermingling signs and practices from an array of different registers. In actively shaping how signs within a particular event make references, an actor establishes "an authoritative voice . . . which is grounded at least in part in the knowledge, ability, and right to control the re-centering of valued texts" (Bauman and Briggs 1990: 77). What is striking in the Ghanaian case is how performers recontextualize signs for new purposes. Actors remake the enduring structures of interpretation within which they are embedded (Eisenlohr 2006; Keane 1997). They manipulate established definitions of traditional, popular, and modern genres to position themselves as knowledgeable.

Audience: Theatre and Television Reception

Concert party's organization, timing, and narrative structure were reshaped to suit the needs of the proscenium stage and remediation on television (R. Williams [1974] 1990). Audience members were imagined as consumers under the rubric of a national citizenry, though they were hierarchically ordered by class taste and differing access to spaces of leisure. The opposition between inclusion and exclusion structured concert party's viewing practices. At the National Theatre and on television, audiences were oriented toward uniform patterns of consumption while simultaneously reproducing class, ethnic, and urban-rural distinctions (Bourdieu 1984). Television versus theatre viewing of concert party contrasted oppositional practices of spatial organization and technological mediation that ordered marginality and class differences as forms of viewership.[34] National audiences understood themselves increasingly in relation to spatially dispersed, electronically mediated forms of collectivity. With privatization, corporate electronic media stand in for the state, becoming powerful "homogenizing agents" (cf. Guss 2000: 92). For *Key Soap Concert Party*, television was crucial to the circulation and recontextualization of symbols and practices that produced a dispersed public. Theatre images were circulated and consumed in context-specific ways, indexing centralized imaginaries to link dispersed viewers (Spitulnik 1996). In this instance, the co-presence of theatre audiences and the dispersal of television audiences operated in conjunction to reinforce class and ethnic inequalities, while simultaneously inculcating rising notions of individuated consumption.

The National Theatre: Centralized Viewing

For less educated, working-class audiences, concert party was a "way in" to the modern space of the National Theatre in downtown Accra as they associated practices of consumption—of theatre and hygiene products—with an elite "modern" urban public; though their continued displacement from the center effectively reinforced their desire for "modernity" and its practices of leisure and consumption. In this sense, the continued displacement of nonelites incorporated them into the ideologies of consumption and class-based desire that structured their marginality. For elites, traditional entertainment—with the negative moral associations of backward traditions and rural, uneducated life it held for them—is made into something accessible and vaguely respectable through association with "modern" institutions and consumption practices. They were drawn in through ongoing ambivalence to ideas of Ghanaian culture.

Concert Party audiences consisted mostly of young working-class people from poor areas around Accra, though an increasing number of middle-class and educated elites patronized the program and watched it on television. For working-class Ghanaians from Accra, as well as those who traveled from rural areas to attend the program, *Key Soap Concert Party* was an event through which patrons could enjoy the spectacle of what they saw as modernity. Many Accra patrons came from poor areas in the capital like Nima and Jamestown, as well as outlying neighborhoods such as Adenta and Teshie-Nungua. Younger, working-class Ghanaians, dressed in the latest urban fashions, enjoyed the spectacle of *Concert Party* as a special social event. For them, going to the National Theatre was an occasion to see and be seen, to enjoy the monumental spaces of the theatre filled with modern African artworks, to relax and appreciate Sunday afternoon as a time for (bourgeois) leisure. Some people traveled from as far away as the city of Cape Coast to attend performances. Others who came to Accra for work or on short visits made a point of going to *Key Soap Concert Party*.

Yaw is a driver in his thirties from the central city of Kumasi and representative of many audience members for whom the trip to the National Theatre was a special event meant to confirm a preexisting idea of what the National Theatre represented about the modernity of Accra.[35] After watching a performance of theatre groups with several friends, he explained to me that he had always loved watching *Concert Party* on television, so when he visited Accra he made sure to come to the National Theatre to see it for himself. Attending a show was live confirmation of the televised, electronically mediated event that he normally encountered at home or in any restaurant, bar, or compound house he might be in. "Normally, I watch *Concert Party* whenever it is on," he explained. "Wherever you are in Ghana you know you can see it at the same time after church. . . . It is relaxing and makes me laugh and reminds me of the old days. I am glad they have brought it back." His nostalgia for the past heyday of concert party aligns leisure time and remembrances of an idealized, simpler time. It links the current show with fond memories, accomplishing one of the primary tasks of marketing, branding, and product placement, which is to get consumers to emotionally identify with their product through an indexical ground. Concert party bridges the gap between past and present in this man's memory. The confirmation that one can watch the show anywhere in Ghana and find the familiar jokes, routines, music, and styles provides indexical links between cultural familiarity and comfort, electronic mediation. The fact that performances are primarily in Twi is important in that native speakers found the use of their language as a de facto lingua franca a sign of comforting familiarity, whereas nonnative speakers sometimes saw it as a sign of Asante cultural domination.

An Ewe girl of thirteen came to Accra from a small village in the Volta Region to work during school vacation. She spoke only a little English and Akan. However, she came to the National Theatre with her older sister, a seamstress who lived in Accra and had been to the program before. For her, the event was exciting, if a bit overwhelming; she was not particularly interested in the specific performances and said that she did not understand most of what was going on. But the sense of the whole event—people wearing fancy dresses; the impressive spaces of downtown Accra and the National Theatre building, which she had only seen on television; the spectacle of cameras, lights, costumes, and music on stage—impressed her. "I really love this place and want to come back as much as I can," she explained.

While some poor Ghanaians who patronized *Key Soap Concert Party* enjoyed it as a spectacle of modern urban life, for many the National Theatre represented an elite place where they were not welcome, not only because of the price of tickets but because, as a social institution, it was alien to them. Especially during popular performances, large groups of children and teenagers, as well as traders and workers, who could not afford to pay the entrance fees created carnivalesque unintended spaces of sociality outside the theatre. They were intimidated and could not "read" the modern theatre space or move through it in socially appropriate ways, even though concert party was supposedly "the people's" form of entertainment. The National Theatre came to represent urbanity, cosmopolitanness, and modernity. Thus, the act of being excluded from it produced resentment and frustration as well as a desire for access to the symbols and practices of "successful modernity." In this sense, the politics of exclusion operated to reinforce marginal class-based identities and their existence in relationship to markers of elite positions. This is one way in which hierarchical forms of personhood associated with the neoliberal state were reinforced.

In contrast, for elite patrons *Key Soap Concert Party* invoked a sense of familiarity and nostalgia for the rural past. But in the urban, modern context of the National Theatre, middle-class Ghanaians could, at the same time, distance themselves from what were seen as bawdy, old-fashioned lifestyles by defining these practices within a bounded, reified notion of "traditional, folk culture." In this sense, traditional culture became something to be circumscribed and viewed as a performance, a spectacle of a past world, no longer something to be lived but rather nostalgically remembered. To add prestige to the high-profile programs around Christmas and New Year's, popular public figures were invited and given seats in the front of the auditorium. Increasingly, middle-class and elite families and couples began attending, dressed in more conservative Western clothes or contemporary African fashions, Nigerian lace *agbadas,* and wax print cloth designs. They experienced the National Theatre as a site for leisure viewing, a practice associated with urban, "modern" elite life. In this sense, the theatre is a place where audiences perform national and class identifications (Kruger 1992).

The audiences were central to concert party performances, both for the live spectacle as well as for its being televised, but not necessarily in the participatory fashion of the more interactive traveling troupes. Being in the audience at the National Theatre was more about being seen reacting rather than actively engaging with fellow audience members or performers. Many viewers came to the show so that people would see them on television when the program was broadcast. It was a chance for local people to perform unfamiliar bourgeois practices, which were marked as elite, to enact modern forms of personhood and be made visible in the eyes of the modern media apparatus. For working-class and upwardly mobile Ghanaians, then, this visibility was a sign of entry into modern urban life, a way of being recognized, made visible in the eyes of the media apparatus, and thus affirmed as participating in the practices of an urban public.

In the performances at the National Theatre, actors and audience members were rigidly regulated spatially and temporally. As I have described, the performers stuck closely to rehearsed, carefully timed performances. Fixed auditorium seating regulated audience interactions, distancing performers from viewers. The landscape of the auditorium discouraged, but did not eliminate, interactions between audiences and performers as well as action in the audience such as singing and dancing. In contrast, older traveling shows were characterized by improvisation and digression. These troupes set up impromptu stages and scenery in compound houses, open courtyards, or community buildings and involved more explicit audience participation. The performances were continually reshaped by audience input and the specificities of each new venue and audience. Audience members enjoyed these shows as festival-like events focused on dancing and music. As one old-timer told me, part of the fun of the old concert party was leaving to get a drink, coming back, and asking some people on a bench near you what had happened. *Key Soap Concert Party*, in contrast, tried to produce a generic, consumer-oriented time-space.

As one of the *Concert Party* organizers pointed out to me one afternoon as we watched a rehearsal in the empty auditorium, promoting concert party at the National Theatre involved two contradictory tasks: on the one hand, encouraging elite audiences to be interested in local programs, which they had often seen as beneath them; and, on the other hand, educating working-class audiences in proper bourgeois viewing practices and the uses of centralized, institutional spaces.[36] *Key Soap Concert Party* brought these elite and working-class audiences together while simultaneously reinforcing their differences. Indeed, these various audiences used concert party to enact their differing ideas of what it meant to be modern in the context of the contemporary Ghanaian state and the global free market. As I noted earlier, most working-class Ghanaians saw formal theatre as a privilege of elites and expatriates. "Concert," on the other hand, was familiar to them. *Key Soap Concert Party* shaped working-class audiences into a theatre-going public that identified itself within undifferentiated bourgeois spaces such as the National Theatre. By "modernizing" concert party and bringing it to the central location of the National Theatre, its sponsors made it a venue that allowed marginalized people to imagine themselves as "modern." Conversely, by creating concert party as a "traditional" form within "modern" institutions, elites were able to appreciate it nostalgically as part of their "folk" heritage, thus seeing themselves as modern in opposition. Elite audiences, who disparaged concert party performances as old-fashioned but enjoyed "modern," more explicitly Western forms of entertainment, patronized the program as it gained prestige through its association with the institutional authority of television, Unilever, and the National Theatre. The practices of commodification—of theatrical entertainment as well as hygiene products—subsumed these various national audiences within liberal ideas of consumption and the role of individuals within a homogeneous national public.

Television: Authoritative Technologies and Dispersed Viewing

In a general sense, television viewing by marginalized people both within Accra and in more geographically remote locations throughout the country reinforced a tense affiliation with centralized spaces and simultaneous exclusion from them. More specifically, the process reinforced desires for imagined symbolic centers—in this case the National Theatre and the consumption of specific leisure entertainment and Unilever products—while emphasizing most viewers' continual exclusion/displacement from these centers. The fact that concert party was a genre with which people identified so closely meant that its movement from rural performances to the National Theatre brought marginalized people into contact with individuated practices of "national" viewership and consumption. In the contradictory recognition of their identification with, but distance from, an imaginary national center, television viewers of *Key Soap Concert Party* were reinforced as marginalized subjects while simultaneously being incorporated into the diffuse structures of the decentralized neoliberal state and its concomitant ideology of individuated consumption.

The television cameras took an active, participatory role in defining *Key Soap Concert Party*'s modern image. The GBC camera crew used three cameras: one set up for the establishing shot in the back of the auditorium, one in the audience just below stage left, and one actually on the stage, downstage right. The conspicuous presence of the camera and cameraman on the stage emphasized the whole event as a continuous performance in which the line between who was performing and who was observing was blurred. As this implies, the role of the audience as part of the spectacle was crucial to the live performance and its television broadcast. The presence of the audience itself, then, became a crucial part of the television broadcast. During performances the cameras often panned the audience, and in the tape editing, audience reactions to the show were cut with reverse shots of the action on stage. In this way, the live audience reactions became a crucial part of the performance as experienced by the television viewer.

A comedic performance in 2000, televised just before the presidential elections, provides an example of how audiences identify themselves through feelings of exclusion provoked by dispersed viewing. It also shows how performers creatively voice complex sets of references to balance the moral regulations of the theatre with the desire to excite and surprise the audience. To begin his routine, a comedian danced adowa, an Asante funeral dance that is familiar to all Ghanaians. However, as a part of the subtle hand gestures of this "traditional" dance he included a downward thumb motion that in recent months had come to symbolize the campaign slogan "Asee Ho," for opposition NPP presidential candidate J. A. Kufuor, who was himself an Asante (as opposed to outgoing President Rawlings, whose mother was Ewe and father was Scottish). "Asee Ho" translated literally as "down there." It referred to the fact that Kufuor's name appeared at the bottom of the voting ballot and called for voters to mark the box "down there" to vote him into power. It also took on obscene, and humorous, sexual connotations. This phrase and its associated gesture were used frequently in public spaces by youth to make sexual innuendos or indicate their political affiliation in both joking and serious ways. At the local bar in Accra where I was watching this program, the mostly male working-class viewers were immediately provoked into heated discussions about political change, ethnic rivalry, and the role of corporations such as Unilever in cushioning, or contributing to, the desperate economic conditions of the nation. The trickster-like indeterminacy of the comedian's intent in using this subtle political hand gesture—and the possible roles of the National Theatre and Unilever in sanctioning or censuring its deployment—further heightened its efficacy in stirring controversy. One man complained about how the previous government had destroyed the nation and bragged that things would change when the new government came. Another man pointed out that the previous government had built the National Theatre that they were all enjoying and had provided color television viewing as well. The first man replied that the theatre was only for "those wealthy government officials to show off for their girlfriends." He explained to me later that he regularly watched concert party when he had the chance but had never been to the Theatre itself. This conversation about inclusion/exclusion was provoked by a political sign embedded within a cultural performance made accessible through television.

Dispersed audiences were included in nationally relevant issues such as those provoked at this bar, though this inclusion was structured by feelings of shared exclusion from the center. National identification was diffused through mass media and the ever more privatized, decentralized manifestations of state. These viewers participated in a national public sphere, though one delineated by the interpenetration of ethnic and state politics, the class distinctions that excluded them from the theatre, and, ultimately, the ambiguous corporate authorization of political and cultural discourse.

The knowledge that the show was broadcast on television made being at the theatre—whether in the audience or on the stage—an act of participation. For example, upon visiting the house of a friend with whom I had attended *Key Soap Concert Party*, we were greeted with, "Hey Challey,[37] you were on TV, I saw you on the *Concert Party!*" Being seen on television was an aspect of participation. By viewing a performance—and being seen by others to be viewing it—audience members were actively engaging in leisure activities, that is, consumptive practices associated with liberal, individuated forms of personhood. In contrast, despite the increasing social prestige of concert party, many educated Ghanaians and those with elite class aspirations did not go to *Concert Party* for *fear of* being seen there. Numerous university graduates told me that they enjoyed the program but did not want others to see them on television for fear they would be ridiculed as being uneducated and backward with insults such as "Hey, village boy!" Some did not even want to admit to watching it on television but then would do so in the privacy of their homes.

For both rural and urban poor, television viewing of *Key Soap Concert Party* was a communal practice. Often there were only a few televisions in a neighborhood or village situated at a provisions kiosk, a hair salon, a drinking spot, or in the courtyard or living room of a relatively well-off family. Here, people congregated to view favorite shows, sporting matches, and local and foreign films. In these public and semipublic spaces, multiple radios and televisions played, each dominating a specific area. Someone might see part of a program while buying food at the roadside and then walk several hundred yards to a drinking spot and watch and discuss another snippet of the program with other people. In these contexts, *Key Soap Concert Party* programs would spark conversations on specific topics in politics, travel, or sports. The show's presence and familiarity, as well as its invocation and recirculation of new and familiar symbols, phrases, and images, marked viewers as participants in a national public. These diffused, marginalized audiences identified with the "traditional" nature of the concert party genre and the contemporary social references within the performances at the same time that they were excluded from access to the privileges of the "modern" elite identifications and individual leisure activities indexed by theatre (and soap) consumption.

Bar Soap's Powerful Cleanliness

Ghana's National Theatre was mandated to be one of first state institutions to make itself economically self-sufficient as the state assessed the value of its resources on the open market. Its struggles to both support theatre arts and make money highlight the structural contradictions of privatization in relation to changing mediations of cultural production. Artists and audiences are oriented toward the gendered moral authority of modern life defined by bar soap's cleanliness. Notions of moral and bodily cleanliness and control are meant to sanitize concert party as a marker of idealized spaces of feminine domestic life for live and televised public consumption. State support for privatization, and belief in the moral and fiscal benefits of the free market, have reshaped the conditions of Ghanaian life as they have around the globe. Crucially, however, this case reveals that marketization entails complex entanglements of corporate and state interests. The tradition of trickster storytelling also encourages audiences and artists alike to approach transformations with indirection, irreverence, and an eye for seeing things two ways simultaneously. While the sanitized concert party is organized by metaphors of moral and theatrical control, the poetics of storytelling that underlie it provoke uncertainty and creative duality.

Ghana's valorization of privatization and the free market is articulated through changing public mediations of culture and the reconfiguration of state institutional control, rather than the withdrawal of the state. Increasingly, public authority and collective affiliation are made and contested through dispersed, mass-mediated performances that blur the generic boundaries between popular, formal, religious, and traditional theatre. The rise of individuated forms of pleasure and consumption reveal a complex intermingling of state, corporate, and local interests. New urban tastes emerge in institutions and technologies for the public display and circulation of culture. Despite the concern of theatre artists of their growing irrelevance, the arts remain significant, though they become subject to the vagaries of a market shaped by corporate interest, and theatre entrepreneurs become dispensable wage-workers. While appropriations of culture remain at the center of Ghanaian public life, they increasingly symbolize a moral tension between collective good and personal desire.

I have tried to tease out individual performance styles, audience tastes, theatrical forms, and moral beliefs that are contested in conflicts among corporate organizers, National Theatre executives, performers, and audience members. *Key Soap Concert Party*, a soap opera if there ever was one, oriented audiences toward the morality of the market, reimagining national citizens simultaneously as consuming subjects. Central to this was the rise of dispersed, electronically mediated audiences. Through a variety of practices, theatre and television audiences were invoked as individuated consumers, while class, gender, ethnic, and urban-rural differences were reinscribed. The privatization of state-run enterprises and the valorization of the free market blur the lines between state and corporate structures and interests, between discourses of consumption and national identification. Performers and audiences are caught in the midst of structural changes that they negotiate. On stage, actors use creative double voicing to navigate an uncertain landscape and debates over what constitutes modern theatrical form and traditional content. Off stage, artists and audiences are increasingly oriented toward consumption as an interpretive and social frame, if in ambivalent ways.

Cole (2001) argues that concert party in the 1950s era of nationalism produced an increasingly homogenous audience by indexing it as an undifferentiated public—as opposed to audiences at funerals, chiefly courts, storytelling events, and other types of public performances, which were hierarchically constructed. Concert party's rise was built on how it harnessed the urban, the modern, and the foreign for reexamination by rural farmers and semieducated workers. At the turn of the millennium, concert party is harnessed by state and corporate interests as a way for elite and nonelite audiences to contemplate the uncertainty and tension between privatization and ideas of national cultural identity. Concert party's evolving structure invokes self-consciousness and debates about the meaning and relevance of performance for audiences and performers. Reflexive negotiations of the formal structures of performance are crucial ways that public speaking authority is produced and contested. Practitioners struggle to maintain a coherent definition of concert party as a genre defined by the use of multimedia, staging, storytelling, and improvisation techniques. In this process, elite audiences, local peoples, administrators, and various artists are tied to state and corporate sensibilities through changing notions of cultural legitimacy.

As National Theatre and Key Soap organizers reshape ideas of tradition and reorganize popular theatre, the trickster—manifest in the historical links between concert party and Anansesem—acts as a structuring figure for conflicts over commodification and the arts. The trickster narrates and translates political change through double-voiced comedic routines and dramatic plays. Staging and timing are reconfigured and commodities are inserted into the program, transforming how theatre artists conceive of their performances and how audiences expect to see them. Corporate sponsors, theatre workers, and artists struggle to reshape the formal aspects of performances into what are considered morally acceptable and pleasurable terms for a changing public. Conflicts arise between creative irreverence characteristic of concert party's eclectic history and the needs of corporate sponsorship.

7 Fake Pastors and Real Comedians
Doubling and Parody in Miraculous, Charismatic Performance

> The pastor pours drinking water, but claims that it's holy water.
> Rap lyrics, Grey of the Mobile Boys

THIS CHAPTER EXAMINES how, in millennial Ghana, the figure of the false prophet or pastor—and fear of fakery more generally—plays a dynamic and productive role in shaping an emerging sphere of moral uncertainty to which performance and its assessment are central. Since the 1980s an increasing number of popular Ghanaian performers have been moved by the Holy Spirit and been "born again" as Charismatic pastors. From highlife musician and concert party theatre leader, Nana Ampadu, known for his sequined jumpsuits and irreverent Ananse-based hit songs, touched by the Holy Spirit in 1988, to Promzy, a hip-hop/hiplife musician known for his tough gangster image who was born again in 2014, artists have rejected their bawdy entertainments in favor of pious celebrations of Christ. However, the public has often remained skeptical of the sincerity of these conversions. Rampant concerns that they are faking their new beliefs in order to garner publicity reveal how intricate links between sincerity and fakery lie just below the surface of all sorts of theatrical social action. Rather than a tale of how new Christian movements reshape the public sphere, the interplay between pastors and artists demonstrates a complex blurring of sacred and profane in popular realms and raises questions about the contextually specific logic of reiteration (Meyer 2004a; J. Shipley 2013b). Ghanaian conversion narratives are not signs of how people make a "complete break with the past," severing ties to older kin and social networks (Meyer 1998a) but demonstrate something of the performance logic in which belief and meaning are made and assessed through public self-presentations. A new identity's coherence relies on authoritatively embodying that self in the moment rather than on maintaining contiguous links to past selves and previous performances.

Over the past two decades, Charismatic preaching has become a powerful form of public speaking around the globe, as megachurches and televangelists have arisen from Sweden to Seoul to Harare (S. Coleman 2000; Schulz 2003, 2012; Van de Port 2006; Van der Veer 1996). Scholars have demonstrated the links between Charismatic spirituality, political-economic liberalization, and changing media landscapes in a variety of locales (De Witte 2005; Engelke 2007; Marshall 2009; Meyer 2006; Pype 2012). As with other fundamentalist movements, pastors and congregation members claim spiritual authority to challenge established moral, legal, and political orders (Comaroff and Comaroff 1997). In Ghana, the structural and moral tensions around state privatization that shaped the struggles at the National Theatre as I described also fostered the rise of Charismatic churches (Gifford 1998, 2004; Meyer 2004b). Their "prosperity doctrines" promise economic success in this life through prayer, emphasizing modes of performativity that display wealth and morally validate an entrepreneurial subject (Hackett 1999). This doctrine emerges in an economic climate in which self-determination, choice, and entrepreneurialism are valorized, even while viable state and business models of success have been undercut. Becoming a pastor has become an increasingly common spiritual calling and an economically viable vocation. The glamorous sheen of successful pastors floods the media, linking the presence of the Holy Spirit to promised wealth for disenfranchised masses with little hope for material success. Promises of economic salvation, however, breed anxieties about how to assess genuine spiritual power through pastors' public performances. And frequent scandals about their financial indiscretions and sexual misconduct raise the specter of spiritual trickery.

In contradiction to studies that claim to "take religion seriously" as well as the radical ontological breaks with the past that some doctrines posit, I take belief with some skepticism, as indeed many believers do.[1] I am not arguing that Charismatic belief is epiphenomenal of political economic change but rather that in order to understand belief we must examine it in its pragmatic enactment, that is, as something made and remade in social action. In this instance, this reveals that the perceived ubiquity of fakery defines the realm of moral and spiritual meaning. Extended observations of Ghanaian public life show that much daily concern with religion and belief is taken up with assessments of fake pastors and fake miracles. In this sense, I take seriously fear of the fake as key to understanding how belief and meaning are made and contested. Miraculous events are not affectively charged ruptures that punctuate and shape neo-Pentecostal life (cf. Marshall 2010). Instead they are relevant in the practical ways that people are obsessed with and anxious about false prophets. Stories of fakery endlessly circulate in the media and through word of mouth. Significantly, the veracity or fakeness of spiritual forces and men of God—much like Ananse tales—are judged in terms of public performance.

I examine fear of the fake as a performance logic that is constitutive of the force of spiritual authority through which key contradictions of neoliberal life are addressed. I focus on pastors and comedians as parallel figures: both are performers who provoke public moral discourse by telling persuasive stories. And as pastors present both the ideal and the threat of the neoliberal, comedians parody this figuration. While trickster storytelling provides pastors with established, viable performance idioms, the rise of Charismatism, with its highly performative logic, provides new opportunities for established theatre artists. The moral contestations I describe center on the evaluation of sincerity and fakeness through performance. Charismatism's permeation of popular entertainment and public life breeds anxieties that spiritual power is faked, performed for entrepreneurial success. Perhaps the greatest fear for participants is that the distance between real and fake, moral and immoral may collapse.

A fake pastor is sometimes referred to as an *osofo meko*, literally a "pepper pastor." As one university student and volunteer Sunday school teacher explained to me, "some of these so-called men of God would put hot pepper in your eyes to deceive you."[2] As the potential to "get the Holy Spirit" is marketized, public attention focuses on assessing spiritual power's authenticity through its visual, performed elements. "Prosperity doctrines" promise sacred access to entrepreneurial success in which a spiritual exchange—receiving the gift of the Holy Spirit—stands for a desired financial exchange. Fakery appears as the margin, the horizon against which a moral center and sincere performances are clarified (Derrida 1988). The fake does not negate value or belief but rather provides a critical comment on the conditions of their emergence. Belief in and obsession with fakery is belief in the potential of its opposite. Uncertainty provokes forms of speech, performance, and assessment that simultaneously legitimize and question the potential of a spiritually validated entrepreneur. If a good performance is a sign of holy anointment, then the dangers of a skilled actor who can, to paraphrase George Burns, fake sincerity become very real.

Strikingly, fears of financial and sexual exploitation of vulnerable women by smooth-talking charlatans mark the entrepreneurial spirit as masculine. And both pastoral preaching and comedic routines are primarily masculine modes of speaking. Anxieties often revolve around illicitly-earned male wealth and control of female sexuality. Salacious stories of pastors exploiting women for money and sex demonstrate that the female body is the locus of anxieties about producing and consuming value as well as the center of notions of the miraculous. While women gain new opportunities to produce and control value with the rising free market and new media, they also become vulnerable to masculinized seductive performances and consumptive practices.

Assessments of fakery in performance are productive of a decentered, moral public, bringing together a variety of electronic and digital media and expressive genres from radio, television, music, the internet, theatre, comedy, preaching, and political speeches and ceremonies. The rise of call-in radio talk shows, the ubiquity of mobile phones that underpin them, the religious conversion of artists, popular video-films, and social media accessed through smart phones all contribute to a diffuse yet discontinuous public world in which the entrepreneurial spirit gains preeminence as it is aligned with spiritual authority and assessed through surface appearances. New communication technologies have sped up the circulation of moral commentary, although they rely on established styles of storytelling, indirection, double voicing, excess, and humor. While Charismatic churches have been characterized by the explicit rejection of "traditional" culture and religion (Meyer 2004a), their formal structures of multimedia worship are built on popular concert party theatre idioms in intermingling preaching, humor, gospel music infused with reggae, highlife, and hip-hop, and popular drumming and dancing. Popular all-night crusades in outdoor theatrical venues around urban areas resemble concert party performances of decades ago in their organization. Indeed, the rise of Charismatic churches in Ghana in the 1980s overtook concert party and highlife concerts as popular social gatherings by appropriating many aspects of these popular genres. Some churches have their own bands and concert party troupes and produce their own radio, video, and television shows and online content, infusing older genres with newly pious messages.

Here, I focus on how links between pastors and comedians rely on the trickster that remains the center of Ghanaian speech culture even as new media reshape a urban community of interpretation.[3] As concert party comedian Ghana Boy explained to me during a theatre rehearsal, Ananse is the prototype for the comedian, and popular entertainment in general emerges from trickster storytelling (cf. Cole 2001: 109). But, to his mind, as neo-Pentecostals dominate Ghanaian public life, other performers are judged increasingly in relation to pastors and asked to be moral voices. For Ghana Boy, as I describe in the previous chapter, the assessment works both ways: "We comedians are like pastors; we are there to entertain and to impart moral lessons to the public. We are all tricking the audience for them to enjoy and learn lessons at the same time."

Fear of fakery raises public interest in the relationship between acting and sincerity; people wonder if there is a gap between who a pastor is and how he acts. Is he just a good actor or is his performance index his sincere belief and spiritual power? A good performance can be either a sign of sincerity or a sign of a skilled performer who is a good liar. With comedians, audiences thrill at being fooled. Mock sincerity becomes a reflexive commentary on acting itself. Mixed with the fear of being fooled is pleasure in trickery and a predisposition to think of public enactments as always double voiced. Ananse is a hero-charlatan whose greed gets him in trouble. He is an entrepreneur of sorts, but it is said that Ananse loves to eat but does not like to work. Trickery is morally condemned but is also the basis for creative wordplay, providing the potential for wealth without work. Recall that Ananse storytelling sessions are often begun with audiences pleading with storytellers to lie to them, and with statements like, "If Ananse tells you to look up, you should look down." But creative performance and persuasive words can seduce audiences away from scrutinizing intent. The trickster, the comedian, and the Charismatic preacher share a set of performance strategies that can seduce their audiences and obfuscate intent, in the process demarcating a dispersed moral public driven by uncertainty and ambiguity.[4]

From State to Church: The Rise of Charismatic Entrepreneurs

In Ghana, the popular, political, and religious have long been closely intertwined (Debrunner 1967). Kwame Nkrumah and Jerry Rawlings were both Christian, and as Charismatic leaders they were both linked in various ways to tales of spiritual salvation. At the same time, rumors swirled around both of them, claiming that their affiliation with traditional spiritual forces gave them magical persuasive powers over the populace. Nkrumah's status as founding national figure was formalized in an appellation *Osagyefo* (redeemer/savior). He incorporated Christian iconography into state protocol, though he also used Akan traditional religious performances in state spectacles. Clandestine accusations also spread during his rule, claiming he visited shrines strengthening the "unholy" powers of persuasion and charisma. When he waved his white handkerchief or wiped his brow, some believed that people watching would be magically persuaded to follow him. It was rumored that when he was overthrown in 1966 fetish shrines were found in his residence. Colonel Acheampong, who assumed command of the country in a coup d'etat in 1972, claimed that his military takeover was inspired and guided by Christian moral authority and that his strong spiritual convictions protected him from harm during combat. When Flight Lieutenant Jerry John Rawlings first took power in his short-lived 1979 coup, he was often praised as a Christ-like savior referred to as "Junior Jesus." When Rawlings again took power in 1981, national newspapers described him in terms of the Christian Messiah with headlines, "Second Coming of Rawlings!" When the public became critical of Rawlings's regime, "Junior Jesus" quickly became "Junior Judas."

As Charismatism took hold through the 1980s, young men left established churches to form new ministries; other non-Christians, mostly uneducated, were also called by God. Orthodox missionary denominations, older Pentecostals, and Spiritual African Independent Churches (AICs) began to lose membership as converts turned to neo-Pentecostals (Meyer 2004a). Numerous small congregations emerged around young leaders claiming the Holy Spirit's presence. In the 1980s Reverend Vagalas, who describes himself as a "former witch doctor" who "received the Holy Spirit," founded Lord's Vineyard International Ministries and became renowned for healing, deliverance, and fighting demons "in the spiritual realm." He explained to me that whereas spiritual leadership in orthodox churches was restricted to those who had long been part of church hierarchy, younger Christians felt faith should not be mediated through official institutional channels but rather that each "individual has a direct spiritual relationship with the Holy Spirit."[5] John Ghartey, a teacher at Action Faith Ministries Bible College, recalled, "We in schools felt that we wanted a new direction for the churches.... The older generation had nothing to tell us."[6] Theological critiques arose out of Bible study groups within established churches, church fellowships, and secondary school religious associations. Brew Riverson Jr., a film and television actor and born-again Christian who is the son of a minister, recalled that for youth growing up in the 1980s, "Charismatic preaching addressed contemporary concerns of spiritual and moral poverty, but gave us the belief and power to make our own future."[7] Pentecostals and neo-Pentecostals emphasize the presence of the Holy Spirit in contemporary life. For Pentecostals, speaking in tongues, the laying on of hands, and the sacraments are primary evidence of the Holy Spirit. However, for neo-Pentecostals or Charismatics, the fruits of the Holy Spirit—faith, joy, and material prosperity—are signs of the Spirit's anointing. Charismatism links spiritual presence to personal aspiration and success.

New churches provided basic community needs. The impoverished state failed to provide social services, although it remained tied to ideals of centralization that prevented the private sector from fulfilling basic needs. As one member of Christian Action Faith Ministries International said to me, he joined because "it *is* community." Churches, with the aid of tax-exempt status, rose through membership donations. Congregations bought land, built churches, and supported the clergy. Members received mail and telephone calls through church offices. In addition, medical procedures, education, marriages, and, in particular, costly funerals were supported. Churches took up older forms of informal collective savings schemes so members could pool resources. As another member explained, "If someone dies, Charismatic churches are there to help with the funeral. [Orthodox] churches are more rigid in their membership. You have to find someone who is a long-time member and beg them to help arrange funerals. For younger people without money, Charismatic churches are more humane. Young and poor members are willing to give because they feel their money is building something and they have a voice. They are a part of something dynamic, you know?" (cf. Addae-Mensah 2000).

Although many orthodox churches were critical of Rawlings's socialist tendencies, young Christians initially supported his vision of moral discipline and generational change. Hierarchical control of orthodox churches came to be seen as part of endemic social mismanagement reflecting the colonial mentality of the older generation. However, new religious movements were soon seen as a threat to state sovereignty. Whereas orthodox churches emphasized the authority of institutional mediation, Charismatic preaching posited a direct relationship between worshipper and spiritual authority (Engelke 2004).

Regulating Churches

Charismatism as a dominant aspect of public life was spurred by the state's struggles to regulate religious institutions. The state unintentionally gave new churches moral legitimacy by positioning them as an alternative to state control. In 1989, PNDC Law 221, the Religious Bodies Registration Act, "required all religious bodies to register with the National Commission on Culture [NCC]" (Nugent 1995: 188). Mohammed Ben Abdallah, chairman of the NCC, argued for state regulation of Pentecostal denominations, which were "not well organized or grounded within the religious traditions of the country" and that appeared at such a rapid rate that "the government could not keep track of them."[8] Around the same time, the government banned the Jehovah's Witnesses and the Church of Latter-Day Saints for "teaching the inferiority of African peoples" and undermining projects of national unity.[9] For government, Law 221 was not aimed at regulating religious freedom per se but addressed the "threat" of religious movements to national culture. Rights to free expression came into conflict with the state's attempt to protect "cultural integrity" from foreign influence.

In an August 1989 speech at the opening of the Association of Episcopal Conferences of Anglophone West Africa, Rawlings argued that "the church must join in the struggle to emancipate the oppressed and to create a new order of justice." Rawlings expressed distress at the immorality and antisociality of wealth:

> The world in which the youth live . . . is characterized by ugly contradictions, wealth, over-consumption, and seemingly unlimited opportunities for a tiny minority whilst the majority are doomed to deprivation and cannot meet their very basic needs. . . . With the immense advances in communications such as video, satellite TV, etc., our youth see the hypocrisy of international figures of power and influence. . . . We learn that success means not getting caught, that beauty and respectability have no local reference points and only have to do with external foreign things. . . . Are we ready to admit that the tentacles of this evil have reached the core of our religious and Christian traditions?[10]

Abdallah recalled: "The use of electronic media by new churches and the flashy styles of Charismatic leaders really concerned some in government. It was not as much specific cases of corruption as the sense that these were not African-oriented movements and they praised individual wealth as if it was a positive moral attribute."[11] Rawlings emphasized the state's right to regulate church financial relations:

> Do we realize that our refusal to condemn our silence about those of our own church members who flaunt ill-gotten wealth is contributing to the society's inability to restore spiritual values. . . . [Church leaders] admit and I quote, "We do not question the right or duty of government to check any activity which goes against public decency and morality, promotes the financial

exploitation of believers, endangers public peace or compromises national unity and honor."

I would agree that if other effective means offered themselves, they would be preferable to making a law to prevent the abuse of freedom of worship. We cannot have our very spirituality exploited for material gain by those who merely wish to control us for their own ends.[12]

Religious regulation was posited as the state's legitimate moral purview. Many, however, read this as a sign of government's refusal to liberalize or recognize individual rights. The Christian Council of Ghana, comprising fourteen prominent churches, protested that government had curtailed liberties promoting religious and ethnic discrimination.[13] Contrary to the law's intent, established churches refused to register whereas new churches were eager for official recognition.[14] Established churches were themselves "concerned at the proliferation of sects whose doctrines they found questionable" (Nugent 1995: 188). However, they were immediately galvanized against government regulation of religious activities. The resistance of orthodox churches to government regulation ironically helped new churches emerge in their midst.

By the mid-1990s, Charismatic churches were the most popular form of worship in Ghana (Hanson 2000: 173).[15] Older denominations developed Charismatic subgroups with lively forms of worship and young leadership to hold on to their members. And although Charismatism emerged through youth rebellion, its proponents increasingly relied on images of success to promote their message. This resonated with the entrepreneurial spirit as well as established West African "Big Man" leadership models linking accumulation and display of wealth to power (McCaskie 2002). New pastors adopted flamboyant personal styles demonstrating established ideas that displays of extreme wealth are part of the production of public power across West Africa. For example, Akan chiefs ceremonially display authority through the richness of their kente cloth and gold adornments. Popular religious and entertainment events involve wealthy patrons publicly giving money as a sign of power. Indeed, affluence requires giving money back to the community. And rumors and jealousy often arise if those who are seen as wealthy do not reinject resources into the economy.

In a society that values the aesthetics of public wealth, a generation of politically disenfranchised youth turned to spiritual realms for new manners of material production (cf. McCaskie 2002). Accra's landscape changed as new churches sprang up, ranging from small wooden shacks with modest signs to huge concrete-and-tile buildings in central locations, providing alternative networks of social support and moral community. Successful congregations established smaller branches throughout the country. For Ghanaians abroad, new churches established branches around the world and online platforms, providing crucial structural and emotional connections to home.

Artists into Pastors

Government curfews in the early 1980s, established to curb moral "indiscipline," also destroyed Accra's vibrant nightlife. State taxes on foreign imports designed to protect local producers made prices on musical equipment prohibitively high, crippling Ghana's entertainment industry.[16] Cheap video production, mobile video screenings, and DJ equipment made live bands and traveling theatre economically untenable. Because religious institutions were exempt from taxes on musical instruments, musicians who did not leave the country began playing in new churches eager to attract mass audiences. They used popular music and dance in worship and sponsored gospel-highlife bands and theatre groups.[17] Many popular entertainers have publicly been "born again." Their religious conversions have helped popularize new churches, though the association between entertainers and Charismatism highlights concerns about fakery and the relationship between staged performance and spiritual anointing.

In 1988 Nana Ampadu, singer, guitarist, leader of African Brothers Band International, and one of the country's most popular highlife musicians, was "touched by the Holy Spirit." Seven prophets came to him saying he should give up his "profane" entertainment lifestyle and, instead, preach about salvation and sin.[18] Since the 1960s Ampadu has toured Ghana as leader of a popular highlife band/concert party theatre group, entertainment forms that dominated mid-twentieth-century Anglophone West African entertainment. His music was particularly noted for drawing on Ananse storytelling (J. Shipley 2013a: 37–38). His songs often told oblique stories about animals or life in traditional rural villages. His fans thrilled at trying to interpret his messages. One fan recalls that his songs were so exciting because they made you think and were not always easy to interpret, "like hearing proverbs or Ananse stories."

When he was born again, he traded in his 1970s rhinestone-studded black jumpsuit, reminiscent of Wilson Pickett, for well-tailored conservative suits. He shifted from the debauchery of popular music to a "respectable" Christian public persona. Although he drew on similar styles of showmanship and music, he began to preach and sing to congregations to follow the word of God and avoid sin. He explained that his performances and the stories he told while preaching were not that different from those he used when he was doing highlife. He said that he always told moral tales to make people think, but that now they were "anointed and oriented to God." Ampadu's critics felt his conversion was a calculated career shift for a notorious showman who wanted to make money by latching onto the rapid rise of charismatic Christianity. As the leader of a rival concert party group told me, "That guy has never had a religious experience in his life. He is just trying to take advantage like so many of these other so-called men of God."

Ampadu was not alone among entertainers in having a sudden religious conversion around the same time. T. O. Jazz, another popular musician, was "born again" in 1986. As Jazz explained to me, his group had been protected against witchcraft and made successful by his allegiance to mmoatia magical dwarfs. However, when the Holy Spirit came to him, he realized that Jesus's spiritual power was superior to traditional spirits, and so he converted. This conversion implies a mystical realm in which there is a pantheon of spiritual forces competing for attention and material success.[19]

In 1999, Ampadu helped establish the first explicitly Christian radio station in Accra, 103.5 FM. Since the privatization of radio in the mid-1990s, Christian programming and gospel music had steadily increased in market share. By 2001, there were three Christian FM stations in Accra. By 2008, Christian radio and television were ubiquitous. The interplay between sacred and secular forms of entertainment continues as several star hiplife/hip-hop rap artists—often seen as profane and immoral in their performance styles and lyrics—have converted (J. Shipley 2013a). For example, rap pioneer Lord Kenya's records around the turn of the millennium were widely popular blends of rap and highlife and crucial in popularizing hiplife music (J. Shipley 2013a: 117). He was known for songs like "Sika Baa" (Money woman) about women who do anything for cash. He was also frequently in the news for drug-use scandals. However, in 2009–2010 he released a gospel album titled *Christ Life*, renounced his old lifestyle, and began calling himself Evangelist Lord Kenya.

While churches have integrated older forms of worship and entertainment with new media, purportedly secular realms of entertainment became permeated with the spirit of Charismatic Christianity. By appropriating the stance of Charismatic leadership, previously profane entertainers gained new public salience. Conversely, they popularized Christian messages, giving churches a stylish sheen as central venues for live entertainment. But as we shall see, the specter of the fake both shadows and drives this transformation.

Ushering in the Millennium

Pastors in performance rely on melodrama, humor, and narratives of personal redemption to position listeners within a Charismatic public (J. Shipley 2013b). Charismatic preaching adopts poetic tropes from popular entertainment, reinforcing spiritual authenticity through media spectacle, double voicing, pleasurable wordplay, images of excess, and complex intertextual references. Pastors both invoke and distance themselves from spiritual fakery through rhetorical style and bodily comportment. The pastor is the ideal neoliberal subject as well as the specter of its opposite. Fear of moral inversion sets the conditions of possibility for legitimate preachers. These performers struggle to maintain the moral dichotomy between real and fake, while it threatens to collapse under assessments that align choice itself with personal greed. Pastors implore worshippers to choose personal faith, with the spiritual choice making possible other material ones. But the promises of individual choice heighten fear of an immoral opposite.

On December 31, 1999, a majority of young urban Ghanaians ushered in the millennium by going to church, demonstrating the centrality of neo-Pentecostal sensibilities to public life (Hanson 2000). Four friends from Ghana's National Theatre and I went to Pastor Mensa Otabil's International Central Gospel Church (ICGC). Established in 1984, ICGC is one of the largest and most respected Charismatic churches in the region. Otabil quit school for financial reasons, founding ICGC at age twenty-four. His church gained recognition when Otabil broadcast sermons on Accra's first successful private radio station, Joy FM, in 1995. He explains, "If Joy FM had not given me the opportunity, I would still have probably remained a 'hidden voice' restricted to a little church somewhere" (quoted in Asamoah-Gyadu 2005). At the same time the growing success of his inspirational radio program called *The Living Word* lent the commercial station an air of respectability and spirituality as it sought audiences and private sponsorship. Later he expanded *The Living Word* to television; his broadcasts are often heard in roadside kiosks and markets throughout Accra (De Witte 2003). Recordings are sold on cassette, VHS, CD, and DVD and circulate online. Kojo, a taxi driver in New York, explained to me that even though he was a Presbyterian, he listened to Otabil's old cassette sermons for inspiration and has friends send new sermons. "Otabil is humble," he said, "not like some arrogant pastors. He is also not afraid to talk about the real problems we face."

Christ Temple, ICGC's four-thousand-seat headquarters, is a point of pride for church members. It is a magnificent open cathedral near central Accra, built in the late 1990s as, at the time, one of the largest venues in Ghana. Through congregational fund-raising, investment, and community organizing, new churches have arisen as centers of urban life. We arrived at 9:30 p.m. that New Year's Eve. Christ Temple was already full, with several thousand people seated outside in folding chairs rapidly set up around three sides of the building. The massive congregation consisted mostly of young adults, well dressed in Western-style suits and dresses or West African formal dress. Although expensive cars filled the parking lot, indicating an elite presence, much of the congregation consisted of laborers, traders, and seamstresses. The service reflected basic neo-Pentecostal liturgy: singing by gospel choir and live band, prayers by various clergy, thanksgiving, and individual prayer. Video cameramen conspicuously recorded the altar. State-of-the-art speakers and ten-foot video screens adorned the walls inside and were mounted outside the temple for the crowds in folding chairs. The spectacle of technology condensed and focused the services on the pastor's bodily presence.

Live Charismatic services are multimedia spectacles, visions of Afromodernity for aspiring Ghanaians (cf. De Witte 2003, 2005). Meyer argues that Pentecostalism calls for "a complete break with the past" and is opposed to the "Ghanaian State which aim[s] at a restoration of national pride" (1998b: 316). In practice, this dichotomy is blurred. Mission Christianity for the most part demonized African music, dance, and worship, although it promoted local languages and culture to facilitate conversions. In 1932 the Gold Coast colony banned anti-witchcraft shrines fostering the popularity of Pentecostal churches and the African Independent Church through their incorporation of witch-finding techniques and African modes of worship (Allman and Parker 2005). Most neo-Pentecostals explicitly denounce African culture while their religious services formally incorporate popular entertainment and traditional worship. Otabil explicitly invokes culture for Africanizing modernity (cf. Meyer 2004a). According to one young member who is a bank clerk, she likes Otabil's church because he is "more Ghanaian" than "Westernized" Charismatics. Appropriating national ceremonial imagery, the choir wears Ghanaian kente and wax-print cloth sewn in African styles. One member states, "Otabil always dresses like an African. He does not wear expensive suits." He preaches in elegant lace agbadas or other African formal wear, although, like most well-known pastors, Otabil preaches in English. He is noted for using simple language and humor deploying the modern authority conferred by English while appearing local and accessible.

As midnight approached, Otabil preached about past failures and future potential. The millennium, he said,

> is a moment of transition, a time for reflection on your situation, personally and as a nation. . . . This is a chance to realize your dreams, to overcome frustrations of the past and lay the foundation for future prosperity. . . . Some of you want to succeed in business, others want to build a new house, some want to have children. Your future can be different than your past.

Individual faith was the key to change, turning spiritual development into material progress. He called audience members to refashion themselves in the personalized language of an African-oriented liberation theology. Otabil often asked congregation members to speak affirmations emphasizing faith as choice. He commanded that everyone turn to the person seated on each side of him or her and say, "You are a beautiful person and you will have your miracle." Emphasizing success through belief and self-confidence, he then asked people to repeat the phrase but this time to say, "You are a beautiful *Black* person and will have your miracle." For broader audiences, this performative enunciation aligned racial affiliation with individuated faith. Individual choice is encouraged through collectivity.

Just before midnight at Christ Temple, excitement peaked as Otabil told people to pray, "in their own individual ways," for their future. As the clock counted down, murmured prayers in English, Ewe, Twi, Fante, and Ga, and the voices of those praying in tongues, built to a polyphonous crescendo trailing off after the stroke of midnight. Abena, a young actress, explained that Otabil, despite his fame and large congregation, "makes you *feel* like he is speaking to *you*."

In the video *Turning Failure into Success,* recorded live and sold at the chapel bookstore, Otabil's sermon uses metaphors of performance, invoking listeners as active participants in God's plan:

> Say with me in Jesus's name, that in this year I will turn my failure into success. Because God is with me, nothing shall be against me. . . . Your life is being rewritten and the part you play has been exchanged from the part of the drunkard to the part of the prince! [*Cheering.*] The script has changed! You are not going to play the role of a failure again. You are not going to play the role of somebody who is down again. You are going to play a new role a role of a successful person in Jesus's name. (Otabil 2000)

The key is the worshipper's active choice. Otabil chastises those who passively wait for salvation. He continues: "Do you know that people fail by choice? You don't fail *by force*. You are the number one contributor to your failure . . . you can't help a person beyond his ability to change" (Otabil 2000). Success is not a gift but rather is achieved through personal labor and active choice (Otabil 2002). Shifting between first-, second-, and third-person forms of address aligns pastor and congregation in past failure, present struggle, and future potential. The pastor himself embodies the image of success. Sermons authorize audience members to make moral choices that will lead to inner spiritual transformation and, in turn, material prosperity. Through shifting participation roles, sermons produce a tension between an agentive speaker and a passive recipient. The pastor is both a passive mediator, a recipient who channels the gift of the Holy Spirit for his followers, and an agentive individual who actively voices his aspiration to unleash inner potential (Agha 2005a; Eisenlohr 2006). Pastoral authority hinges on the potential ambiguity between the Holy Spirit as the giver of the spiritual gift and the gift, the power, in itself. This ambiguity is reflected onto the pastor, who can defer authorship of his words and deeds by claiming to be only a medium of divine action and animator of divine words or who can claim credit for positive actions, since the Holy Spirit's gift gives individuals the power to choose and author their own salvation and future success (Goffman 1981).

Humor frames the transformative dangers and potentials of speaking. In one segment of *Turning Failure into Success,* Otabil preaches, "God is about to answer your prayers, even those of you who pray casually. So be careful what you say. Be careful what you pray for." The potency of choice as well as its corrupting potential is at the heart of his message. Informality includes listeners as part of a shared intimate community with the pastor. Comic asides are important in church events and, despite their seeming irrelevance to the message and occasional irreverence, are usually included in the video edited versions of sermons.

For example, in one *Turning Failure into Success* tape, Otabil directs the congregation to find a biblical passage in Luke. "Luke is easy to find. It's Matthew, Mark, Luke, and John. If you don't know where Luke is . . . pray to God. [*Laughter.*]" Humor breaks frame and includes listeners as privy to insider knowledge. These informal moments highlight other parts of the sermon as sincere. Parodying the power of words, Otabil points to spiritual struggle as an ongoing battle over meaning and agency. It is continual and messy rather than being an easy opposition of good and evil. Otabil calls on his listeners to actively choose success, creating a moral interiority that dictates the performance of public actions. The pastor weaves together overlapping voices that populate Accra's urban chronotope, reimagining a hopeful future in contrast to a flawed past and corrupt present. Otabil's mediatized Pan-African Charismatism provides worshippers with a spiritual language to engage racial, gendered, and economic inequality as anointed entrepreneurs. Although material success is a sign of spiritual power, the potential for fakery haunts its performative potential.

Pastor Kodjoe Amankwa's sermon at a small branch of Christian Action Faith Ministries in suburban Accra, not long after the turn of the millennium, demonstrates how the threat of fakery both haunts and mobilizes pastoral authority.[20] Situated at one end of a dirt compound, the one-story concrete structure with a corrugated roof holds about 150 worshippers.[21] The congregation of local workers wears their Sunday best. One reason many young adults give for attending Charismatic churches is that they provide a feeling of success by association. As one young woman explained, "Charismatics are very rich. . . . They dress well so when you go to church you have to match up to their class. . . . If you go there you feel that you will be somebody someday."

The pastor is dressed in a tailored powder-blue suit, crisp white shirt, silk tie, and gold watch. He stands on a crowded pulpit amid cluttered musical equipment, surrounded by church officials. A cordless microphone is clipped to his lapel and connected to large dusty speakers. He exudes personal confidence:

> Many supposed men of God . . . present themselves as spiritually pure. They drive fancy cars and wear beautiful suits and get fat off of their poor congregations. People want to believe but then see these men drive off and leave them to walk and sweat on a dusty road. And you shake your head and say are you sure this is a man of God? . . . We are all of the same flesh . . . the Spirit is in *you*.

The threat of spiritual fakeness is a sign of failed moral and economic circulation, warning congregations to be wary of false prophets. Invoking fakeness in a sermon positions the speaker as an authoritative judge of moral right and distancing the taint of impropriety. Charismatic preaching challenges indirect speaking characteristic of Ghanaian public life, emphasizing immediacy, sincerity, and directness as metacodes for moral authority (cf. Kwesi Yankah 1995). This is characterized by the repetitive layering of active commands in the first and second person. Warnings about false prophets distance the speaker from rumors of impropriety, especially as congregational donations provide primary revenue for church and pastor. During services, gospel-highlife music plays as worshippers line up to dance or walk down the aisles, placing donations in large boxes near the pulpit. The pastor implores, "In the Lord's name, what you give you shall receive back a thousandfold!" The ethos of giving and building the church confers the promise of moral right and future material success. Congregations also hold fund-raisers for specific building projects and members make donations when they have achieved success or for deliverance and healing services. As one member explained, "You give especially when you have found success yourself." For example, many musicians and concert party artists pray and make donations to their church when they are successful and fear what will happen if they do not. Active material exchanges animate spiritual ones.

Religious performance is removed from traditional hierarchies and placed in the hands of creative performers whose self-presentations can garner belief. Whereas orthodox churches emphasize the authority of institutional mediation, Charismatic preaching invokes a direct relationship between worshipper and spiritual authority (Engelke 2004). A worshipper becomes agentive by reflexively choosing the ideology of choice itself. This choosing subject potentially authorizes both the pious entrepreneur and the corrupt charlatan. The individual's direct relationship to the Spirit is, contradictorily, made possible only through the mediation of the pastor and the institutional support of the church. Pastors become successful through public belief in their success and the authenticity of their struggle. Fakery and failure mark the horizon against which pastors produce their respectability. Church rituals frame and magnify the power of words linking spiritual struggle to entrepreneurial potential.

Comedians Parody Pastors

While pastors drew on established modes of performance, comedians conversely appropriated the rising popularity of Charismatic preaching for their own ends. At the National Theatre of Ghana on December 26, 1999, the fifteen-hundred-seat theatre was standing room only for the fifth annual national finals of the *Key Soap Concert Party* "Who Is Who" competition to pick the best comedian and best concert party theatre troupe. At the National Theatre I became friends with Ghana Boy, an up-and-coming comedian. We often talked about theatre and politics. On stage his routines relied on the growing affinity between pastoral preaching and comedic parody. Many comedians self-consciously invoke the genre of preaching and poke fun at audience expectations of salvation and deliverance. Comedians inhabit and critique the ambivalences of pastoral preaching, making themselves into legitimate social commentators.

As part of the *Key Soap Concert Party* revitalization of the genre at the National Theatre and on Ghana Television (see chapter 6), organizers sought to replace its older raucous image with commodity marketing under the rubric of traditional values and Christian morality. With the transformation of the genre to television and formal stages, comedians focused on short stand-up routines, telling a series of humorous moral vignettes, creatively incorporating props, costume, dance, and music but increasingly focused on the power of the solo performer.

Backstage at the competition, Ghana Boy put on his costume, a foam cut-out map of Ghana, and applied red, yellow and green face paint. A few minutes later the crowd cheered as he came to the microphone smiling. He flatly stated a connection between comedy and pastoral preaching. "I am a pastor, telling you stories for your salvation." He told several humorous stories with serious moral messages: about three naïve Ghanaians who travel abroad and get arrested for a murder they did not commit, and about a young man who smokes marijuana and is burned to death because he is too stoned to realize his house is on fire. As Ghana Boy's twenty-minute routine concluded, the crowd laughed and cheered as he rode off on a hand-cranked paraplegic's bicycle.

Next came the contestant everyone was waiting for: Bishop Bob Okalla, Ghana Boy's mentor and the favorite to win the competition. His name reflected the comedian's irreverence and mimicry. As he was announced, he slipped into the auditorium by a side door and the crowd erupted at his unexpected appearance. Okalla wore a ragged colonial police uniform stuffed with a pillow and tied with a giant wristwatch around his stomach. He had a cooking pestle for a necktie, along with two dirty neckties loosely hanging around his collar. Snow boots adorned his feet and his hands were covered with long red stockings. On his left wrist was strapped a wall clock. He wore messy white face paint, oversized glasses, and a police inspector's cap. Okalla casually walked through the audience to the stage, as a "small boy" carried his arm and the oversized clock attached to it as if he were carrying a heavy load for his master. His character was a pastiche of symbols, simultaneously evoking multiple registers: colonial, domestic, state, storytelling trickery (Donkor 2013). The oversaturated markers of the mundane created a character both naïvely embedded within daily life and pushed to the extreme through an excessive display of the normal. In emphasizing the absurdity of daily life, he called attention to the impossibility of normalcy for struggling Ghanaians.

Mounting the stage, Okalla performed his signature awkward dance and face contortions to resounding cheers. With comic seriousness, his left arm strapped with the clock held stiffly away from his body, he greeted the audience as if he were an old woman welcoming them home from a long journey. He asked if they had had anything to eat. As the crowd shouted, "No, we are hungry!" he shifted registers, adopting a pastor's authoritative speaking stance (Goffman 1981). He told the crowd with mock seriousness that he knew that on Sunday everyone went to church and prayed hard so that the rumored Millennium Comet would not destroy the country. One manifestation of millennium anxiety was in humorous rumors circulating around Accra about a Millennium Comet coming to destroy the country. For some, a foreign body hurtling through space toward the small country symbolized frustration at the nation's economic instability. One audience member later told me, "We Ghanaians lack control over our predicament. Like this silly comet rumor; we can be crushed at any time."[22]

Okalla mused that he did not want people to get hurt, so he went up to the sky and fetched the comet. He began to sing the tune of a popular local rap song, calling the rock to come down. An audience member shouted "In the name of Jesus!" as the crowd howled with laughter. Descending from the ceiling was a papier-mâché comet with an old-fashioned pocket watch. It hovered behind Okalla amid Key Soap advertising that decorated the set. Audience members recognized themselves in the performer's invocation of the framing devices of church services, shouting "Hallelujah!" and "Amen!" and waving handkerchiefs, parodically adopting the stances of a church congregation, if only for a moment. They were remade in the performative force of comedian as Charismatic preacher, just as they adopted the bodily affects of a hip-hop audience in response to the performer's use of this popular music. A comic's skill is to rapidly interweave a diverse set of speech genres, to realign and push to excess various types of singing, preaching, and storytelling.

Bishop Bob Okalla's command of the Millennium Comet directly invoked pastoral preaching by mimicking the claims pastors make about the power of words to reshape Ghanaians' material circumstances. In contradistinction to the weight of spiritual and economic problems, the trickster's solution was absurdly direct. Using the power of words, he called down the unseen danger of the comet for all to scrutinize. A fantastical millennial rumor was rendered visible and absurd through its literal enactment. As the rock hovered behind him on stage through the rest of his monologue, the colonial-style watch ominously invoked both nostalgia and foreignness. Although Pastor Otabil's preaching oriented subjects toward a new future, Okalla's comedy emphasized symbols of time and the past, framing the future through the layered, unspoken presence of the past in daily life. Structuring his comedic routine through formal aspects of Charismatic preaching allowed Okalla to inhabit and comment on the struggles and hopes of material life in the metalanguage of performance.

Bishop Bob Okalla won the competition: three million cedis and a trip to Toronto to perform at Anansekrom, a festival for the Canadian Ghanaian community.[23] Ghana Boy took second place, also winning a trip to perform in Toronto.

Comedians are legitimate fakes. Comedians and pastors both draw on the tradition of Ananse the trickster in telling moral stories. Trickster storytelling relies on slippage between notions of trickery and talking. Comedians mimic and explode pastors' claims about the power of words by focusing on the pleasure of storytelling and trickery itself. Although a pastor is judged by the sincerity of his spiritual connection, a comedian is judged on the authenticity of his mimicry and how masterfully he juxtaposes and condenses different forms of public discourse. They both link daily life to moral lessons for public scrutiny within a multimedia aesthetic. The pastor represents an idealized neoliberal subject who is liberated to make individual moral choices. The comic is the perversion of this ideal, demonstrating the performance skills of a pastor while explicitly eschewing the claims to moral right. They stage comedic routines as moral lessons that explode the idea that words can be transformative, although in the process they highlight and recontextualize words and actions for further public scrutiny. The comic points to critical agency embodied in the ideal of parody itself. Comedians mock pastoral authority by inhabiting, condensing, and amplifying rhetorical and bodily styles. But in parody they validate the language of individual aspiration as central to public moral deliberation.

Mediating Scandals: Exploiting Sexual and Financial Value

The threat of charlatans haunts public discourse; some fear being tricked whereas others fear being accused of trickery. The prevalence of these figurations reveals the fake at the symbolic center of moral discourse assessed in terms of performance. Scandalous, shocking tales commonly focus on male pastors' sexual exploitation of female subjects who seek help for bearing children, moral purity, and business success. The gendered nature of pastoral misconduct shows how the female body often marks anxieties about the production and consumption of value. Stories about fake pastors and their sexual and material corruption infuse radio, television, video-films, newspapers, and the internet. Public talk is often mediated through texting and radio call-in programs dominated by mobile phone users. Tales of trickery have a broader life than each specific controversy, suffusing media and daily talk. Audiences try to discern whether a story's subject intends to deceive or is animating the word of God. Threats of moral trickery create spaces for public deliberation over hopes for spiritual and material wealth and fears of failure (Beidelman 1980).

Electronica confer the sheen of modernity. Technological forms speed up and multiply how rumors of fakeness circulate. Less reputable newspapers displayed at wooden kiosks along roadsides often have prominent photos and large headlines. As one newspaper worker explained to me, "These stories sell papers. People love to hear these controversies." These tales are not simply pulp entertainment but instead permeate state-sponsored and private media. The same stories move among media from newsprint to radio to the internet, linking dispersed audiences around moral titillation. For example, in 2003, the national press reported that the chief administrator of a major Kumasi state hospital "warned the public against the tricks of some fake pastors who make unnecessary claims to outwit them . . . he described such pastors as tricksters and warned radio stations to screen pastors who, in radio broadcasts, make . . . misleading claims at the peril of the lives of the members of the public."[24]

On radio, the Prophet Reverend Doctor Ebenezer Adarkwa Opambour Yiadom, founder of Ebenezer Miracle Worship Center, claimed that a woman came to him complaining of stomach pain after having surgery at the hospital. He prayed for her and a surgical knife "fell from the woman's private part." The medical administrator described the pastor as a liar who was only exposing his ignorance of the anatomy of the human body. He advised people seeking "counseling in life to go to good pastors . . . like Mensa Otabil." Ebenezer's actions are judged false; the pastor is cast as a trickster taking advantage of public suffering and naïveté. But as the saying goes, there is no such thing as bad press. Rather than destroy his legitimacy, controversies of this sort appear productive of Ebenezer's spiritual potential. Indeed, as I describe later, Ebenezer Miracle Worship Center grew to include major revival meetings and a television show despite various accusations.

Pastoral controversy is a common trope linking common concerns about sexuality, money, and family to the dangers and potencies of the spiritual realm. Moral shock provides a space for engaging with day-to-day moral ambivalences. Tales have stock characters emplaced within narratives of struggle, outrageous degradation, and potential redemption. A newspaper story titled "All Night Prayer Service in Hotel Room: Married Woman in Big Trouble" describes a woman attending a new church, the Come to Jesus Ministry.[25] Soon afterward, she stopped sleeping with her husband. He "found out that his wife's spate of all-night [prayer session] outings were false and that she had been secretly meeting the pastor of her church in a hotel." The pastor told her that he "had prophesied that she would die . . . if she continued living" with her husband. The pastor had "a vision" that the husband was "a wizard . . . possessed with 65 demons and has been communing with evil spirits each night." The pastor told the man to find another wife as "the marriage . . . had been spiritually annulled." In another newspaper story, "Pastor Runs Away from Pregnancy," a pastor claims "to have seen God in a vision asking him to marry a woman."[26] The woman consequently moved in with him. But as soon as she became pregnant, the pastor accused her of "being a witch who wanted to break his relationship with God." The woman's family took him to court for violating the marriage.

These stories link Ghanaians at home and abroad through a contested sense of moral community. Another recent article in the *Daily Guide* (reprinted online at ghanaweb.com) describes a thirteen-year-old girl told by her mother to visit a pastor for prayers and to receive an anointed handkerchief. The pastor was accused of having sex with the girl. The mother alerted the authorities, not initially because of sexual impropriety but rather because the pastor had shaved the girl's pubic hair and the mother feared he would spiritually harm the daughter. Within a day of being posted on the popular Ghanaian news website, three hundred responses were posted from Ghanaians in the country and around the globe. This story provoked passionate discussion on topics ranging from state political corruption to the history of the misconduct of white-devil colonial missionaries who had acted in similar ways toward Africans. Many responses lament the ubiquity of spiritual fakes. Several argue that Christian worshippers should take a lesson from Islam and read the Bible personally and more with personal discipline. One wrote, "Brothers & SISTERS, PLEASE OPEN YOUR EYES AND READ THE BIBLE YOURSELF. I can tell you that if any of this pastors [sic] comes to you and realize that you know the word then they get choke [sic] with their tricks."[27] Here is an argument against needing pastors to mediate God's word. Unmediated personal knowledge of God can circumvent the trickery of opportunistic preachers. In this logic, pastors insidiously make themselves appear necessary as spirit mediums for a generation freed from the hierarchies of older churches. The online posting continues, "Being a pastor is a call from God . . . [and] is not about money." In a conversation with Bronx-based Ghanaians about this case, one young man criticized linking material wealth and spirituality. "You case your body in gold and diamonds. But what does God need with diamonds? It is what is in your heart that matters. That is what concerns God."[28]

Spiritual trickery, although condemned morally, becomes a form of social mobility animated in electronic circulation. Stories of impropriety glamorize material temptations for powerful entrepreneurial men focused on sexual consumption of women and other forms of value. Newspapers, the internet, and radio replicate and circulate stories for Ghanaians to question and assess, creating a discursive space of moral deliberation. The saturation of electronic and print news with sexual and financial fakes blur the lines between desire and threat. Indeed, desire often emerges for that which is morally repugnant. Moral subjects are produced and contested through ambiguity of mediatized talk that links spiritual power to material success, spiritual trickery to entrepreneurialism. Moral ambivalence to pastoral authority and obsessions with discerning real from fake is itself an engine of public circulation. A poetics of public life relies on linking the two.

Radio and Gendered Moral Mediation

By the late 1990s, radio call-in programs were a staple of daily life, with stations competing for audiences with both the promise of spiritual deliverance and titillating topical discussions. They are built on ubiquitous circulating stories of trickery and public moral titillation, anxiety, and outrage. The fact that the most popular radio host is a woman points to the ways that highly visible and successful women become vulnerable under free-market conditions but also shows how the reinvention of established forms of gendered speaking and women's conversations (*mba nkomo*) can act as a form of moral regulation. New electronic media are well suited to address moral anxieties about the misuse of the Holy Spirit's power. The speed and repetition of electronic circulation magnifies the effect of moral stories. The formal aspects of radio call-in programs coupled with the ubiquity of mobile phones create a dispersed moral community of participant-listeners. This community centers on the public circulation of the idealized figure of the pastor and his model of aspiration and success. Tales of spiritual disaster provide a frame for understanding personal predicaments. The radio call-in format confers authority through technology's association with modernity's power. But the medium also lends itself to manipulation and trickery.

One example is Pastor Kwesi Bonsu,[29] who had a call-in program in Accra for several months. He claimed that the Holy Spirit gave him the power to heal ailments. People called and he healed their physical maladies over the phone. The program became a popular talking point around Accra. During one program a man called to be healed and the pastor prayed for him several times, but the man said he was not getting better. It was discovered that the pastor had been paying people to call and pretend to be healed. The program was quickly taken off the air. I had heard this program during theatre rehearsals with several popular groups in Accra. While discussing the debunking of this fake healer, one young actor jokingly placed his hands on a female friend's shoulders and went into a mock trance, speaking in tongues. Shaking violently, he shouted, "In the name of Jesus give me money! Amen." Everyone laughed. Another, more pious actor was upset at the mockery of prayer even though he agreed it replicated what had happened. He lamented quietly, "You see what people will do for money." Spiritual fakery—and the replicating parodies surrounding it—produces a space for debating and contesting ideologies of individual choice and deliberating on moral right.

The most significant radio call-in show in the first decade of private radio has been *Odo Ne Asomdwee* (Love and peace). It has been a platform for unmasking rampant fake pastors and other public scams. Grace Omaboe, a nationally renowned television and film actress, is popularly known as Maame Dokono, the comic name of the market woman she portrayed in the weekly soap opera *Ofoso Dadze* (Pastor Dadze).[30] In 1997 she began hosting her call-in show on Choice FM in Accra, focusing on solving problems for people whom neither family nor local authorities would help. The program is conducted entirely in Akan and Ga, targeting popular audiences. For Maame Dokono and her audiences, the program provides a dispersed moral community. Whereas many programs last for a short time, Maame Dokono has been on air continuously for over a decade and expanded the show to broadcast on Metro TV.[31] As one listener waiting outside the radio station one evening to speak with her explained to me, "She tells the truth, not like politicians or these fake religious leaders you can find everywhere."

During the broadcast of Maame Dokono's show, a large portion of shops, roadside markets, taxi ranks, public transportation vehicles, and work sites around the city were tuned in to listen to Maame Dokono. Outside Choice FM's studios, hundreds of people with a variety of problems often congregated, waiting to speak with Maame Dokono. For each program she picks several cases to investigate and bring onto the show. "The purpose of the program is to compensate the victims of spiritual and financial scams . . . and bring these false pastors and such people to public justice." Without legal authority she relies on the power of talk as public shaming. This draws on older oral traditions where rumor becomes a form of community moral discipline through shaming (Kwesi Yankah 1995). During the program, the host interviews various parties involved and broadcasts live phone calls for listeners to present their opinion on the case. Surprisingly, those accused of sexual misconduct or financial impropriety often come on air to defend themselves and try to save face. Reflecting the show's public importance, a common joke in Accra was to tell someone, "if you cheat me I will take you to Maame Dokono." This in fact replicates an older saying that shows the power of oral circulation as social discipline: "If you fool me, everyone will know what you have said."[32] Moral community is posited in the judgment of sincerity and consistency of language use. There is an expectation that the value of words will emerge in the process of their circulation.

Those accused of trickery often defend taking money for uncompleted spiritual acts by arguing that they are only a medium for powerful spirits they cannot control or that the ritual conditions were not met. Victims demystify secret rituals and prayer sessions by revealing them in titillating detail. Maame Dokono responds in the language of business exchange, pushing guests to admit that they do not have spiritual powers or that they have failed to fulfill their promises. For many, the exchange of money for spiritual favors is not the question. In Christian, Islamic, and traditional religions, congregations support religious leaders and institutions. Those who seek special attention for a funeral, wedding, or mediumship make donations. Piousness and spiritual sincerity are judged retroactively through successful exchanges of material for spiritual power.

The transformation of an actress into a radio call-in host seeking to unmask spiritual fakes shows the interpenetration of popular entertainment and Charismatism. Maame Dokono's acting fame magnifies her sense of pious duty and her authority to assess fakery. In an increasingly Charismatic public sphere, threats of spiritual fakeness and corruption provide a moral language through which legitimate public behavior is assessed. Moral authenticity is measured in the language of public performance. The struggles to discern real and fake spiritual power creates a deliberative space and a language for talking about the threat and promise of individuated desires. Maame Dokono's program has contributed to public discourse delineated by ubiquitous electronically circulating talk about corrupt preachers. The desperate hope for divine healing is haunted by fake pastors' duplicitous fluency in the language of spiritual power. The more someone is in need, the greater the anxiety at being led astray or taken advantage of sexually or financially. Radio call-in programs provide the potential for a female entrepreneur such as Maame Dokono to reinvent established social roles in which older respected women are seen as repositories of wisdom and moral regulators in times of societal crisis.[33] The circulatory potential of radio, internet, and mobile phone technologies allows the moral regulatory effect of women shaming men about male sexual and financial indiscretions to operate on broader urban and international scales.[34]

Ghana Boy Seeks Spiritual Help

Ghana Boy's story illustrates another aspect of the interplay between theatre artists and Charismatism. After placing second in the "Who Is Who" competition, Ghana Boy was poised for success. He traveled back and forth to North America several times for performances for Ghanaian events and academic programs. He had been making money painting signs but increasingly focused on his comedy. On one trip to the United States he decided to overstay his visa and try to make a life in New York. He searched for performance gigs and tried to make money to help his entertainment career. He worked as a security guard in the Bronx and passed out flyers in Times Square. His comedy was primarily in Akan, and the few gigs he could find for Ghanaian organizations in the United States did not pay much. He could not find steady work, and after several years he returned to Ghana with very little money. There were, of course, high expectations from family and friends that he would support them after traveling abroad. He explained to me, "When people travel everyone expects them to come back with riches, but they don't know the struggles 'over there.'" He was frustrated because he did not have the financial means to produce the films and albums he was planning. "I won't lie to you: things have been hard. But, by God's grace everything will be okay."

In 2007 Ghana Boy faced an unexpected tragedy. Slowly he went blind. "First I lost sight in one eye, and then the other one started to go. September 5, 2007, was the last day that I saw anything." When he lost his vision he was forced to return to his family's house in Kumasi. A group of friends and artists from Accra came to visit him at his mother's house in Kumasi after hearing rumors of his plight. We sat under a tree in the mud-block compound house tucked between an evangelical Pentecostal church and a garbage dump on the outskirts of the city.

When he started to go blind he went to Korle Bu, Accra's main hospital, but they did not find any physical causes for his lost vision. "When they told me that they did not see any problem with my eyes, I went to see my mother. I never told you this, Jesse, but she is a fetish, an Okomfo. She is at a powerful shrine in my hometown in Brong Ahafo Region. When I went there the shrine told me that the gods and ancestors were angry because I had traveled and had not come to them to pay my respects properly . . . you know when you go abroad people get jealous so it could also be that people are using witchcraft to bring me down." Spiritual attacks are usually understood to be committed by those closest to the victim. Those who are successful are subject to spiritual attack by friends and family who feel neglected and entitled to share in their kin's success. Many who seek supernatural protection do so out of anxiety that they have already been attacked by unknown assailants close to them. After returning to Kumasi, Ghana Boy was confined to a small cement-block room he shared with ten male relatives. During the day he was mostly alone with only his mobile phone and radio for companionship. He showed us how he saved numbers on his Nokia phone by memorizing and counting how many buttons to push.

Ghana Boy explained that he called several radio pastors. He finally got in touch with one of most popular, the Prophet Reverend Doctor Ebenezer Adarkwa Opambour Yiadom, whom I described earlier. Ghana Boy explained that he went to Ebenezer Miracle Worship Center, where the Prophet pre-interviewed him before the service, asking details about losing his vision. Ghana Boy told him that he had traveled abroad, lost his passport on returning to Ghana, and soon after lost his vision.

Reverend Ebenezer is young, handsome, well dressed. His church attracts young, active audiences and is broadcast on radio and television across the country. At his most animated, his performance emphasizes forceful intonation, convoluted facial expressions, and tense trance-like bodily movements that accentuate that he is struggling to channel forces from another realm. The television show uses dramatic editing to emphasize Ebenezer's miraculous powers of healing. It is at its most dramatic when the prophet gestures toward the crowd with prayers and the camera pans across the audience as they collapse in waves as if directly hit by the spiritual force of his words and gestures. The camera movements imagine power flowing from his body into the audience. Sitting in the congregation of the megachurch, Ghana Boy was called on stage during the healing section of the service. "He acted like we had not met. He started asking me have I recently traveled and I replied 'yes.' The crowd shouted with excitement. 'Heeey!' He then asked if I lost my passport and I said yes. The crowd screamed. Then he prayed intensely and said that someone was attacking my eyes but that I would be better in four weeks. Everyone shouted with joy and praised the Lord. I went to sit down again . . . that was three months ago."

As we contemplated his plight, Ghana Boy mused on the techniques pastors use to appear spiritually powerful. He joked about a man with a high-pitched voice who called in to a radio pastor who healed people over the radio. "Most of the women calling claim to have problems giving birth, you see. But this pastor was not clever enough when he received a call. 'Hello?'" Ghana Boy says in an exaggerated falsetto voice. "Don't say anything else, ma'am. I can see that you have a problem with your womb," Ghana Boy says, shifting into the smooth authoritative voice of a radio preacher. He pauses for comic effect. Again in an exaggerated high voice he intones, "Please, Pastor, I am a man, ooh!" His small audience laughs as Ghana Boy shakes his head, telling jokes he has performed for large crowds.

After Ebenezer's failure, Ghana Boy explained, "I am covering all my bases." He was going to finish the traditional shrine rituals in his home village to "appease the gods." He is also seeing medical doctors at Kumasi's Akomfe Anokye Teaching Hospital in case they can find something physically wrong with him. And he hoped to find a pastor to really heal him. His friend Serwaa Koto sells tea and bread in Adom, a central shopping area of Kumasi, and comes after work to help him. She is a religious Christian but is upset that he has spent so much money going to see pastors who have cheated him. Another friend (who is an actress) confided her concern that Ghana Boy had given several hundred dollars given to him to pay for food and shelter to several others who claimed they could heal him through spiritual means. Sitting in his room, Serwaa Koto says there is only one option left. "What else can we do? You have been to the doctors and to several pastors who claim they will help, but all they do is take your money."

As Ghana Boy's story circulated, it picked up speed, intertwined with other tales of spiritual malfeasance. In August 2008, someone in the Concert Party Union, of which Ghana Boy was a member, was accused of sending a photograph of the wife of recently deceased comedian Bob Santos to a fetish priest to have her killed "out of jealousy around his success," as another member says. She was interviewed on Hot FM in Accra, broadcast by its affiliate Fox FM in Kumasi, where Ghana Boy heard the program. She mentioned Ghana Boy's lost vision as an example of the kinds of spiritual attacks that are made out of jealousy. She discussed how artists and Ghanaians more generally "bring each other down" using spiritual means. The radio DJ called Ghana Boy to talk about his case on air. He described how spiritual attacks are commonly used to prevent fellow Ghanaians from succeeding. "Out of jealousy we hold ourselves back."

This common discourse of national lament connects the spiritual realm to material gain by positing the collectivity as opposed to individual aspiration.

Witchcraft accusations and rumor-circulation in Ghanaian societies are old disciplinary forms for punishing individuals who put personal interests ahead of the national, ethnic, village, or family collective (Field 1962). Aspiration takes many forms. Foreign travel produces value in the imagination of those left at home. Entertainers are self-fashioning public figures, making them susceptible to scrutiny. Because of these two factors Ghana Boy felt especially vulnerable to spiritual attack. He traced his physical ailment to his neglect of traditional spiritual forces and the perception that he had not looked after collective needs in favor of his aspirations. "When people think you make money and you don't donate to your church or to the shrine they think you are holding out on them. They will punish you. But my problem is I never made any money, but they did not believe me. What was I to do?" In seeking to counteract these forces, Ghana Boy was again victimized by pastors who preyed on his neediness.

In September 2008, Ghana Boy was interviewed live on 104.5 FM's regular evening program. He related to me, "The host challenged the public, calling anyone who can help me get my sight back. Since the interview my phone has not rested. We have selected and interviewed two or three people who by God's grace will help me." Ghana Boy's continued hope and public search for miraculous solutions is played out through his mobile phone. Despite recognition that he has been tricked by spiritual frauds, he seeks those who are morally good and spiritually giving.

Ghana Boy's tragic story shows how aspiration and struggle are refracted in spiritual terms. And loss can be replicated, performed, and made productive. By January 2009 he was recording music and acting again in several video-films, in fact portraying a false prophet in one. I called Ghana Boy and we talked while he was on set. "My character is very funny. I give counseling to people. When they come and say, 'I need a husband. I want to travel,' I lie to them. I tell them I will pray, I will use special oils, and then I take their money. The film is tentatively titled *Onyame Huhunue Wo*, 'God Sees You.' And the cameraman is shooting it so that you cannot tell that I am blind."

Indeed Ghana Boy latched on to the sudden rise of a Twi-language video-film industry in Kumasi. Whereas Accra-based video producers focused on trying to reach high production values and portray "modern" scenarios and English-language dialogue, in Kumasi, films tended to be absurdist, comedic tales in Akan. Younger comedians, unable to reach live audiences, found a new audience by shooting raucous, improvised scenarios and rapidly releasing films in two, three, or four parts, selling them from vans and in markets and as digital downloads quickly and cheaply to outcompete bootleggers. Ghana Boy was trying to reach Agya Koo, a peer comedian who had risen rapidly to fame through Kumasi-based video-films, to see if he would help him get into the new market.

"He says he will help and then doesn't pick [up] my calls. . . . Now that he is successful he acts like a stranger, but we came up together."

Doubling as Moral Affect

Despite the continued dominance in local Ghanaian political discourse that the nation-state and its related forms of civil society be judged in singular, universal terms, ideas of moral citizenship circulate across public life through culturally specific ideas of performance and its interpretation. A shared poetic configuration endures across genres. As actors adopt stances and deploy signs and styles, they encourage references to the historical authority of various signifiers that remain part of a shared public aesthetic, which is both enduring and evolving with new usages. Their reiteration contributes to the making of an enduring set of new media circuits through which Charismatism increasingly blends into other realms, and popular performance forms blend into religious worship. Pastors and comedians adopt similar stances and parodically inhabit each other's styles of delivery, linking dispersed genres of performance within single frames. Both create pleasurable performances that impart moral stories for contemplation but balance these sentiments with different intents. By creating a poetics of Charismatism that builds on the established performance values of staged performance, actors structure disparate participation roles into a lasting discourse of performative moral duality, a duality that is productive in enticing participants to critically engage in public moral discourse by assessing performances in terms of their authenticity and force.

As the previous chapters show, electronically mediated popular and religious genres neither oppose nor replace state-centered theatre but rather intertwine various technological and institutional realms through shared performance idioms, combining sacred with profane pleasures in performance. Fakes are productive, not only of pastoral authority but also of sustained moral discourse built on older popular genres. The threat of the fake is generative in structuring this critical discourse cultivated across performance genres.

Moral deliberation provoked by storytelling demonstrates the gendered aspects of Ghanaian public culture, in which freedoms associated with the free market unleash masculine anxieties about female sexuality and economic accumulation while also providing new possibilities for female entrepreneurs and speakers, such as Maame Dokono, as public moral voices. She draws on older ideas of women being the bearers of wisdom and regulators of social mores to claim a voice as an entrepreneur on air. The intense public focus on women's sexual exploitation locates concerns about the real and the fake in bodily ideas of value production. Ghana Boy's case highlights a public obsession linking travel to the production of value and the circulation of wealth.

Public obsession with the fake becomes a form of belief and moral discipline that produces what it claims to mitigate against. The pastor is an idealized entrepreneurial subject creating a market and audience in performance. Participants become agentive by reflexively choosing the ideology of choice itself. Marketization presents new agencies as well as new uncertainties. Publics struggle to maintain clear moral dichotomies that threaten to collapse in the affinity between individual choice and personal greed. Entertainers often capitalize on this shifting terrain between moral clarity and collective anxiety.

Local understandings of performance are rooted in assessments of actors' moral dispositions. Audiences and congregations strain to discern the spiritual legitimacy of converts and pastors claiming authority through the Holy Spirit. The threat of the fake's inversion of value conveys the hopes and dangers of individual choice. Electronic media accelerate pastoral influence as well as anxiety about fakeness. Moral assessment of performance blurs the lines between entertainment and worship, political-economic concerns and spiritual struggle. Theatre artists mix religious and entertainment genres permeating public life with Charismatic moral sensibilities.

Aspiration in the mid-twentieth-century Gold Coast colony was for political autonomy and access to the promises of modernity. Workers strove for stable wage labor and control of state institutions formerly denied to African peoples. In the new millennium, the failures of postcolonial centralized states have shifted into precarious imaginaries of entrepreneurial prosperity underpinned by faith in the divine and in marketization. Personal aspiration becomes a divine mirror of the mediatized, sped-up landscape, as aspirants copy successful pastors, football stars, business leaders, popular singers, and movie actors. The idea of choice itself is a fetish for freedom, structured as moral ideal for the individual and immoral nightmare for the collective. Neoliberalism structures individual freedom as desirable but increasingly out of reach (Comaroff and Comaroff 2000). The ubiquity and speed of electronic and digital technologies—radio, the internet, mobile phones—and the overlapping realms of religion, entertainment, news, and politics blend into an overlapping mediatized spectacle (Debord 1994: 16; Virilio 1977). Sermons circulate on radio, on television, and in digital forms. Private anxieties are made public in mobile phone calls to radio stations that are then streamed online for Ghanaians abroad. Secret rituals are described for mass newspaper and radio audiences. Business, pleasure, and spirituality merge through the language of lament and moral anxiety. The fake becomes a ubiquitous part of the daily circulations of media and talk, creating an inverted image of public Christian morality.

Debates about fakeness recall concerns with witchcraft accusations unleashed in the modern colonial state in 1930s West Africa (Allman and Parker 2005). There is a similar logic of inversion and anxiety in which spiritual forces are used in defense against others thought to already be on the spiritual attack. E. E. Evans-Pritchard explains that the logic of sorcery and witchcraft is retroactive in that misfortune is subsequently explained by attributing malevolence to individuals who—intentionally with sorcery and unintentionally with witchcraft—produce destructive action (cf. Evans-Pritchard 1937). Gluckman (1965: 220) argues that witchcraft is both a "theory of morality" and of causality. In Charismatic discourse, prosperity defines moral legitimacy, and a retroactive logic frames success as positive and failure as negative.

The language of moral action allows people to both inhabit and critique individuated aspirations and personal consumptive practices. Counterfeit moral and economic value is often tied to modernity's aspirations; fakes and fetishes mobilize spirituality in imagining moral and immoral agencies (Comaroff and Comaroff 2006: 13–16). As André Gide (1949) explores through counterfeit currency, neither real nor fake has ultimate referents but gains legitimacy through practices of circulation. But the threat of the counterfeiter also breeds anxiety about the origins of value, unleashing a crisis of authority. As postcolonial Africa is reshaped by neoliberal concerns, national publics become moral landscapes of individual potential and threat. In Nigeria the confluence of fabulous oil wealth and authoritarian military rule produced what Andrew Apter (2005) has called a "simulacra state" that supported fantastical schemes for wealth production. The disjuncture between the public display of wealth and structural modes of production helped 419 scams and various forms of economic trickery become almost-acceptable forms of wealth creation (D. Smith 2008). As with electronically mediated Charismatism, these forms rely on circulation itself to produce legitimacy.

Neoliberalism produces suspicion that things are not as they appear. The specter of the fake pastor manifests fear of a bad transaction, of uneven exchange. Prevalent accusations of fakery reveal a disconnect between ideals of entrepreneurship and the lived experience of an economy reliant on service industries, travel, and consumption as productive engines. Having faith is an agentive moral stance—a belief in the performative potential of public life—that sets conditions for the miraculous to occur. Moral anxieties about spiritual attacks and fakery are animated by the performative doubleness associated with this postcolonial version of neoliberalism (Comaroff and Comaroff 2006). In neoliberal Ghana, the renewable morality of hope belies promises of economic success and threats of failure, while fear of fakery is a marker of belief.

8 Copying Independence
Backstage at the Fiftieth-Anniversary Reenactment of Nkrumah's Independence Speech

> Almighty Kwame receive your drink
> Heaven and earth, receive your drink
> Ancestors receive your drink
> Let's pray to Kwame Nkrumah, Ghanaians!
> Rap lyrics, *Kwame Nkrumah*, Obrafour[1]

HIDDEN IN THE BACK of the Arts Centre in downtown Accra, over one hundred actors prepare for the annual reenactment of Kwame Nkrumah's March 6, 1957 midnight speech declaring Ghana a free, independent nation. It is the evening of March 5, 2007. A variety of performers have come for the event; concert party comedians like Ghana Boy, television actors like David Dontoh, dancers, and old-time actors and musicians mingle. Some relax at a drinking spot in a blue wooden kiosk. Others chat as they change into period costumes in the open-air theatre that once was a center for theatrical activity in the city. This speech is one of Nkrumah's best known, quoted in a wide variety of contexts, with snippets regularly appearing on television and radio. The iconic photograph of Nkrumah waving a handkerchief from a podium—which is even replicated by hip-hop group Native Funk Lords for an album cover—was taken at this event (J. Shipley 2013a: 141).

The Rawlings NDC government had commissioned the Ghana Actors' Guild (GAG) annually to perform a carefully scripted, condensed, and staged copy of the original independence celebrations. The event continued under the NPP government. Whereas in most years the reenactment has been a relatively small remembrance, 2007's celebration is imbued with heightened expectations and receives broad public attention due to the milestone fiftieth anniversary (Akyeampong and Aikins 2008). A state committee, with the aid of private marketing consultants, has branded the event "Ghana@50." They have organized highly publicized events throughout the year, culminating in Nkrumah's re-created midnight speech to be attended by President Kufuor and foreign dignitaries. Kufuor's New Patriotic Party (NPP) is anxious to align itself with Nkrumah's reputation as Pan-Africanist visionary as Ghana positions itself as a leader of Africa's liberalization movement (Pierre 2012). The government is especially interested in eliding the memory that, as most Ghanaians know, the NPP is the political descendant of Nkrumah's opposition, which actually voted against independence from British rule in a 1956 referendum. Heightening the sense of spatio-temporal overlap, the independence speech will be reenacted next to the Arts Centre at the Kwame Nkrumah Mausoleum, which was built as a memorial aimed at tourists to celebrate the first leader's Pan-African vision. The layerings of past significance over the same space shows how this urban landscape is built through historical memory. Nkrumah's body was—after several interim gravesites—reinterred here, the very spot where his original proclamation of independence was made.

Reenactment is a performance genre that relies on explicit copying as a form of reference, calling on audiences and performers to reflexively assess the closeness and distance of the current moment from the event being replicated. However, a doubling is inevitable in reframing past events. As past and present run simultaneously, participants can assess the relationship between them. While in content, this mimetic performance strives for verisimilitude, the formal framing devices of the theatrical event condense, circulate, and distance the performance from its original. On a micro level, Nkrumah's speech and celebration are copied with great skill. David Dontoh, the actor portraying Nkrumah, turns in a virtuoso performance, copying with uncanny precision the former leader's speech. Supporting roles are played by concert party performers, television soap-opera actors, dancers, and other artists in need of work. They dress in authentic period costumes, performing intricate dances that represent various cultural groups from around the nation. The performers' detail-oriented skill in copying the moment of independence—achieved through replicating the bodily gestures and words from the original event—is meant to bring past and present into alignment in broader social registers. But the processes of copying, condensing, and carefully staging a transformative political event highlight the dissonance between the uncertainty and excitement of the original moment and the lack of emotional transformation or conflict in its dramatic replica. Indeed, the closeness of the copy to the original has the opposite effect from that intended. For audiences and actors, the sincerity of a reenactment precludes the irreverence and transgression that made Ghana's independence an international sign of Africa's emergence from colonial rule. For many participants, reframing this event emphasizes the gap between the nation as a historical locus of socialism and Pan-Africanism and its present position as a celebrated emblem of free-market reform. In examining why this performance, and the Ghana@50 events more generally, are met with cynicism from performers and audiences, I demonstrate how the poetics of public performance are objectified and circulated. The state's imagination of itself in a moment of anxiety, and the ways that actors relate to its performance, reveal how an enduring poetics of theatre shapes Ghanaian interpretations of state spectacle.

What is the difference between parodying and reenacting (Bhabha 1994; J. Shipley 2013b; Yurchak 2005)? Various types of copying are signifying practices that impart meaning to words and deeds based on shifting contextual frames and on how performers are cast as authors or animators of speech within them. As I have discussed, Goffman's (1981) ethnographic approach to talk and communicative action separates the speaker/actor into a triad—author, animator, principal—complicating the various aspects of performance participation and their relationship to culturally legitimated positions. According to Goffman, the animator is one who actually speaks, the principal is the subject whose positionality is established through semiotic action, and the author is the one who is ascribed responsibility for the signs used (Kockelman 2004: 131). As opposed to many theories of performance that assume that subjects that emerge from ritual and performance events are coherent and singular and perdure across other social registers and over time, Goffman's work disentangles participation role-taking from totalizing ideas of subjectivity (Kockelman 2006a). As subjects reference and link multiple registers, participants are interlocked in positions of authority and passivity. But the ways that participants embody, enact, and realign aesthetic and moral values within a performance point to socially specific ways that a community conceives of coherence and the stability of identity.

In the previous chapter, I show how pastors and comedians copy and reference performance styles and recontextualize them to gain speaking authority. Exaggeration and irreverence dominate the emotional valence of their pastoral and comedic performances, as does an ethos of improvisation and uncertainty. Audiences struggle to discern pastoral sincerity and spiritual validity in how they animate the Holy Spirit. Listeners hang on a comedian's every word, waiting to catch unexpected references and, as in Ananse storytelling, avoid being tricked. In the process, observers assess the authorship of words and gestures and judge speakers' moral positions and performance abilities accordingly. In parodies, while a speaker is understood to be simply reporting or animating another's words, he or she inflects and recontextualizes references to give them new meaning. Doubling for a comedian is an intentional form of parody, and for a pastor, perhaps, an unintentional one.

In contrast, monumental reenactments attempt to preclude parody and uncertainty that shape other Ghanaian theatrical genres. Various types of copying differ in how they use references and how they predispose participants to interpret and connect signs and actions. Performers must navigate the gaps between character and actor accordingly, showing that forms of copying and embodiment are contextually specific. Replicating a political speech from a moment of national transformation is intended as a respectful representation that lends legitimacy to present speakers—as proxies for their patrons—by creating a present intimacy with memories of past greatness. In re-creating independence, actors take on the roles of political leaders and celebrants in a foundational, mythic moment of the nation. While the content of the reenactment is framed in a sincere realistic style, the blending of other genres—cultural display, media commentary, tourist spectacle, formal staged drama—creates a multimedia event with parodic potential. In objectifying independence as a cultural performance, an exact replica to be consumed live and on television, participants are distanced from the original moment and from identification as sincere, national subjects. In the dramatization of Nkrumah's speech, Ghana's originary political transformation is remade as historical copy. In this reiteration, meant to bring audiences closer through a moment of sincere nationalism, participants are distanced in the reflexive awareness of the copy.

Generational Change: Theatre as Nostalgia and Wage Labor

Informal talk in the lead-up to the performance marks generational differences regarding nostalgia and possibility and ideas of theatre as a form of labor. While young actors appear pragmatic and cynical about Nkrumah's historical legacy and participate in the performance as wage laborers, the older generations lament the lost hope that the anniversary brings forth. The contrast between how younger and older actors imagine the links between independence and the present is stark. Older artists born around the end of colonial rule identify with the independence-era state and its leadership, which promised to fight for its citizenry and the equality of Ghanaians and Africans as they entered a skeptical and unequal global ecumene. The younger generation, born in the 1970s and 1980s, were raised in the midst of state privatization with its valorizations of free markets, individual earning, and personal consumption.

As evening falls, performers in their teens and twenties wearing Ghana@50 T-shirts and waving Ghanaian flags have just returned from parading through the streets of Accra on a large truck with Kwame Nkrumah's Rolls-Royce strapped to the back. Behind the Arts Centre, actors prepare, eat, and discuss the upcoming event. Goldfinger, a veteran actor and concert party group leader, talks loudly to comedian Ghana Boy about the old days as younger Ghana Actors' Guild members drink and play checkers. "You kids do not remember what we were fighting for in those days." Switching between English and Twi to emphasize his points, Goldfinger recalls the political struggles of fifty years ago. He quotes several of Nkrumah's speeches at length with both bitterness and nostalgia in his voice.

"I was a teenager in Kumasi but I remember well what Nkrumah was trying to do. He called on Ghanaians to stand up to be seen in the world. He built the Organization of African Unity. He declared that Ghana's independence was meaningless unless linked up with the total liberation of Africa."

As he gets more passionate, the younger actors gently tease him. "Hey, old man, sit down. You no go fit start a revolution now?"

Goldfinger's tone reflects a discourse of lament for past hope familiar among older Ghanaians. He continues ignoring the taunts. "Since Nkrumah was overthrown this country has been in trouble. I'm telling you. These kids don't even know who fought and died for them." A former boxer and soldier, Goldfinger had spent time in Europe before returning to Ghana to focus on acting in concert party popular theatre shows. He remains an officer of the Concert Party Union, though he has not had much work in recent years and makes money selling *akpeteshie,* a local distilled alcohol, and other drinks. As I have said, the Arts Centre is on the site of a colonial-era membership club for elite Africans, the Rodger Club. In the 1980s when the state built regional cultural centers, it became the Centre for National Culture (CNC) in Accra. In the 1990s, the place developed into a tourist center selling arts and crafts to foreigners. In the back, local artists and performers inhabit their own realm separate from tourist economies. Goldfinger gets up from the porch of the drinking spot and goes to his rooms, which, like those of many poor artists, are in the back of the Arts Centre. He returns carrying a plastic bag full of worn and warped 78 rpm records. He speaks to me and to Ghana Boy as the others are ignoring him. "Shipley! Do you know what these are? Do you see this record? It is an original copy of Lord Kitchener's 'Birth of Ghana.'" This song is the Trinidadian Calypso star's well-known celebration of Nkrumah. Goldfinger begins to sing the calypso highlife song with a powerful voice trained by years on the stage:

> Dr. Nkrumah went on his way
> to make the Gold Coast what it is today . . .
> Ghana is the name
> we wish to proclaim
> We will be jolly merry and gay
> Sixth of March, Independence Day

His voice cuts out as some younger men parodically join in while others try to contain their amusement as the old man sings the familiar highlife melody. While the song is still well known, young people do not attach the same sentiment to it as those for whom it marks lost hopes of independence-era Ghana.

Most of the actors present are in their teens and twenties. I find out that many older-generation actors, frustrated by this government's lack of support, have refused to perform. While some are interested in the historical importance of reenacting Nkrumah's speech, for these youths this is a paid gig, one among many state and private sponsored shows they put on, incorporating various kinds of costuming, dialogue, music, and dance, into a theatrical framework. Ghana Boy smirks at me. "I think they will be late declaring independence today. [*Laughter.*] It is almost midnight and we have not even gotten into costume. But today we can celebrate getting a paycheck. Last year the government only bought us *kenkey* and a small piece of fish for the reenactment."[2] He holds up his little finger to indicate the size of the fish they were given for payment. Goldfinger intercedes: "Especially considering that this government was the very party opposed to Nkrumah and independence at the time, [and] people forget they actually voted against it, they are lucky that anyone showed up this year to perform at all." The artists have been promised they will be paid in cash, though there is some concern as many bills for Ghana@50 events throughout the year have gone unpaid by government organizers.

Goldfinger continues his recollections of Nkrumah. "He was the original *Showboy!* When he spoke everyone paid attention. He was a trickster and magician. . . . His enemies were afraid of him; women loved him." Part of Nkrumah's resilience as a politician was his widely recognized abilities as a masterful orator. He was referred to as a trickster partly because of his ability for a time to play Soviet and Chinese interests off Western demands in maintaining Ghana's balance between cold-war allegiances. When I ask Goldfinger why Nkrumah was seen as a trickster, he explains, "He was a powerful speaker and could persuade anyone to do anything." The art of persuasive speaking is crucial to the actor and the politician. Nkrumah was nicknamed "Showboy" in a popular highlife tune celebrating his rhetorical skill and masterful performance sensibility. The fact that many saw him as a kind of trickster points to his ability to improvise, to draw on multiple symbolic registers, to sway an audience while rendering performative intent ambiguous. Having beliefs that are internally consistent is a moral principle of purportedly universal modern subjects. However, picking and choosing to survive is a morally legitimate position for those on the margins living alternate modernities.

Walking around the Arts Centre I talk with performers, some of whom I have known for ten years through my research on participation in Ghanaian theatre, television, video-films, music, and state cultural institutions. Others I am just meeting. While some have attended secondary school and university and have formal theatre training, most are from semieducated backgrounds, having grown up in rural areas or on the margins of bigger cities. They occupy what Karin Barber (1987, 1997) describes as an in-between class. I have come unannounced to this event, so the actors improvise a role for me as a participant. As an ethos of improvisation pervades popular theatre, Ghana Boy asks if I want to get into costume. I am not sure whether he is serious or making fun of me. What roles I could play? I could be American vice president Richard Nixon or perhaps a member of the Soviet delegation present at independence, who were notable observers at the 1957 event. I decline, instead helping to organize equipment and costumes.

The actors gather in small groups across the open courtyard to get into their costumes. They dress as stock characters using traditional cloth, beads, and hairstyles to generically represent, as one actor tells me, "a typical person" from the various regions and cultural groups of the country. The performance is supposed to replicate the actual moment of independence, but the costuming betrays the actors' visual and bodily acknowledgment of the distance between today and their images of past generations. The actors representing the Fante people from the coastal region dress in colonial-era Bermuda shorts, white shirts, and knee socks, while the Asante put on kente cloth. The Ewe group wears ceramic and glass beads, Ewe kente, and white powder. Women stuff pillows and cloth under their dresses, a common technique to emphasize their backsides when they dance. Some use exaggerated makeup to whiten their hair and beards. "We are supposed to stand for the different regions of the country," one artist explains. "We represent that by our dress and our dance, to show [that] the different cultures were united in celebrating independence. This is a performance, though. Artists do not have to represent their own cultural groups."

Staging Independence

The coup that overthrew Nkrumah on February 24, 1966, was led by dissident military officers backed by the U.S. government. Seidu Bananzi, from Tongo in the Upper East Region, who was one of his personal bodyguards, recalls that the opposition was "too scared to plot something while Nkrumah was in the country because he was too powerful . . . and charismatic. So they waited until he was on a diplomatic mission to Asia."[3] After the coup Nkrumah lived in exile in Guinea, where President Sékou Touré made him an honorary co-president. He died in 1972 in Bucharest, though his body has not had a restful time since his death. Its movements reflect the Ghanaian state's ambivalence to recuperating Nkrumah's legacy. His body was first buried in Guinea, though his remains were subsequently moved to his mother's home village in Ghana's Western Region. Then, on July 1, 1992, he was reinterred for a second time in the mausoleum built at the old polo grounds in downtown Accra, where he had declared Ghana's independence. This was part of the Rawlings state's recuperation project spearheaded by the new National Commission on Culture in the late 1980s and early 1990s, building urban monuments to the political and cultural legacy of Pan-Africanism, to attract tourism and to imbue Accra with a national cultural sensibility.[4] The government reimagined Accra as a space of return for African diasporic peoples united through common struggles against the slave trade and colonialism. Nkrumah's mausoleum was meant to be a site of pilgrimage for people from across the African diaspora, memorializing the founding of Ghana. While Rawlings drew heavily on Nkrumah's legacy, some close to him felt he was personally more ambivalent. The large concrete monument was designed as a giant traditional executioner's sword planted in the ground. A story circulates that late one night during construction of this monument, Rawlings was driving around Accra as he tended to do and decided that the statue would be too tall, so he dictated that the handle should be left off, rendering the intended sword an abstract sculpture. In this personal ambivalence he seems to recognize that reawakening the symbolic power of Nkrumah's political and intellectual image was instrumental for maintaining power as well as being crucial to the development of the Ghanaian state.

On High Street, several hundred meters down from Nkrumah's mausoleum, a giant stage is being erected for "The President's Show," an all-night popular music concert to follow the replication of Nkrumah's independence speech. The concert will feature the latest popular hiplife artists—an electronically driven musical form combining rap, highlife, *kpanlogo*, and other popular styles (J. Shipley 2013a). Youth begin to congregate in the streets as night falls. In contrast to the ordered reenactment, a jubilant crowd of several thousand youths slowly gathers around the large stage set up in High Street outside the mausoleum to listen to the popular musicians.

Close to midnight the actors are finally in costume. Excitement mounts as the artists leave the Arts Centre gates; leaders shout last-minute directions for the show as they move en masse through crowds in the streets toward the gates of the mausoleum only a few hundred meters away. As they attempt to enter the Kwame Nkrumah Mausoleum, there is confusion as the mass of actors push at the gates but are stopped as they have no official escort or paperwork. The soldiers at the gates are unsure of themselves and overwhelmed by the crowds. As regular Ghanaians in the streets attempt to enter to watch the reenactment, soldiers shout for order. At the same time, the flatbed truck enters the gates carrying Nkrumah's Rolls-Royce, retrieved, some say, after decades of being hidden in the bush.

An argument breaks out as soldiers, ordered to restrict entry to the mausoleum, prevent the artists from entering the grounds. Performers are dressed in traditional styles—kente cloth, northern smocks—that mark different regions of the country circa 1957; some, wearing colonial civil-service khaki shorts and short-sleeved white shirts, surge to the gate. "Can't you see we are in costume? We do not have our identification with us. Everyone dressed in old styles for the show is with the group!" one performer shouts. The actors' period costumes do not seem to convince the military guards, who are preparing for the arrival of President Kufuor, President Olusegun Obasanjo of Nigeria, and a high-powered retinue of diplomatic and political officials from across the continent. One artist jokes to the guard, "My friend, do you want to be responsible for stopping independence from happening?" While the artists argue half in jest, half in outrage, the soldiers push back in agitation, and several even unsling their rifles. For a few minutes everyone is stuck, unable to enter and unable to turn around as the crowd surges behind them. Finally, the artists are separated from the crowd members and let in as lead artists indicate for the soldiers who are the performers. Several actors tell the guards that I am with the group and I am ushered in, trying to be helpful with minor stage-managing tasks, before taking a seat in the audience. The performers disperse among the audience, awaiting their moment.

The yearlong Ghana@50 programs aim to present historical continuity and political consensus by collapsing and linking the history of independence into the contemporary state (Akyeampong and Aikins 2008). One way this is achieved is visually. Digitally manipulated photographs of Kufuor and Nkrumah sharing a moment of laughter are posted all around the city and epitomize the political struggle to bring together disparate spaces and times in the search for public consensus. The previous day while driving with an older popular-music producer, I comment on the waving flags lining most streets in the capital emblazoned with images of President Kufuor and Kwame Nkrumah together. In the photograph Kwame Nkrumah looks out toward the viewer with determination, while Kufuor grins and stares at the first president. Driving his run-down Mercedes, my friend explains, "At first the government tried to celebrate independence without Kwame Nkrumah. When they realized this wouldn't work, they have tried to retell the story and take Nkrumah's story as their own. These goofy pictures of Kufuor smiling at Nkrumah! What are people supposed to think, they are best friends? But young people don't know. And for foreigners, Ghana is the face of progress, African democracy; that's how the government keeps getting aid money. So they need to maintain the image, you know?" The state at independence posited African culture as the moral core of the nation and a new Ghanaian citizen-subject. Ghana@50 in copying this image seems to unwittingly mock its own attempts to get close.

The staging of Nkrumah's speech was scripted and directed by Efo Kojo Mawugbe. A proponent of Rawlings's revolutionary government of the early 1980s, he is a prolific playwright who has worked since the 1990s in various capacities with the National Commission on Culture. I met him in 1998 when he returned to the School of Performing Arts to do a new M.F.A. course in theatre directing.[5] In 2007 he is director of the National Theatre of Ghana. I have not seen him in several years and congratulate him on the prominence of the reenactment this year, which often has had small crowds and little media recognition. He wears a newly tailored shirt sewn from special fiftieth-anniversary celebration cloth emblazoned with Kwame Nkrumah's face. As with all major public events in Ghana, the anniversary is marked by printing special cloth, which men and women can sew into dresses and shirts. I comment that there are several different wax-print and batik cloth patterns in the markets commemorating the anniversary but that I had not seen any with Nkrumah's face. He tells me that though the cloth with Nkrumah's face had been one of the early patterns for sale, no one was wearing it. "The government bought up all of it [and got rid of it]. They did not want people celebrating and displaying his face. They do not want people to be reminded that they were in the opposition when independence was declared."

Mawugbe originally intended the independence play to link Nkrumah's political legacy to the Rawlings Revolution. But Kufuor has worked hard to align himself with public reverence for Nkrumah's declaration of independence as the inaugural moment of Ghanaian nationhood while skipping over Nkrumah's overthrow, military rulers, and the Rawlings era. Public discourse around Ghana@50 has been dominated by images of Nkrumah declaring independence and discussions of his vision of the unity of African nations, but as Mawugbe points out, they are "sanitized images. The NPP do not want to remind people of the revolutionary implications of Nkrumah. They just want to look good by association." As Nkrumah's Pan-Africanist legacy is celebrated, there is a loud silence about Nkrumah's overthrow in 1966 by forces aligned with NPP forebears and criticisms that he focused national resources on foreign struggles across the continent at the expense of his own people. The discrepancies of this revisionist history were not lost on many observers as radio talk shows and private newspapers circulated criticisms of the government's handling of the affairs.

Mawugbe explains to me how he condensed the events of independence into a viewable, timed performance. "We watched the films of the event and talked to people who were there. I exactly replicated the speech with his switching languages and hand gestures and dress. The dances are performed to show how all the people of Ghana were symbolically part of the new nation." The original event is already mediated by its iconic representation on film and in photographs. To show the unity of the nation, each group moves to the center of the staging area under Nkrumah's podium and do a dance for about five minutes that is meant to represent a typical cultural performance from their region while Nkrumah stands waiting to speak.

At the reenactment, government officials, embassy staff, invited guests, tourists, and elite Ghanaians are seated around the periphery of the fountain in front of Nkrumah's statue. Perhaps a thousand are in attendance. A special box is designated for the presidents of Ghana and Nigeria. They have come from a session of parliament with UN Secretary General Kofi Annan and the Duke of Kent as the queen of England's representative commemorating the 1957 vote, attended by the Duchess of Kent, approving the motion for independence.[6] At the gates, guards continue to keep people from entering despite rows of empty seats in the large compound. Two African American colleagues are stopped at the gates and call my mobile phone. I go to the front gate and, acting with authority conferred only by my being a respectably dressed white man, I ask the guard to let them in, which he does (Pierre 2012). The mausoleum, a popular tourist and pilgrimage site, has recently been renovated, though the work has not been completed in time for the event. Statues of traditional Akan chiefly attendants and symbols of chieftaincy surround the Nkrumah statue. Nkrumah's statue is dressed in traditional cloth with one arm raised, frozen as he strides forward. It dwarfs the actors on their podium. The main monument, towering behind the proceedings, is a concrete executioner's sword rising one hundred feet out of the ground, on a grand scale like the kind carried by courtly executioners who protect and enforce the words of Akan chiefs (Kwesi Yankah 1995). On a national scale the language of the chiefly court has been appropriated as a visual marker of the state's moral and cultural legitimacy.

Replicating these symbolic logics developed in the struggle for independence that I describe in chapter 1, national unity is represented as a condensed set of visual signs manifest in culturally specific performances and their juxtaposition within a multicultural logic of nationhood. This logic of display follows the strategy of British colonial objectification of traditional culture and its subsequent reappropriation under Nkrumah for ceremonies and by the Ghana Dance Ensemble and National Theatre Movement as representations of the different cultural groups of the nation, each symbolized by a staged, stereotypic dance and cultural costume. Actors in groups of twenty representing each region of the country wait in the aisles around the main podium and come forward one group at a time performing regional dances. Fante from the Central Region perform highlife, Ga from the Accra in the Eastern Region perform kpanlogo, the Ewe from the Volta Region dance *agbekor,* Asante Region performers dance adowa, Northern Region dancers do a Dagomba dance, and Eastern and Western Region dancers also do Akan dances. One group plays songs from Malawi, as one actor explains, "to represent other Africans' role in independence." Demonstrating regional and cultural identity through dances has been a crucial ongoing national idiom of Ghanaian performance. The performers are not necessarily from the regions they represent but have mastered the dances as part of their repertoire. Highlife and kpanlogo are both social popular genres evolving in the mid-twentieth century, but in the logic of this event they stand for traditional forms representing cultural identities. While all regions contain multiple cultural groups, certain dances come to stand in for entire regions. After brief individual performances, all the groups congregate around the rickety wooden podium where actors dressed as the Big Six political leadership stand. It is positioned between a platform with numerous video cameras set up monitoring the action and a twenty-foot video screen projecting the action below. Two formally dressed smiling masters of ceremonies are positioned to the side of the screen as pleasant hosts and commentators for the entire event. Their commentary frames the ceremony with snappy, upbeat television-awards-show-style banter designed to introduce the uninitiated to the reenactment. They begin, "Welcome to Ghana at Fifty celebrations, inaugurating that great night when Kwame Nkrumah declared Ghana a free nation." They mark the event as a highly structured, easily consumed, made-for-television image.

Being Kwame Nkrumah

David Dontoh has been the preeminent portrayer of Nkrumah in Ghana for many years. He has a degree from the School of Performing Arts at the University of Ghana, Legon. He is one of the most respected and sought-after actors in the country. He features in numerous films and hosts an Akan-language television quiz show called *Agro* (Play) in which contestants win prizes for answering questions on topics including history, politics, and proverbial speech. He is president of the Ghana Concert Party Union and a member of Abibigromma: The National Theatre Players. Dontoh reached international audiences in the HBO film *Deadly Voyage* (1996) starring Omar Epps and based on a true story. Dontoh plays one of a group of African stowaways on board a Russian freighter bound for Europe who are killed by the crew. He was a member of Ghana Theatre Club when he first earned national fame through his role in the popular television soap opera *Obra* (Life), which went on the air in the early 1980s. The weekly Akan-language program told comedic morality tales about greed, jealousy, and sexual indiscretion that built on Anansesem storytelling styles (J. Shipley 2013b: 56–57). In the first several episodes of *Obra*, he portrayed a character named Ghanaman; Dontoh told me that this character was so popular because he essentially portrayed an everyman trickster. "People loved it because there were always two sides to what was happening; you know the Ananse sensibility. I would always have some scheme as a womanizer or trying to make money. . . . In public the character was always smiling and charming, but there would be some inner scheme or plot he would be working on. It actually took me a long time to get away from that stereotype because people would associate me with the character and assume I was also like that." Decades later, people continue to call him Ghanaman and assume his personal character is as duplicitous as his television role. In private he is a soft-spoken, intellectually informed artist equally comfortable in English and Fante.

Dontoh's unexpected childhood encounter with Nkrumah shaped his vision of his lifelong role as a Nkrumah imitator. Dontoh is from Gyegyeano, a small town in the Central Region near Cape Coast. His mother smoked and sold fish in a roadside market. After his grandfather passed away, he went to live with his father in 1966. His father was in charge of animal husbandry at the Kwame Nkrumah Ideological Institute in Winneba. The institute was a training center for radicals from around Africa. Nkrumah would come to stay on occasion, and Dontoh's father relished conversations with him about animals, food, and the running of the institute. One day young David was waiting for his father in the main hall when Nkrumah himself passed by. "He saw me sitting there and called me over. He asked me who I was and I told him who my father was. . . . A few weeks later in 1966, the coup happened and Nkrumah was overthrown. My father disappeared and my brothers and I had to eat from garbage cans for months. Finally, we made our way . . . moved to Accra in 1969 to rejoin my father."

After Nkrumah's overthrow in 1966, statues were toppled amid general jubilation. His supporters were punished, jailed, and ostracized. Bananzi, one of the president's personal bodyguards, recalls being in the presidential Flagstaff House when the rebels took over. He was beaten, jailed, and starved.[7] When he was eventually released, he once again became bodyguard for the next head of state, and indeed faithfully guarded each of the next five heads of state in turn through the mid 1980s. For several years after Nkrumah's overthrow, as the opposition government attempted to undo his legacy, images of Nkrumah were removed and his status as founding father was disavowed. However, after the overthrow of Ghana's Second Republic, Nkrumah's legacy was gradually recuperated.

Greene Odoi was purportedly the first person to portray Nkrumah in 1974 in the play *The Trial of Kwame Nkrumah* by Kweku Mensa-Bonsu. Dontoh first played Nkrumah at the World Youth Festival in Moscow in 1985. In 1986 he played Nkrumah in a revival of *The Trial of Kwame Nkrumah*. He recounts, "I was always particularly interested in watching him through the public media, on film. I was a Ghana film club member and got to watch a lot of films. I would watch him critically and pay attention to all the details. I would listen to how my dad told me he behaved, and listening to my dad I could feel Nkrumah. He was a very dynamic speaker. When I first played him people said, 'That is Nkrumah, he sounds like him! Even the gestures!' So any time they wanted Nkrumah, a festival or sketch or play, they would call me. Being Nkrumah has been one of the hallmarks of my acting career."

Copying: Closeness/Distance from the Past

Dontoh has perfected Nkrumah's speech, through personal recollection, stories from his father, and long-term film study. His performance is a detailed copying of Nkrumah's voice, timing, gestures, and movements. He replicates Nkrumah's forceful, staccato English and his rapid shift to the Fante language in the middle of the speech. He tries to capture the passion, charisma, and spontaneity of a leader known as a master performer. Dontoh and the other five actors playing the Big Six leadership mount the rostrum and closely copy bodily poses and hand and facial gestures learned from studying the famous documentary film footage shot on this spot fifty years ago. While the dancers move below, Dontoh's

Nkrumah waves his handkerchief in time with the crowd's pulsing jubilations. At times they move literally in slow motion, seemingly replicating the jumpy, degraded sixteen-millimeter film version of the events that is often played on television. It is as if they are illustrating half-recalled memories, copying a copy of an event so often repeated in different forms that it is the copies that become the referent, circulating as memories of memories. At the mausoleum the large group of performers and hundreds of seated guests are dwarfed by the monumental space and echoes of conservatively estimated crowds of over 100,000 who were present for Nkrumah's independence speech. The podium looks isolated in front of the serene fountains, captured by a sea of camera crews, loudspeakers, and big-screen projectors. In contrast to the pressing crowds in 1957, the elite audience now watches while lounging in rows of plastic chairs distanced from the performers. The flow of events is carefully orchestrated for television broadcast and for foreign eyes; it is not a celebration as much as a document of the idea of a celebration.

The performers complete their dances and turn to watch the podium. Dontoh's exacting gestures replicate and bring to life the inaugural moment of nationhood. He flawlessly duplicates Nkrumah's speech, which begins in English, then switches to Fante, and then back to English. Nkrumah was noted for speaking English with a Ghanaian inflection rather than with the studied English accent of many of his political peers who studied abroad and returned home with new modes of speaking. In a short address Nkrumah highlighted many of the themes that have remained crucial to the next fifty years of political discourse—the meaning of freedom, self-determination, sovereignty, racial prejudice, the responsibilities of nationhood, Pan-Africanism. Formally, his words and actions inaugurated the speech forms and ritual performances of the nation. The speech highlights independence as the end of a struggle and the beginning of new psychological and political possibilities. For Nkrumah, if independence was to be a long-term success Ghanaians must take responsibility for the nation's destiny.

> At long last the battle has ended. [*Cheers.*] And thus Ghana your beloved country is free forever. [*Cheers.*] From now on today we must change our attitudes, our minds; we must realize that from now on we are no more a colonial people but a free and independent people. . . . That also entails hard work. I am depending upon the millions of the country, the chiefs and people, to reshape the destiny of this country. We are prepared to build up to make it a nation that will be respected by every other nation in the world.

Hope for the future is predicated on political and spiritual unity in Ghana and across Africa. Nkrumah emotionally overwhelms the crowd, just as he appears to be overwhelmed by the moment and its implications. He pauses to wipe away tears. "It doesn't matter how far my eye goes; I can see that you are here in your millions." Dontoh mimes looking out over the huge crowd that Nkrumah must have seen; his words are flattened by the actual smallness of the elite crowd, the mass of cameras and electronic equipment, and the VIP observers as he looks out into emptiness. Nkrumah's rhetoric is both regal and populist. He is a leader whose emotions and dictates point the crowds to identify as part of a new nation. He is also one of the crowd, a local product observing the processes of history with his people. The promises of the nation are a challenge, a hope, and a threat. "And my last warning to you is that you are to stand firm behind us so that we can prove to the world that when the African is given a chance he can show to the world that he is somebody. . . . We shall no more go back to sleep anymore. Today from now on there is a new African in the world. . . . That new African is ready to fight his own battles and show that after all the black man is capable of managing his own affairs."

For Nkrumah, the possibilities of Ghana as a new state were tied to resymbolizing the shared historical oppression of African peoples as a form of powerful unity. Dontoh masterfully speaks as Nkrumah about Pan-Africanism: "As I said in the assembly just minutes ago. I made the point that we will create our own African personality and identity. It is the only way we can show the world that we will fight our own battles. . . . Our independence is meaningless unless linked up to the total liberation of the African continent."

Moving to the conclusion, he slows the tempo of his speech, marking the seriousness of the occasion and its transformative nature. "Fellow Ghanaians, let us now ask for God's blessing. And for only two seconds in your thousands and millions I want to ask you to pause only for one minute. And give thanks to almighty God for having led us through obstacles, difficulties, imprisonments, hardships, and suffering. To have brought us to the end of our trouble today. Ghana is free forever!" For the conclusion of the speech, Dontoh's image is simulcast to the pop music stage outside in the street, and the musicians pause. As Nkrumah did, Dontoh removes his cap, directing the crowd in how to show ritual respect for their new national anthem. He declares, "Ghana is free forever. And here I will ask the band to play the Ghana national anthem." After the anthem, Dontoh appears on the verge of tears, as Nkrumah did. He waves his hand, overcome with emotion, shouting a call-and-response. "Freedom!" the crowd replies, repeated three times. He cuts his words short as if overwhelmed and unable to continue. At the reenactment, Dontoh replicates Nkrumah's intense spontaneous emotional climax as the staging lights go off and cameras cut. The actors dissipate as an impressive, if brief, fireworks display over the mausoleum lights the sky. The crowd exits the mausoleum, spilling into the street. Fireworks explode as a hit hiplife song, "Konkontibaa" by musician Obour, plays over the speakers that moments ago transmitted Dontoh's version of Nkrumah's speech, merging this historical reenactment with popular entertainment.

Reenacted independence is a reflexive event in which actors and audiences engage with politics and with the telling of history. Through condensation, magnification, projection, and quotation, they reimagine the closeness and distance of the original to the reenactment. Progress and failure, hope and irony emerge in the gaps between the original and the copy and how participants reflexively experience them. For visitors and casual observers, the event provides a sanitized, spectacular version of Ghana's history suitable for media transmission, seamlessly linking its present aspirations to past glory. The grand, well-orchestrated ceremony is impressive as a spectacle, though it provokes questions about the links between the present government and Nkrumah as well as questions about the financial cost of the events. Later that night, I hang out backstage at the President's Show on High Street. One young music producer expresses a common frustration to a group of artists. "We are a developing country. Why is Kufuor spending all this money to buy a hundred [expensive] new cars for visiting dignitaries and to celebrate when we don't have proper water and education. It is a façade."

The reiteration and amplification of this inaugural moment of the nation-state reframes it as both mourning and celebration, an ambivalent marker of the hopes and failures of Ghana's political history and the role that public spectacle has played in it. Dontoh's expert replication of Nkrumah's performance seems to emphasize the distance of contemporary Ghana from the older vision of what independence promised. Stark economic disparities of contemporary urban life—represented most visibly by the spectacle of impoverished actors enticed by lower wages to reenact independence—are juxtaposed with the current state's attempt to portray itself as an emblem of stability on the world stage.

In 1957 the Ghanaian state self-consciously portrayed itself as the embodiment of hope for the political aspirations of the African continent, people of African descent around the world, and indeed all colonized people, by proclaiming its moment of independence a beacon to ignite future global transformations. In 2007 the legacy of Nkrumah's Ghana is rendered unstable through its repetition in which the public are powerless and passive observers. The tensions between racial affiliation, national aspiration, and personal disappointment are intentionally concealed, though in their neglect perhaps all the more visible for a national audience. Contested national memories are reinvoked in the public enactment of Nkrumah's speech. Individual and collective freedoms are framed, foregrounded, and assessed against a contemporary landscape of economic struggle and state dissimulation. These contradictions are especially obvious to actors who are both on stage and behind the scenes in the making of these public artifices.

The official state reenactment of Nkrumah's speech attempts to portray continuity between the independence leaders' Pan-Africanist stances and the contemporary state's policies of liberalization. Nkrumah as the iconic hero of the

Ghanaian and African fight for independence is linked to the current government's notion of progress through promoting private investment and developing civil society and service industry infrastructure. The violent split between Nkrumahists and the political ancestors of the current government is ignored. It is simulated evidence of the present government's link to an imagined past glory rather than a sincere invocation of historical connection.

Framing devices for the event include stylish television commentators, cameras and lights, guarded gates that kept out most local people, highly rigid timing and spatial demarcations of the performance, and strict separations between actors and audience that prevented the drama from drawing on the emotional valence of a spectacular uncontrolled celebration akin to the original declaration. For the actors, the lack of remuneration and the contrast between the state's lavish spending on the Ghana@50 celebrations and their personal and artistic predicaments framed the performance, as a reminder of financial promises. The interplay between backstage and frontstage at the reenactment shows that while popular artists are marginalized within social and economic hierarchies, they are simultaneously close observers of and participants in the poetics of public moral discourse.

The event is a replication of a film copy of the original event. Its spatial and temporal framing makes it highly suitable for television circulation and excerpting. On stage and behind the scenes the neat, official portrayal of independence is framed by stories of struggle, financial uncertainty, moral contradiction, and individual desire. Audiences and performers see not only the intended events on stage but juxtapose official scripts and unintended framing devices. Frustration and the irony of impossibility emerge for many observers in the disjuncture of watching the state's dissimulation, placing itself as a direct descendant of the independence struggle.

Traditionalization, Lament, and National Memory

Narratives and debates about Nkrumah's personal charisma have been central to national memory as it oscillates between reverence and melancholia. In 2007, in the shadow of the new Wembley Stadium in northwest London, Alexander A. Ekumah, a soft-spoken man with thick glasses, is parked behind the shop where his son-in-law works as a barber. His daughter Ekua Ekumah is a friend of mine, an actress, director, and lecturer at the School of Performing Arts, Legon. She studied theatre in London before returning to Accra to earn her M.F.A. at SPA. She and her husband, Kudjo, move back and forth between Accra and London. Her father moved from Accra in the early 1960s, remaining in London for over forty years. He speaks with quiet intellect, looking through the London drizzle. "Since Nkrumah was overthrown things have not been the same. That man believed in education and the arts; things used to be vibrant. I still don't understand what happened.... We had everything. The U.S. and Britain could not stand to see a black country succeed. So they had to destroy our economy and get rid of Nkrumah." Kwame Nkrumah's rise and fall remain the narrative of the nation's hopes and failures. For people across the political spectrum his story to anchors a moral economy of memory.

"Are you going to Ghana for the fiftieth-anniversary celebrations of independence?" I ask, and am met with a sharp reproach. "These people in power now [President Kufuor and the NPP], they were against independence at the time. Everyone forgets. The Asante voted against independence. Now they want to poison people's minds with false stories about what happened. There are still some of us around who remember, but they don't want people to know the truth about what a great man Nkrumah was and that they were against him." I ask him where he was at independence in 1957. He stares through the windscreen into the darkening street.

"I was at the old polo grounds for Independence on 6 March. I was a teacher in Accra at the time. In front of the new parliament building, that is where it all happened. It was such a memorable scene with so many programs and music and people dancing everywhere. It was a huge, mixed crowd, you grabbed people and danced, we were all holding hands; you didn't care who it was. The whole place was full of human beings.... And when the British flag came down and the Ghana flag went up? Oh my God! You felt it in your heart. And you found yourself crying. Tears were coming down. Then, on the podium he said, 'Ghana is now free forever.' When Nkrumah said this, oh ... it was as if something was holding down on the people ... and suddenly it was released. Everyone was weeping ... I can't even talk about it." His voice trails off.

Like many of his generation, Alex narrates his memories of Nkrumah's public charisma as a personal relationship. "If you met Nkrumah like I did, you would never go against him. He was a powerful man. He had charisma, the strength to fight for a new Africa; and after what his enemies tried to do to him they pushed him to the edge. That is when he started detaining people. In those days we were not fighting for ourselves like people are today. Nkrumah taught us to fight for the nation and for the whole of Africa. He pulled us together as a people. Today you look at Ghana and we have lost a lot. People are interested only in themselves. It is heartbreaking."

I get out of the car and head to the barbershop where my friend Kudjo, the old man's son-in-law, works. Wembley's space-age metal glows neon blue through the plate-glass window. Kudjo discusses his plans to sell used laptops in Accra as young Londoners of African and Caribbean descent crowd the seats around the four barbers' chairs waiting for haircuts. While he cleans his hair clippers between customers, I tell him I am struck by the old man's unprovoked passion for Nkrumah. But my friend is less nostalgic. "Oh, he's an old Gold Coaster. You know they are full of stories . . . but what have we got now?" Remembering, as a personal, emotional form of contemplation, is refracted for the old and the young through current emotional concerns and external representations that reinforce or contradict ideas of the past. While the independence generation feels increasingly distant from previous hopes and promises, younger people resignify the meaning of independence, often distancing themselves from it as they assess the relative importance of the past to their present predicaments.

Fragments of Nkrumah's independence speech and symbols of the ceremony are circulated and reiterated across personal stories, public performance genres, and various media platforms: in popular hiplife songs, such as the one quoted in this chapter's epigraph, which invokes the loss of Nkrumah's leadership to lament the moral degradation of the nation, and by religious leaders like Pastor Mensa Otabil, described in the previous chapter, who replicate Nkrumah's poses and styles to claim speaking authority and invoke Pan-African pride among his constituents. These references mark the ritual birth of the nation and Nkrumah's role as foundational of Ghanaian identity both in his person and in the complex ambivalence Ghana has cultivated toward his legacy. The image of Nkrumah proclaiming independence, waving his white handkerchief from high on the podium, is simultaneously a symbol of hope and a lament about lost agency and the nation's failure to meet expectations.

In the Pan-Africanist imaginary of Nkrumah's Ghana, colonial routes of extraction were redirected as channels for circulating black capital and maintaining global African affiliations. Pan-Africanism in this guise was a collective, trans-state project. In state celebrations of Ghana's fiftieth anniversary, Pan-Africanism becomes a nostalgic spectacle, meant to aid free-market success and attract wealth and investment through the performance of stability and success. Ideologies of the free market create the image of success, invoking the market as productive of wealth, while avoiding direct questions like why workers are not paid and how Nkrumah's words relate to contemporary politics.

Independence as Reobjectified Cultural Performance

In its 2007 reenactment, Nkrumah's declaration of independence is objectified as cultural performance for contemplation, recontextualization, and circulation. As chapters 1 and 2 describe, the objectification of culture and tradition as performance styles is a primary way that affective affiliations, and reflexive engagements with them, have been produced and maintained across Ghanaian public life. Nostalgia for various cultural traditions is crucial to creating those traditions and to the formation of a modern collectivity in opposition to them. Cultural tradition is made as words, gestures, signs, and practices that reference ideas of the past are circulated across media and genres, connecting present and future to the making and remaking of a past. For performance analysis, "the focus of attention is the strategic process of traditionalization rather than a quality of traditionality that is considered to inhere in a cultural form conceived of as akin to a persistent natural object" (Bauman 1992: 128). Processes of traditionalization actively position pieces of discourse as markers of the past, producing value in aligning them with established authority. Actors create abstract value and personal authority by linking moral stances to the past.

But, of course, ideas of tradition change in relation to the power dynamics of the present. The logic of decentralized colonial rule was validated through traditionalizing spectacles of African cultural practices. With independence, cultural tradition was appropriated in service of a centralized Pan-African state. The rising state aligned economic and political sovereignty, Pan-African cultural affiliation, a citizenry's rights to self-determination, and obligations to a black (inter)national public. Over time, independence—with Nkrumah's role first as protagonist of the national struggle, then as fallen icon, and finally as reanointed, lost hero—was no longer a marker of newness and possibilities for Ghanaian modern nationhood but became a symbol of tradition, objectified and deployed in the service of the state, its meaning contested and debated as an index of Ghana's future.

Ghana@50 celebrations in Accra attempted to link Nkrumah's struggle for independence to the NPP government's focus on portraying Ghana as a stable place for investment and tourism. Reenactment as a performance genre authorizes actors and audiences to reflexively engage with the politics of history. It tries to harness the residual power of the initial event for new purposes (Kruger 1999: 5). In condensing and magnifying the original as a set of performance practices and repeating and copying its enactment across various media, contemporary performers and audiences assess the symbolic distance between the original and the reenactment (Turner 1982). Local ideas of the future and discourses of progress and failure are mediated and judged in the gaps between the original and the copy. Ghana's independence day in 1957 was a transformative ritual moment with uncertain short- and long-term potentials (Kruger 1999: 5). It called on participants to be agents, actively transforming themselves from colonial subjects into citizens of a new black nation-state. While the original was a ritual event in which theoretically all viewers were participants, the reenactment was ceremonial theatre in the sense that it emphasized the distance between the staged drama and the viewers (Kruger 1999). The reenactment distanced its public from the transformative potential of the original that it was trying to capture through highly mediated framing devices both in the actual performance and in the public circulation of Ghana@50 more generally. Unintentionally, participants were made passive consumers of a lost, potential future. Actors appear bored, disillusioned, and frustrated, not affectively engaged in the event, confined to copying previous events without room for creative interpretation. Each chose to perform for a wage, or not, without the promise of future revenue that comes with group membership or long-term state sponsorship or the hopes of a collective artistic project. This incident shows a tale of high modern liberal political possibility—the birth of a nation-state and its diverse, united citizenry—reframed as a multimedia sign of state dissimulation within a neoliberal present.

This remediated event demonstrates crucial themes of this book—how the contradictions of privatization are refracted through a theatrical poetics of duality and irreverence; how new technologies and urban transformations shape performance aesthetics; how on-stage and off-stage practices and state and private interests intertwine in making public theatricality; how actors and audiences reflexively engage with the line between performance and reality. Another crucial aspect of Ghanaian performance theory is how performances make the future through a presentist version of the past. That is to say, this reenactment is an example of a performance of nationhood and self-making that is decidedly not about making singular, perduring identities. Here, the performance of a personal or national identity is a representation of the past, not as a cumulative progressive history of progress (or failure) that leads to a shared idea of self in the present, but rather as a set of signs, stances, and practices that can coexist out of time and indeed in contradictory configurations. In one sense, then, it portrays a clearly uncertain future.

Various types of public performance, as I have described, are linked by a perduring theatrical poetics defined by its storytelling structure and focus on trickster-oriented narrations. Actors aim to reach audiences by drawing on multiple references and stances from popular and religious realms to establish moral legitimacy and emotional force. Ghanaian theatrical poetics emphasize the ways actors acknowledge that they are performing and play with the lines between narrating, observing, and participating in a story. In a reenactment these shifts take on specific implications. Behind the scenes and on stage at the state-sponsored reenactment of independence, actors index the original celebration, revealing disconnections between past and present political regimes that free them of singular, consistent subject positions. By reframing the celebrations through spatio-temporal compression, the electronic media apparatus, and various types of narration, the reenactment highlights the distance and dissonance between the original and the copy. David Dontoh's virtuoso performance in recreating Nkrumah's speech word for word and gesture for gesture actually emphasizes, in the exactness of the copy, the contemporary implausibility of Nkrumah's words as morally authoritative. The similarity of the replica to its original highlights how much the social context has changed.

In classic models of language use, performance roles are divided between roles of speaker and hearer. In these analyses, a speaking position within micro-level performances correlates to a unified social role that is consistent over time and across social realms. In this reenactment the fractured forms of reference and simultaneous contradictory positions distance participants from the enduring national citizen-subject the event purports to envision. Focusing on specific participant roles that actors inhabit in particular moments of performance foregrounds the shifting, unstable ways that event participants take effective stances that can be the opposite of the literal intent of the words and deeds performed. In the reflexive acknowledgment of stance-taking, subjects recognize themselves and are recognized (Keane 1997; Kockelman 2006b). But reenactment as a genre must avoid exaggeration, reflexivity, and parody as modes of reflexivity in favor of exactness and reverence as per Dontoh's masterful performance. Actors cannot reinterpret the original or break performance frame to acknowledge the fact that the performance is a reference to another foundational event. For Ghana@50, the contrast between the exactness of the speech and the spectacular multimedia show and changing political conditions with which it is reframed, provides the reflexive function that the actors themselves, in this context, cannot. The performed sincerity acts to undermine itself.

Epilogue
Unfreedom as Critical Theory

Unfreedom

In examining an apparently disparate set of performances, styles, and interactions, this book shows how theatre discourse animates creative possibilities for urban life on the global margins. Theatre has been central to shaping Accra's landscape and sensibility. These ethnographic and historical tales show how, as forms of cultural mediation change, the idiom of the trickster/storyteller shapes how audiences imagine new moralities and futures simply in the telling. Social actors claim moral power by realigning multiple historical and cultural contexts for their own purposes. Words and actions are made meaningful by linking them to past traditions, present collective beliefs, future wealth, and otherworldly spiritual anointing, conferring on speakers and listeners transformative potential. The focus of public life in urban Ghana has shifted from state political pageantry and cultural nationalist displays to dispersed media, religious, and popular imaginaries. Pan-African cultural spectacle was crucial to the moral authority of early independence nationhood. However, with the precarious conditions of the free market, various, diffuse, electronically mediated genres are reoriented toward individual success as a moral project, rather than collective national redemption. In Accra's vernacular spaces, authority is conferred through a performer's fluency in multiple symbolic registers: national, ethnic, religious, racial, stylistic, linguistic, commercial. Fluid code-switching delineates the possibilities of multiplicity as critical practice in the daily life of Accra.

Theatrical idioms provide ways for Ghanaians to turn social potential into future success. Opportunities come and go, and actors, social and theatrical, have to constantly adjust. One young actor traveling to the United States to perform confided in me that he felt the skills he learned doing music, dance, and drama would serve him well in other realms. "Ghanaians are like tricksters. Wherever they go in the world they hustle to make money and make themselves into successes, so when they return to Ghana they can be big men and build a big house." Acting on stage is linked to hustling off stage and to Ghana's place in the global hierarchy; being a trickster is about doing whatever is necessary to achieve success, using wit and cunning in the face of structural obstacles.

With marketization comes an entangled fantasy of freedom. In the postmillennial world, notions of freedom align not with political liberation from colonial rule or economic sovereignty in the face of neocolonial corporate extraction, but with personal freedoms to consume, travel, spend, and claim an identity. In these practices the imagination of a Pan-African Ghana is mediated through popular culture, new religious movements, and electronic and digital technologies. The neoliberal state transforms older ideas of liberation associated with national independence into dreams of personal freedom and its inverse unfreedom—the structuring of activities that entangle aspirants in webs of frustration made out of their own hopes. The fight for freedom from colonial rule was a collective action focused on achieving cultural-political self-determination. In a free-market world, the entrepreneur is imbued with the moral right to succeed outside national responsibility.

State and corporate struggles to control local peoples have shifted from the production of place and moral belonging toward the appropriation of circulatory mechanisms themselves. A structural antagonism is established between freedom and the institutions deemed necessary for its existence. But freedom is deferred at the moment it emerges as a possibility and people chase their aspirations from an increasing distance. Class, ethnic, political, and religious collectivities use the language of privatization and marketization to stake claims on social and natural resources. Corporations and entrepreneurial subjects redeploy the language of culture and belonging for various types of value production and profit. As we have seen, actors, playwrights, comedians, politicians, and religious leaders performatively speak the language of success to produce immanent prosperity. These forms of copying the future provide critical commentary on the desires they represent.

Ananse as Post-neoliberal Critical Theorist, but Also the Same as Ever

Ananse the spider is traditionally understood as a greedy and selfish, though sympathetic, character; his trickery creates illicit pleasure and excitement, raising questions about collective moral action. In Ghanaian public culture, persuasive and authoritative speaking is assessed in relation to a performer's ability to use indirection, humor, innuendo, metaphor, and dense sets of references concentrated in proverbial and proverb-like statements. The trickster remains a figure of mediation useful across a broad range of urban public genres, where performers find excitement and power in the elegant play of words. The trickster is often referenced in popular culture, politics, religion, and daily life in urban Ghana. Highlife and hip-hop musicians explicitly and implicitly draw on Ananse tales and images of the trickster. Everything from television advertisements to rap lyrics to children's entertainment to religious preaching to casual conversations regularly draw on trickster tales. In focusing attention on the process of mediation itself, the trickster points to a prevailing social contradiction pitting individual aspiration against collective obligation. As the public's attention shifts from centralized state politics toward private institutions, these forms of cultural mediation that emerge through national theatre continue to shape public speaking across a broad array of urban contexts.

The figuration of the trickster—with his predilection for moral flexibility, humor, and creative greed—takes on new connotations in the world of millennial Ghana. A central problem in adapting storytelling for the modern stage was codifying its improvisational and dialogic aspects. Playwrights, in scripting the character of the storyteller or including a storytelling frame for narrative action, mimicked improvisational interactions between performers, narrators, and audience members. This focus on the formal and metapragmatic aspects of drama has predisposed theatre to absorb broader structural tensions. In the context of social change, staged drama has the ability to agitate audiences and performers into thinking about moral and aesthetic value. The examples I have given throughout this book of conflicts and misunderstandings on and around the stage are moments of disruption in which artists and audiences renegotiate how to act and how to interpret action.

Subtlety speaks loudly in Ghana. In contemporary contexts, a poetics of indirection and reflexive mediation gives public figures tools to redirect an audience's attention and creatively realign multiple discursive registers, genres, and stances—for example, the ways that comedians and pastors draw on each other's styles to reach their audiences. Performers claim voice by manipulating the polarities between the visible and the concealed, on stage and off stage, authorship and animation, directness and mediation. Through the valorization of obfuscation, narration and action collapse on one another. Actors create spaces within which they narrate their own actions, authorizing the indexical groundings for their symbolic work. Ananse's example allows performers to blend genres and performance strategies through which a speaker's words become authoritative.

Yet life in contemporary urban Ghana entails an explicit sense of the potentials and threats of mixing unrelated political, religious, and popular social registers. If entrepreneurial self-fashioning is the embodiment of the neoliberal, then Ananse's parodic copying of this stance is post-neoliberal critique. If Ananse's sensibility has authorized entrepreneurial activity since the early days of concert party, his explicit awareness of the artifice of copying critically undermines popular, religious, or state prosperity doctrines. This awareness helps shape the forms of recognition, intent, desire, anxiety, and the certainty and uncertainty with which people relate to the failures of the neoliberal state. Creativity and innovation are defined through an actor's ability to position himself or herself at the intersection of multiple interpretive frameworks, opening new angles for producing socially legitimate positions. The performative aspects of postmarketized urban life present creative strategies through which cosmopolitan Ghanaians of various statuses claim authority. They do so by inhabiting the idea of multiplicity itself (Mbembe 2001). Multiple registers and genres remain both co-present and incommensurable within a performer's repertoire, ready for deployment in the right situation and simultaneously ready for satire. Recent social theory has focused on the potentials of multiplicity and radical difference to critically engage European philosophical assumptions about the singularity of modern subjects and related political sovereignties. I am concerned with how contextually specific forms of alterity exist in the midst of a purportedly uniform modernity.

The figure of the trickster links past, present, and future forms of cultural mediation to individual agency, providing a semiotic node around which Ghanaian publics can espouse or criticize the economic and liberatory potential of the words and actions of national citizens and consuming subjects. Ghanaians navigate recent global shifts in the relationships of capital to the nation-state and its citizenry through ambivalent, double-voiced readings. The ways in which the lines are drawn and redrawn between stage drama and cultural display, moral fable and religious ceremony, corporate media and political power are telling of how theatre artists mediate social change.

Ghanaians move across a social landscape populated with actors and pastors, politicians and comedians, radio hosts and businessmen. In the daily and the spectacular, they encounter and negotiate historical layers of political encounters and popular expression. A community of interpretation is built on a productive uncertainty. People scrutinize actions and words for hidden intent, always ready to find double meanings (Mbembe 2001). The trickster figuration is immanent; that is, anyone is potentially a trickster. Successful people are accused of being fakes in jealousy; unsuccessful people are accused in disgust. Those in the public eye try to adopt an effortless authoritative style to deflect accusations of hidden motives. Jean Rouch's narrative film *Jaguar* follows three youths from rural Niger who come to seek their fortunes in Accra and Kumasi. The film's climactic scene captures the sensibility of Baudelaire's *flâneur*, as the main character, Damouré, strolls through Accra's streets cool and detached, smoking a cigarette, his hat casually cocked to the side. Master of his world, he glides through busy urban environs as highlife music plays. Some say "being jaguar," a term for being cool, came from Bob Cole, star concert party leader, famed for his style and stage presence. In the 1960s, he drove around Accra in a Jaguar convertible, wearing a white suit (Collins 2007). He was so dazzling that as one actor recalls, "He was more famous than Nkrumah." Successful tricksters are jaguars or flâneurs or *kubolors*—a Ga-language term for vagabonds—who navigate a dangerous and exciting urban landscape with cool detached attention, carefree observers, brimming with potential and unknowable moral agendas.

The trickster provides a local, critical discourse on agency and creativity, pointing to the freedoms of individual action as well as its limits. Success creates its own moral authority. Anxieties about fakeness that the trickster breeds, however, provide criteria for judging and disciplining individual desires in the language of authenticity and belief. With the ever-looming threat of the fake pastor, for example, who may trick his congregation into believing he has powers from the Holy Spirit, audiences are provoked to actively engage with ideas of fakery or be left wondering who, in fact, is the fool. The immanent fake lurks behind politicians who make promises of anticorruption and progress, hip-hop artists who present themselves as celebrities and brag about working with American record labels and rappers, and successful-looking businessmen who claim to have international connections. Because of the haunting double, performers in general are scrutinized for signs of insincerity. If contradictions between public performance and private desire emerge, moral performance authority is transformed into the embarrassment of a failed hustler. Uncertainty both drives and calls into question the morality of actions.

Ethnographers have sought to understand the structuring of social life while maintaining humanist hopes for the emergent potentials of vitality and agency. The trickster figuration subverts such hopes, offering instead a local ordering of action as always both creative and destructive. In formal theatre, the trickster/storyteller often breaks the frame of the proscenium stage to address both characters and audience members. The realism of the Western proscenium stage is eschewed in favor of the self-conscious recognition of the line between on stage and off stage that comes from the potentials of trickery. In reflexive navigation of performance form, actors and audiences assess the ability to maintain public face and hide private desires. The promise of choice gives individuals freedom but then shackles them with their own desire.

Three Things I Know about Ananse as Sublime Cultural Citizen

Ananse is a cultural citizen in three ways: First, Ananse is multiple. Second, Ananse is power-hungry. Third, Ananse fails, though as an antihero he opens up new possibilities.

In September 2013, playwright Mohammed Ben Abdallah stands on the apron of the main stage at Ghana's National Theatre waiting for several of the key actors, who are two hours late returning from buying props to prepare for the final dress rehearsal. His new play, *Song of the Pharaoh*, will open the next day. But the set is unfinished; nothing has been painted; the head designer does not answer his phone and has not been seen for days; the lighting crew and stagehands do not know their cues and lights and gels have not been set up; the music director struggles to coordinate the drummers and musicians with the recorded tracks; cordless microphones for actors have not yet arrived. Normally calm and in command, Abdallah finally loses his temper, angrily exclaiming, "This is what happens in a nation whose hero is Kweku Ananse." He is referring to this series of last-minute disappointments and competing allegiances that threaten to derail the show even when everything had been planned and promised for months and all of the pieces of the production appear ready for assembly. Only a few days earlier, one of the lead actors got married to a foreigner and left the country without notice; her replacement struggles to learn the part; another actor claims she is being threatened with imprisonment for illegally tapping into the electricity grid; another is missing much of the time while working on a more lucrative private contract. In this major theatre production, the selfish, contingent, and unexpected threaten to undo collective work, though also provide the tools for fixing things at the last minute and allowing the production to come off successfully through a spirit of entrepreneurship and improvisation. The trickster is immanent, providing the potential for any public event or persona to either succeed or implode through a haunting uncertainty.

For Abdallah, this play is the apotheosis of his Abibigro style of drama that blends music, dance, and theatre from a variety of African styles into a proscenium-staged format. It has a large cast of over sixty, including collaborations between the National Theatre Players and the National Dance Company, and a theme song performed by the National Symphony Orchestra. The dance and music draw together new composition and choreography with Yoruba, Akan, and Ga music and dance through a story set in ancient Egypt. A young Accra fashion designer, Patrick, creates costumes through a combination of contemporary Afro-chic style and ancient Egyptian imagery with sheer gold lamé and well-tailored kente cloth. The staging expands on the trickster storytelling idiom with three main storytellers who move on and off stage as they chat with each other and the audience and travel in time and space. Amenhotep plays the role of another storyteller, an ancient Egyptian scribe who is reincarnated back in time from a modern fetish priest tasked with recording the play for future generations; he moves between realms, talking and joking with various characters and audience members while being unable to communicate with others. Building on historical research, the play posits the pharaoh Akhenaten as the model for both Oedipus and Moses. The playwright explores these connections by portraying sexual tension between Akhenaten and his mother and religious conflicts between his proto-monotheism and established Egyptian gods. Akhenaten marries his childhood friend, the beautiful Nefertiti, and they battle with her father and uncles for religious and political power of the kingdom. In the final scene, Akhenaten leads a procession of followers—made up of the National Dance Company moving in slow-motion, funeral-march choreography—across the desert, downstage right, into exile, through the audience, as his newly built "City of Light" is destroyed upstage.

If trickster storytelling's reflexivity and powers of inversion are good for theatre, and audiences enjoy being tricked, the same skills are annoying off stage and undermine the process of theatrical production itself. As Abdallah's precurtain frustration illustrates, Ananse's legacy can be used to explain moral transgressions, corruption, confusion, and poor organization. Incidental problems threaten to undo the production from within. But they do not. As is often the case in theatre, at the last moment, the sets are painted, the actors arrive, and the opening run of the play is a success. Backstage drama and lack of resources are common to many theatres. But explaining them through Ananse's immanence shows how the trickster provides a local order of action and explanation. But this is an explanation that rather avoids its own question. The power of the trickster figuration comes from his ability to subsume a long history of large and small encounters and power struggles within an idea of tradition and a genre of storytelling with a propensity for obfuscating intent, humorous undoing, and pointed innuendo. Ananse allows people to locate encounters in a local episteme and use uncertainty as a productive and entertaining style of social interaction. Over the course of the twentieth century, this mode of indirection is marked as a signifier of traditional culture, in which culture becomes both the problem and the solution. That is, if some see Akan or Ghanaian or African cultural values and ethnic and linguistic ties as holding back the progress of the Ghanaian nation-state, others see cultural revival as the way to reinvigorate local identities for the modern world (Mamdani 1996). The polarizing tension between these positions suspends ideas of the future in limbo.

From before Ghana's independence, the National Theatre Movement has itself been an ethnographic project of sorts. It has been a form of cultural translation, in which the tools of translation do not lend themselves to making sense but rather to a sublime absurdity and uncertainty and to eluding narrative closure (Asad 1973; Žižek 1989). Ananse makes fun of people without them realizing it. Ghanaian cultural citizenship emerges in this elision—this pleasurable potential misrecognition. It is the blurring of recognition—that is, being while hiding in plain sight—that makes Ananse sublime; maddening but sublime in a way that confounds political, historical, and ethnographic sense. Following the struggles and frustrations of the cast and crew, *Song of the Pharaoh*'s successful production is powerful for everyone involved precisely because it almost imploded at the last minute. Trickster sublime is built on the immanent dissolution of order and the potential of transforming the world in the image of the self, but a self that is unstable and threatens to turn in to its opposite.

Ghanaian national culture is meant to be a sincere enterprise built on belief in an individual's moral responsibility to the collective whether it is a theatre company or the nation. The philosophical foundations of the modern nation-state imply a citizen whose moral positions are consistent across social contexts. The citizen-subject is meant to have two main attributes: being an individual unfettered by premodern ties and fulfilling moral and legal obligations to the state that, in turn, entitle the citizen to a set of basic and consistent rights. Modern citizenship requires subjects to be responsive to the state over all other political, spiritual, cultural, and kin allegiances that pull at them and requires subjects to accept the idea that citizenship is universal despite the ways that race, class, and gender shape forms of belonging. National theatre, as a project for building cultural foundations for state cohesion and progress, is inherently modern in its earnestness. But in the case of Ghana, contradictions emerge because the theatrical poetics that underlie this national project of cultural unity is one of multiplicity and mockery. Ananse is a model for a different modern subject. While trickster storytelling provides a shared national cultural idiom, it is one that valorizes the pleasure and efficacy of multiplicity and copying; of inhabiting stances of power in ways that make it hard to discern mockery from sincerity (Yurchak 2005). Trickster performances critique the foundations of the projects they claim to support.

In some instances, Ananse blatantly seeks power. Yaw Asare's play *Ananse in the Land of Idiots* tells a tale of Ananse as a seditious power-hungry usurper.[1] Here, he is willing to do anything for success. Based on an old tale, the play is framed by the storyteller, who tells the audience in detail of Ananse's immoral activities: "In his encounter with the people of Dim-nyim-Lira: Land of Idiots, Ananse tactfully blends his skills to persuade, coax, flatter, ridicule, entrap, court, insult, blackmail, coerce, and lure King Dorsey and his credulous citizenry to realize his personal dreams as he finds himself suddenly lifted from a gloomy position of one condemned (for defiling a sacred ritual process) into a veritable Prince—complete with a royal bride, a whole chiefdom, power, and wealth!" Asare's characters directly confront the audience with questions about their actions.

The play's action follows Ananse as he "first extricates himself from a tight corner that his greed had placed him in and then secures a favoured position in 'the Land of Idiots.' Eventually, through subterfuge, disguise, murder, and the elimination of a man who assists him along his devious path, he secures the hand of the daughter of the local ruler. . . . Ananse departs with his bride to enjoy life on an island he has been given."[2]

Ananse's illicit action is only possible because of the trust of others. For playwright Asare, Ananse is contradictory and misrecognized, the custodian of tradition who is constantly hustling for the future. He also provides a warning about trusting surface interpretations. The storyteller asks, "Why were they caught in Ananse's web of cunning, despite the caution from the gods?" Ananse himself later scolds the audience for not appreciating his deceptions and disguises. "You see? What did I say? Your world misunderstands me! No one accords me my proper place as the prime custodian of ethical, moral and philosophical norms. You say my methods are crude and sly. Hmm! Now tell me; what is wrong with a man employing his god-given talents to cope with the challenges of a hostile world?" Ananse invokes outrage and becomes outraged in turn at his audience's naïve view of morality. But Ananse does not usually succeed in getting what he seeks, as he seems to in Asare's tale.

Critics have argued about whether West Africa's notorious 419 and Sakawa internet scams should be seen as criminal (Burrell 2012). To some, the originators of these e-mails are creative entrepreneurs making wealth through their wits, indeed inventing a sector of the informal economy. Is it these computer-savvy kids' fault if someone is greedy enough to want to earn fabulous wealth from a fictitious prince and gullible enough to send money to a stranger? Perhaps their marks are paying for a good performance; they just do not know it. It is said that Ananse loves to eat but does not like to work. But he is also misunderstood. Hustling is serious work, labor that produces new forms of value. Is it wrong for him to succeed if others do not recognize a lie? It is their obligation to search for the truth. If they cannot tell when someone is tricking them, they deserve to be fooled. But again, this raises the question, what does it mean if this custodian of tradition, this national icon, is a liar?

Give Ananse the final word, as his stories enter the mouths of others. "Ananse and the Wisdom Pot" is perhaps the best-known Ananse tale, retold and transformed in multiple versions. It tells how Ananse accidentally introduces wisdom into the world (Carroll 1984). It appears in Rattray's 1930 collection. Efua Sutherland uses it for a children's tale. Kwesi Yankah (1995) retells it in his book on speech culture of the Akan chief's court to illustrate how Akan forms of communication and indirection are transposable to a broader Ghanaian public sphere.

Abibigromma member Kwesi Brown turned it into a short play in which Ananse is an elder and Okyeame, a courtly linguist and spokesperson serving the chief of his village. But Ananse aspires to be chief himself. Abrewa (old woman) is the storyteller who is telling the tale to a child who represents the audience and shifts attention between on and off stage. Ananse moves between acting and addressing the storyteller and audience. At one point he warns people of his predilection for deception and inversion. "I am Kweku Ananse. . . . When I tell you to look up . . . you better look down." As the action progresses, Ananse's wife is concerned as he has not been himself since he entered the chief's court and gained some power.

> Kweku Ananse pretended to be seriously sick so he would be excused from his daily activities at the chief's palace and also from going to the farm. . . . Ananse

often sat quietly under a baobab tree, talking and laughing to himself like a lunatic at the marketplace. Passersby looked confused as to what was going wrong with such a respected elder. This went on for a long time and one day Kweku Ananse finally found a solution to his worries.

Ananse decides to collect all the wisdom in the world in a big pot.

He wants "to control this village, I must collect all wisdom belonging to the people of Menpeasem [a town called 'I don't want trouble'] including the chief and elders, and hide it somewhere no one could find [it]." Ananse secretly gathers all the wisdom to keep for himself so he can outsmart anyone. He ties the pot to his stomach in order to climb a tree to hide it. Because of the pot's awkwardness he is stuck, but if he drops the pot he will lose all the wisdom. Ananse's son finds him there and suggests that his father place the pot behind him and then climb up to hide it. Having received his son's advice, Ananse realizes he does not have all of the wisdom in the world.

The tale ends with frustration. "Kweku Ananse . . . could not stand the humiliation of being outwitted by his own son, so he dropped the pot and it broke into pieces scattering the wisdom all over in the village. Ananse climbed up the tree, without the wisdom pot and lived the rest of his life in misery and shame up there. This is the reason the spider is seen on trees all the time." Ananse ignores family and village obligations in his greed. His desires cloud his judgment and get him in trouble. He is publicly embarrassed by his failure. The storyteller ends with a question for the audience: "*Nkolaa* [children] tell me what you learned from this story?"

A denizen of a traditional mystical realm, Ananse makes his way into urban life in multiple guises. As with the myth of Pandora's box, this tale describes the unintended ways social life is produced through a selfish act. Ananse's attempt and failure to capture all the world's wisdom is a story of endless hope and skill, of incompetence and frustration. Contemporary audiences use his lessons to make sense of changing social landscapes, continually reassessing moral choices and being watchful for seduction and false promises. Ananse's tireless desire is both amoral and endlessly compelling.

The unintended consequences of presenting the trickster as an idealized Ghanaian cultural citizen create a blend of sincere and parodic stances viable in various popular, religious, commercial, and political performance styles. A poetics of duality and a logic of trickery highlight an actor's ability to appear authentic and a character's ability to think quickly, manipulate audiences, and navigate fantastical scenarios. Trickster tales endure as they simultaneously celebrate and warn of individual desire and the pleasures and dangers of persuasive speaking. Ananse is an everyman character navigating impossible situations through wit and guile. Trickery is a central trope of contemporary Ghanaian public life, shaping interpretive frames of performances on and off stage and grounding a moral public in the art of storytelling itself.

Notes

Introduction

1. This moral drama is reminiscent of the South African play *The Island* by Athol Fugard, John Kani, and Winston Ntshona, in which two prisoners held in an apartheid-era jail perform the play *Antigone* for themselves. Watching this *Hamlet*-like play within a play is intended to push characters and audiences to think about theatricality itself and in the process question the relationship between moral conviction and law, activism and self-preservation in the context of South Africa's Apartheid authoritarian regime.

2. The different colonial legacies—Portuguese, French, Belgian, and British—and the complex layerings of multiple performance traditions with politics have created a wide variety of public cultures in postcolonial Africa. Debates about autochthony, tradition, Pan-Africanism and Négritude, and the relationship between culture and political sovereignty characterize much postcolonial discourse around the continent. In some contexts the archiving and objectification of cultural and religious practices within urban and national frames—as in Senegal under first president Léopold Senghor, a poet, scholar, and leading voice of Négritude— facilitated a flexible decentralized politics that allowed for eclectic inclusion and contentiousness within a shared idiom. In other contexts—like Nigeria, which came to independence under Pan-African thinker first president Nnamdi Azikiwe—the contradictions fostered by colonial rule between cultural belonging and political borders led to postindependence violence, dissolution, and civil war (Achebe 2012; Geschiere 2009; Geschiere and Nyamnjoh 2000). Through an in-depth study of culture, theatre, and politics in Ghana, I hope to contribute to comparative thinking across postindependence Africa.

3. Scholars are examining how eclectic genres, technologies, and media forms have been crucial to the making of modern and postcolonial Africa (Abu-Lughod 2004; Fabian 1998; Goodman 2005; Hirschkind 2006; Pype 2012; Spitulnik 2001). As African performance genres travel across and are intertwined in political-economic networks, they shape the creative, evolving experiences of urban Africa and link disparate rural and urban spaces and temporalities in Africa to other parts of the world (Ebron 2002; Goodman 2005; Sasha Newell 2012; Nuttall and Mbembe 2008). Studies of African expressive forms focus on, among other forms, hiplife (J. Shipley 2013a), radio and film (Larkin 2008), Pan-African expression and festivals (A. Apter 2005; Jaji 2014), literary culture (Stephanie Newell 2002), cultural education (Coe 2005), jazz (Feld 2012), newsprint (Hasty 2005), Bata (Klein 2007), Afrobeat/Fela (Veal 2000), Yoruba popular theatre (Barber 2000), concert party popular theatre (Cole 2001), video-film (Garritano 2013; Meyer 1998b), highlife (Collins 1994a, 1994b; Plageman 2012), Juju music (Waterman 1990), and drama (Banham 2008; Banham, Gibbs, and Osofisan 2001; Donkor 2008; Gibbs 2009; Kerr 1995; Kruger 1999).

4. Max Gluckman's (1965) early concerns with traditional authority, urbanization, and social change challenged anthropological assumptions about the stasis of African political and cultural authority. James Ferguson's research in the urban Zambian Copperbelt recalls the Rhodes-Livingstone Institute's earlier insistence on studying African societies in flux rather than as stable entities. Recently ethnographies in a variety of urban contexts examine how cities constitute and are constituted by infrastructure, creative and mobile practices, and global

flows and the excesses and leakages these entail (Anand 2011; Carse 2014; Fisch 2013; Hoffman 2011; Larkin 2013; Mazzarella 2013; McGovern 2013; Sasha Newell 2012; Peterson 2010; Tsing 2004).

5. An abbreviated version of this chapter appears as J. Shipley (2004).
6. An abbreviated version of this chapter appears as J. Shipley (2009).

1. Making Culture

1. Colonial Reports—Annual. No. 1559. Gold Coast Report for 1930–1931, 31–32.
2. Colonial Reports—Annual. No. 1559. Gold Coast Report for 1930–1931, v.
3. See Parker (2000) for more on the development of Accra and the relationship between British rule and chieftaincy. Accra was developing as an eclectic multiethnic city on the land of the Ga peoples. As Accra became a regional and international cosmopolitan hub, there was a rush to own, control, and develop land and property. The British administration recognized the Ga Mantse (chief) and other subchiefs as traditional rulers and owners of land as a way to control and tax the rapid growth of the city and curb the power of African educated elites who had access to liberal civic society and its legal and economic ends and means. By recognizing "traditional" customary authorities, Gold Coast administrators controlled development. Taxation, development of markets and trade routes, and enlistment of wage laborers, then, were built on colonial categorizations of local cultural difference and their links to national sovereignty.
4. Private interview with John Collins, December 2003.
5. For a comprehensive examination of literary clubs in the Gold Coast, see Stephanie Newell (2002: 27–82).
6. "Music and the Stage: Is Drama Not Literature: Call to Critics to Show Wider Interest," *Gold Coast Spectator*, August 6, 1932, 1059. Other clubs Musing Light mentions that did music and drama include Accra Cheery Ocas, Old Students of the Accra Government Teachers Training College, Merry Deccas, Omar Khayyams, Accra Social Reformers, the Madrona, Reformers Club, and Musical Dragons.
7. "Human Orchestra: Four Negro Lads Who Orchestrate Vocally," *Gold Coast Spectator*, March 12, 1932, 339.
8. "Announcements," *Gold Coast Spectator*, March 12, 1932, 339.
9. Musing Light, *Gold Coast Spectator*, August 19, 1933, 1123. Quoted in Agovi (1990: 15).
10. Musing Light, *Gold Coast Spectator*, May 28, 1932, 715. Quoted in Agovi (1990: 14). See also Cole (2001: 37).
11. Musing Light, *Gold Coast Spectator*, December 12, 1931, 2727. Quoted in Agovi (1990: 14).
12. "Music and the Stage," 1059.
13. "Listening-in by School Children," *Gold Coast Spectator*, May 27, 1933, 673. John Collins (2007: 19) states that the Gold Coast ZOY radio rediffusion station had begun operating in Accra in 1935.
14. "Brunswick Gramophone and Record Service: Why the Palladium Is Popular?" *Gold Coast Spectator*, March 12, 1932, 360.
15. "His Majesty's Xmas Message," *Gold Coast Spectator*, December 24, 1932.
16. *Report of the Committee Appointed in 1932 by the Governor of the Gold Coast Colony to Inspect the Prince of Wales' College and School, Achimota*. Published on behalf of the Government of the Gold Coast by the Crown Agents for the Colonies, 4 Millbank, Westminster, London, 14.

17. Anonymous interview, June 2011.
18. Private interview with Albert Mawere Opoku, October 1999.
19. *Visit of His Royal Highness the Prince of Wales to the Gold Coast 1925*, 208.
20. Ibid., 132–33.
21. *Report of the Committee Appointed in 1932*, 57.
22. Ibid., 34.
23. Ghana's Public Records and Archives Administration Department [PRAAD] Report on Achimota College of the year 1928–1929. Accra, Ghana: Government Printer.
24. *Report of the Committee Appointed in 1932*, 34.
25. Ibid.
26. Private interview with Professor Edward Ayensu, May 2013.
27. *Report of the Committee Appointed in 1932*, 39.
28. Private interview with Albert Mawere Opoku, October 1999.
29. Ibid.
30. Ibid.
31. All quotations are from private interviews with Guy Warren (Kofi Ghanaba), December 2000.
32. Anonymous interview, May 2004.
33. It was not uncommon for African artists, scholars, writers, and musicians to attribute their politicization to stays in the United States. Ghanaian scholar/novelist Ayi Kwei Armah describes such experiences. Nigerian Afrobeat musical pioneer Fela Anikulapo Kuti also attributed his politicization and focus on Pan-Africanism and African music and culture to his experiences of racism and political-racial struggle in the United Kingdom and the United States (Collins 2009; Veal 2000).
34. Indirect rule led to rising interests in understanding African cultures. In 1926 the International Institute of African Languages and Cultures (now the International African Institute) was founded in London under the leadership of Frederick Lugard, the architect of indirect rule. Rattray retired in 1930, leading to the closing of the department. The government further politicized studies of culture by then training "select political officers in the field" (Bourret 1952: 46). In 1933 the second edition of Christaller's Akan dictionary was published.
35. PRAAD. CSO 21/9/12. "Enclosure in Circular Dispatch Dated 26th August 1937," 1–2.
36. PRAAD. CSO 18/B/160. "Extract from a Report of the Committee Appointed in 1938 by the Governor of the Gold Coast Colony to Inspect the Prince of Wales' College, Achimota," 2–3.
37. Ibid., 3.
38. Ibid.
39. Ibid., 2.
40. The establishment of the Westermann script to standardize writing of local vernacular languages was a crucial aspect of the language and culture policies of the 1920s; see Stephanie Newell (2002).
41. *Report of the Committee appointed in 1932*, 39.
42. PRAAD. CSO 18/B/160. "Extract from a Report of the Committee Appointed in 1938," 3.
43. Ibid., 1.
44. Ibid.
45. Ibid.
46. British administrators recognized and reacted to the differences between French colonial approaches to the erasure of local difference and advocating for ideas of French civilization and British notions of indirect rule that endeavored to rule through local cultural and social institutions. One report asks, "Can Christianity be widely introduced without destroying the

tribal system along with its religious basis? Can African organisation and customs survive the spread of Western economic influences, and with what modification? . . . The answers are vital for the work of Achimota, unless it is to proceed on the lines of French Colonial Education, which tries to make those to whom it gives a higher education into good Frenchmen with little regard for the preservation of African elements in their life, whether good or bad." Accra PRO. CSO 18/B/160. "Extract from a Report of the Committee appointed in 1938," 2.

47. *Report of the Committee appointed in 1932*, 34.

48. Agbodeka 1977 also reports a successful production of *The Mikado* in 1930.

49. Accra PRO. CSO 18/6/156—0154.

50. PRAAD. Unnumbered. "Memorandum on the Proposed Institute of West African Research in Arts & Industries & Social Studies," 10.

51. Ibid.

52. In South Africa, ethnographic work underpinned apartheid's racial segregation by showing that Africans were purportedly cultural beings and that without their traditions they would not survive in the modern world. This type of research led to the creation of South African homelands where they were confined in the name of cultural preservation and denied the access of Africans to the rights, spaces, and obligations of citizenship. In this context culture became a language for controlling African labor.

53. William Ofori Atta, *West Africa*, August 24, 1935, quoted in Jenkins (1994: 175).

54. Ethnomusicologist J. H. K. Nketia begins his foundational 1962 book *African Music in Ghana* with an ambivalent if generous reading of Ward's work as a proto-ethnomusicologist. While at Achimota, Ward made observations based on the music played by students and a few short trips to rural areas. Nketia lauds him for playing "an important role in Ghanaian music education in the 1930s and anticipating later more complete interpretations of rhythm and scale in African music," though he criticizes Ward for being mostly interested in African music for "its creative possibilities" and stating that African music could grow into a great art form if it learned from European "modern developments in form and harmony" (Nketia 1962: 1).

55. PRAAD. 1250 SF2. "Telegram from the Governor to Secretary of State," October 28, 1940, 17.

56. PRAAD. 1250 SF2. "Gold Coast Railway, General Manager's Office No. 179/9188," October 31, 1940, 23.

57. PRAAD. 1250 SF2. "From the Governor," November 22, 1940, 32.

58. Ibid., 33.

59. The development, consolidation, and diffusion of radio, recorded music, and cinema were crucial to the postwar Gold Coast. During the war, propaganda films along with comedies and dramas were played at urban cinemas and by mobile film units that traveled the country (Collins 2007: 19–20). In 1947 Decca established a record-pressing plant in the Gold Coast, and in 1954 radio became part of the Gold Coast Broadcasting System (2007: 19–20).

60. For descriptions of the British view of indigenous African drama and African understandings of theatre, see "Native Drama" (1932) and Stevens (1930). (Archival sources for the early history of Gold Coast drama are recorded in Gibbs 2006.)

2. The National Theatre Movement

1. Ghana's Public Records and Archives Administration Department [PRAAD]. 3/7/60. "The Ghana Drama Studio presents Two Ananse Plays," October 14 (n.d.).

2. The IAS opened in 1961, though the official opening was held in 1963. Kwame Nkrumah, quoted in Addo (1965).

3. Recent scholarly interest in infrastructure has led ethnographers to focus on the built environment. Concern with technology and infrastructure grounds semiotic studies in materiality and social practice (Larkin 2013). These studies begin with things like roads and health clinics (Masquelier 2001, 2002), oil (A. Apter 2005; Coronil 1997; Watts 2011), radios, generators, and electricity (Larkin 2008, 2013), water and pipes (Anand 2011), canals (Carse 2014), media technology (Boyer 2013), and computer code (G. Coleman 2012). In these studies, materiality of the built world shapes and is shaped by social action, reenacting and reconfiguring historical forms of meaning and power. Considering theatre through the development of state, religious, and private infrastructures that appear to participants to underlie and precede aesthetic sensibilities avoids the common sense that art is an abstraction or a set of idealized texts/representations. The notion of infrastructure is useful in showing how social groups, built spaces, and media forms organize disparate signs, influences, and arguments into new, structured theatrical practices.

4. Private interview with J. H. K. Nketia, November 1999.

5. PRAAD. Unnumbered document. *Program Published for First National Festival of the Arts*, Accra, 1957.

6. Populations of Accra by decade: 1960—338,396; 1970—636,667; 1984—969,195; 2000—1,658,937. National Population Census, http://ama.ghanadistricts.gov.gh/?arrow=atd&_=3&sa=3004. Accessed November 2014.

7. Private interview with Bob Vanns, January 15, 1999.

8. Ibid.; private interview with T. O. Jazz, February 1999.

9. Private interview with John Collins, June 2005.

10. Private interview with Bob Vanns, December 2000.

11. Private interview with J. H. K. Nketia, November 1999.

12. "African Studies: The Vision and the Reality." Program for the thirtieth anniversary of the Institute of African Studies. University of Ghana, March 13, 1992.

13. The school was inaugurated on February 1, 1965. See http://www.ug.edu.gh/index1.php?linkid=840).

14. Private interview with J. H. K. Nketia, February 1999. See also Nketia (1965) and Gibbs (2006).

15. PRAAD. ACG 7 & ACG 4/SF2. Ministry of Education. Reorganization of the Arts Council of Ghana. Closed file. "The Ghana Drama Studio," supplement to letter on "advancement in Ghana's Cultural Programme" by Efua Sutherland sent to Oheneba Kwaw Richardson, June 25, 1970.

16. Private interview with Mohammed Ben Abdallah, April 2013.

17. Private interview with J. H. K. Nketia, February 1999.

18. Private interview with Martin Owusu, November 1999; see also Botwe-Asamoah (2005).

19. Private interview with Asiedu Yirenkyi, November 1998.

20. PRAAD. ACG 7 & ACG 4/SF2. "The Ghana Drama Studio," June 25, 1970.

21. Private interview with Mohammed Ben Abdallah, November 1999.

22. PRAAD. "The Ghana Drama Studio Presents Two Ananse Plays," March 7, 1960.

23. PRAAD. ACG 7 & ACG 4/SF2. "The Ghana Drama Studio," June 25, 1970.

24. Anonymous, "Writers' Workshop Notes," School of Music and Drama. See also Gibbs (2006).

25. PRAAD. ACG 7 & ACG 4/SF2. "The Ghana Drama Studio," June 25, 1970.

26. Private interview with Sandy Arkhurst, March 1999.

27. Private interview with Mohammed Ben Abdallah, October 1999.

28. Private interview with Nana Ampadu, May 1999.

29. "African Drama" (1934).

30. Ibid.
31. Private interview with Yaw Asare, February 2000.
32. In 1999 I did research in Atwia with Abibigromma member Samuel Dawson, who was also studying storytelling and the rural community's relationship to this storytelling house built with support from Ghanaian urban elites and foreign funders in the 1960s.
33. There are different variations on this call-and-response formula. A further reply can be, "Ye sisi aara" (We are tricking still, we haven't stopped). *Sisi* can be translated as "hoax," "bully," or "lie." Private correspondence with David Donkor, November 2002.
34. Private interview with Sandy Arkhurst, October 1999.
35. Private interview with Martin Owusu, January 1999.
36. Private interview with Mohammed Ben Abdallah, November 1999.
37. See Scott Kennedy's 1973 book *In Search of African Theatre* for descriptions of the theatre scene in Accra and at the University of Ghana, Legon, in the late 1960s and early 1970s. It is a first-person account, from the perspective of an African American artist-teacher, of various strands of Ghanaian theatre.
38. Private interview with anonymous former student of de Graft's, March 1999.
39. Developments in Pan-Africanism and the arts in Ghana influenced and were to some extent in dialogue with what was happening in Francophone West Africa, Nigeria, and the Caribbean. In 1966 the Première Festival Mondial des Arts Nègres in Dakar was a major international event. Alioune Diop's journal *Presence Africain*, the work of Léopold Senghor of Senegal and Sékou Touré of Guinea, the Ballet National du Sénégal, and Les Ballets Africains of Guinea were part of the Francophone movement to think about the role of the arts in linking black peoples together as part of a cultural-political collectivity. The second World Black and African Festival of Arts and Culture (FESTAC) in Nigeria in 1977 continued this tradition as a major global event for the display of black cultures and arts and their relationship to African political sovereignty and state authority.
40. Private interview with Sandy Arkhurst, March 1999.
41. Ibid.
42. Ibid.
43. Private interview with Asiedu Yirenkyi, October 1998.
44. Private interview with Sandy Arkhurst, March 1999.
45. Private interview with Asiedu Yirenkyi, October 1998.
46. Ibid.
47. Ibid.
48. Private interview with Solomon Sampah, May 2013.
49. PRAAD. Ref. ACG.62/5. "Arts Council of Ghana."
50. PRAAD. RG 3/7/168. Félix Morisseau-Leroy, "Report on the Training of the Workers' Brigade Concert Party," October 8, 1962.
51. Ibid.
52. PRAAD. RG 3/7/168. To Chief Promotions Officer on Workers' Brigade Drama Group from George Andoh Wilson and F. Morisseau-Leroy, April 1, 1963. In one document the Venezuelan group is called "El Retalo do Marvillas."
53. Ibid.
54. PRAAD. RG 3/7/168. Félix Morisseau-Leroy, "Report on the Training of the Workers' Brigade Concert Party," October 8, 1962.
55. PRAAD. RG 3/7/168. To Chief Promotions Officer on Workers' Brigade Drama Group from George Andoh Wilson and F. Morisseau-Leroy, April 1, 1963.
56. PRAAD. RG 3/7/168: 164. "Kumasi Tour of 'Awo Ye' and Doguicimi"; Unnumbered document. "Workers' Brigade Drama Group Performances." January 7 to November 6, 1963.

57. PRAAD. RG 3/7/168. Ref. 16/164. Workers' Brigade Drama Group. October 12, 1963.
58. Ibid.
59. Ibid.
60. PRAAD. RG 3/7/168. Ref. 16/164. Workers' Brigade Drama Group. October 12, 1963; Accra PRO. RG 3/7/168. Unnumbered document. Memo from B. Casely-Hayford, Chief Promotions Officer, Ghana Institute of Arts and Culture, report on meeting, December 18, 1962.
61. Ibid.
62. Ibid.
63. PRAAD. RG 3/7/171: 180–82. "List of Member of The National Drama Company."
64. PRAAD. RG 3/7/171: 165–66. "Miss Lucy Addo, Resignation"; 175. "Lucy Addo—It is time that I failed to turn up for the performance of 'Akosombo' . . ."; 176. "Case of two members of the National Drama Company."
65. PRAAD. 186. "Memorandum F. K. Fiawoo to F. Morisseau-Leroy"; 190. Memo to Mr. J. C. de Graft, Director, Ghana Drama Studio from F. Morisseau-Leroy, May 30, 1966; 191. Press release, "The Dagger of Liberation"; 308. "Sons and Daughters," February 24 and 25, 1967. Documents refer to Faiwoo's play as *Tuinese*; elsewhere it is *Tuniese*.
66. PRAAD. RG 3/7/168: 164. "Kumasi Tour of 'Awo Ye' and Doguicimi"; Unnumbered document. "Workers' Brigade Drama Group Performances." January 7 to November 6, 1963.
67. Accra PRO. RG 3/7/168: 164. Ref. F. 16/164. "Workers' Brigade Drama Group," October 18, 1963, 2.
68. PRAAD. Unnumbered document. "Confidential U.S. State Department Central Files." GHANA 1960–January 1963 Internal Affairs and Foreign Affairs.
69. Private interview with Solomon Sampah, August 2013.
70. http://nkrumahinfobank.org/article.php?id=446&c=51. Accessed January 5, 2015.
71. Private interview with Edward Ayensu, August 2013.
72. Private interview with Mohammed Ben Abdallah, August 2013.
73. Private correspondence with Nii Addokwei Moffatt, February 2011.
74. Private interview with Mohammed Ben Abdallah, August 2013.
75. Nketia became a professor of music and at various times head of both IAS and the School of Music and Drama.
76. Nketia's research was central to providing the cultural materials for formulating the aesthetics of Nkrumah's state, particularly around ceremonial occasions like Independence Day and Republic Day. As Nketia and other intellectuals and politicians became involved in developing Ghana's statecraft after independence, many African countries employed "traditional" arts to "make a contribution to nation building . . . creating and maintaining new institutional frameworks and loyalties that transcend the boundaries of ethnicity" (Nketia in Altbach and Hassan 1996: 129).
77. Private interview with Albert Mawere Opoku, December 1998.
78. Ibid.
79. Private interview with Guy Warren (Kofi Ghanaba), 2000.
80. Opoku worked with the group until his death in 2001.
81. Private interview with J. H. K. Nketia, February 1999.
82. Private interview with Albert Mawere Opoku, December 1998. Also see Lokko (1980: 312).
83. Private interview with Albert Mawere Opoku, December 1998.
84. Ibid.
85. Opoku explained that festivals like the Akan Odwira and the Ga Homowo celebrations were researched for their dramatic structures, such that their key elements could be discerned,

divided into easily teachable movements, ordered and timed for narrative organization, and blocked to aid staging and display for audience observation. Ibid.

86. Ibid.

87. Private interview with Albert Mawere Opoku, December 1998.

88. Ibid.

89. Later, as director of the Ghana Dance Ensemble, Ampofo Duodu expanded on dances from non-Akan cultures, arguing that the celebration of community should not be defined by Asante royal imagery. Since Nketia and Opoku were Akan elites, dancers and choreographers from other groups were at times concerned that their dances were being subsumed into an Akan idiom. As one dancer explained, "including dances from other ethnic groups shows that Ghanaian societies are multicultural and not limited by dominant groups." Private interview with anonymous Dance Ensemble member, July 2011.

90. Private interview with anonymous Dance Ensemble member, November 1999.

91. Nonreferential aspects of signs are grounded through indexical relations between signs and the "emergent structures" of new contexts (Bauman and Briggs 1990: 76). The performative aspects of performances are those elements that both point to and transform "certain aspects of the [figures] and contexts of interaction" (Lee 1997: 93).

3. Revolutionary Storytelling

1. Private interview with Mohammed Ben Abdallah, July 2013.

2. Private interview with Solomon Sampah, November 1999.

3. Ghana's Public Records and Archives Administration Department [PRAAD]. ACG 7 & ACG 4/SF2. Ministry of Education. Reorganization of the Arts Council of Ghana. Closed file. Letter on "advancement in Ghana's Cultural Programme" by Efua Sutherland sent to Oheneba Kwaw Richardson, June 25, 1970.

4. Ibid.

5. Ibid.

6. Ibid.

7. PRAAD. ACG 7. Ministry of Education. Reorganization of the Arts Council of Ghana. Closed file. "Notes on the Reorganization of the Arts Council." Dr. Seth Cudjoe, undated, in 1970 file.

8. Ibid.

9. PRAAD. ACG 7. Ministry of Education. Reorganization of the Arts Council of Ghana. Closed file. "The Arts of Ghana and Their Need of Social and Aesthetic Criteria." Dr. Seth Cudjoe, August 7, 1974.

10. Anonymous interview, June 2005.

11. NationalPopulationCensusdata.http://ama.ghanadistricts.gov.gh/?arrow=atd&_=3&sa=3004.

12. Anonymous interview, November 1999.

13. Private interview with Mohammed Ben Abdallah, February 2000.

14. See Rawlings (1983).

15. Private interview with Ama Ata Aidoo, July 2013.

16. Ibid.

17. Ibid.

18. Ibid.

19. "Towards a Creative National Culture," April 2, 1982, acquired from Asiedu Yirenkyi.

20. Private interview with Asiedu Yirenkyi, October 1998.
21. Private interview with Mohammed Ben Abdallah, October 1999.
22. PRAAD. Closed files on PNDC Ministry of Education and Culture. Unnumbered documents. "Cultural Agreement between Ghana and Czechoslovakia." PNDC Secretary of Education and Culture. April 26, 1988; "Cabinet Memorandum. Visit to the German Democratic Republic for Discussions of Ghana/GDR Cultural Exchange Programme for 1980/81." Dr. Kwamena Ogran, Minister of Education Culture and Sports. Undated.
23. PRAAD. Closed files on PNDC Ministry of Education and Culture. Unnumbered documents. "Protocol for Cultural Co-operation between the Republic of Cuba and the Republic of Ghana for the Years" and "Provisional National Defence Council Memorandum: Ratification of Agreement on Cultural Co-operation between Ghana and Cuba." Dr. Obed Asamoah, Secretary of Foreign Affairs, June 22, 1982.
24. Private interview with Mohammed Ben Abdallah, March 1999.
25. Private interview with Mohammed Ben Abdallah, February 2000.
26. PRAAD. ACG 4/SF2. Reorganization of the Arts Council of Ghana. Closed file. Speech by Dr. Mohammed Ben Abdallah, PNDC Secretary for Culture and Tourism at the Inauguration of the Central Regional Cultural Committee, August 1, 1986.
27. PRAAD. ACG 4/SF2. Reorganization of the Arts Council of Ghana. Closed file. Speech by Dr. Mohammed Ben Abdallah, PNDC Secretary for Culture and Tourism at the Inauguration of the Begoro District Cultural Committee, July 20, 1986.
28. Ibid.
29. Private interview with Mohammed Ben Abdallah, November 1999.
30. Private interview with Mohammed Ben Abdallah, March 1999.
31. Personal communication with an ex-PNDC official, February 2002.
32. Private interview with Mohammed Ben Abdallah, January 2000.
33. Private interview with Mohammed Ben Abdallah, March 1999.
34. Unpublished document describing the founding of Abibigromma Theatre Company, 1984.
35. Private interview with Mohammed Ben Abdallah, March 1999.
36. Private interview with Mohammed Ben Abdallah, June 2004.
37. Private interview with Oh! Nii Kwei Sowah, April 1999.
38. Private interview with Mohammed Ben Abdallah, March 1999.
39. Private interview with Edinam Atatsi, December 1999.
40. Private interview with Agnes Panfred, July 2013.
41. Private interview with Edinam Atatsi, December 1999.
42. Private interview with Solomon Sampah, July 2013.
43. Private interview with Edinam Atatsi, December 1999.
44. Private interview with Francis Nii-Yartey, March 1999.
45. Private interview with Nana Bosompra, director of *Osofo Dadze* and *Obra*, March 1998.
46. Private interview with Edinam Atatsi, December 1999.
47. Private interview with Nana Brefo Boateng, assistant commissioner, National Commission on Culture, February 1999.
48. Private interview with Mohammed Ben Abdallah, January 2000.
49. Ibid.
50. Private interview with Korkor Amarteifio, October 1999.
51. *National Theatre in Retrospect: An Overview of the First Four Operational Years 1994-1997*, 13–14. Unpublished document.
52. Private interview with Mohammed Ben Abdallah, January 2000.

53. Private interview with Mohammed Ben Abdallah, April 2013.
54. Private interview with Nana Brefo Boateng, May 1999. As Boateng describes, rather than encouraging innovation and artistic risk, over time the National Theatre and the National Commission on Culture became institutions that ossified culture, "tasked to promote, preserve, and develop Ghana's culture."
55. *National Theatre in Retrospect*, 12.
56. Private interview with Komla Amoako, December 1999.
57. Private interview with Mohammed Ben Abdallah, October 1999.
58. Anonymous interview, November 1999.
59. Private interview with Mohammed Ben Abdallah, October 1999.
60. Ibid.
61. Ghana National Theatre Law, Article 7, PNDC L.259, 1991.
62. National Commission on Culture Law, Article 3, PNDC L.238, 1990.
63. Private interview with Yaw Asare, December 1998.
64. Private interview with Mohammed Ben Abdallah, October 1999.
65. *National Theatre in Retrospect*, 12.

4. A Man of the People

1. Ama Ata Aidoo and James Gibbs (in Banham, Gibbs, and Osofisan 2001: 84–87) offer an excellent biography of Abdallah.
2. Unpublished interview conducted by Dr. John Collins with Mohammed Ben Abdallah upon the occasion of his being appointed secretary of culture and tourism in 1983. Obtained from Dr. John Collins.
3. Private interview with Mohammed Ben Abdallah, February 2000.
4. Private interview with Mohammed Ben Abdallah, July 28, 2013.
5. Private interview with Chinua Achebe, April 24, 2004.

5. Total African Theatre

1. All quotations from Mohammed Ben Abdallah in this chapter are taken from a series of private interviews and conversations with him in late 1998 and early 1999.
2. Private interview with Emmanuel Mantey, October 1998.
3. In the 2000s the student population grew rapidly, quickly outpacing the capacity of existing facilities. While new studio and classroom spaces were built, Abibigromma was moved to a large storage shed in the back of the university's maintenance yard.
4. Private interview with Yaw Asare, December 1998.
5. Private interview with Oh! Nii Kwei Sowah, December 1998.
6. Ibid.
7. At the time the exchange rate was around three thousand Ghana cedis to one U.S. dollar, though there was rapid inflation.
8. Private interview with Ishak al-Mumminin, October 1998.
9. Private interview with Kwesi Brown, November 1999.
10. Ibid.
11. Ibid.
12. Ibid.
13. Ibid.

14. Private interviews with Kwesi Brown, December 1998 and November 2008.
15. Private interview with Emmanuel Mantey, October 1998.
16. Private interview with Ishak al-Mumminin, October 1998.
17. Private interview with Emmanuel Mantey, October 1998.
18. Private interview with Margaret Cudjoe, November 1999.
19. Private interview with David Akramah Cofie, November 2008.
20. The dondo is a talking drum from northern Ghana. "Dondology" was an insult aimed at those studying African music, making fun of the notion that it was a scientific endeavor.
21. Private interview with David Akramah Cofie, October 1998.
22. The debate on language among characters in the play points to both informal and institutional concerns about language fluency and use. As I have described, Abdallah spearheaded PNDC education policy reform requiring the teaching of local languages and culture. Abdallah explains, "African states have been stuck in the contradictions of colonial languages since independence. Learning local languages is crucial for cultural identity; but Ghanaians also must be fluent in English to engage with globalization." Private interview with Mohammed Ben Abdallah, February 2000.
23. Anonymous interview, November 1999.
24. Private interview with Ishak al-Mumminin, October 1998.
25. Official programs for Abibigromma list his name as Mamdou Bole Ndiaye, though he spelled his name Amadou in interviews for this research.
26. Private interview with Habib Chester Iddrisu, November 1999.
27. Private interview with Margaret Cudjoe, November 1999.
28. Anonymous interview, Drama Studio, December 1998.
29. Private interview with Kwesi Brown, December 1998.
30. Private interview with Margaret Cudjoe, October 1998.
31. Private interview with Kwesi Brown, December 1998.
32. The group's versatility and stamina was evident during this festival designed to showcase their skills for the public. They performed Martin Owusu's *Story Ananse Told* on November 18–20, 1999; Abdallah's *Verdict of the Cobra*, directed by Margaret Cudjoe, and traditional dances on November 22–24; *The Witch of Mopti* on November 25–27; *Tipawumli*, a dance drama choreographed by Habib Chester Iddrisu, and *Lovenet* by Aseidu Yirenkyi, stage managed by Jesse Offei, on November 30 and December 1; *Rape of the Ramatu Sisters*, choreographed by Cecilia Yelpoe, and *The Queue*, written by Bill Marshall and directed by Margaret Cudjoe, on December 2–4; and *Midnight Hotel*, written and directed by Professor Femi Osofisan, on December 9–11. Osofisan had directed the play with the group two years prior when he had been visiting SPA from Nigeria.
33. Anonymous interview, November 1998.
34. Anonymous interview with audience member, November 1998.
35. Private interview with Oh! Nii Kwei Sowah, November 1998.
36. Anonymous interview, December 1998.
37. Private interview with Kwesi Brown, December 1998.
38. Ibid.
39. Ibid.

6. "The Best Tradition Goes On"

1. "Concert Party" is capitalized when referring to the specific *Key Soap Concert Party* program at the National Theatre. It is in lowercase when referring the general theatrical genre.

2. Unilever Ghana Ltd. is a subsidiary of Unilever Overseas Holdings Ltd. and CWA Holdings Ltd., which are both subsidiaries of Unilever PLC, which is incorporated in England. Unilever is a multinational corporation that has a wide range of products in Ghana, including food, personal hygiene, and household care items. During the colonial period, the parent company controlled 70 percent of the soap sold worldwide.

3. In the initial presidential and parliamentary elections held on December 6, 2000, six candidates ran for president. No clear majority was won by any candidate, though J. A. Kufuor of the NPP party received the most votes, winning 46 percent of votes cast, and Vice President John Atta Mills of the ruling NDC party came in second with 38 percent. A runoff election was held on December 27, 2000, between the top two candidates. Kufuor's victory was announced on December 30, 2000, and the inauguration was set for January 7, 2001.

4. At the time the exchange rate was approximately seven thousand Ghana cedis to one U.S. dollar.

5. Anthropological texts such as Isaac Shapera's work on Tswana law, Meyer Fortes's description of Tallensi social structure, and Rattray's works on Ashanti law, religion, and society have been used by later generations in these locales to codify and define tradition.

6. Private interview with Seth Ashong-Kitae, May 1, 2000.

7. Ibid.

8. Private interview with a Unilever marketing manager, April 2001.

9. Opiah (Y. B. Bampoe), A. B. Crentsil, and Araba Stamp, among others, performed in the initial programs.

10. At Unilever, the brands manager for Key Soap is in charge of *Key Soap Concert Party* and liaisons with the National Theatre and Unilever's advertising agency, Lintas Ghana Ltd. The marketing manager for home care (i.e., products used in care of the home) is his superior, and the marketing director oversees this whole operation.

11. Key Soap is a pale yellow soap sold in footlong bars or smaller, cut-up pieces. It is used for washing clothes and dishes as well as for personal hygiene.

12. Private interview with a Unilever executive, April 2001.

13. Unilever Ghana Ltd., while a subsidiary of Unilever PLC, has relative autonomy in terms of local decision making. Most of its employees are Ghanaians, while a few Europeans occupy upper managerial and specialist positions.

14. In the late 1990s Sir Frank Lowe was president of Lowe Lintas and Partners, of which Lintas Ghana was an affiliate. While they claim no political affiliation, Jake Obetey Lampetey, a prominent NPP party member and former television actor, has served as their CEO.

15. Private interview with a Unilever executive, April 2001.

16. *National Theatre in Retrospect: An Overview of the First Four Operational Years 1994–1997,* 17. Unpublished document.

17. Private interview with a Unilever executive, April 2001.

18. Private interview with a Lintas production assistant, November 2000.

19. Private interview with Bob Vanns, March 1999.

20. "Bishop Bob Okalla: Man of the Moment," *People and Places,* March 27, 1996.

21. Private interview with a Concert Party Union official, January 2000.

22. Private interview with a concert party performer, December 1999.

23. "Bishop Bob Okalla: Man of the Moment."

24. Private correspondence with Ama Boabeng, April 1999.

25. *Cultural Splash* was a concert party program run at the Arts Centre in Accra from 1997 to 1999 featuring the concert party artists who had left the National Theatre. It was managed by Bristman Advertising Company and sponsored by Accra Brewery Company (ABC). The

show was taped and shown on TV3, the first private television station in Ghana, which was established by a Malaysian firm in 1996. According to several of the artists involved, when the sponsorship ran out, the management began having problems, and the program was canceled.

26. "Bishop Bob Okalla: Man of the Moment," *People and Places*, March 27, 1996.
27. Private interview with a Unilever marketing manager, April 2001.
28. Private interview with a Unilever executive, April 2001.
29. Ibid.
30. Y. B. Bampoe at a Concert Party Union meeting, March 1999.
31. Skin bleaching by artists on stage was banned and has been used as a way to detract from performers' scores. While some saw this as a positive social message by Unilever, others have said that it was a way for the corporation to distance themselves from practices they have promoted in the past and promote their new skin-related hygiene products.
32. Private correspondence with a concert party performer, November 2000.
33. Comedian Bishop Bob Okalla, "Who Is Who" *Key Soap Concert Party* finals, January 1, 2001. Translated from the Akan with assistance from Emma Agyei Dwarko.
34. Kelvin Asare-Williams and Sarah Dzorgbadze assisted with audience interviews and performance assessments on numerous dates.
35. "Yaw" is a pseudonym.
36. Private interview with a National Theatre official, October 1999.
37. *Challey* is a vernacular term generally used as a familiar form of address for friends and acquaintances, especially by young men.

7. Fake Pastors and Real Comedians

1. The study of religion and myth has been a locus in anthropology for understanding alterity. Recently, there has been concern in anthropology of religion and ethnography more generally to "take seriously" difference and religious experience. However, this often means that ethnographers take religious doctrine literally, focus on texts and myths as abstract representations of fundamental difference, assume the boundedness of groups, and return to naïve ideas of voice and presence, all in the name of critiquing historically grounded ethnography, concerns with representation, and focus on history and power. Situating culture, meaning, and belief in rich historical and social contexts and in relation to semiotic fields and power dynamics does not preclude understanding these as self-contained and meaningful in their own right and their own terms. I take religion, belief, and incommensurable difference seriously but consider how radical difference is historically situated and produced as a form of experience that shapes and is shaped in social interactions.
2. Private correspondence with Delali Noviewoo, December 2002.
3. In examining Ghanaian popular video-films and images, Meyer (1998a: 321) argues that the devil is central to Pentecostal public culture in making dichotomies of tradition and modernity. Meyer focuses on the Pentecostalization of the public sphere, taking popular images of spiritual battle and diabolic figures as reflective of structuring signs (Meyer 2004a, 2004b). Here, good and evil are not separate realms in spiritual battle but two sides of the performative struggle over authority.
4. The television show *Kejetia*, which went into production in 2000, was a series for considering trickery in Ghanaian popular drama. Its main character was a small-time hustler and Pentecostal preacher who staged fake healing prayer sessions in the markets of the city of Kumasi. In each episode the fake pastor got into some new predicament in which he barely

escaped getting caught. Yaw Asare, one of the main writers of the series, created this pastor/ trickster character to resonate with the daily frustrations and predicaments many Ghanaians face. Private interview with Yaw Asare, January 2000.

    5. Private interview with Reverend Vagalas, June 1999.

    6. Private interview with Reverend John B. Ghartey, November 2001. He explained that in the early days of Rawlings, the spirit of "people's power" affected youth attitudes toward Christianity around the country. "It was part of the spirit of political change that came with Rawlings. At first we were with him. It was not until later that he started to turn against the churches."

    7. Private interview with Brew Riverson Jr., January 2000.

    8. Private interview with Mohammed Ben Abdallah, November 1999.

    9. Private correspondence with Mohammed Ben Abdallah, January 2000.

    10. Jerry John Rawlings, "The Church Must Join in the Struggle to Emancipate the Oppressed and Create a New Order of Justice," opening of the Association of Episcopal Conferences of Anglophone West Africa. Accra, Ghana: Information Services Department, August 20, 1989.

    11. Private interview with Mohammed Ben Abdallah, January 2000.

    12. Ibid.

    13. Private interview with Reverend Akrong, Institute of African Studies, January 2000.

    14. I would like to thank an anonymous reviewer for this point.

    15. The proportion of the country claiming Christianity as their religion remained fairly static at almost 70 percent in the 2000 census.

    16. Private interview with Paa Kwesi Holdbrook-Smith, February 2005.

    17. Private correspondence with John Collins, October 2002.

    18. Private interview with Nana Ampadu, February 2000.

    19. Private interview with T. O. Jazz, May 1999.

    20. This is a pseudonym. All quotations are from sermons at Christian Action Faith Ministries.

    21. Duncan-Williams's Christian Action Faith Ministries International is also one of the largest "new" churches in Ghana (Duncan-Williams 1997). Its styles of worship are more generally indicative of what are seen as Westernized neo-Pentecostal modes of performance. As with all megachurches it has many branches throughout the country. A small church in a poor northern suburb of Accra is typical of churches in peri-urban residential areas.

    22. Interview with audience member at National Theatre, December 1999.

    23. At the time, the exchange rate was approximately seven thousand Ghanaian cedis to one U.S. dollar.

    24. "KATH Boss Dares Kumasi Pastor," *Ghanaian Chronicle*, May 15, 2003.

    25. *People and Places*, December 23, 1998–January 6, 1999, 3.

    26. *Weekly Spectator*, October 9–October 15, 1999, 1, 13.

    27. This comment is in response to Kwaku Duah, "Pastor Shaves 13 Year Old Girl," *Daily Guide*, January 27, 2008, http://www.ghanaweb.com/GhanaHomePage/NewsArchive/artikel.php?ID=138281.

    28. Anonymous conversation, March 2008.

    29. This is a pseudonym.

    30. *Dokono* (or *kenkey*) is a staple food made of pounded yam, cassava, or corn, mashed, fermented, and wrapped in banana leaves or plastic.

    31. Private interviews with Grace Omaboe, March and April 1999.

    32. This is translated from "Se wo sisi me a obia be ti yen ka."

33. Private interview with Esi Sutherland-Addy, December 2005.
34. Ibid.

8. Copying Independence

1. Lyrics translated by Kwesi Brown and David Donkor. Obrafour's hit rap song from 1999 described Nkrumah's continued relevance to the national imaginary. See J. Shipley (2013a: 108–33) for an extended discussion.
2. *Kenkey* (or *dokono*) is a staple food made of pounded yam, cassava, or corn, mashed, fermented, and wrapped in banana leaves or plastic.
3. Private interview with Seidu Bananzi, November 1998.
4. Private interview with Mohammed Ben Abdallah, March 1999.
5. In 2000 I directed his one-act play *The Gods Are to Blame* with Abibigromma: National Theatre Players. This play is an existentialist critique of the IMF's control of African economic conditions.
6. For an online account, see http://www.monstersandcritics.com/news/africa/news/article_1273246.php/Fireworks_re-enactments_usher_in_Ghanas_50th_independence_day.
7. Private interview with Seidu Bananzi, November 1998.

Epilogue

1. Yaw Asare was the director of Abibigromma: National Theatre Players for several years and taught at the School of Performing Arts. By Abdallah's account he was his star student, a dancer turned scholar, playwright, and director. A number of his plays have been regularly done by Abibigromma and other groups. *Ananse in the Land of Idiots* was performed as part of the 2007 fiftieth-anniversary independence celebrations at the National Theatre, directed by Africanus Aveh. One of the actors in the production told me, "We all heard this story growing up in the village. . . . Yaw has creatively shaped it for the stage, doing blocking and writing, fixing dialogue for the characters." Yaw Asare was deeply invested in trying to translate Guan, Ewe, and Akan expressive culture for contemporary audiences. Asare, who died suddenly in 2002, according to Abdallah, "pushed Abibigro as a theatre concept to its furthest potential. . . . If I defined it, he could talk about it and write it better than anyone."
2. http://www.ghana50.gov.gh/events/index.php?op=classic12.

Bibliography

Abdallah, Mohammed Ben. 1987. *The Trial of Mallam Ilya and Other Plays.* Accra, Ghana: Woeli.
———. 1989. *The Fall of Kumbi and Other Plays.* Accra, Ghana: Woeli.
Abu-Lughod, Lila. 2004. *Dramas of Nationhood: The Politics of Television in Egypt.* Chicago: University of Chicago Press.
Achebe, Chinua. 2012. *There Was a Country.* New York: Penguin.
Acquah, Ione. 1972. *Accra Survey.* Accra: Ghana Universities Press.
Adams, Anne V., and Esi Sutherland-Addy, eds. 2007. *The Legacy of Efua Sutherland: Pan-African Cultural Activism.* Banbury, U.K.: Ayebia Clarke.
Addae-Mensah, Apostle Matthew. 2000. *Walking in the Power of God: Thrilling Testimonies about Supernatural Encounters with God.* Belleville, Ontario: Guardian Books.
Addo, G. B. 1965. "1964 Drama Workshop." *Ghana Cultural Review* 1 (1).
Adjei, Mike. 1993. *Death and Pain: Rawlings' Ghana—The Inside Story.* London: Black Line.
"African Drama and the British Drama League." *Overseas Education* 5 (April 1934): 125–28.
Afrifa, Colonel A. A. 1966. *The Ghana Coup: 24th February 1966.* New York: Humanities Press.
Agawu, Kofi. 1995. *African Rhythm: A Northern Ewe Perspective.* Cambridge: Cambridge University Press.
———. 1996. "The Amu Legacy: Ephraim Amu 1899–1995." *Africa* 66 (2): 274–79.
———. 2003. *Representing African Music: Postcolonial Notes, Queries, Positions.* New York: Routledge.
Agbodeka, Francis. 1971. *African Politics and British Policy in the Gold Coast 1868–1900: A Study in the Forms and Force of Protest.* Evanston, Ill.: Longman / Northwestern University Press.
———. 1977. *Achimota in the National Setting: A Unique Educational Experiment in West Africa.* Accra, Ghana: Afram.
Agha, Asif. 2005a. "Introduction: Semiosis across Encounters." *Journal of Linguistic Anthropology* 15 (1): 1–5.
———. 2005b. "Voicing, Footing, Enregisterment." *Journal of Linguistic Anthropology* 15 (1): 38–59.
Agovi, Kofi E. 1990. "The Origin of Literary Theatre in Colonial Ghana." *Institute of African Studies Research Review* 6 (1): 1–23.
———. 1992. "Joe de Graft." In *Dictionary of Literary Biography.* Vol. 117: *African and Caribbean Writers,* edited by Bernth Lindfors and Reinhard Sander, 134–40. Detroit: Bruccoli Clark Layman.
Agyekum, Peter Kwame. 1980. *The Gold Coast—Her March to the Independent State of Ghana: A Bird's Eye View.* Accra, Ghana: New Times.

Agyeman, Opoku. 1992. *Nkrumah's Ghana and East Africa: Pan-Africanism and African Interstate Relations*. Rutherford, N.J.: Fairleigh Dickinson University Press.
Akoto, Baffour Osei. 1992. *Struggle against Dictator*. Kumasi, Ghana: Payless Printing Press.
Akpala, Kwesi. 1964. "The Theatre in Socialist Ghana." *The Ghanaian* (April): 13.
Akudinobi, Jude G. 2001. "Nationalism, African Cinema, and Frames of Scrutiny." *Research in African Literatures* 32 (3): 123–42.
Akyeampong, Emmanuel. 1996. *Drink, Power, and Cultural Change: A Social History of Alcohol in Ghana, c. 1800 to Recent Times*. Portsmouth, N.H.: Heinemann.
Akyeampong, Emmanuel, and Ama de-Graft Aikins. 2008. "Ghana at Fifty: Reflections on Independence and After." *Transition* 98:24–34.
Allman, Jean, and John Parker. 2005. *Tongnaab: The History of a West African God*. Bloomington: Indiana University Press.
Allman, Jean Marie. 1993. *The Quills of the Porcupine: Asante Nationalism in an Emergent Ghana*. Madison: University of Wisconsin Press.
———. 2013. "Kwame Nkrumah, African Studies, and the Politics of Knowledge Production in the Black Star of Africa." *International Journal of African Historical Studies* 46 (2): 181–203.
Allman, Jean Marie, and Victoria B. Tashjian. 2000. *I Will Not Eat Stone: A Women's History of Colonial Asante*. Oxford: Heinemann.
Altbach, Philip G., and Salah M. Hassan, eds. 1996. *The Muse of Modernity*. Trenton, N.J.: Africa World Press.
Amamoo, Joseph G. 1988. *The Ghanaian Revolution*. London: Jafint.
Anaba, Eastwood. 1998. *God's End-Time Militia: Winning the War Within and Without*. Accra, Ghana: Design Solutions.
Anand, Nikhil. 2011. "Pressure: The PoliTechnics of Water Supply in Mumbai." *Cultural Anthropology* 26 (4): 542–64.
Anderson, Allan H. 2001. *African Reformation: African Initiated Christianity in the 20th Century*. Trenton, N.J.: Africa World Press.
Anderson, Benedict. 1983. *Imagined Communities: Reflections on the Origin and Spread of Nationalism*. London: Verso.
Angelou, Maya. 1991. *All God's Children Need Traveling Shoes*. New York: Vintage Books.
Anyidoho, Akuosua. 1994. "Tradition and Innovation in Nnwonkoro, an Akan Female Verbal Genre." *African Literatures* 25 (3): 141–59.
Anyidoho, Kofi. 1983. "Oral Poetics and Traditions of Verbal Art in Africa." Ph.D. diss., University of Texas, Austin.
———. 1996. "Dr. Efua Sutherland: A Biographical Sketch." *African Literature Association Bulletin* 22 (3): 9–12.
———. 2000. "National Identity and the Language of Metaphor." In *FonTomFrom: Contemporary Ghanaian Literature, Theatre and Film*, edited by Kofi Anyidoho and James Gibbs, 12–28. Matatu 21–22. Amsterdam: Rodopi.
Appiah, Kwame Anthony. 1992. *In My Father's House: African in the Philosophy of Culture*. Oxford: Oxford University Press.
Apter, Andrew. 1996. "The Pan-African Nation: Oil-Money and the Spectacle of Culture in Nigeria." *Public Culture* 8 (3): 441–66.
———. 1999. "The Subvention of Tradition: A Genealogy of the Nigerian Durbar." In *State/Culture: The Study of State Formation after the Cultural Turn*, edited by George Steinmetz, 213–52. Ithaca, N.Y.: Cornell University Press.

———. 2005. *The Pan-African Nation: Oil and the Spectacle of Culture in Nigeria.* Chicago: University of Chicago Press.
———. 2007. *Beyond Words: Discourse and Critical Agency in Africa.* Chicago: University of Chicago Press.
Apter, David. 1963. *Ghana in Transition.* Princeton, N.J.: Princeton University Press.
Arhin, Kwame, ed. 1993. *The Life and Work of Kwame Nkrumah.* Trenton, N.J.: Africa World Press.
Arkhurst, Sandy. 2007. "Kodzidan." In *The Legacy of Efua Sutherland: Pan-African Cultural Activism,* edited by Anne V. Adams and Esi Sutherland-Addy, 165–74. Banbury, U.K.: Ayebia Clarke.
Armah, Ayi Kwei. (1971) 1995. *Fragments.* London: Heinemann.
Aryeetey, Ernest, Jane Harrigan, and Machiko Nissanke. 2000. *Economic Reforms in Ghana: The Miracle and the Mirage.* Oxford: James Currey.
Asad, Talal, ed. 1973. *Anthropology and the Colonial Encounter.* Atlantic Highlands, N.J.: Humanities Press.
Asamoah-Gyadu, J. Kwabena. 2005. "Reshaping Sub-Saharan African Christianity." archive.waccglobal.org/wacc/publications/media_development/2005_2/reshaping_sub_saharan_african_christianity.
Asare, Alphonse Yaw. n.d. "Ananse in the Land of Idiots." Unpublished play script, School of Performing Arts, University of Ghana, Legon.
Asare, Charles Agyin. 1997. *It Is Miracle Time: Experiencing GOD's Supernatural Working Power.* Vols. 1–2. Accra, Ghana: Type Company.
Asempa Publishers, eds. 1990. *The Rise of Independent Churches in Ghana.* Accra, Ghana: Asempa.
Ashton, S. R., and S. E. Stockwell, eds. 1996. *Imperial Policy and Colonial Practice, 1925–1945.* London: Institute of Commonwealth Studies, University of London.
Asiedu, Awo. 2001. "Interview with Mohammed Ben Abdallah." In *African Theatre: Playwrights and Politics,* edited by Martin Banham, James Gibbs, and Femi Osofisan, 95–106. Oxford: James Currey.
Askew, Kelly M. 2002. *Performing the Nation: Swahili Music and Cultural Politics in Tanzania.* Chicago: University of Chicago Press.
Austin, Dennis. 1964. *Politics in Ghana, 1946–1960.* London: Oxford University Press.
Austin, John L. 1975. *How to Do Things with Words.* Cambridge, Mass.: Harvard University Press.
Baah-Nuakoh, Amoah. 1997. *Studies on the Ghanaian Economy.* Vol. 1: *The Pre-"Revolutionary" Years, 1957–1981.* Accra: Ghana Universities Press.
Bakhtin, M. M. 1982. *The Dialogic Imagination: Four Essays.* Austin: University of Texas Press.
Baku, D. E. Kofi. 1990. "History and National Development: The Case of John Mensah Sarbah and the Reconstruction of Gold Coast History." *Institute of African Studies Research Review* 6 (1): 36–48.
Bame, Kwabena N. 1985. *Come to Laugh: African Traditional Theatre in Ghana.* New York: Lilian Barber.
Banham, Martin, ed. 2008. *A History of Theatre in Africa.* Cambridge: Cambridge University Press.
Banham, Martin, James Gibbs, and Femi Osofisan, eds. 2001. *African Theatre: Playwrights and Politics.* Oxford: James Currey.

Barber, Karin. 1987. "Popular Arts in Africa." *African Studies Review* 30 (3): 1–78.
———. 1997. "Preliminary Notes on Audiences in Africa." *Africa* 67 (3): 347–62.
———. 2000. *The Generation of Plays: Yoruba Popular Life in Theatre.* Bloomington: Indiana University Press.
Barber, Karin, John Collins, and Alain Ricard. 1997. *West African Popular Theatre.* Bloomington: Indiana University Press.
Bauman, Richard. 1992. "Contextualization, Tradition, and the Dialogue of Genres: Icelandic Legends of the *Kraftaskald.*" In *Rethinking Context: Language as an Interactive Phenomenon,* edited by Alessandro Duranti and Charles Goodwin, 125–45. Cambridge: Cambridge University Press.
Bauman, Richard, and Charles Briggs. 1990. "Poetics and Performance as Critical Perspectives on Language and Social Life." *Annual Review of Anthropology* 19:59–88.
———. 2003. *Voices of Modernity: Language Ideologies and the Politics of Inequality.* Cambridge: Cambridge University Press.
Baynham, Simon. 1988. *The Military and Politics in Nkrumah's Ghana.* Boulder, Colo.: Westview.
Beeman, William O. 1993. "The Anthropology of Theatre and Spectacle." *Annual Review of Anthropology* 22:369–93.
Beidelman, Thomas. 1980. "The Moral Imagination of the Kaguru: Some Thoughts on Tricksters, Translation, and Comparative Analysis." *American Ethnologist* 7 (1): 27–42.
Berry, Jack. 1961. *Spoken Art in West Africa.* London: School of Oriental and African Studies, University of London.
Berry, Sara S. 2001. *Chiefs Know Their Boundaries: Essays on Property, Power, and the Past in Asante, 1896–1996.* Oxford: James Currey.
Bhabha, Homi K. 1994. *The Location of Culture.* London: Routledge.
Birmingham, W. B., and G. Jahoda. 1955. "A Pre-election Survey in a Semi-literate Society." *Public Opinion Quarterly* 19 (2): 140–52.
Boahen, Adu. 1975. *Ghana: Evolution and Change in the Nineteenth and Twentieth Centuries.* London: Longman.
Bobo, Benjamin F. 1974. "Black Internal Migration: U.S. and Ghana—A Comparative Study." Professional Paper 3, Center for Afro-American Studies, University of California, Los Angeles.
Botwe-Asamoah, Kwame. 2005. *Kwame Nkrumah's Politico-cultural Thought and Politics: An African-Centered Paradigm for the Second Phase of the African Revolution.* New York: Routledge.
Bourdieu, Pierre. 1984. *Distinction: A Social Critique of the Judgement of Taste.* Cambridge, Mass.: Harvard University Press.
Bourret, F. M. 1952. *The Gold Coast.* London: Oxford University Press.
Boyer, Dominic. 2005. *Spirit and System: Media, Intellectuals, and the Dialectic in Modern German Culture.* Chicago: University of Chicago Press.
———. 2013. *The Life Informatic: Newsmaking in the Digital Era.* Ithaca, N.Y.: Cornell University Press.
Briggs, Charles L., and Richard Bauman. 1995. "Genre, Intertextuality, and Social Power." In *Language, Culture, and Society: A Book of Readings,* edited by Ben G. Blount, 567–608. Prospect Heights, Ill.: Waveland.

Brown, Aaron. 1956. "The Phelps-Stokes Fund and Its Projects." *Journal of Negro Education* 25 (4): 456–62.
Brown, Godfrey. 1964. "British Educational Policy in West and Central Africa." *Journal of Modern African Studies* 2 (3): 365–77.
Buah, F. K. 1998. *A History of Ghana*. London: Macmillan.
Buell, Raymond Leslie. 1928. *The Native Problem in Africa*. New York: Macmillan.
Burke, Timothy. 1996. *Lifebuoy Women and Lux Men: Commodification, Consumption, and Cleanliness in Modern Zimbabwe*. Durham, N.C.: Duke University Press.
Burrell, Jenna. 2012. *Invisible Users: Youth in the Internet Cafés of Urban Ghana*. Cambridge, Mass.: MIT Press.
Busia, Kofi Abrefa. 1951. *The Position of the Chief in the Modern Political System of Ashanti*. London: Oxford University Press.
———. 1962. *The Challenge of Africa*. New York: Praeger.
Butler, Judith. 1990. *Gender Trouble: Feminism and the Subversion of Identity*. New York: Routledge.
———. 1997. *Excitable Speech: A Politics of the Performative*. New York: Routledge.
Cannadine, David. 1983. "The Context, Performance, and Meaning of Ritual: The British Monarchy and the 'Invention of Tradition,' c. 1820–1977." In *The Invention of Tradition*, edited by Eric Hobsbawm and Terence Ranger, 101–64. Cambridge: Cambridge University Press.
Carroll, Michael P. 1984. "The Trickster as Selfish-Buffoon and Culture-Hero." *Ethos* 12 (2): 105–31.
Carse, Ashley. 2014. *Beyond the Big Ditch: Politics, Ecology, and Infrastructure at the Panama Canal*. Cambridge, Mass.: MIT Press.
Casely Hayford, Joseph Ephraim. 1903. *Gold Coast Native Institutions*. London: Sweet and Maxwell.
Cecil, Lord Edward. (1921) 1984. *The Leisure of an Egyptian Official*. London: Century.
Chalfin, Brenda. 2004. *Shea Butter Republic: State Power, Global Markets, and the Making of an Indigenous Commodity*. London: Routledge.
———. 2010. *Neoliberal Frontiers: An Ethnography of Sovereignty in West Africa*. Chicago: University of Chicago Press.
Chatterjee, Partha. 1993. *The Nation and Its Fragments: Colonial and Postcolonial Histories*. Princeton, N.J.: Princeton University Press.
Chernoff, John. 2003. *Hustling Is Not Stealing: Stories of an African Bar Girl*. Chicago: University of Chicago Press.
Clarence-Smith, William Gervase. 1994. "The Organisation of 'Consent' in British West Africa, 1820s to 1960s." In *Contesting Colonial Hegemony: State and Society in Africa*, edited by Dagmar Engels and Shula Marks, 55–78. London: British Academic Press.
Clark, Gracia. 1994. *Onions Are My Husband: Survival and Accumulation by West African Market Women*. Chicago: University of Chicago Press.
Clarke, Kamari. 2004. *Mapping Yoruba Transnational Networks: Power and Agency in the Making of Transnational Communities*. Durham, N.C.: Duke University Press.
Coe, Cati. 2005. *Dilemmas of Culture in African Schools: Youth, Nationalism, and the Transformation of Knowledge*. Chicago: University of Chicago Press.

Cohn, Bernard S. 1983. "Representing Authority in Victorian India." In *The Invention of Tradition,* edited by Eric Hobsbawm and Terence Ranger, 165–209. Cambridge: Cambridge University Press.
———. 1996. *Colonialism and Its Forms of Knowledge.* Princeton, N.J.: Princeton University Press.
Cole, Catherine M. 1997. "'This Is Actually a Good Interpretation of Modern Civilisation': Popular Theatre and the Social Imaginary in Ghana, 1946–66." *Africa* 67 (3): 363–88.
———. 2001. *Ghana's Concert Party Theatre.* Bloomington: Indiana University Press.
Coleman, Gabriella. 2012. *Coding Freedom.* Princeton, N.J.: Princeton University Press.
Coleman, Simon. 2000. *The Globalization of Charismatic Christianity: Spreading the Gospel of Prosperity.* Cambridge: Cambridge University Press.
Collins, John. 1994a. "The Ghanaian Concert Party: African Popular Entertainment at the Crossroads." Ph.D. diss., State University of New York, Buffalo.
———. 1994b. *Highlife Time.* Accra, Ghana: Anansesem.
———. 2007. "Popular Performance and Culture in Ghana the Past 50 Years." *Ghana Studies* 10:9–64.
———. 2009. *Fela: Kalakuta Notes.* Amsterdam: KIT.
Colonial Reports. 1933. *Annual Report on the Social and Economic Progress of the People of the Gold Coast, 1931–32.* London: His Majesty's Stationery Office.
———. 1936. *Annual Report on the Social and Economic Progress of the People of the Gold Coast, 1934–35.* London: His Majesty's Stationery Office.
Comaroff, Jean. 1985. *Body of Power, Spirit of Resistance: The Culture and History of a South African People.* Chicago: University of Chicago Press.
Comaroff, John L., and Jean Comaroff. 1992. *Ethnography and the Historical Imagination.* Chicago: University of Chicago Press.
———. 1993. *Modernity and Its Malcontents: Ritual and Power in Postcolonial Africa.* Chicago: University of Chicago Press.
———. 1997. *Of Revelation and Revolution: The Dialectics of Modernity on a South African Frontier.* Vol. 2. Chicago: University of Chicago Press.
———. 2000. "Millennial Capitalism: First Thoughts on a Second Coming." *Public Culture* 12 (2): 291–343.
———, eds. 2006. *Law and Disorder in the Postcolony.* Chicago: University of Chicago Press.
Cooper, Frederick, and Ann Laura Stoler, eds. 1997. *Tensions of Empire: Colonial Cultures in a Bourgeois World.* Berkeley: University of California Press.
Coronil, Fernando. 1997. *The Magical State: Oil Money, Democracy, and Capitalism in Venezuela.* Chicago: University of Chicago Press.
Crobsen, Kodjo. 1984. *Power to the People: Reflections on Retrogressive Politics.* London: Kodjo Crobsen.
Dake, J. Mawuse. n.d. *Lamentations of a Patriot: A Political Indictment of J. J.* Accra, Ghana: Concerned Citizens Platform.
Danquah, J. B. 1928. *Gold Coast: Akan Laws and Customs and the Akim Abuakwa Constitution.* London: Routledge.
Davidson, Basil. 1973. *Black Star: A View of the Life and Times of Kwame Nkrumah.* London: Allen Lane.

De Boeck, Filip. 2011. "Inhabiting Ocular Ground: Kinshasa's Future in the Light of Congo's Spectral Urban Politics." *Cultural Anthropology* 26 (2): 263–86.
De Certeau, Michel. 1984. *The Practice of Everyday Life*. Berkeley: University of California Press.
De Graft, J. C. 1970. *Through a Film Darkly*. London: Oxford University Press.
——. 1979. *Sons and Daughters*. London: Oxford University Press.
De Witte, Marleen. 2003. "Altar Media's 'Living Word': Televised Christianity in Ghana." *Journal of Religion in Africa* 33 (2): 172–202.
——. 2005. "The Spectacular and the Spirits: Charismatics and Neo-traditionalists on Ghanaian Television." *Material Religion* 1 (3): 314–35.
Debord, Guy. 1994. *The Society of the Spectacle*. New York: Zone Books.
Debrunner, Hans W. 1967. *A History of Christianity in Ghana*. Accra, Ghana: Waterville.
Dent, Alexander. 2009. *River of Tears: Country Music, Memory, and Modernity in Brazil*. Durham, N.C.: Duke University Press.
Derrida, Jacques. 1988. "Signature Event Context." In *Limited Inc*. Evanston, Ill.: Northwestern University Press.
Donkor, David. 2008. "Spiders in the City: Trickster and the Politics/Economics of Performance in Ghana's Popular Theatre Revival." Ph.D. diss., Northwestern University, Evanston, Ill.
——. 2013. "Selling the President: Stand-up Comedy and the Politricks of Indirection in Ghana." *Theatre Survey* 54 (2): 255–81.
Du Bois, W. E. B. 1947. *The World and Africa: An Inquiry into the Part Which Africa Has Played in World History*. New York: Viking.
Dumett, Raymond E. 1998. *El Dorado in West Africa: The Gold-Mining Frontier, African Labor, and Colonial Capitalism in the Gold Coast, 1987–1900*. Athens: Ohio University Press.
Duncan-Williams, Bishop Nicholas. 1997. *Taking the Promises of God in Battle*. Middlesex, U.K.: Bishop House.
Dunn, John, and A. F. Robertson. 1973. *Dependence and Opportunity: Political Change in Ahafo*. Cambridge: Cambridge University Press.
Dupuis, Joseph. (1824) 1966. *Journal of a Residence in Ashantee*. London: Frank Cass.
Duranti, Allesandro, ed. 2001. *Linguistic Anthropology*. London: Blackwell.
Ebron, Paulla. 2002. *Performing Africa*. Princeton, N.J.: Princeton University Press.
Eisenlohr, Patrick. 2006. *Little India: Diaspora, Time, and Ethnolinguistic Belonging in Hindu Mauritius*. Berkeley: University of California Press.
Ellis, A. B. 1887. *The Tshi-Speaking Peoples of the Gold Coast of West Africa*. London: Chapman and Hall.
Eluwa, G. I. C. 1971. "Background to the Emergence of the National Congress of British West Africa." *African Studies Review* 14 (2): 205–18.
Engelke, Matthew. 2004. "Text and Performance in an African Church: The Book, 'Live and Direct.'" *American Ethnologist* 31 (1): 76–91.
——. 2007. *A Problem of Presence: Beyond Scripture in an African Church*. Berkeley: University of California Press.
Esedebe, P. Olisanwuche. 1994. *Pan-Africanism: The Idea and Movement, 1776–1991*. Washington, D.C.: Howard University Press.
Evans-Pritchard, E. E. 1931. "Sorcery and Native Opinion." *Africa* 4 (1): 22–55.

———. 1937. *Witchcraft, Oracles and Magic among the Azande*. Oxford: Oxford University Press.
Fabian, Johannes. 1998. *Moments of Freedom: Anthropology and Popular Culture*. Charlottesville: University Press of Virginia.
———. 2007. *Memory against Culture: Arguments and Reminders*. Durham, N.C.: Duke University Press.
Facey, Ellen E. 1997. "Kastom and Nation Making: The Politicization of Tradition on Nguna, Vanuatu." In *Nation Making: Emergent Identities in Postcolonial Melanesia*, edited by Robert J. Foster, 207–25. Ann Arbor: University of Michigan Press.
Fanon, Frantz. 1963. *The Wretched of the Earth*. New York: Grove Press.
———. 1991. *Black Skins, White Masks*. New York: Grove Press.
Feld, Steven. 2012. *Jazz Cosmopolitanism in Accra: Five Years in Ghana*. Durham, N.C.: Duke University Press.
Ferguson, James. 1999. *Expectations of Modernity: Myths and Meanings of Urban Life on the Zambian Copperbelt*. Berkeley: University of California Press.
———. 2006. *Global Shadows: Africa in the Neoliberal World Order*. Durham, N.C.: Duke University Press.
Field, Margaret J. 1962. *Search for Security: An Ethno-psychiatric Study of Rural Ghana*. Evanston, Ill.: Northwestern University Press.
Fisch, Michael. 2013. "Tokyo's Commuter Train Suicides and the Society of Emergence." *Cultural Anthropology* 28 (2): 320–43.
Fortes, Meyer. (1950) 1987. "Kinship and Marriage among the Ashanti." In *African Systems of Kinship and Marriage*, edited by A. R. Radcliffe-Brown and Daryll Forde, 252–84. London: KPI.
Fraser, Alexander G. 1933. "Native Education in Africa." *Journal of the Royal Society of Arts* 81 (4208): 813–31.
Fugard, Athol, John Kani, and Winston Ntshona. 1976. *Sizwe Bansi Is Dead and The Island: Two Plays*. New York: Viking.
Fuller, Francis. 1921. *A Vanished Dynasty—Ashanti*. London: J. Murray.
Fyfe, Christopher. 1992. "Race, Empire, and the Historians." *Race and Class* 33 (4): 15–30.
Gaines, Kevin. 2006. *American Africans in Ghana: Black Expatriates and the Civil Rights Era*. Chapel Hill: University of North Carolina Press.
Gal, Susan. 2005. "Language Ideologies Compared: Metaphors of Public and Private." *Journal of Linguistic Anthropology* 15 (1): 23–37.
Garritano, Carmela. 2013. *African Video Movies and Global Desires: A Ghanaian History*. Athens: Ohio University Press.
Gates, Henry Louis, Jr. 1988. *The Signifying Monkey: A Theory of African-American Literary Criticism*. Oxford: Oxford University Press.
Geertz, Clifford. 1985. *Negara: The Theatre State in Nineteenth-Century Bali*. Princeton, N.J.: Princeton University Press.
Geschiere, Peter. 2009. *The Perils of Belonging: Autochthony, Citizenship, and Exclusion in Africa and Europe*. Chicago: University of Chicago Press.
Geschiere, Peter, and Stephen Jackson. 2006. "Autochthony and the Crisis of Citizenship: Democratization, Decentralization, and the Politics of Belonging." *African Studies Review* 49 (2): 1–7.
Geschiere, Peter, and Francis B. Nyamnjoh. 2000. "Capitalism and Autochthony: The Seesaw of Mobility and Belonging." *Public Culture* 12 (2): 423–52.

Gibbs, James. 1995. *Ghanaian Theatre: A Bibliography*. Llangynidr, U.K.: Nolisment.
———. 2001. "Joe de Graft: Theatrical Prophet with Strange Honours." In *African Theatre: Playwrights and Politics*, edited by Martin Banham, James Gibbs, and Femi Osofisan, 72–83. Oxford: James Currey.
———. 2006. *Ghanaian Theatre: A Bibliography of Primary and Secondary Sources—A Work in Progress*. Llangynidr, U.K.: Nolisment.
———. 2009. *Nkyin-Kyin: Essays on the Ghanaian Theatre*. Amsterdam: Rodopi.
Gide, André. 1949. *The Counterfeiters*. New York: Knopf.
Gifford, Paul. 1993. *Christianity and Politics in Doe's Liberia*. Cambridge: Cambridge University Press.
———. 1994. "Some Recent Developments in African Christianity." *African Affairs* 93 (373): 513–34.
———. 1998. *African Christianity: Its Public Role*. Bloomington: Indiana University Press.
———. 2004. *Ghana's New Christianity: Pentecostalism in a Globalizing African Economy*. Bloomington: Indiana University Press.
Gil, Jose. (1985) 1998. *Metamorphosis of the Body*. Minneapolis: University of Minnesota Press.
Gilbert, Michelle. 2000. "Hollywood Icons, Local Demons." Exhibit catalog, Trinity College, Hartford, Conn.
Gilroy, Paul. 1993. *The Black Atlantic: Modernity and Double Consciousness*. Cambridge, Mass.: Harvard University Press.
Ginsburg, Faye D. 2002. "Screen Memories: Resignifying the Traditional Media." In *Media Worlds: Anthropology on New Terrain*, edited by Faye D. Ginsburg, Lila Abu-Lughod, and Brian Larkin, 39–57. Berkeley: University of California Press.
Gluckman, Max. 1949. "The Village Headman in British Central Africa." *Africa* 19 (2): 89–106.
———. 1965. *Politics, Law, and Ritual in Tribal Society*. Chicago: Aldine.
Godelier, Maurice. 1977. *Perspectives in Marxist Anthropology*. Cambridge: Cambridge University Press.
Goffman, Erving. 1959. *The Presentation of Self in Everyday Life*. New York: Anchor Books.
———. 1981. *Forms of Talk*. Philadelphia: University of Pennsylvania Press.
Goldberg, David Theo. 1993. *Racist Culture: Philosophy and the Politics of Meaning*. Oxford: Blackwell.
———. 1997. *Racial Subjects: Writing on Race in America*. New York: Routledge.
Goodman, Jane. 2005. *Berber Culture on the World Stage: From Village to Video*. Bloomington: Indiana University Press.
Goodwin, Charles, and Alessandro Duranti. 1992. "Rethinking Context: An Introduction." In *Rethinking Context: Language as an Interactive Phenomenon*, edited by Alessandro Duranti and Charles Goodwin, 1–42. Cambridge: Cambridge University Press.
Government Publications Relating to Africa. n.d. *Annual Departmental Reports Relating to the Gold Coast and British Togoland 1843–1956*.
Green, Sandra E. 1998. "Developing the Arts for Development: Perspectives on Ghana." *Africa Notes* 1998:1–8.
———. 2002. *Sacred Sites and the Colonial Encounter: A History of Meaning and Memory in Ghana*. Bloomington: Indiana University Press.

Greenhouse, Carol J., ed. 2009. *Ethnographies of Neoliberalism*. Philadelphia: University of Pennsylvania Press.
Guenther, Mathias. 1999. *Tricksters and Trancers: Bushman Religion and Society*. Bloomington: Indiana University Press.
Guss, David M. 2000. *The Festive State: Race, Ethnicity, and Nationalism as Cultural Performance*. Berkeley: University of California Press.
Guyer, Jane. 2004. *Marginal Gains: Monetary Transactions in Atlantic Africa*. Chicago: University of Chicago Press.
Gyekye, Kwame. 1987. *An Essay on African Philosophical Thought: The Akan Conceptual Scheme*. Cambridge: Cambridge University Press.
Gyimah-Boadi, E., ed. 1993. *Ghana under PNDC Rule*. Oxford: CODESRIA.
Habermas, Jürgen. 1991. *The Structural Transformation of the Public Sphere*. Cambridge, Mass.: MIT Press.
———. 1996. "Further Reflections on the Public Sphere." In *Habermas and the Public Sphere*, edited by Craig Calhoun, 421–61. Cambridge, Mass.: MIT Press.
Hackett, Rosalind. 1999. "The Gospel of Prosperity in West Africa." In *Religion and the Transformations of Capitalism*, edited by Richard H. Roberts, 199–214. London: Routledge.
Hagan, George P. 1993. "Nkrumah's Leadership Style—An Assessment from a Cultural Perspective." In *The Life and Work of Kwame Nkrumah*, edited by Kwame Arhin, 177–206. Trenton, N.J.: Africa World Press.
Handler, Richard. 1988. *Nationalism and the Politics of Culture in Quebec*. Madison: University of Wisconsin Press.
Hanks, William F. 1996. *Language and Communicative Practices*. Boulder, Colo.: Westview.
Hannerz, Ulf. 1987. "The World in Creolisation." *Africa* 57 (4): 546–59.
Hansen, Emmanuel. 1991. *Ghana under Rawlings: Early Years*. Lagos: Malthouse.
Hansen, Thomas Blom, and Finn Stepputat, eds. 2005. *Sovereign Bodies: Citizens, Migrants, and States in the Postcolonial World*. Princeton, N.J.: Princeton University Press.
Hanson, Susan. 2000. *A Nation Touched by the Fire of Heaven*. Accra, Ghana: Journagrafx.
Hart, Keith. 1973. "Informal Income Opportunities and Urban Employment in Ghana." *Journal of Modern African Studies* 11 (1): 61–89.
Hartman, Saidiya. 2007. *Lose Your Mother: A Journey along the Atlantic Slave Route*. New York: Farrar, Straus and Giroux.
Harvey, David. 2005. *A Brief History of Neoliberalism*. Oxford: Oxford University Press.
Hasty, Jennifer. 2002. "Rites of Passage, Routes of Redemption: Emancipation Tourism and the Wealth of Culture." *Africa Today* 49 (3): 47–76.
———. 2005. *The Press and Political Culture in Ghana*. Bloomington: Indiana University Press.
Haugerud, Angelique. 1997. *The Culture of Politics in Modern Kenya*. Cambridge: Cambridge University Press.
Herbst, Jeffrey. 1993. *The Politics of Reform in Ghana, 1982–1991*. Berkeley: University of California Press.
Hertzfeld, Michael. 2004. *Cultural Intimacy: Social Poetics in the Nation-State*. London: Routledge.

Hess, Janet Berry. 2000. "Imagining Architecture: The Structure of Nationalism in Accra, Ghana." *Africa Today* 47 (2): 35–58.
Hetherington, Penelope. 1978. *British Paternalism and Africa 1920–1940.* London: Frank Cass.
Hill, Jane H. 2005. "Intertextuality as Source and Evidence for Indirect Indexical Meanings." *Journal of Linguistic Anthropology* 15 (1): 113–24.
Hilson, Gavin M. 2004. "Structural Adjustment in Ghana: Assessing the Impacts of Mining-Sector Reform." *Africa Today* 51 (2): 53–77.
Hirschkind, Charles. 2006. *The Ethical Soundscape: Cassette Sermons and Islamic Counterpublics.* New York: Columbia University Press.
Hobsbawm, Eric, and Terence Ranger, eds. 1992. *The Invention of Tradition.* Cambridge: Cambridge University Press.
Hoffman, Daniel J. 2007. "The City as Barracks: Freetown, Monrovia, and the Organization of Violence in Postcolonial African Cities." *Cultural Anthropology* 22 (3): 400–428.
———. 2011. "Violence Just in Time: War and Work in Contemporary West Africa." *Cultural Anthropology* 26 (1): 34–57.
Holsey, Bayo. 2007. *Routes of Remembrance: Refashioning the Slave Trade in Ghana.* Chicago: University of Chicago Press.
Horst, Heather, and Daniel Miller. 2005. "From Kinship to Link-Up: Cell Phones and Social Networking in Jamaica." *Current Anthropology* 46 (5): 755–78.
Huber, Magnus. 1999. *Ghanaian Pidgin English in Its West African Context: A Sociohistorical and Structural Analysis.* Amsterdam: John Benjamins.
Hughes, David McDermott. 2005. "Third Nature: Making Space and Time in the Great Limpopo Conservation Area." *Cultural Anthropology* 22 (1): 1–65.
Hunt, Stephen, and Nicola Lightly. 2001. "The British Black Pentecostal 'Revival': Identity and Belief in the 'New' Nigerian Churches." *Ethnic and Racial Studies* 24 (1): 104–24.
Hunter, Linda, and Chaibou Elhadji Oumarou. 1998. "Towards a Hausa Verbal Aesthetic: Aspects of Language about Using Language." *Journal of African Cultural Studies* 11 (2): 157–70.
Hutchful, Eboe. 1987. "Ghana and the Ghanaian Revolution." *Canadian Journal of African Studies* 21 (3): 420–23.
Hyam, Ronald, ed. 1992. *The Labour Government and the End of Empire 1945–1951.* British Documents on the End of Empire. London: Institute of Commonwealth Studies, University of London.
Hyde, Lewis. 1998. *Trickster Makes This World: Mischief, Myth, and Art.* New York: Farrar, Straus and Giroux.
Iddrisu, Habib Chester. 2011. "The Price of Adaptation: Hybridization of African Music and Dance from Village to International Stage." Ph.D. diss., Northwestern University, Evanston, Ill.
Irvine, Judith T. 2005. "Commentary: Knots and Tears in the Interdiscursive Fabric." *Journal of Linguistic Anthropology* 15 (1): 72–80.
Jackson, Kofi Abaka. 1999. *When Guns Rule: A Soldier's Testimony of the Events Leading to the June 4 Uprising in Ghana and Its Aftermath.* Accra, Ghana: Woeli.
Jaji, Tsitsi. 2014. *Africa in Stereo: Modernism, Music, and Pan-African Solidarity.* Oxford: Oxford University Press.

Jakobson, Roman. 1960. "Linguistics and Poetics." In *Style in Language,* edited by Thomas A. Sebeok, 350–77. Cambridge, Mass.: MIT Press.
James, C. L. R. (1962) 1977. *Nkrumah and the Ghana Revolution.* London: Allison and Busby.
Jenkins, Ray. 1994. "William Ofori Atta, Nnambi Azikiwe, J. B. Danquah and the 'Grilling' of W. E. F. Ward of Achimota in 1935." *History in Africa* 21:171–89.
Jeyifo, Biodun. 2007. "When Anansegoro Begins to Grow: Reading Efua Sutherland Three Decades On." In *The Legacy of Efua Sutherland: Pan-African Cultural Activism,* edited by Anne V. Adams and Esi Sutherland-Addy, 24–37. Banbury, U.K.: Ayebia Clarke.
Johnston, Sir Harry H. 1899. *A History of the Colonization of Africa by Alien Races.* Cambridge: Cambridge University Press.
July, Robert. 2007. "'Here, Then, Is Efua': Sutherland and the Drama Studio." In *The Legacy of Efua Sutherland: Pan-African Cultural Activism,* edited by Anne V. Adams and Esi Sutherland-Addy, 160–64. Banbury, U.K.: Ayebia Clarke.
Jung, Carl G. (1956) 1972. "On the Psychology of the Trickster Figure." In *The Trickster: A Study in American Indian Mythology,* edited by Paul Radin. New York: Schocken.
Kapchan, Deborah. 1996. *Gender on the Market: Moroccan Women and the Revoicing of Tradition.* Philadelphia: University of Pennsylvania Press.
Keane, Webb. 1997. *Signs of Recognition: Powers and Hazards of Representations in an Indonesian Society.* Berkeley: University of California Press.
———. 2002. "Sincerity, 'Modernity,' and the Protestants." *Cultural Anthropology* 17 (1): 65–92.
Keenan, Thomas. 2005. "Drift: Politics and the Simulation of Real Life." *Grey Room* 21:94–111.
Kemoli, Arthur, and Helen Mwanzi. 1981. *Notes of Joe de Graft's Muntu.* Nairobi: Heinemann.
Kennedy, Scott. 1973. *In Search of African Theatre: A Unique Personal Account of the African Theatre by an American Black Who Has Been Both Observer and Participant.* New York: Scribner's.
Kerr, David. 1995. *African Popular Theatre: From Precolonial Times to the Present Day.* London: James Currey.
Kimble, David. 1963. *A Political History of Ghana, 1850–1928.* Oxford: Oxford University Press.
King, Kenneth James. 1971. *Pan-Africanism and Education: A Study of Race Philanthropy and Education in the Southern United States of America and East Africa.* London: Clarendon.
Klein, Debra L. 2007. *Yoruba Bata Goes Global: Artists, Culture Brokers, and Fans.* Chicago: University of Chicago Press.
Kockelman, Paul. 2004. "Stance and Subjectivity." *Journal of Linguistic Anthropology* 14 (2): 122–50.
———. 2005. "The Semiotic Stance." *Semiotica* 157:233–304.
———. 2006a. "Agent, Person, Subject, Self." *Semiotica* 162:1–18.
———. 2006b. "A Semiotic Ontology of the Commodity." *Journal of Linguistic Anthropology* 16 (1): 76–102.
Konadu-Agyemang, Kwadwo, ed. 2001. *IMF and World Bank Sponsored Structural Adjustment Programs in Africa: Ghana's Experience, 1983–1999.* Aldershot, U.K.: Ashgate.

Kruger, Loren. 1992. *The National Stage: Theatre and Cultural Legitimation in England, France, and America*. Chicago: University of Chicago Press.
———. 1999. *South African Theatre*. Chicago: University of Chicago Press.
Larkin, Brian. 2008. *Signal and Noise: Media, Infrastructure and Urban Culture in Nigeria*. Durham, N.C.: Duke University Press.
———. 2013. "The Politics and Poetics of Infrastructure." *Annual Review of Anthropology* 42:327–43.
Lawrenson, T. E. 1954. "The Idea of a National Theatre." *Universitas* 1 (3): 6–10.
Lee, Benjamin. 1997. *Talking Heads: Language, Metalanguage, and the Semiotics of Subjectivity*. Durham, N.C.: Duke University Press.
Lee, Benjamin, and Edward LiPuma. 2002. "Cultures of Circulation: The Imaginations of Modernity." *Public Culture* 14 (1): 191–213.
Lentz, Carola, and Paul Nugent, eds. 2000. *Ethnicity in Ghana: The Limits of Invention*. London: Macmillan.
Levi-Strauss, Claude. 1955. "The Structural Study of Myth." *Journal of American Folklore* 68 (270): 428–44.
Lokko, Sophia D. 1980. "Theatre Space: A Historical Overview of the Theatre Movement in Ghana." *Modern Drama* 23 (3): 309–19.
Lubiano, Wahneema, ed. 1997. *The House That Race Built: Black Americans, U.S. Terrain*. New York: Pantheon.
Lugard, Lord. (1922) 1965. *The Dual Mandate in British Tropical Africa*. London: Frank Cass.
Maduakor, Obi. 2001. "Joe de Graft and the Ghana Cultural Revival." In *African Theatre: Playwrights and Politics*, edited by Martin Banham, James Gibbs, and Femi Osofisan, 65–71. Oxford: James Currey.
Mamdani, Mahmood. 1996. *Citizen and Subject: Contemporary Africa and the Legacy of Late Colonialism*. Princeton, N.J.: Princeton University Press.
Manning, Paul, and Ilana Gershon. 2013. "Animating Interaction." *HAU: Journal of Ethnographic Theory* 3 (3): 107–37.
Manoukian, Madeline. 1964. *Akan and Ga-Adangbe People*. London: International African Institute.
Marshall, Ruth. 2009. *Political Spiritualities: The Pentecostal Revolution in Nigeria*. Chicago: University of Chicago Press.
———. 2010. "The Sovereignty of Miracles: Pentecostal Political Theology in Nigeria." *Constellations* 17 (2): 197–223.
Marx, Karl. 1994. *The Eighteenth Brumaire of Louis Bonaparte*. New York: International.
Masquelier, Adeline. 2001. "Behind the Dispensary's Prosperous Façade: Imagining the State in Rural Niger." *Public Culture* 13 (2): 267–91.
———. 2002. "Road Mythographies: Space, Mobility, and the Historical Imagination in Postcolonial Niger." *American Ethnologist* 29 (4): 829–56.
Massing, Andreas W. 1994. *Local Government Reform in Ghana: Democratic Renewal or Autocratic Revival?* Saarbrücken, Germany: Breitenbach.
Maxwell, John, ed. 1928. *The Gold Coast Handbook*. London: Crown Agents for the Colonies.
Mazzarella, William. 2013. *Censorium: Cinema and the Open Edge of Mass Publicity*. Durham, N.C.: Duke University Press.
Mbembe, Achille. 2001. *On the Postcolony*. Berkeley: University of California Press.

———. 2005. "Sovereignty as a Form of Expenditure." In *Sovereign Bodies: Citizens, Migrants, and States in the Postcolonial World*, edited by Thomas Blom Hansen and Finn Stepputat, 148–66. Princeton, N.J.: Princeton University Press.
McAnany, Emile G., and Kenton T. Wilkinson, eds. 1996. *Mass Media and Free Trade: NAFTA and the Cultural Industries*. Austin: University of Texas Press.
McCaskie, T. C. 2002. *State and Society in Pre-colonial Asante*. Cambridge: Cambridge University Press.
McGovern, Mike. 2013. *Unmasking the State: Making Guinea Modern*. Chicago: University of Chicago Press.
Mendoza, Eugene L. 2001. *Continuity and Change in a West African Society: Globalization's Impact on the Sisala of Ghana*. Durham, N.C.: Carolina Academic Press.
Mensah, Ronald. 1975. *Masterpieces of Christian Philosophy*. Accra: Ghana Publishing.
Meyer, Birgit. 1998a. "Commodities and the Power of Prayer: Pentecostalist Attitudes towards Consumption in Contemporary Ghana." *Development and Change* 29 (4): 751–76.
———. 1998b. "'Make a Complete Break with the Past': Memory and Postcolonial Modernity in Ghanaian Pentecostal Discourse." In *Memory and the Postcolony: African Anthropology and the Critique of Power*, edited by Richard Werbner, 182–208. London: Zed Books.
———. 1998c. "The Power of Money: Politics, Occult Forces, and Pentecostalism in Ghana." *African Studies Review* 41 (3): 15–37.
———. 1999a. "Popular Ghanaian Cinema and 'African Heritage.'" *Africa Today* 46 (2): 93–114.
———. 1999b. *Translating the Devil: Religion and Modernity among the Ewe in Ghana*. Edinburgh: Edinburgh University Press.
———. 2004a. "Christianity in Africa: From African Independent to Pentecostal-Charismatic Churches." *Annual Review of Anthropology* 33:447–74.
———. 2004b. "'Praise the Lord': Popular Cinema and Pentecostalite Style in Ghana's New Public Sphere." *American Ethnologist* 31 (1): 92–110.
———. 2006. "Religious Revelation, Secrecy and the Limits of Visual Representation." *Anthropological Theory* 6 (4): 431–53.
Meyer, Birgit, and Annelies Moors, eds. 2006. *Religion, Media, and the Public Sphere*. Bloomington: Indiana University Press.
Meyerowitz, Eva L. 1952. *Akan Traditions of Origin*. London: Faber and Faber.
———. 1962. *At the Court of an African King*. London: Faber and Faber.
Mireku, Ebenezer. 1991. *Which Way Ghana? Restoring Hope and Confidence in the Ghanaian*. Accra, Ghana: Asuo Peabo.
Mitchell, Timothy. 1991. *Colonizing Egypt*. Berkeley: University of California Press.
Morisseau-Leroy, Félix. 1965. "The Ghana Theatre Movement." *Ghana Cultural Review* 1 (1): 10, 14.
Morrow, Curtis J. "Kojo." 2000. *Return of the African-American*. Huntington, N.Y.: Kroshka Books.
Mudimbe, V. Y. 1988. *Gnosis, Philosophy, and the Order of Knowledge*. Bloomington: Indiana University Press.
Munn, Nancy. 1986. *The Fame of Gawa: A Symbolic Study of Value Transformation in a Massim Society*. Durham, N.C.: Duke University Press.
"Native Drama, an Enquiry." *Drama* 32 (November 1932): 27–29.

Newell, Sasha. 2012. *The Modernity Bluff: Crime, Consumption, and Citizenship in Côte d'Ivoire*. Chicago: University of Chicago Press.
Newell, Stephanie. 2002. *Literary Culture in Colonial Ghana*. Bloomington: Indiana University Press.
Ninsin, Kwame A. 1996. *Ghana's Political Transition 1990–1993: Selected Documents*. Accra, Ghana: Freedom Publications.
———. 1998. *Ghana: Transition to Democracy*. Dakar, Senegal: CODESRIA.
Nketia, J. H. K. 1962. "The Problem of Meaning in African Music." *Ethnomusicology* 6:1–7.
———. 1965. "The School of Music and Drama." *Ghana Cultural Review* 1 (July–September): 28.
———. 1976. *Cultural Development and the Arts*. Legon: Institute of African Studies, University of Ghana.
———. 1982. "Developing Contemporary Idioms Out of Traditional Music." *Studia Musicologica Academiae Scientiarum Hungarica* 24:81–97.
———. 1996. "National Development and the Performing Arts of Africa." In *The Muse of Modernity: Essays on Culture as Development in Africa*, edited by Philip G. Altbach and Salah M. Hassan, 117–49. Trenton, N.J.: Africa World Press.
Nkrumah, Kwame. (195/) 1979. *The Autobiography of Kwame Nkrumah*. New York: International.
———. 1961. *I Speak of Freedom: A Statement of African Ideology*. London: Heinemann.
———. 1997. *Selected Speeches: Kwame Nkrumah*. Vols. 1–5. Compiled by Samuel Obeng. Accra, Ghana: Afram.
Nugent, Paul. 1995. *Big Men, Small Boys and Politics in Ghana*. London: Pinter.
Nuttall, Sarah, and Achille Mbembe, eds. 2008. *Johannesburg: The Elusive Metropolis*. Durham, N.C.: Duke University Press.
Obeng, Samuel Gyasi. 1997. "Language and Politics: Indirectness in Political Discourse." *Discourse and Society* 8 (1): 49–83.
———. 1999. "Requests in Akan Discourse." *Anthropological Linguistics* 41 (2): 230–51.
———. 2000. "From Praise to Criticism: A Pragmalinguistic Discussion of Metaphors in African (Ghanaian) Political Rhetoric." In *The CVC of Sociolinguistics: Contact, Variation, and Culture*, edited by Julie Auger and Andrea Word-Allbritton. Working Papers in Linguistics 2. Bloomington: Indiana University Linguistics Club.
Okeke, Barbara E. 1982. *4 June: A Revolution Betrayed*. Enugu, Nigeria: Ikenga.
Olaniyan, Tejumola, and Ato Quayson, eds. 2007. *African Literature: An Anthology of Criticism and Theory*. Malden, Mass.: Wiley-Blackwell.
Omari, T. Peter. 1971. *Kwame Nkrumah: The Anatomy of an African Dictatorship*. New York: Africana.
Oosthuizen, G. C., and Irving Hexham. 1992. *Empirical Studies of African Independent/ Indigenous Churches*. Lewiston, N.Y.: Edwin Mellen.
Osei, Akwasi P. 1999. *Ghana: Recurrence and Change in a Post-independence African State*. New York: Peter Lang.
Osofisan, Femi. 2007. "'There's a Lot of Strength in Our People': Efua Sutherland's Last Interview." In *The Legacy of Efua Sutherland: Pan-African Cultural Activism*, edited by Anne V. Adams and Esi Sutherland-Addy, 201–8. Banbury, U.K.: Ayebia Clarke.
Otabil, Mensa. 2000. *Turning Failure into Success*. Accra, Ghana: AltarMedia. Videocassette (VHS).

———. 2002. *Buy the Future: Learning to Negotiate for a Future Better than Your Present.* Lanham, Md.: Pneuma Life Publishing.

Owomoyela, Oyekan. 1997. *Yoruba Trickster Tales.* Lincoln: University of Nebraska Press.

Owusu, Maxwell. 1970. *Uses and Abuses of Political Power: A Case Study of Continuity and Change in the Politics of Ghana.* Chicago: University of Chicago Press.

Pare, Osei. 1988. *Towards a Better Ghana.* Accra, Ghana: Pare Publications.

Parker, John. 2000. *Making the Town: Ga State and Society in Early Colonial Accra.* Portsmouth, N.H.: Heinemann.

Parmentier, Richard J. 1994. *Signs in Society: Studies in Semiotic Anthropology.* Bloomington: Indiana University Press.

Pellow, Deborah. 2002. *Landlords and Lodgers: Socio-spatial Organization in an Accra Community.* Westport, Conn.: Praeger.

Pellow, Deborah, and Naomi Chazan. 1986. *Ghana: Coping with Uncertainty.* Boulder, Colo.: Westview.

Pelton, Robert D. 1980. *The Trickster in West Africa: A Study of Mythic Irony and Sacred Delight.* Berkeley: University of California Press.

Peterson, Marina. 2010. *Sound, Space, and the City: Civic Performance in Downtown Los Angeles.* Philadelphia: University of Pennsylvania Press.

Pickard-Cambridge, A. W. 1940. "The Place of Achimota in West African Education." *Journal of the Royal African Society* 39 (155): 143–53.

Pierre, Jemima. 2012. *The Predicament of Blackness: Postcolonial Ghana and the Politics of Race.* Chicago: University of Chicago Press.

Pierre, Jemima, and Jesse Weaver Shipley. 2003. "African/Diaspora History: W. E. B. Du Bois and Pan-Africanism in Ghana." In *Ghana in Africa and the World: Essays in Honor of Adu Boahen,* edited by Toyin Falola. Trenton, N.J.: Africa World Press.

Piot, Charles. 2010. *Nostalgia for the Future: West Africa after the Cold War.* Chicago: University of Chicago Press.

Plageman, Nate. 2012. *Highlife Saturday Night: Popular Music and Social Change in Urban Ghana.* Bloomington: Indiana University Press.

Pobee, John S. 1991. *Religion and Politics in Ghana.* Accra, Ghana: Asempa.

Povinelli, Elizabeth. 2001. "Radical Worlds: The Anthropology of Incommensurability and Inconceivability." *Annual Review of Anthropology* 30:319–34.

———. 2002. *The Cunning of Recognition: Indigenous Alterities and the Making of Australian Multiculturalism.* Durham, N.C.: Duke University Press.

———. 2011. *Economies of Abandonment: Social Belonging and Endurance in Late Liberalism.* Durham, N.C.: Duke University Press.

Prais, Jinny. 2014. "Representing an African City and Urban Elite: The Nightclubs, Dance Halls, and Red Light District of Interwar Accra." In *The Arts of Citizenship in African Cities,* edited by Mamadou Diouf and Rosalind Fredericks, 187–208. New York: Palgrave Macmillan.

Pype, Katrien. 2012. *The Making of the Pentecostal Melodrama: Religion, Media, and Gender in Kinshasa.* Oxford: Berghahn.

Quayson, Ato. 2014. *Oxford Street, Accra: City Life and the Itineraries of Transnationalism.* Durham, N.C.: Duke University Press.

Radin, Paul. (1956) 1972. *The Trickster: A Study in American Indian Mythology.* New York: Schocken.

Rattray, R. S. (1923) 1969. *Ashanti*. New York: Negro Universities Press.
———. 1927. *Religion and Art in Ashanti*. Oxford: Oxford University Press.
———. 1929. *Ashanti Law and Constitution*. Oxford: Oxford University Press.
———. 1930. *Akan-Ashanti Folk-Tales*. Oxford: Clarendon.
Rawlings, Jerry John. 1983. "Radio Broadcast to the Nation on 31 December 1981." Reprinted in *Revolutionary Journey: Selected Speeches of Flt. Lt. Jerry John Rawlings, Chairman of the PNDC, Dec. 31st 1981–Dec. 31st 1982*. Vol. 1. Accra, Ghana: Information Services Department.
Reed, Susan A. 2002. "Performing Respectability: The *Berava*, Middle-Class Nationalism, and the Classicization of Kandyan Dance in Sri Lanka." *Cultural Anthropology* 17 (2): 246–77.
Robertson, A. F. 1975. "Anthropology and Government in Ghana." *African Affairs* 74 (294): 51–59.
Rubin, Don, ed. 1997. *World Encyclopedia of Contemporary Theatre*. Vol. 3: *Africa*. London: Routledge.
Scally, Anthony, Anson Phelps Stokes, The Freeman Publishing Co., and C. G. Woodson. 1991. "Confidential Memorandum for the Trustees of the Phelps-Stokes Fund Regarding Dr. Carter G. Woodson's Attacks on Dr. Thomas Jesse Jones." *Journal of Negro History* 76 (1/4): 48–60.
Schramm, Katharina. 2000. "The Politics of Dance: Changing Representations of the Nation in Ghana." *Africa Spectrum* 35 (3): 339–58.
Schulz, Dorothea. 2003. "'Charisma and Brotherhood' Revisited: Mass-Mediated Forms of Spirituality in Urban Mali." *Journal of Religion in Africa* 33 (2): 146–71.
———. 2012. *Muslims and New Media in West Africa: Pathways to God*. Bloomington: Indiana University Press.
Scott, David. 2004. *Conscripts of Modernity: The Tragedy of Colonial Enlightenment*. Durham, N.C.: Duke University Press.
———. 2014. *Omens of Adversity: Tragedy, Time, Memory, Justice*. Durham, N.C.: Duke University Press.
Scott, James C. 1990. *Domination and the Arts of Resistance*. New Haven, Conn.: Yale University Press.
Sekyi, Kobina. (1918) 1974. *The Blinkards: A Comedy and the Anglo-Fanti—A Short Story*. Oxford: Heinemann.
Shaloff, Stanley. 1974. "The Africanization Controversy in the Gold Coast, 1926–1946." *African Studies Review* 17 (3): 493–504.
Shaw, Rosalind. 2002. *Memories of the Slave Trade: Ritual and the Historical Imagination in Sierra Leone*. Chicago: University of Chicago Press.
———. 2007. "Displacing Violence: Making Pentecostal Memory in Postwar Sierra Leone." *Cultural Anthropology* 22 (1): 66–93.
Shepperson, George. 1960. "Notes on Negro American Influences on the Emergence of African Nationalism." *Journal of African History* 1 (2): 299–312.
Shillington, Kevin. 1992. *Ghana and the Rawlings Factor*. London: Macmillan.
Shipley, H. Thorne. 1995. *Intersensory Origin of Mind: A Revisit to Emergent Evolution*. London: Routledge.
Shipley, Jesse Weaver. 2004. "'The Best Tradition Goes On': Popular Theatre and Televised Soap in Neoliberal Ghana." In *Producing African Futures: Ritual and Reproduction in a Neoliberal Age*, edited by Brad Weiss, 106–40. Leiden, Netherlands: Brill.

---. 2009. "Comedians, Pastors, and the Miraculous Agency of Charisma in Ghana." *Cultural Anthropology* 24 (3): 523–52.

---. 2013a. *Living the Hiplife: Celebrity and Entrepreneurship in Ghanaian Popular Music.* Durham, N.C.: Duke University Press.

---. 2013b. "Television Tricksters: Parody and Contradiction in Ghanaian Melodrama." *Social Text* 31 (4 117): 49–76.

---. Forthcoming. "Trickster Ethnography." In *International Encyclopedia of the Social and Behavioral Sciences.* 2nd ed. Oxford: Elsevier.

Shorter, Aylward, and Joseph N. Njiru. 2001. *New Religious Movements in Africa.* Nairobi: Paulines.

Sillah, Mohammed-Bassiru. 1984. *African Coup d'Etat: A Case Study of Jerry Rawlings in Ghana.* Lawrenceville, Va.: Brunswick.

Silverstein, Michael. 1976. "Shifters, Linguistic Categories, and Cultural Description." In *Meaning in Anthropology*, edited by Keith Basso and Henry A. Selby Jr., 11–55. Albuquerque: University of New Mexico Press.

---. 1998. "Contemporary Transformations of Local Linguistic Communities." *Annual Review of Anthropology* 27:401–26.

---. 2005. "Axes of Evals: Token versus Type Interdiscursivity." *Journal of Linguistic Anthropology* 15 (1): 6–22.

Silverstein, Michael, and Greg Urban, eds. 1996. *Natural Histories of Discourse.* Chicago: University of Chicago Press.

Silvio, Teri. 2010. "Animation: The New Performance?" *Journal of Linguistic Anthropology* 20 (2): 422–38.

Skinner, Elliott P. 1963. "Strangers in West African Societies." *Journal of the International African Institute* 33 (4): 307–20.

Smith, Daniel Jordan. 2008. *A Culture of Corruption: Everyday Deception and Popular Discontent in Nigeria.* Princeton, N.J.: Princeton University Press.

Smith, Edwin W. 1928. *The Golden Stool: Some Aspects of the Conflict of Cultures in Modern Africa.* Garden City, N.Y.: Doubleday, Doran.

---. 1929. *Aggrey of Africa.* London: Student Christian Movement.

Spitulnik, Debra. 1996. "The Social Circulation of Media Discourse and the Mediation of Communities." *Journal of Linguistic Anthropology* 6 (2): 161–87.

---. 1998. "Mediating Unity and Diversity: The Production of Language Ideologies in Zambian Broadcasting." In *Language Ideologies: Practice and Theory*, edited by Bambi B. Schieffelin, Kathryn A. Woolard, and Paul V. Kroskrity, 163–88. Oxford: Oxford University Press.

---. 2001. "The Social Circulation of Media Discourse and the Mediation of Communities." In *Linguistic Anthropology*, edited by Alessandro Duranti, 95–118. London: Blackwell.

Stevens, G. A. 1930. "The Aesthetic Education of the Negro." *Overseas Education* 1 (April): 3.

Stoeltje, Beverly. 2000. "Gender Ideologies and Discursive Practices in Asante." *Political and Legal Anthropology Review* 23 (2): 77–88.

---. 2003. "The Global and the Local with a Focus on Africa." *Oral Tradition* 18 (1): 93–95.

Stoller, Paul. 1995. *Embodying Colonial Memories: Spirit Possession, Power, and the Hauka in West Africa.* New York: Routledge.

Stopford, R. W. 1943. "The Institute of West African Arts, Industries and Social Science: The Society's Afternoon Meeting for the Rev. R. W. Stopford, Principal of Achimota College, Gold Coast, 26th May, 1943." *Journal of the Royal African Society* 42 (169): 183–90.
Sutherland, Efua. 1970. *The Original Bob: The Story of Bob Johnson—Ghana's Ace Comedian.* Accra, Ghana: Anowuo.
———. 1971. *Foriwa.* Accra-Tema: Ghana Publishing.
———. 1975. *The Marriage of Anansewa.* London: Longman.
Sutherland-Addy, Esi. 2002. "Drama in Her Life: Interview with Adeline Ama Buabeng." In *African Theatre: Women,* edited by Jane Plastow, 66–82. Oxford: James Currey.
Thomi, W., P. W. K. Yankson, and S. Y. Zanu, eds. 2000. *A Decade of Decentralization in Ghana: Retrospect and Prospects.* Accra, Ghana: EPAD Research Project.
Trouillot, Rolph. 2003. *Global Transformations: Anthropology and the Modern World.* New York: Palgrave Macmillan.
Tsing, Anna Lowenhaupt. 2004. *Friction: An Ethnography of Global Connection.* Princeton, N.J.: Princeton University Press.
Turner, Victor. 1982. *From Ritual to Theatre: The Human Seriousness of Play.* New York: PAJ.
Van de Port, Mattijs. 2006. "Visualizing the Sacred: Video Technology, 'Televisual' Style and the Religious Imagination in Bahian Candomblé." *American Ethnologist* 33 (3): 444–62.
Van der Veer, Peter, ed. 1996. *Conversion to Modernities: The Globalization of Christianity.* New York: Routledge.
Veal, Michael. 2000. *Fela: The Life and Times of an African Musical Icon.* Philadelphia: Temple University Press.
Vecsey, Christopher. 1981. "The Exception Who Proves the Rule: Ananse the Akan Trickster." *Journal of Religion in Africa* 12 (3): 161–77.
Virilio, Paul. 1977. *Speed and Politics: An Essay on Dromology.* Los Angeles: Semiotext(e).
Walcott, Rinaldo. Forthcoming. *Black Diaspora Faggotry: Frames, Readings, Limits.* Durham, N.C.: Duke University Press.
Wallbank, T. Walter. 1934. "The Educational Renaissance in British Tropical Africa." *Journal of Negro Education* 3 (1): 105–22.
———. 1935. "Achimota College and Educational Objectives in Africa." *Journal of Negro Education* 4 (2): 230–45.
Waterman, Christopher Alan. 1990. *Juju: A Social History and Ethnography of an African Popular Music.* Chicago: University of Chicago Press.
Watts, Michael. 2011. "Blood Oil: The Anatomy of an Insurgency in the Niger Delta." In *Crude Domination: An Anthropology of Oil,* edited by Andrea Behrends, Stephen P. Reyna, and Günther Schlee, 49–80. Oxford, Berghahn.
Waugh, Linda R. 1980. "The Poetic Function in the Theory of Roman Jakobson." *Poetics Today* 2 (1a): 57–82.
Weiss, Brad, ed. 2004. *Producing African Futures: Ritual and Reproduction in a Neoliberal Age.* Leiden, Netherlands: Brill.
———. 2009. *Street Dreams and Hip Hop Barbershops: Global Fantasy in Urban Tanzania.* Bloomington: Indiana University Press.
Werbner, Richard. 2011. *Holy Hustlers, Schism, and Prophecy: Apostolic Reformation in Botswana.* Berkeley: University of California Press.

Werbner, Richard, and Terence Ranger, eds. 1996. *Postcolonial Identities in Africa*. London: Zed Books.
Westwood, John. 2001. *The Amazing Dictator and His Men: A Story of Intrigue, Murder, Presidential Zealousness, Mayhem in Ghana*. Legon, Ghana: Legon Digest / NESTRECO.
White, Bob W. 1999. "Modernity's Trickster: 'Dipping' and 'Throwing' in Congolese Popular Dance Music." *Research in African Literatures* 30 (4): 156–75.
Wilks, Ivor. 1993. *Forests of Gold: Essays on the Akan and the Kingdom of Asante*. Athens: Ohio University Press.
Williams, C. Kingsley. 1962. *Achimota: The Early Years 1924–1948*. Accra, Ghana: Longmans.
Williams, Raymond. (1974) 1990. *Television: Technology and Cultural Form*. London: Routledge.
Wilson, Henry S. 1969. *Origins of West African Nationalism*. London: Macmillan / St. Martin's.
Wiredu, Kwasi. 1996. *Cultural Universals and Particulars: An African Perspective*. Bloomington: Indiana University Press.
Wright, Richard. 1954. *Black Power: A Record of Reactions in a Land of Pathos*. New York: Harper and Brothers.
Wyllie, Robert W. 1980. *The Spirit Seekers: New Religious Movements in Southern Ghana*. Missoula, Mont.: Scholars Press.
Yankah, Kojo. 1986. *The Trial of J. J. Rawlings: Echoes of the 31st December Revolution*. Accra: Ghana Publishing.
Yankah, Kwesi. 1983. *The Akan Trickster Cycle: Myth or Folktale*. Bloomington: Indiana University Press.
——. 1989. *The Proverb in the Context of Akan Rhetoric: A Theory of Proverb Praxis*. Bern: Peter Lang.
——. 1992. "Traditional Lore in Population Communication: The Case of the Akan in Ghana." *Africa Media Review* 6 (1): 15–24.
——. 1995. *Speaking for the Chief: Okyeame and the Politics of Akan Royal Oratory*. Bloomington: Indiana University Press.
——. 1998. *Free Speech in Traditional Society: The Cultural Foundations of Communication in Contemporary Ghana*. Accra: Ghana Universities Press.
Yeebo, Zaya. 1991. *Ghana: The Struggle for Popular Power*. London: New Beacon Books.
Young, Crawford. 1994. *The African Colonial State in Comparative Perspective*. New Haven, Conn.: Yale University Press.
Yurchak, Alexei. 2005. *Everything Was Forever, until It Was No More*. Princeton, N.J.: Princeton University Press.
Ziorklui, Emmanuel Doe. 1989. *Ghana: Nkrumah to Rawlings*. Vol. 1. Accra: Ghana Publishing.
Žižek, Slavoj. 1989. *The Sublime Object of Ideology*. London: Verso.

Index

Abbas, Ferhat, 106
Abdallah, Mohammed Ben, 8, 76, 87, 150; on Abibigromma move, 99–100; Abibigromma Theatre Company and, 9–10, 93–96; as artist-politician, 103–12; on culture's significance to politics, 108; as director, 118–19, 122–23; on first production of *The Witch of Mopti*, 118–19; government positions, 90–92, 103, 108, 109, 118–19; influences on, 104–7; letter to Rawlings, 104, 108–9, 112; National Commission on Culture and, 97; political disillusionment, 83; on radical theatre, 145; returns to School of Performing Arts as lecturer, 120; on state regulation of Pentecostal denominations, 181; trip to Soviet Union, 104. Works: *Land of a Million Magicians*, 110; *The Slaves*, 107; *Song of the Pharaoh*, 230–32; *The Trial of Mallam Ilya*, 2–4, 8, 16, 144; *Verdict of the Cobra*, 93, 119; *The Witch of Mopti*, 21, 115–46
Abibigro '99: A Festival of Total African Theatre Productions, 141
Abibigro genre, 93–94, 150, 251n1 (epilogue); reflexive aspects, 130, 134; "total African theatre," 9, 122–25
Abibigromma Theatre Company, 21, 85; 1980s, 9–10, 93–96; categories of performance, 93–94; *Fortunes of the Moor*, 123; junior members, 127, 128; at Legon, 118–20, 126–28; linguistic and class hierarchy, 126–29; original production of *The Witch of Mopti*, 118; repertoire, 10–11, 121, 136; salaries, 119; split in 1990s, 98–99, 119. *See also* National Theatre Players (Abibigromma)
Abibiman Concert Party group, 110
Aborigines' Rights Protection Society, 28, 47
Accra, Ghana, 238n3; as capital, 1877, 27; as center for radicals, 4; entertainment, 1960s, 58; as Gold Coast colony capital, 6; growth, 1900s, 28; mid-twentieth-century urbanization, 31; multiethnic and multilingual space, 11; population, 1960, 58; under Rawlings regimes, 87; self-image of city, 26
Accra Drama Group, 74
Accra Philharmonics, 32

Acheampong, I. K., 83, 179
Achebe, Chinua, 54, 111
Achimota College: anthropology, art, and criticism at, 42–46; appropriation of rural culture, 26, 52; arts education, 42–43; contesting history and racialized education, 46–51; daily routine, 37; formalized drama program, 45–46; Institute of West African Culture, 42, 59; making and contesting culture at, 34–41; Nkrumah at, 56; subjects taught, 37–38; Tribal Night and Tribal Drumming Night, 38–39, 49, 77. *See also* University College of the Gold Coast (UCGC)
Acquaye, Saka, 76
Action Faith Ministries Bible College, 180
actor-character relationship, 117
actors: authority of, 3, 4, 13, 165–66; control of audience, 124, 136, 162, 170–72; economic difficulties, 11, 119–20, 157–58; generational change, 119–20, 207–10; male, rise of, 150; multiple subject positions, 17–18; Nigerian vs. Ghanaian, 124; as pastors, 175, 180, 183–84; rehearsals, 116, 122–36, 137, 138, 143, 146
Addo, Joyce, 96
Addo, Willie, 156
Adinku, William, 93
Adisadel College, 29
adowa (Akan dance), 12, 78, 171
Afahye (Festival; play), 74
Africa before the White Man Came (Ward), 48
African American community in Ghana, 72
African Brothers Band International, 183
"African personality," 7, 53, 69
Africans: contesting history and racialized education, 46–51; as culture-bound subjects, 28, 52; "fragility" of, 44, 47, 52, 240n52
"afternoon jump" dances, 87, 94
agbekor/atsiagbekor (Ewe dance), 78, 79
Aggrey, James, 36, 47, 56
Agovi, Kofi E., 30
Agro (television quiz show), 11, 215
Aidoo, Ama Ata, 88–89
Akan Ceremonial (Opoku), 78–79, 81, 121
Akan chiefly courts, 19, 121
Akan Drama (television show), 95

273

Akan folkloric revival, 4, 13–14
Akan languages and performance, 1, 11, 71, 129, 153, 195; adowa, 12, 78, 171
Akan-Ashanti Folk-Tales (Rattray), 13–14, 55, 64, 234
Ako-Adjei, Ebenezer, 56
Akuffo, William, 153
akutia (innuendo), 64
Allman, Jean, 59
Amankwa, Kodjoe, 188–89
Amarteifio, Korkor, 97
American racial theory, 47
Amoako, Komla, 99
Amore Cultural Troupe, 110
Ampadu, Nana, 63, 175, 183–84
Amu, Ephraim, 38, 40, 42, 51, 123
"Ananse and the Wisdom Pot," 234–35
Ananse in the Land of Idiots (Asare), 233–34
Ananse the Spider, 1–2; as antihero, 14, 68, 230; as basis for Pan-African political project, 54; duality of, 15, 65–68; as entrepreneur, 178; as genre blender, 13; as narrator, 14; poetics of mediation and, 13–20; as post-neoliberal critical theorist, 227–30; as prototype for comedian, 178; as sublime cultural citizen, 22, 230–35; urban appropriation of, 6, 15, 21
Anansegro (Ananse theatre), 7, 9, 65, 88, 93, 122; aesthetics of indirection and doubleness, 65, 68; as communal art, 67; storyteller as mediator, 13–20, 67, 72
Anansekrom (Canada), 191
Anansesem (Ananse the Spider trickster storytelling), 7, 13–14, 122, 183; as body of stories and performance, 63; entrepreneurial sensibilities, 151; foundational narrative, 14; as indirect parodies of particular people, 55, 65, 67; mboguw (mboguo) songs, 125; parody of particular people, 55, 65; as removed from history and politics, 64; soap operas based on, 215
Angelou, Maya, 70, 97
animator, 206
Annan, Kofi, 213
Anokye Players, 107
Anowa (Aidoo), 88–89
anthropology, 42–44
anticolonial struggle, 4, 46, 49
Antigone (Morisseau-Leroy), 75
Antubam, Kofi, 43
appropriation: of concert party, 150–52; logic of, 4, 26, 51–52; of rural culture by urban publics, 15, 20–21, 26, 52, 53–54, 60

archetype, trickster, 64
Arkhurst, Sandy, 66, 70, 71, 118
Armah, Ayi Kwei, 70
Armed Forces Revolutionary Council (AFRC), 84
Arts Centre (Accra), 2, 57, 74, 76, 91, 94, 110, 157; Nkrumah reenactment and, 204, 207–8
Arts Council of Ghana, 60, 73, 84
Asante courtly music, 77, 78
Asare, Yaw, 101, 119, 233–34, 251n1 (epilogue)
Ashong-Kitae, Seth, 152–53
Askew, Kelly, 15
Atatsi, Edinam, 94, 95, 96
audience: as active participants, 4, 55, 63, 65–66, 71, 125, 143, 162, 169, 190–91; as actors, 149; actors' control of, 124, 136, 162, 170–72; being seen on television, 169, 172; changes from 1980s to 1990s, 141–45; Charismatic churches and, 186–87, 190–91; communal participation, 71; as consumers, 149, 166, 169–70; double voicing and, 124; emotional affiliation, 136; fourth wall, 14–15; framing and, 131, 132; interaction with performers, 2–3, 15; *Key Soap Concert Party* and, 155, 162–63; laughter at tragedy, 143; local, discouragement of, 141; participation, in *The Witch of Mopti*, 116, 130–34; for radio, 33–34, 51; response to *The Witch of Mopti*, 141–42; socialist theatre traditions and, 71, 73, 95; television and, 148, 170–71; theatre and television reception, 166–72; unsettling of, 3; at "Who Is Who" competition, 147–49
Austin, John L., 117
authority, 53, 206, 229; of performers, 3, 4, 13, 166–65; producing and contesting, 160–62; questioning, 3; speaking authority, 13, 19, 130; spiritual, 176
Awo Ye (Giving birth is good; musical comedy), 74, 75
Azikwe, Nnambi, 48

Bampoe, Y. B. (Opiah), 157
Bananzi, Seidu, 210, 216
Barber, Karin, 9, 10, 16
Bauman, Richard, 165–66, 222–23
bawa (Dagara/Dagati dance), 78
Beckett, Samuel, 123
"The Best Tradition Goes On" slogan, 147, 160–61
Big Six, 50, 214, 216
"Birth of Ghana" (Lord Kitchener), 208

Index | 275

Blinkards, The (Sekyi), 29, 50
Boabeng, Ama, 156
Boateng, Nana Brefo, 96
Bomukasa dance group, 121
Bonsu, Kwesi, 195
boundary-making, 13, 18, 80
Brecht, Bertolt, 107, 110, 145
Briggs, Charles, 165–66
Brown, Kwesi, 123, 124, 125, 141, 142–43, 234–35
Busia, Kofi, 59, 83
Butler, Judith, 117

Caesaris Incursio in Oram Auream (play), 45
Casely-Hayford, Beattie, 75
Central Regional Cultural Committee, 91
Centre for National Culture (CNC), 91
Charismatic churches: concert party theatre idioms, 163, 178; direct spiritual relationship with Holy Spirit, 180, 189; doubling as moral affect, 201–3; Holy Spirit, emphasis on, 180, 187; individual choice emphasized, 185, 186–87, 189, 195, 202; marketization and, 177, 202; millennium and, 184–89; neo-Pentecostals, 176, 178, 179, 185; Pentecostal, 163, 181, 186; performance metaphors used, 187; preaching, 175–76; prosperity doctrines, 176, 177, 181–82, 186–88, 203; radio and gendered moral mediation, 194–97, 201; regulation of, 181–82; rise of, 179–80; sexuality, scandals and fears of exploitation, 171, 177, 192–94, 196–97; spirituality and personal success linked, 179–80; younger generation and, 179–80, 182. See also churches, orthodox; pastors
Chekhov, Anton, 72
chieftaincy, 27–28; education of elite children, 36; Nkrumah's overturning of, 56; Okyeame (linguist), 19, 133, 234; public displays of wealth, 182; symbols of, 97, 135–36, 214; in The Witch of Mopti, 135–36
Choice FM, 195–96
Christ Temple, 185, 186
Christian Action Faith Ministries International, 180, 188, 250n21
Christian Council of Ghana, 182
churches, orthodox, 181–82. See also Charismatic churches
citizen: Ananse the Spider as, 22, 230–35; good performance and, 55; consumer as, 150; model national, 20
civil servants, 84
class divisions, 6, 166–70

cloth, for anniversary events, 212–13
code-switching, 54, 125–29
Cofie, David, 121, 130, 131
Cole, Bob, 110, 151, 174, 229
Cole, Catherine, 10, 30
colo entertainment, 154, 161
colonial era: administration, performance and, 25–26; African "character," development of, 28, 35, 39, 42–46; anthropology, 42–44; contestation by African intellectuals, 26, 27, 35; forms of public spectacle, 4, 6; Gold Coast identity, 25; indirect rule, 26–34, 239n34
Colonial Welfare and Development Act (1942), 45
comedians, 12, 21–22, 147, 148–49; as legitimate fakes, 192; as masculine, 177; parallel to pastors, 177; parody pastors, 163–64, 189–92; as performance stars, 150, 151
Communist projects, 57
community of interpretation, 18, 82, 178, 229; The Witch of Mopti and, 141–45
concert party popular theatre, 6–7, 14, 21, 31–32, 147–74; 1900s, 29, 30; Charismatic churches and, 163, 178; contradictory public image, 151; cultural legitimacy, 160; decline of, 152–53; double voicing, 151, 162–66; humor, 143–44; as independent, 147, 150, 151, 153, 155–56; marketization and privatization, 150; in multimedia worship, 178; National Theatre and, 147–48, 153–54, 155, 173–74; rebirth of, 153–57; resignified, 150–52; state and corporate appropriation of, 150–52; subversive aesthetic sensibilities, 164–65; theatrical form, 150–52, 156–58, 168–70; "Who Is Who" competition, 147–49, 162–63, 189; women and, 71, 94, 160. See also Key Soap Concert Party
Concert Party Union, 153, 156, 157–60, 199, 208, 215
consumerism, 150–52, 166, 169–70
Convention People's Party (CCP), 56, 58
conversion narratives, 175
copying, 22, 205, 206, 223, 227, 228, 233; distancing and, 216–20
Cosmopolitan Club, 29
coups, 2–3, 8, 83, 84–85, 86, 144, 148
critical agency, 20, 52, 66, 192
critical discourse, 5, 51, 145–46, 201, 230
criticism, 45–46
Cudjoe, Margaret ("Maggie"), 125, 127
Cudjoe, Seth, 84
cultural, linguistic, and kin networks, 11

Cultural Centre (Kumasi), 91, 107
cultural debates: reflexivity, 25–26; theory of performance, 26, 60–62
cultural mediation, 6–8
cultural nationalism, 21, 72; Ananse as icon for, 14; morality stories, 95–96; under Rawlings, 85; recuperating, 88–89; state control of, 91–92
cultural particularity, 42, 43, 51, 56
Cultural Revolution, 1980s, 8, 21, 85
Cultural Revolution, 1982, 89–92
cultural-national model, 72
culture: as ahistorical, 25–27, 53; British notions, 6; contesting history and racialized education, 46–51; despiritualizing, 27; indirect rule and, 26–34; as object and technology, 25; as preservation, 84; structuring theatrical reflexivity by arguing about, 51–52; used to administer, 25–26, 53; used to deny Africans political authority, 53. *See also* tradition

Dagara/Dagari peoples, 78
Dagbamba peoples, 78, 80
Dagger of Liberation, A (Kwamuar), 75
Dagomba peoples, 126, 135, 214
Damas Choir, 76
damba/takai dance (Dagbamba dance), 78
dance, 76–80, 95; disrespect and misrecognition, 79; at Nkrumah reenactment, 213–14; Pan-African aesthetic, 134–36, 244n89
Danquah, J. B., 48, 50, 56, 72
de Graft, Joe, 61–62; concert party, support for, 68–69; influence of, 72. Works: *Hamile,* 69; *Mambo,* 69, 95; *Muntu,* 69; *Sons and Daughters,* 75; *Through a Film Darkly,* 69
Deadly Voyage (film), 215
decentralization, 56, 91, 170–72, 177, 223, 237n2
Defense Commission of the Organization of African Unity, 74
depoliticized practices, 20, 26, 53, 72; education, 28, 41
Diabolo (film; Akuffo), 153
Dilemma of a Ghost (Aidoo), 88
district cultural committees, 91
Dokonoe, Maame, 11
Donkor, David, 125
Dontoh, David, 11, 154, 204; *Agro,* 11, 215; Concert Party Union president, 157, 215; encounter with Nkrumah, 215–16; equated with Ghanaman, 215; portrayal of Nkrumah, 205, 215–20, 224, 225

double voicing, 66, 116, 122–25, 130; in concert party popular theatre, 151, 162–66. *See also* duality
Drake, St. Clair, 59
Drama Studio, 53, 61, 62–63, 70, 88; Abdallah at, 106–7; attendance and performances, 141; rebuilt, 98
Drama Studio Players, 71–72
drummers, 40–41, 78–79, 120, 121, 127, 134–35; Tribal Night and Tribal Drumming Night, 38–39, 49
Du Bois, Shirley, 70
Du Bois, W. E. B., 70
duality, 19, 26, 55, 173, 235; of Ananse the Spider, 15, 65–68; moral affect, 201–3; performative, 52, 65, 68, 116, 123–24, 201, 203, 224; in reenactment, 205–6. *See also* double voicing
Durkheim, Émile, 116

Ebenezer Miracle Worship Center, 193, 198
education, 29, 65; arts, 42–43; of chieftaincy children, 36; depoliticized practices, 28, 41; for girls, 89; reform under Nkrumah, 58–59; reform under Rawlings, 89, 92; role in understanding difference, 37; theories of racial inequality in, 46–49; tribal focus, 37–40; vernacularization policies, 36. *See also* Achimota College
Education Code of 1925, 36
Efiritete Concert Party group, 158, 159
Efua Sutherland Drama Studio, 98
Eighteenth Brumaire of Louis Napoleon, The (Marx), 85
Ekumah, Alexander A., 220–22
Ekumah, Ekua, 220
Ekumah, Kudjo, 220, 221
electronic media, 1; church use of, 181, 182, 185, 202; concert party, effect on, 147, 152–53, 166; fears of fakery and, 177–78, 202; rise of, 108, 141, 144
e-mail scams, 234
Empire Day, 27, 33, 39
Encyclopedia Africana, 70
English-language theatre, 6, 7, 29, 32, 72, 125–26; of de Graft, 68
English-language use, authority and, 128–29, 133, 186
entrepreneurial sensibilities, 20, 227; Ananse as entrepreneur, 178; "Big Man" leadership models, 182; fakeness as social mobility, 194; as masculine, 177

Eternal Idol, The (Adinku), 93
ethnographic research, 21, 42–44, 64, 206, 249n1
European staging conventions, 14, 61, 63
Evans-Pritchard, E. E., 203
Events, 95
Ewe language and performance, 36, 37, 38, 40, 50, 75, 78, 79, 210; atsiagbekor (Ewe war dance), 78, 79
exclusion, politics of, 166, 168–72
Experimental Theatre Players, 61, 62

fakeness, 175–203; sincerity vs. acting, 178; as social mobility, 194
fakery, fear of, 21–22, 176, 188, 230; born-again entertainers, 183; challenged by pastors, 188–89; doubling as moral affect, 201–3; inversion, 184, 202; mediating scandals, 192–94
Fanon, Frantz, 4, 106, 112
Fante language and performance, 36, 37, 39, 57, 70, 71, 74, 79, 210, 217
FESTAC 77 (Nigeria), 67, 97
festivals, rural, 90, 91
Fiawoo, F. K., 50, 74, 75
Fifth Landing Stage (Fiawoo), 50, 74
flâneur figure, 229
folk opera, 76
Folk's Place Theatre, 153
Foriwa (Sutherland), 66
form, theatrical, 68, 173–74, 230; Abdallah's experiments, 2–4, 9, 130, 145–46; concert party, 150–52, 156–58, 168–70; debates about, 54, 80–82, 174; emphasis on, 72, 80–82, 147–48, 150; experiments with, 95, 99
Fortes, Meyer, 42, 59
Fortunes of the Moor, 123
Fragments (Armah), 70
Fraser, Alexander G., 35–36
freedom, 5, 7, 54, 86, 112, 202, 217–19, 227, 230; artistic, 72, 99; religious, 181–82
freedom fighting, theatre as, 60
funding issues, 83–84, 96, 98–102, 119
future, reimagining, 85–86, 223–24, 226

Ga language and performance, 11, 36, 37, 39, 41, 76, 128–29; kpanlogo dance, 78, 211, 214
Gal, Susan, 116
Gbeho, Philip, 38, 57
gender: dramatic conflict in terms of, 116, 124, 137, 138; moral ordering of bodies, 160; radio and moral mediation, 194–97, 201; tradition as feminine, 150, 156, 160. *See also* sexuality; women

genre blending, 1, 8–13, 80, 93, 95; concert party and Charismatic churches, 178; reenactment and, 206–7. *See also* Abibigro genre
Get Involved Drama Group, 96
Ghana: ancient, 48; Central Region, 70, 71; ceremonies, 77, 78–79, 90; constitution, 1925, 28; coups, 2–3, 8, 83, 84–85, 86, 144, 148; elections, 148, 248n3; foreign visitors, 121; Fourth Republic, 85, 97, 148; independence, 1, 21, 53; Northern Territories, 27, 42; presidential elections, 2000, 103; Second Republic, 59, 83; tension between socialist and capitalist thought, 7–8. *See also* Accra, Ghana; state
Ghana Actors' Guild (GAG), 204, 207
Ghana Arts Council, 56–57, 61–62
Ghana Boy (Samuel Otoo), 163–64, 189–90; on Ananse as prototype for comedian, 178; Nkrumah reenactment and, 204, 207, 208–9; seeks spiritual help, 197–201
Ghana Broadcasting Corporation (GBC), 57, 105, 154–55, 156
Ghana Broadcasting House, 87
Ghana Dance Ensemble, 36, 76–80, 95, 99, 100, 120, 135, 214, 244n89
Ghana Drama Studio, 53, 62
Ghana Institute of Arts and Culture, 73
Ghana Society of Writers, 61
Ghana Television, 21, 70, 71, 147
Ghana Theatre Club, 73, 95, 215
Ghanaba, Kofi (Guy Warren), 40–41, 77
Ghartey, John, 180
Gibbs, James, 62, 66, 68, 107
Gide, André, 203
Gizo (Hausa spider trickster), 18, 105
Goffman, Erving, 206
Gold Coast colony, 6; bans anti-witchcraft shrines, 186; identity, 25; protonationalism, 26. *See also* Achimota College; colonial era; indirect rule
Gold Coast Leader, 47
Gold Coast Spectator, 32
Goldfinger (actor), 207–9
Good Samaritans Society, 74
Good Woman of Setzuan (Brecht), 110
Government Training College, 35, 44
Grant, George Alfred, 56
Guggisberg, Decima (Moore), 28
Guggisberg, Frederick Gordon, 28, 34, 37, 47
Gyekye, Kwame, 19

Haitian Creole language, 73
Half Moon Club, 32

278 | Index

Hall, Stuart, 5
Harrison, H. S., 42
Hausa language and performance, 11, 18, 36, 51, 105
Hegel, G. W. F., 85
highlife music, 6, 31, 32, 58, 64, 183, 208
hiplife songs, 204, 222
Hodgkin, Thomas, 59
Hood, George, 45, 46
hope and possibility, tropes of, 68
Hsiung, S. I., 66
humor, 143–44, 145–46, 163–64
Hunwick, Uwa, 95

Ice Water, 156
Iddrisu, Habib, 78, 80, 121, 134, 137
idealism, 8, 70, 87, 112, 119
identity politics, 15, 36; centralized identity under Nkrumah, 60; teaching of history to students, 48–49
in-between class, 209
independence, 1; ceremonies (1957), 22, 53, 57; drive to, 56–60; memories of, 221; as reobjectified cultural performance, 222–25. *See also* Nkrumah's Independence Speech, Fiftieth-Anniversary reenactment (2007)
indirect rule, 26–34, 239n34; divide-and-rule tactics, 40, 41, 60; education and, 34–41
indirection, 16, 19, 228; aesthetics of, 65, 68; African personhood and, 19; in Ananse stories, 63, 66; challenged by Charismatics, 188; chieftaincy used, 27–28; humor, 143; ignoring opposition, 111–12; in proverbs, 66; purposeful misunderstanding, 129
Information Services Department, 58
infrastructure, 56–60, 85, 90–91, 241n3
Institute of African Studies (IAS), 53, 59–60, 63
Institute of Arts and Culture, 57, 74
Institute of West African Arts, 45
Institute of West African Culture, 42, 44, 59
inter- and intraethnic harmony, 77–78
International Central Gospel Church (ICGC), 185, 186
International Monetary Fund (IMF), 8, 96, 110
"invented traditions," 51
irreverence, 7, 10, 15, 18, 41, 63, 187, 205–6, 224; of Ananse, 55, 175; concert party and, 173, 174

Jaguar (film; Rouch), 229
Jakobson, Roman, 16
Jazz, T. O., 183–84

Jeyifo, Biodun, 67
Johnson, Bob, 30, 74
Joy FM, 185
Jung, C. G., 64
juxtapositions, 12

Kasina/Kasem people, 78
Kawawa, Rashidi, 106
Kenyatta Conference Centre (Nairobi), 69
kete (Akan dance), 78
Key Soap Concert Party, 147–49, 189–90; actors boycott, 158; "The Best Tradition Goes On" slogan, 147, 160–61; corporate takeover of, 157–60; format, 155; payments to actors, 158; political references, 171–72; producing and contesting authority, 160–62; regulation of performances, 160–62; staging and performances, 154–55; television cameras, role of, 170–71; topical themes, 161–62. *See also* concert party popular theatre
Kodzidan ("House of Stories"; Atwia), 70–71
Kofitiah, Diana, 126, 129
"Konkontibaa" (song), 218
Koo, Agya, 200
kpanlogo (Ga dance), 78, 211, 214
Kufuor, J. A., 148, 171, 210, 211, 219
Kumasi, Ghana, 91, 104, 107
Kusum Agromma (culture/tradition players), 62, 71
Kusum Agromma group, 62, 71, 156
Kwame Nkrumah Ideological Institute (Winneba), 215–16
Kwame Nkrumah Mausoleum, 205, 210–11, 214, 217, 218
Kwamuar, Sebastian Y., 75

Ladipo, Duro, 76
Lady Precious Stream (Hsiung), 66
lament, language of, 199, 202, 208, 220–22
Land of a Million Magicians (Abdallah), 110
Landon, Letitia Elizabeth, 29
language: about language use, 17; adaptation, 136; appropriate, for public speaking, 19, 132–33; classic models of use, 224–25; debate about practices, 54, 116, 125–26, 247n22; ideologies, 125–29; linguistic and class hierarchy, 126–29, 131–33, 142–43; metalanguage, 55, 80, 131–33, 191; policy under Rawlings, 92, 108; use by pastors, 186–88, 192; vernacularization policies, 36
Lee, Robert, 72

Legon 7, 107
Legon Road Theatre, 107
Lever Brothers, 154
Levi-Strauss, Claude, 64
Light, Musing, 32, 33
Limann, Hilla, 84–85
Lintas Ghana Ltd., 154, 156
literary clubs, 6, 29, 32
Lord Kenya (Evangelist Lord Kenya), 184
Lord Kitchener, 208
Lord's Vineyard International Ministries, 179
Lost Fishermen, The (opera), 76
Louis Napoleon, 85–86
lunga drum, 80

Maame Dokono (Grace Omaboe), 195–97, 201
Maclean, George, 29
Makerere University (Kampala, Uganda), 54
Malcolm X., 106
Mali, 136
Mamdani, Mahmood, 41
Man of the People, A (Achebe), 111
Mantey, Emmanuel, 127
marketization, 4–5, 7–8, 21, 85, 102, 112; Charismatic churches and, 177, 202; concert party popular theatre and, 151, 173; freedom, fantasy of, 227
Marriage of Anansewa, The (Sutherland), 66–68, 81
Marx, Karl, 85–86
Mawugbe, Efo Kojo, 212–13
mba nkomo (women's conversations), 195
mboguw (mboguo) songs, 125
mediation: African personhood and, 19; cultural, 6–8; drama as point of, 85; by pastors, 187–88; poetics of, 13–20; radio and moral, 194–97, 201; storyteller as mediator, 13, 67, 72
memorials, 92
memory, national, 220–22
memory, theatre of, 88–89, 217
Mensa-Bonsu, Kweku, 95, 216
Mensah, E. T., 58
metalanguage, 55, 80, 131–33, 191
metaphor, 63–67, 72
metapragmatic elements, 55, 80, 146, 152, 228
Methodist Wesleyan High School (Mfantsipim School), 29
Meyer, Birgit, 185–86
Meyerowitz, H. V., 42, 43
microlevel events, 152, 224
millennium, 184–89, 191

Millennium Comet, 191
Mills, John Evans Atta, 148
missionaries, 27, 29–30, 60, 158, 194
mmoatia magical dwarfs, 14, 184
Moffatt, Nii Addokwei, 76
Mollette, Carlton, 123
Mopti, Mali, 136
moral affect, doublings as, 201–3
moral community, 182, 193–97, 201
moral storytelling, 4, 17, 21, 201–3; by Charismatic pastors, 183–84; comedians and pastors compared, 189–92; split subject, 117. *See also* storytelling
moral values, 2–3, 95–96; *Key Soap Concert Party* and, 150, 173–74; in *The Witch of Mopti*, 138–41, 145–46
Morisseau-Leroy, Félix, 65, 70, 73, 74–75, 156; *Antigone*, 75; Workers' Brigade Drama Group and, 73
multiplicity, 17–18, 116, 117, 229
Mumminin, Ishak al-, 127, 133, 135
music, 38, 40–41
musicians, 123, 127, 134–35, 183
mystical realm, 7, 184, 235

nagla (Kasina/Kasem dance), 78
National Academy of Music, 84
National Commission on Culture (NCC), 91–92, 96, 97, 181, 210, 212
National Congress of British West Africa, 28, 47
National Cultural Troupe, 75
National Dance Company, 100–101, 231
National Democratic Congress (NDC), 148
National Drama Company, 75
National Festival of the Arts, 57
national imaginary, 4–5, 57, 80
National Symphony Orchestra, 57, 99, 231
National Theatre (Ghana), 85, 96–98; Abibigromma moves to, 99–100, 119; centralized viewing at, 166–70; concert party popular theatre and, 147–49, 153–54, 155; promotes younger artists, 158; resident companies, 99–101; as state-owned enterprise, 99; television reception, 166–72; "Who Is Who" competition, 147–49, 162–63, 189
National Theatre (Nigeria), 97
National Theatre in Retrospect, 98
National Theatre Movement, 4, 7, 60–63; competing theories of African theatre and, 63–76; development of, 21; as ethnographic project, 232; Ghana Dance Ensemble, 76–80; legacy

National Theatre Movement (*continued*)
of, 85, 89, 90, 95; linking of styles, 7; potentials and failures, 83; protection of, 100, 101; as state-based project, 60, 74; traditional culture codified, 150
National Theatre Players (Abibigromma), 10, 99–101, 111, 214, 231. *See also* Abibigromma Theatre Company
national unity, poetics of, 49–50, 78, 181–82, 214
nation-formation: drive to independence, 56–60; in plays, 74; theatre used for, 55; through totality of public cultural forms, 55–56, 57–58
nation-state, 20, 201, 233
Native Administration Ordinances, 28
Native American societies, 13, 64
Native Funk Lords, 204
Nayo, N. Z., 84
Ndiaye, Amadou Bole, 134–35
Négritude, 56, 73
neocolonialism, critiques of, 21, 85, 86, 87, 91–92, 94, 108
neoliberalism, 20, 150, 202, 203, 227
Nettleford, Rex, 77
New Patriotic Party (NPP), 148, 204–5, 213, 223
Newman, Asare, 93
Ngugi wa Thiong'o, 54
Nigeria, 83, 87, 110, 121; FESTAC 77, 67, 97; National Theatre, 97
Nigerian Broadcasting Corporation, 111
Nii-Yartey, Francis, 95, 101
Nketia, J. H. K., 59, 61, 76, 77, 240n54, 243n76
Nkomode, 163
Nkrumah, Kwame, 7, 8; at Achimota College, 56; "African personality," 7, 53, 69; assassination attempts on, 75; call for self-rule, 50, 60; centenary celebrations of, 111–12; centralized identity under, 60; charisma of, 179, 210, 216, 220, 221; culture and arts as key, 53, 56–59; education reform under, 58–59; encouragement of Africanness, 41; at inauguration of IAS, 59; interment, 205; legacy of, 108, 210–11; midnight speech on March 6, 1957, 22; as Osagyefo (redeemer/savior), 179; overthrow of, 7–8, 75, 83, 86–87, 179, 210, 216; overturning of chieftaincy, 56; parodied in Ananse theatre, 67; picks Osagyefo Players, 75–76; statue, 211, 213–14; Sutherland and, 61–62; as trickster, 209; vision of linking scholarship to political projects, 59. *See also* Nkrumah's Independence Speech, Fiftieth-Anniversary reenactment (2007)

Nkrumah-Ni . . . Africa-Ni (Osofisan), 111–12
Nkrumah's Independence Speech, Fiftieth-Anniversary reenactment (2007), 204–25; dancing, 213–14; distancing effects, 219, 222; Dontoh portrayal of Nkrumah, 205, 215–20, 224, 225; financial cost of, 219; generational change, discussions of, 207–10; "Ghana@50" events, 204–5, 207, 212, 215, 223–24; guests, 211, 213, 219; independence as reobjectified cultural performance, 222–25; made for television, 217, 218, 219; Nkrumah's Rolls-Royce, 207, 211; Pan-Africanism in reenactment, 217–18; "The President's Show," 211; staging independence, 210–15; traditionalization, lament and national memory, 220–22
Non-Aligned Movement, 110
nostalgia, 21, 22, 85–86, 160–61; postrevolutionaries and, 112; theatre as, 207–10
Novisi dance group, 121, 137
Nyame (God), 14, 65
Nyankonsem (Fables of the celestial; Danquah), 50

Obasanjo, Olusegun, 211
Obeng, Samuel, 19
Obour (musician), 218
Obra (Life; soap opera), 215
Odasani (Sutherland), 62
Odo Ne Asomdwee (Love and peace; radio show), 195–96
Odoi, Greene, 216
Of Brecht (play), 107
Offei, Jesse, 138
Ofori Atta, William, 48, 50
Ofoso Dadze (Pastor Dadze; soap opera), 195
Okalla, Bishop Bob, 147, 163, 164–65, 190–91
Okyeame (linguist), 19, 133, 234
Okyeame (literary magazine), 62
Omaboe, Grace (Maame Dokono), 195–97, 201
Onyame Huhunue Wo (God sees you; film), 200
Opoku, Albert Mawere, 36, 38–39, 76–79, 95
Organization of African Unity (OAU), 118, 208
Osagyefo Players, 75–76
Osofisan, Femi, 111–12
Otabil, Mensa, 185, 186–88, 193, 222
Otunla, Olu, 110
Our Sister Killjoy (Aidoo), 88
Owusu, Martin, 72, 118

Padmore, George, 56, 70
Pan-African Historical Theatre Festival (PANAFEST), 92

Pan-Africanism, 4, 6, 7, 26, 56; at Achimota College, 46; as Anglophone, 73; attempts to limit, 49; centralized socialist state infrastructures, 56–57; as collective, trans-state project, 222; as nostalgic, 222; in reenactment of Nkrumah's speech, 217–18; shattered, 83; in *The Witch of Mopti*, 134–38
Pan-Africanist Congresses, 48, 56
pan-cultural anti-imperial nationalism, 51
Panfred, Agnes, 94
parody, 22, 206; of particular people, 55, 65, 67
participation roles, 17, 66, 140, 187, 201
pastors, 21–22; comedians parody, 163–64, 189–92; concert party popular theatre and, 163–64; economically viable vocation, 176; as mediators, 187–88; mock sincerity, 178; osofo meko (pepper pastor), 177; performance styles, 21–22, 183–84; performers as, 175, 180; scandals, 176, 192–94, 196. *See also* Charismatic churches
Peace FM, 164
Peirce, Charles, 19–20
Pelton, Robert, 64
Pentecostalism. *See* Charismatic churches
People's Republic of China, 97
performance: British administration and, 26–27; for ceremonial occasions, 30; debates about acceptable modes of, 54, 68; elite concerns with categorizing, 31; as excuse for denying equal treatment, 48; good citizenship as, 55; reflexive discourse on, 17
performance, poetics of, 102, 150, 151; shared traditions and principles, 1–2, 14–15, 26, 56–60, 78, 96, 151, 237n2
performance logic, 60, 175–76
performance research, 7; Atwia collaborative project, 70–71; blended genres, 8–13; dance, 77
performance theory, 4, 15–16, 22; competing views, 63–76; complexity of, 55; cultural debates, 26, 60–62; developing, 80–82; ritual theory, 116–17; structuring theatrical reflexivity by arguing about culture, 51–52
performativity, 15–16, 82, 117, 176, 244n91
personhood, 19, 52, 165, 168, 172
Phelps-Stokes Commission, 47
pidgin, 40, 54, 128, 138, 143
PNDC Law 221, the Religious Bodies Registration Act, 181–82
poetics: of mediation, 13–20; of national unity, 49–50, 78, 181–82, 214; of performance, 1–2, 14–16, 26, 56–60, 96, 102, 150, 151, 237n2; of public life, 194, 201; of reflexivity, 4, 16, 55; theatrical, 10, 224, 233; of uncertainty, 2
political anxiety, as spiritual battle, 136–38
political parties, 103
Portuphy, Kofi, 95
possession, 79, 138
postcolonial African politics, 112
post-neoliberal critical theory, 227–30
postrevolutionaries, 112
Preventive Detention Acts (1960, 1962), 75
private social clubs, 6, 29, 31, 32–33, 57
privatization, 4, 101–2; concert party and, 150, 173–74; state-owned enterprises (SOEs), 99
Promzy, 175
proscenium stage, 1, 61, 63, 71, 88, 130; dance and, 78; *Key Soap Concert Party* and, 166
prosperity doctrines, 176, 177, 181–82, 186–88, 203
proverbs, 19, 31, 64, 66, 79, 183, 227
Provisional National Defence Council (PNDC), 85, 89, 90–91, 118, 204
public life, poetics of, 194, 201
public wealth, aesthetics of, 182

Quartey, Richard, 153
questioning as self-fashioning, 145–46

racial and cultural affiliations, 6, 80, 88, 136, 186, 219, 223
racial objectification, 4, 25, 40; Africans as culture-bound, 27–29, 51; contesting racialized education, 46–50; naturalization of, 6
radical theatre, 107, 110–11, 145
radical thinkers, 4, 26
Radin, Paul, 64
radio, 164; Christian stations, 184; gendered moral mediation, 194–97; Ghana Broadcasting Corporation (GBC), 57; Joy FM, 185; *The Living Word*, 185; local service, 50–51; public participation, 33–34, 50–51
Raisin in the Sun, A (Hansberry), 75
Rattray, R. S., 13–14, 42, 55, 64–65, 66, 234
Rawlings, Jerry John, 2, 8, 86–87, 146, 171; Abdallah's letter to, 104, 108–9, 112; as Christian, 179; comes to power, 84–85; criticism of, 148; Nkrumah's legacy and, 108, 210–11; on religious denominations, 181
Rawlings Revolution, 84–85, 103, 108, 213
recontextualization of symbols and practices, 61, 135–36, 160, 165–66, 192, 206
recordings, 33–34, 240n59

reenactment, 22, 205; genre blending and, 206–7. *See also* Nkrumah's Independence Speech, Fiftieth-Anniversary reenactment (2007)
reflexivity: cultural debates, 25–26; double, 55; poetics of, 4, 16, 55; of reenactment, 219; in rehearsals, 122; structuring by arguing about culture, 51–52; in *The Witch of Mopti*, 122, 130, 134
rehearsals: reflexivity in, 122; *The Witch of Mopti*, 122–36, 137, 138, 143, 146
Religious Bodies Registration Act, 181–82
repetition, 85–86
Republic Day (1960), 58
revolution, repetition and, 85–86
ritual theory, 116–17
Riverson, Brew, Jr., 11, 180
Rodger Club, 31, 57, 208
Rouch, Jean, 229
rumor circulation, 196, 197
rural culture, appropriation of for urban publics, 15, 20–21, 26, 52, 53–54, 60

Sampah, Solomon, 76, 83–84
satire, 2, 3, 16
School of Music and Drama, 60, 61, 68, 107
School of Performing Arts (SPA), 9, 60, 71, 95, 120, 121
Scott, David, 86
Second Republic of Ghana, 83
Second World Black and African Festival of Arts and Culture (FESTAC 77), 67, 97
Sedition Ordinance of 1934, 49
Sekyi, Kobina, 29, 50
self-consciousness, 4, 18, 34, 45–46; offstage discussions, 116; reflexivity and, 55, 80
self-fashioning, 145–46, 228
self-recognition, 50, 52, 83, 85
self-rule project, 27, 47, 50, 60
semiotic appropriation, 1, 22
Senegal, 73; dances from, 134–35, 136
sexuality: Charismatic pastors and, 171, 177, 192–94, 196–97; concert party themes, 160, 161, 164, 171. *See also* gender; women
Shakespeare, William, 69
Sherif Ali, 104–5
Short History of the Gold Coast, A (Ward), 48
simulacra state, 203
Slaves, The (Abdallah), 107
social organization, 116–17
socialist ethos, 1–2, 7, 73

socialist theatre traditions, 71, 73, 95
Song of the Pharaoh (Abdallah), 230–32
Sophocles, 2
Sowah, Oh! Nii Kwei, 94, 119
Soyinka, Wole, 107
spatial organization, 166
speaker/actor triad, 206
speaking authority, 13, 19, 130
spiritual attacks, 198, 199–200, 203
spiritual power, 79, 137
staging, 17, 63
state: concert party, appropriation of, 150–52; control of cultural nationalism, 91–92; regulation of churches, 181–82; sovereignty, 1–2, 5, 6, 7, 19, 21, 27–28, 53, 54, 57, 115, 137, 180, 227, 237n2. *See also* Ghana
state-owned enterprises (SOEs), 99
Story Ananse Told, The (Owusu), 72
storytellers, 15, 233–34; as mediators, 13, 67; multiple, 116, 117; role of, 17; in *The Witch of Mopti*, 115–18, 130–34
storytelling: formal, 93; links with concert party popular theatre, 7; metapragmatic elements, 55, 80, 146, 152, 228; performance frame, 65–66; principles of, 116; as social event, 65. *See also* moral storytelling; trickster storytelling
Structural Adjustment Program (SAP), 8, 96, 104
Studio Players, 62
subject formation, 15, 82, 116–17, 206
Sutherland, Bill, 61
Sutherland, Efua, 7, 30, 106, 150; advocacy for arts, 84; Atwia collaborative research project, 70–71; develops *Anansegro*, 122; Drama Studio and, 53; formal and informal elements in works of, 67; Kusum Agromma group, 62, 71, 156; National Theatre Movement and, 61–63; performance theory of, 64–65; students of train new generation, 118. Works: *Edufa*, 66; *Foriwa*, 66; *The Marriage of Anansewa*, 66–68, 81
symbols, recontextualization of, 61, 135–36, 160, 165–66, 192, 206

Talents Theatre Company, 95
talking drums, 80
Tamakloe, Allen, 69, 95
Teacher of Africa, The: Black Star (Hunwick), 95
television, 11, 95–96, 215; audience and, 148, 170–71; audience reception, 166–72; audience seen on, 169, 172; authoritative technologies

and dispersed viewing, 170–72; communal viewing, 172; concert party popular theatre and, 151; reenactment of Nkrumah's speech and, 217, 218, 219
theatre: for community development, 71, 158; as cultural mediation, 6–8; decreased funding, 83–84; financial and structural problems, 11; as form of labor, 207; legitimizing, 10, 55, 82, 115, 144, 152, 177; as nostalgia, 207–10; politics removed from, 64, 72; as research technique, 71; values, 5
Theatre Club, 75
theatre-in-the-round, 63, 145
theatrical poetics, 10, 224, 233
Third Woman, The (Danquah), 50
Thompson, Bob, 74
"total African theatre," 9, 122–25
Touré, Sékou, 105, 111, 210
"Towards a Creative National Culture" (Yirenkyi), 90
tradition: Ananse as embodiment of, 68; colonial era performance of, 6, 30, 38–39; commodification of as morally positive, 151, 153, 154, 157–62, 168; culture as ahistorical, 25–27, 53; as feminine, 150, 156, 160; negative associations, 160–61, 166; reinvention of, 7, 41, 53; religious aspects, 178, 179–80, 184, 186, 190, 192, 196, 199; shared, 1–2, 14–15, 26, 56–60, 78, 96, 151, 237n2. *See also* Anansesem (Ananse the Spider trickster storytelling); culture; National Theatre Movement
traditionalization, 220–22
tragedy, 85–86
Trial of Kwame Nkrumah, The (Mensa-Bonsu), 95, 216
Trial of Mallam Ilya, The (Abdallah), 2–4, 8, 16, 144, 237n1
Trial of Wole Soyinka, The (Gibbs), 107
trickster characters: contradictory moral positions, 17; as mediators, 13, 67, 72; new connotations, 227–28; as protagonists and narrators, 72–73
trickster storytelling, 1, 6, 7, 18, 231–32; Charismatic churches and, 21–22, 177–79; ethnographic research, 64; Gizo (Hausa spider trickster), 18, 105; in National Theatre Movement, 54–55; reimagining future, 86; in *The Witch of Mopti*, 115. *See also* Anansesem (Ananse the Spider trickster storytelling); concert party popular theatre; indirection

Tuniese (Fiawoo), 75
Turner, Victor, 116–17
Turning Failure into Success (Otabil), 187–88
Twi language and performance, 10, 11–12, 36, 37, 50, 67, 167

uncertainty, 3–4; copying and, 205; fear of fakery, 177; poetics of, 2; productive potentials of, 19–20; Rawlings coups and, 86, 148; in *The Witch of Mopti*, 117
unfreedom, 5, 226–27
Unilever, 21, 99, 147, 149, 151, 152, 153–64, 170, 171; colonial economics and, 154; Direct Consumer Contact (DCC) program, 159; takeover of concert party, 157–60
United Gold Coast Convention (UGCC), 56
University College of the Gold Coast (UCGC), 58–59. *See also* Achimota College
University of Ghana, Legon, 53; Abibigromma Theatre Company at, 118–20, 126–28; Institute of African Studies (IAS), 59–60; Resident Professional Theatre Company, 93; School of Performing Arts (SPA), 9, 60, 71, 95, 120, 121
urban publics: appropriation of rural culture, 15, 20–21, 26, 52, 53–54, 60; aspirational, 6, 8, 12, 31–34; colonial era, 25–26

Vagalas, Reverend, 179
Vanns, Bob, 156
Verdict of the Cobra (Abdallah), 93, 119
vernacularization policies, 36
video production technology, 152–53, 200

Wachuku, Jaja, 106
Waiting for Godot (Beckett), 130
Walcott, Rinaldo, 5
Ward, W. E. F., 48–49, 240n54
Warren, Guy (Kofi Ghanaba), 40–41, 77
W. E. B. Du Bois Centre for Pan-African Culture, 92, 106
West African National Club, 32
Williams, Dapper, 33
Williams, Kofi Awoonor, 72
Wilson, George Andoh, 76
Wiredu, Kwasi, 19
Witch of Mopti, The (Abdallah), 21, 115–46; community of (mis)interpretation, 141–45; double voicing, 116, 122–25, 130; formalist focus, 116, 142; framing as issue in, 131, 132,

Witch of Mopti (continued)
140; indirection in, 129, 145; interludes, 125; language use, 116, 125–29; moral choice in, 138–41, 145–46; music, 122–23, 125; original production, 118; Pan-African dance aesthetic, 134–36; principles of storytelling, 116; questioning as self-fashioning, 145–46; reflexivity in, 122, 130, 134; rehearsals, 116, 122–36, 137, 138, 143, 146; script, 118, 130–34, 138–40; spiritual and political conflicts, 136–38; staging, 123–25, 130, 133–34; storytellers, 115–18, 130–34, 139–40, 145; as "total African theatre," 122–25; unscriptedness, 116, 130, 133–34, 142–43; U.S. performance, 136

witchcraft accusations, 200, 202
Woeli Publishing Services, 118
women, 7; pastors and fears of exploitation, 177, 192–94, 197; as performers, 71, 73; radio show host, 195–97; in theatre, 88–89, 94. *See also* gender; sexuality
Workers' Brigade, 57, 73, 74
Workers' Brigade Drama Group (Workers' Brigade Concert Party), 58, 73, 74, 156
World War II, 50

Yaa Asantewaa War, 105
Yalley, Teacher, 30
Yankah, Kwesi, 14, 19
Yelpoe, Cecilia, 129
Yiadom, Prophet Reverend Doctor Ebenezer Adarkwa Opambour, 193, 198
Yirenkyi, Asiedu, 70, 71–72, 87, 89–90
Yirenkyi, Kofi, 70
Young People's Literary Club, 33, 49
Young Pioneers, 57, 106
youth, 11–12, 31–32; actors and generational change, 119–20, 207–10; Charismatic churches and, 179–80, 182; generational change, discussions of, 207–10

Zinabu (film; Akuffo and Quartey), 153

JESSE WEAVER SHIPLEY is an ethnographer, filmmaker, and artist. He is Associate Professor of Anthropology at Haverford College. His work focuses on performance, music, technology, youth, urban life, labor, and cultures of circulation. He is the author of *Living the Hiplife: Celebrity and Entrepreneurship in Ghanaian Popular Music* (2013). His films include the feature documentary *Living the Hiplife: Musical Life in the Streets of Accra* (2007) and *Is It Sweet?* (2014) and the multichannel video installations *Black Star* (2012) and *High Tea* (2014).

www.ingramcontent.com/pod-product-compliance
Lightning Source LLC
Chambersburg PA
CBHW050432240426
43661CB00055B/2354